The European Monetary System

STEP

STEP (Centro Interuniversitario di Studi Teorici per la Politica Economica) is a joint research centre of the economics departments of the universities of Bologna and Venezia and the institute of economics of Bocconi University, Milan. The centre promotes research in the area of economic policy and, through its collaboration with the Centre for Economic Policy Research, provides another STEP in furthering the Italian contribution to European economics.

Directors
Giorgio Basevi, Mario Monti, Ignazio Musu

Scientific Advisory Board
Fiorella Padoa-Schioppa, Richard Portes, Luigi Spaventa

Centre for Economic Policy Research

The Centre for Economic Policy Research is a registered charity with educational purposes. It was established in 1983 to promote independent analysis and public discussion of open economies and the relations among them. Institutional (core) finance for the Centre has been provided through major grants from the Economic and Social Research Council, the Leverhulme Trust, the Esmée Fairbairn Trust and the Bank of England. None of these organisations gives prior review to the Centre's publications nor do they necessarily endorse the views expressed therein.

The Centre is pluralist and non-partisan, bringing economic research to bear on the analysis of medium- and long-run policy questions. The research work which it disseminates may include views on policy, but the Board of Governors of the Centre does not give prior review to such publications, and the Centre itself takes no institutional policy positions. The opinions expressed in this volume are those of the authors and not those of the Centre for Economic Policy Research.

The European Monetary System

Edited by

FRANCESCO GIAVAZZI
STEFANO MICOSSI

and

MARCUS MILLER

Proceedings of a conference organised
by the Banca d'Italia, STEP and CEPR

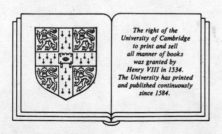

The right of the
University of Cambridge
to print and sell
all manner of books
was granted by
Henry VIII in 1534.
The University has printed
and published continuously
since 1584.

CAMBRIDGE UNIVERSITY PRESS

Cambridge
New York Port Chester Melbourne Sydney

Published by the Press Syndicate of the University of Cambridge
The Pitt Building, Trumpington Street, Cambridge CB2 1RP
40 West 20th Street, New York, NY 10011, USA
10 Stamford Road, Oakleigh, Melbourne 3166, Australia

First published 1988
First paperback edition 1989

Printed in Great Britain by the University Press, Cambridge

British Library cataloguing in publication data

The European Monetary System.
1. European Community. Monetary system:
European Monetary System
I. Giavazzi, Francesco
II. Micossi, Stefano
III. Miller, Marcus H.
332.4'566'094

Library of Congress cataloguing in publication data

The European monetary system / edited by Francesco Giavazzi,
Stefano Micossi, and Marcus Miller.
   p.   cm.
Includes index.
ISBN 0-521-36271-7
1. Money – European Economic Community countries.
2. Monetary policy – European Economic Community countries.
I. Giavazzi, Francesco.
II. Micossi, S.
III. Miller, M. H. (Marcus H.)
HG930.5.E8685 1988
332.4'94 – dc19   88-23266 CIP

ISBN 0 521 36271 7 hard covers
ISBN 0 521 38905 4 paperback

CE

Contents

IV THE FUTURE OF THE EUROPEAN MONETARY SYSTEM

Figures

Tables

Preface

The European Monetary System (EMS) has just celebrated its ninth birthday. Increasingly, neglect of its experience and scepticism regarding its ability to survive have given way to admiration for its success and a desire to explain its resilience.

During the lifetime of the EMS, the world economy has passed through a period of exceptional instability, with large swings in the main currencies' exchange rates and rapid disinflation, together with the build-up of unprecedented imbalances in the leading countries' external payments. While severe strains have occasionally arisen, the EMS has on the whole been remarkably successful in resisting exchange-rate variations when these were not warranted by fundamentals, managing central-rate realignments (relatively) smoothly, and fostering the convergence of inflation performances.

Two other factors have contributed to an enhanced interest in the EMS. Firstly, there seems now to be some consensus of opinion that exchange rates, even for the leading currencies, need to be managed and cannot be left entirely to market forces. Second, there is an increasing perception within the EMS that the system may be entering a new phase, in which members accord lower priority to disinflation among their policy objectives, capital controls are lifted, and the weakness of the dollar persists: all combine to weaken the cohesion of the EMS.

The convictions that there are useful lessons to be drawn from the EMS that may be relevant to the international monetary system as a whole, and that at the same time it may be necessary to adapt the system to changing circumstances and policy priorities if it is to continue to exist, led us to assemble some fifty distinguished academics and central bankers from Europe and the US to take stock of the EMS experience and to discuss its problems and prospects. The conference, sponsored by the Banca d'Italia, the Centro Interuniversitario di Studi Teorici per la Politica Economica (STEP) and the Centre for Economic Policy

Research (CEPR), was held in Perugia on 16–17 October 1987, at the Banca d'Italia School of Automation for Commercial Bank Executives (SADiBa).

The present volume contains the proceedings of that conference. All the areas of current research on the EMS are reviewed, and new contributions to the analysis and interpretation of the system's functioning are contained in the volume. The final panel discussion singled out the main policy issues and future prospects.

We incurred many debts of gratitude during the organisation of the conference and the preparation of this volume. Professor Richard Portes, Director of CEPR, encouraged and advised us on the conference programme from its inception. The success of the conference was due to many factors: the high standard of the papers presented; the stimulating comments contributed by the panelists, discussants and other participants, all of which made for a most lively discussion; and the smooth organisation and pleasant atmosphere created by the efficiency and competence of SADiBa's Director, Paolo Sanguinetti, and his staff, as well as the staff of CEPR and the Banca d'Italia Research Department.

Luisa Dell'Armi and Raffaella Giannini of the Banca d'Italia deserve special gratitude in this regard. The preparation of this volume for publication is due largely to the efforts of Paul Compton, Publications Officer at CEPR, and of the production editor, Keith Povey. The conference was funded by grants to CEPR from the Ford Foundation and the Alfred P. Sloan Foundation, and to STEP from the Consiglio Nazionale delle Ricerche, as well as by the Banca d'Italia; we gratefully acknowledge this support.

FRANCESCO GIAVAZZI
STEFANO MICOSSI
MARCUS MILLER

Conference Participants

Michael J. Artis, *University of Manchester and CEPR*
Gunter D. Baer, *Bank for International Settlements*
Giorgio Basevi, *Università di Bologna, STEP and CEPR*
David Begg, *Birkbeck College, London, and CEPR*
Luis Miguel Beleza, *Banco de Portugal*
Lorenzo Bini Smaghi, *Banca d'Italia*
William H. Branson, *Princeton University and CEPR*
Ralph C. Bryant, *The Brookings Institution*
Emil-M. Claassen, *European University Institute*
Susan M. Collins, *Harvard University*
David Currie, *Queen Mary College, London, and CEPR*
Henning Dalgaard, *Danmarks Nationalbank*
Lamberto Dini, *Banca d'Italia*
Rudiger Dornbusch, *MIT and CEPR*
John Driffill, *University of Southampton and CEPR*
Francesco Giavazzi, *Università di Venezia, STEP and CEPR*
Alberto Giovannini, *Columbia University and CEPR*
Margaret L. Greene, *Federal Reserve Bank of New York*
Daniel Gros, *Centre for European Policy Studies*
Peter B. Kenen, *Princeton University and CEPR*
John Kirby, *Bank of England*
Rainer S. Masera, *Banca d'Italia*
Cristina Mastropasqua, *Banca d'Italia*
Jacques Melitz, *Institut National de la Statistique et des Etudes Economiques and CEPR*
Stefano Micossi, *Banca d'Italia*
Marcus H. Miller, *University of Warwick and CEPR*
Mario Monti, *Università Commerciale 'Luigi Bocconi', Milan, and STEP*
Maurice Obstfeld, *University of Pennsylvania*
Tommaso Padoa-Schioppa, *Banca d'Italia*

Lucas Papademos, *Bank of Greece*
Antonio Pedone, *Università degli Studi di Roma 'La Sapienza'*
Theo Peeters, *Katholieke Universiteit Leuven*
Heracles Polemarchakis, *Columbia University and Centre of Planning and Economic Research, Athens*
Richard Portes, *CEPR and Birkbeck College, London*
Jean-Jacques Rey, *Banque Nationale de Belgique*
George Reynolds, *Central Bank of Ireland*
Wolfgang Rieke, *Deutsche Bundesbank*
Roberto Rinaldi, *Banca d'Italia*
Massimo Russo, *International Monetary Fund*
Fabrizio Saccomanni, *Banca d'Italia*
Luigi Spaventa, *Università degli Studi di Roma 'La Sapienza'*
Niels Thygesen, *University of Copenhagen*
Robert Triffin, *Institut de Recherches Economiques, Louvain*
Giuseppe Tullio, *Banca d'Italia*
José Viñals, *Banco de España*
Stefano Vona, *Banca d'Italia*
Jacques Waitzenegger, *Banque de France*
Charles Wyplosz, *Institut Européen d'Administration des Affaires and CEPR*

1 Introduction*

NIELS THYGESEN

The European Monetary System (EMS) has attracted great attention as a framework for policy coordination ever since it was conceived in 1978. Disillusioned by the prospects for global monetary reform and by the performance of the floating exchange-rate system, the EMS founding fathers wanted to restore, within as large a part as was possible of the European Communities, a system of 'fixed but adjustable' exchange rates. Such a system would protect the large intra-European trade flows against the sharp shifts in competitiveness which were seen as quite possible in its absence. It would also contain divergence of national inflation rates among participants and permit lower and more stable inflation throughout. It was seen, finally, as a stabilising complement to the expansionary fiscal programme to facilitate global economic adjustment which the Europeans – and Germany in particular – had undertaken at the Bonn Summit in July 1978.

This vision of the evolution of 'a zone of monetary stability' had a strong element of damage limitation in it. Yet it was rightly regarded as highly ambitious at the time because it brought back into European management the currencies of some countries – France and Italy in particular – which had stayed apart from earlier efforts; the system had subsequently evolved well beyond its original intentions, despite the absence of any institutional step. The exchange-rate mechanism has become tighter, monetary policy coordination is now closer, and capital mobility higher than was the case in the early years of the EMS.

Since the system was on the drawing board ten years ago it has inspired a massive literature. The present volume is an impressive example of the contribution academic economists and those involved in economic policy making can make to the understanding of how the EMS works, how some of its effects may be measured, and how it might be improved, according to certain well-defined criteria. Macroeconomic theory and careful use of econometric analysis can bring out some of the main implications of the particular blend of exchange-rate management and external constraint represented by the EMS. These tools can also facilitate the evaluation of the more operational, short-term problems encountered in managing the system and the national monetary policies that underpin it. It is interesting to note that the research reported and the evaluations offered are not only European; the analysis of the EMS has also benefited greatly from the attention this extended policy experiment has always received in universities and research institutions in the United States, for example.

The following chapters are divided into four parts: the international environment, the implications for macroeconomic variables and policies, monetary and exchange-rate management, and the future of the EMS.

1   The international environment

The first chapter by Rudiger Dornbusch is critical of the present EMS in three respects: (1) it questions the wisdom of pursuing convergence of inflation rates in Southern Europe towards the near-zero level reached in Germany; (2) it argues that the European Community should consider carefully whether to pursue full liberalisation of capital movements without allowing more flexibility in the exchange rate for financial transactions; and (3) it reminds EMS participants that the international adjustment of imbalances is far from complete and that the US dollar may still have to fall, hence continuing to pose a major challenge to the cohesiveness of the EMS currencies. Underlying all three issues is the author's doubt whether a high degree of nominal exchange-rate fixity is either desirable or feasible for all present and potential members of the system.

The argument against further disinflation in Southern Europe is novel in that it rests less on the output costs of such a policy than on the sustainability of public debt in a phase of declining inflation and hence narrowing scope for financing part of the public sector deficit by money creation. By pursuing disinflation and pegging the exchange rate more firmly to countries with minimal inflation, the authorities give up a seigniorage gain and make necessary a large effort to reduce the deficit through tax increases or expenditure cuts which may not be politically feasible. They may also, in the course of their defence of the exchange rate, have to push up real interest rates at a time when these rates are already dampening the growth rate of the capital stock. This line of reasoning is inspired by the stabilisation and disinflation experience and costs observed in Latin America and in some other countries.

While the attention paid in the traditional analysis of the feasibility of monetary integration in Europe to the interaction of exchange-rate policy and the sustainability of a sizeable public deficit may be insufficient, it is not obvious that a country with high public debt and deficit would have an incentive to reduce its financing problems through devaluation and inflation. The public might perceive such an incentive when it exists and expect higher inflation, hence pushing up interest rates and worsening the budget position rather than the opposite. By aiming for a stable nominal exchange rate with strong EMS currencies, a 'Mediterranean' government might be able to lower real interest rates further and generate more growth (and the associated budgetary improvement) than it could achieve by assuming a less disinflationary stance. But if some countries – notably the new entrants in the European Community and Italy – were to follow the Dornbusch prescription and accept more explicitly a permanently higher inflation rate than Germany and other members aiming at price stability, rules would have to be found for accommodating the required exchange-rate changes. Dornbusch suggests a crawling peg with frequent, almost continuous, adjustments between the two groups of currencies so as to maintain competitiveness stable. Domestic monetary and fiscal policies would then have to assure that inflationary instability does not take over.

A system in which competitiveness is held stable through crawling-peg devaluations of the group of more inflationary currencies would have some resemblance to the EMS in its pre-1983 operation – and to the joint float of four currencies in the 'snake' during the three years that preceded the launching of the EMS. It would, for the more inflationary currencies – which would have no easy common denominator – give up the simplicity of the rules of the present EMS, comprising both relative behaviour of defending the grid of exchange rates *and* a nominal anchor through pegging to low-inflation currencies; in return, it would prevent the misallocation of resources involved in premature pegging of the nominal exchange rate and the consequent real appreciation. It is a choice facing EC countries that have not joined the EMS; but the crawling-peg option is difficult to envisage for countries that are already participating fully in the system. They would lose the nominal anchor and the credibility that goes with it; joint interventions and the credit mechanisms would no longer underpin their currency. It will appear a risky option, in particular, for those countries that have already undertaken significant liberalisation of capital movements.

It is logical, therefore, for a proponent of this option as the best framework for widening exchange-rate management in Europe to complement it with a proposal to introduce dual exchange rates. Real exchange rates, or competitiveness, would be stabilised, but the rates at which financial transactions take place would not be constrained by intervention limits. Such a dual system would require a difficult separation of current and capital transactions; it was tried in the early 1970s by some European countries (France and Italy), and for a much longer period prior to 1979 for the portfolio and direct investment transactions of UK residents, and it has remained in operation in the Belgium–Luxembourg Economic Union since 1948. The general verdict in countries that have tried the system is that it is administratively complex, but that it still offers considerable scope for evasion if the incentives thereto become important, as the financial rate begins to diverge significantly from the commercial rate; but it is also recognised that the existence of a floating financial rate offers some short-run protection to a beleaguered currency. Like Tobin, who originally proposed more widespread use of a dual exchange-rate system a decade ago, as long as full economic and monetary integration is not a realistic option, Dornbusch recognises that a global, moderate transactions tax on all foreign-exchange purchases may constitute a simpler alternative deterrent to excessive capital mobility than a dual exchange-rate system, but with the added inconvenience of imposing a tax also on current account transactions.

The approach runs counter to the efforts in the European Community to increase capital mobility by removing residual restrictions on capital flows and advancing liberalisation in the trade of financial services. Some other authors, notably Driffill and Obstfeld (Chapters 8 and 9 in this volume), discuss the compatibility of advancing financial integration and the continued smooth operation of the EMS as a 'fixed but adjustable' exchange-rate system. The official view in most EMS countries is clearly that monetary integration has advanced sufficiently within the system to make the first of Tobin's two options for dealing with potentially destabilising capital flows – full monetary integration – realistic; in a late stage of monetary integration with nearly fixed exchange rates, increasing capital mobility may reinforce rather than undermine the system.

Dornbusch makes the perceptive comment that the EMS countries today benefit from what is *de facto* a system of dual rates. EMS participants do the bulk of their trade amongst themselves at tightly managed exchange rates which do not permit sudden shifts in competitiveness, while a large share of their financial transactions involve floating currencies, notably the dollar. The very different degree to which Germany (and other EMS countries) on the one hand and the United States on the other have managed to contain swings in their real effective exchange rate is remarkable. But it does not follow from this observation that the EMS countries would have an interest in extending a dual exchange-rate system into their own interrelationships, as financial transactions within Europe assume gradually greater importance.

Dornbusch finally reminds us that the US external deficit still looms large, and that a major further depreciation of the dollar is in store. One may disagree with the size of the required or likely adjustment mentioned by Dornbusch – 30 per cent from the levels observed in October 1987 – while recognising that even a smaller adjustment might put additional strains on the cohesion of the EMS and the macroeconomic performance of its participants.

In several respects the international tensions in 1987–8 are similar to those observed a decade earlier, which provided part of the inspiration for the launching of the EMS: large US current account deficits, a weakening dollar and strong US pressure on Europe to coordinate policies internationally. The policy response in 1978 was some demand stimulus in Europe led by Germany, and the set-up of the EMS to make the participating currencies less vulnerable to international financial disturbances. It may be a sign of greater confidence – and of a perception of having become more self-contained over the past decade – that there is less of a clearly defined policy response from Europe in 1987–8, despite the much larger size of the international imbalances, except for the tightening of the ranks within Europe through the Internal Market programme and a strengthening of the EMS. But the questions of how Europe will absorb the one-third to one-half of the US current deficit that may be its share, and how that process will affect the EMS, will not go away. These questions are not addressed explicitly in the present volume, but the chapter by Vona and Bini Smaghi (Chapter 6) presents some elements for an answer as regards the distribution within Europe of this adjustment.

2 Disinflation, external adjustment and cooperation

The four chapters in the second part of the volume offer a detailed assessment of the EMS as a framework for cooperation for its participants, of the implications for key macroeconomic variables, notably inflation and output, and of the determinants of trade imbalances for the three largest participants.

Jacques Melitz (Chapter 3) asks what incentives countries have to participate in an arrangement like the EMS. Most observers have tended to focus on the disinflationary mechanism operating on the weaker participants in the system. By pegging to the less inflationary currencies over long intervals, with the prospect that they cannot fully devalue in accordance with their excess inflation on the infrequent occasions of a realignment, the authorities of the weaker currencies gain credibility for their disinflationary stance. Private agents will interpret an EMS commitment as more constraining than a national monetary target or other intermediate objectives by which a disinflationary intention may be signalled by a country individually. Inflationary expectations come down faster, and it becomes easier to reduce actual inflation. Other benefits to the weak-currency country may take the form of improving the efficiency of other policy instruments as the inflation uncertainty is reduced.

These benefits of 'tying one's hands', to use the expression of Giavazzi and Pagano (1986), seem attainable and tangible in the context of the EMS. In principle, as Melitz notes, they are transitory; presumably the disinflation effort could be pursued individually by the countries concerned without the external commitment of the EMS. The benefits from joining will disappear only when there is no difference between the reputation of the domestic monetary authority and that of the Bundesbank; convergence in the inflation rate towards the German rate is not in itself a sufficient condition for carrying on individually, because such convergence may be regarded as temporary. Melitz anticipates the discussion of the desirable autonomy of a European central banking institution to replace the present mechanism where weaker-currency countries – I hesitate to identify this case with France, as proposed by Melitz, in view of the performance of the French franc and the low French inflation – draw on the reputation of the Bundesbank. Greater autonomy for other national central banks could facilitate the construction of a European institution, or might even be regarded as a partial alternative to it. In this sense, the benefits of participation in the present EMS to a country truly committed to medium-term price stability are transitory.

In much of the EMS literature, the focus is on this particular aspect. It is clearly not the whole story, even from the perspective of the weaker currencies. An assessment of output costs and losses of competitiveness is also required; without that it is impossible to explain why and when countries occasionally choose to escape from discipline by devaluing. Melitz offers a model in which each participant minimises both the deviation of output from desired levels and the inflation rate. But the most interesting part of the chapter is the analysis of the reasons why Germany too has found the EMS attractive. After all the initiative to launch the system came at least as much from Germany as from France. Why does Germany prefer the EMS to the alternative of individual pursuit of price stability? In the latter case, Germany would export stability to those countries that want to peg their currencies through their own efforts to the DM, but without undertaking the commitments to support these other currencies through intervention and having to accept 'excessive' money creation and some imported inflation.

In the final part of his study, Melitz develops an extended version of his model in which competitiveness enters the welfare function of both Germany and France. Both countries aim at expanding the traded goods sector, but the tendency for trendwise real depreciation of the DM that is implicit in keeping nominal exchange rates stable while inflation rates have not yet fully converged, makes this aim easier to attain for Germany than for other participants. According to this argument, Germany gains more in terms of gradually improving her competitiveness than she loses in terms of upsets to her monetary policy. Melitz argues that these gains may prove more durable than those of Germany's partners pursuing disinflation through the EMS.

This assessment of the benefits and costs of the EMS to Germany is no doubt relevant to an understanding of why the German government took the initiative to set up the EMS in 1978, at a time when fears of excessive appreciation of the DM and a consequent squeeze on profits, investment and growth were widespread. It may also be relevant in understanding the major German interest in preventing any major disruption in the functioning of the EMS. It seems less accurate as an analysis of how the system operates in the short to medium run; Germany has several times initiated realignments, and the Bundesbank has often expressed concern about the implications for monetary management of bringing the DM into a position of undervaluation. Such a position, and Germany's large current account surplus, greatly complicates monetary management and forces a reassessment of the costs and benefits formulated by Melitz. In that sense, the net benefits of participation in the EMS, given the constellation of policies, might also come to be seen as transitory.

Given the emphasis placed on inflation convergence towards a low and stable rate within the EMS, it is natural that the evidence on the determinants of inflation should be examined carefully. To what extent can the remarkable deceleration of inflation that has been observed in all participating countries since 1979 – or rather since inflation peaked in 1980 after the second oil price shock – be attributed to the EMS? This question is taken up in both theoretical and empirical terms in the chapters by Francesco Giavazzi and Alberto Giovannini and by Susan M. Collins (Chapters 4 and 5).

Having reviewed the recent literature on the channels through which a commitment to the EMS may help a process of disinflation, Giavazzi and Giovannini look for evidence of a downward shift in inflationary expectations following the EMS inception. They estimate a reduced-form system of equations for the (quarterly) dynamics of wages, prices and output for three high-inflation EMS countries (Denmark, France and Italy), Germany and the United Kingdom over the 1960s and 1970s, prior to the formation of the EMS, and confront the predictions from this structure with actual observations of wages, prices and output over 1979–87. The results correspond broadly to what one would expect: lower wage and price inflation in the three countries trying to squeeze their inflation through EMS membership than could be predicted from the pre-EMS experience; and higher inflation in Germany. The evidence further suggests that there was no loss in output in Denmark and Italy – rather a gain – some loss in France between 1980 and 1984 and, surprisingly, a substantial loss in Germany. On the whole the evidence is relatively weak; a downward shift in inflationary expectations does appear to have taken place, but only gradually and less dramatically than in the United Kingdom where actual inflation drops sharply below predicted from 1981.

It is not surprising that econometric techniques fail to uncover dramatic shifts in wage–price behaviour following the start of the EMS. The system was initially fairly soft as a disinflationary mechanism; there were seven realignments in the first four years and the nominal anchor of the DM did not initially set a high standard of monetary stability. A tight disinflationary mechanism was not – and could not have been – perceived in the first 3–4 years.

Collins reaches a similar conclusion by using other data and methods; she also brings in the experience of a group of non-EMS countries as a standard of reference and finds little or no evidence of greater convergence of inflation rates in the EMS since 1979 than outside – but that seemed to be a feature of the period up to 1978 as well. There is evidence of only a gradual effect within the EMS, and from about 1983 onwards. There appear to been two issues concerning EMS membership: one is that the behaviour of the authorities is modified, because the instruments available work differently in regimes which peg the exchange rate. Second, a disinflationary commitment may become more credible to the public – in fact, this did not occur until a few years after the EMS was instituted.

The interest of the Collins study arises from careful discussion of how sensitive the conclusions are to the particular way in which the interaction of countries in the EMS and outside it is modelled. Non-cooperative behaviour could well have led to sharper disinflation and lower output for the EMS countries than a cooperative arrangement or

German leadership, the two main models for the EMS. The story has some plausibility: in a non-cooperative situation, where a group of countries do disinflate individually, they will try to use appreciation – or slower depreciation – of the domestic currency as a transmission channel. For example, had they been unconstrained by the EMS, France and Italy might have tried to disinflate by strengthening their exchange rate (or by allowing it to weaken more slowly against the dollar over 1981–5). But if several EMS countries had engaged in such efforts simultaneously, a process of competitive appreciation would have followed, driving both inflation and output below the outcome of the EMS. Conversely, in an international environment of historically low inflation and output well below target, individual countries might, in the absence of the EMS, have tried to stimulate their economies by allowing their currencies to depreciate, hence engaging in a process of competitive depreciation leading to more inflation and output than would have occurred in an EMS framework. The EMS has the merit of limiting, or removing, such inefficiencies resulting from non-cooperative use of national policy instruments.

It is somewhat embarrassing for economists to be unable to state firmer conclusions on the central issues: How much did the EMS contribute to the deceleration of average inflation, to better inflation convergence and to a lowering of the output costs associated with disinflation? There is weak evidence that the system achieved all three results, but the gradual evolution of the EMS itself, the general disinflationary environment also in non-EMS industrial countries in the first half of the 1980s, and the difficulty of constructing the counterfactual scenario in the absence of the EMS perhaps make it impossible to ask for more. Maybe the main contribution of economists to the analysis of these issues is more conceptual than empirical: to clarify how the transmission channels and strategic interactions are modified by the EMS constraints, and how these modifications are gradually perceived by price-setters in the economy and by financial markets. The three studies are helpful in developing such a framework.

On the empirical side, it may be more productive to focus in some depth on case studies of the occasions when the EMS framework was used emphatically to reinforce domestic stabilisation and is generally considered by policymakers to have contributed significantly. An EMS realignment, constrained in size by other participants, helped to trigger major efforts of fiscal tightening in Belgium, Denmark and France in 1982–3; the system provided a more cooperative (and arguably more efficient) framework than the aggressive strategies of competitive devaluation adopted at that time by some other industrial countries (e.g.,

Sweden and Australia). The benefits of continued EMS membership prompted the adoption of domestic policies of budgetary consolidation and deindexation which were anyway desirable, but would have been more controversial in the absence of the EMS. Similarly, membership in the EMS prompted the Italian authorities to modify the high degree of monetary financing of their public deficit in the early 1980s and their system of wage indexation in 1984. Though these reforms were desirable in themselves, it was a perception of the longer-run incompatibility of previous arrangements with the rules of a system to which the country wanted to adhere that made their adoption possible. In this qualitative sense, the EMS has contributed to disinflation and convergence.

While Melitz, Giavazzi and Giovannini and Collins focus on the inflation and output consequences of the EMS, the fourth study in this part of the volume by Stefano Vona and Lorenzo Bini Smaghi (Chapter 6) examines the determinants of goods exports and imports in the three main EMS countries. Their results permit them to address a number of questions of central importance to the sustainability of an EMS where realignments have been relegated to a minor role in external adjustment. Three main conclusions from their study stand out:

(a) Changes in trade balances for Germany, France and Italy are strongly influenced by relative demand growth in the three countries and by growth outside the EMS. Price elasticities are significant, and sufficient for a devaluation to bring about a trade balance improvement. But devaluation is, even within the partial equilibrium approach adopted by the authors, far less efficient as an instrument for shifting demand between the three countries than measures that affect the relative growth of demand more directly, notably fiscal policy.

(b) The boom in the United States from 1983–4 and the appreciation of the dollar and several other non-EMS currencies between 1980 and 1985 improved trade balances of the EMS countries significantly. Though there are no major structural differences between them in their sensitivity to events outside the EMS, the positive influence of these events up to 1985–6 was, however, more valuable to France and Italy which were in that period trying to disinflate and stick to their exchange rate in the EMS. As these favourable factors have been reversed by the massive depreciation of the dollar and the convergence of US to slower European demand growth, external weaknesses have reappeared in a number of EMS countries, while in Germany slow growth of domestic demand has implied a rising trade surplus despite the unfavourable external factors.

(c) For Germany and Italy parallel growth in demand at home and abroad would give rise to no major trade imbalance. For France, however, the income elasticity in the demand for imports seems to be well above that of the foreign demand (from both EMS and non-EMS countries) for French goods. With similar growth rates in France and elsewhere, a trendwise deterioration in France's trade balance may appear and require correction through an improvement in competitiveness; owing to rapid feedbacks on domestic prices, the required devaluation may have to be larger than the desired improvement in competitiveness. The authors contend that resort to the exchange rate as a main adjustment tool could jeopardise the cohesion of the system, since it would undermine its disciplinary element. A more constructive approach would be to utilise the fiscal and structural instruments available for correcting the external position.

The message from the Vona and Bini Smaghi study is that tensions have been building up within the EMS in the form of growing trade imbalances which may threaten the system. If financial markets believe that current account deficits or surpluses are important clues as to how exchange rates will move, the task of the authorities in managing the EMS smoothly will be greatly complicated. There is less reason why they should think so in an increasingly financially integrated Europe. One of the advantages of having the EMS in place, and high capital mobility associated with it, is that participants are given more time within which to choose the best – not necessarily the fastest – method for adjustment. The intra-EMS imbalances would best be dealt with by some mixture of redistribution of demand through fiscal policy – some easing in Germany, accompanied by tightening in other countries – and structural measures.

3   Exchange rates, capital mobility and monetary coordination

In this part of the volume a series of five studies raises a number of issues relating to the performance of the EMS in the short term and the degree of monetary coordination required to underpin the system.

Most observers have concluded that the EMS has succeeded in reducing exchange-rate volatility among its participants. The reduction is obvious if the comparison is made with either the pre-EMS performance of the participating currencies or with a sample of non-EMS currencies. Nor does stability inside the system appear to have been obtained at the expense of more instability *vis-à-vis* the floating currencies. The study by Michael J. Artis and Mark P. Taylor (Chapter 7) goes well beyond these straightforward (but unsatisfactory) standards of reference. Using high-technology econometrics they compute the conditional variance of EMS exchange rates, taking into account the higher degree of stability in the underlying macroeconomic determinants and without making assumptions as to the specific characteristics of the distribution of exchange-rate changes. But their conclusion is similar: the volatility of monthly nominal and real bilateral DM exchange rates for five other EMS currencies is found to have been significantly reduced while similar measures for the dollar (and to a lesser extent sterling) have increased since 1979.

The authors further investigate whether volatility has been transferred from the foreign-exchange markets to domestic financial markets. One plausible hypothesis is that stabilisation of the exchange rate has required more flexible use of interest-rate differentials to sustain the EMS. This is not borne out by the careful empirical work of Artis and Taylor; the volatility of short-term nominal interest rates in all four of the domestic markets considered (Germany, the Netherlands, France and Italy) has been reduced after 1979, though significantly so only in the Netherlands and Italy. This is in contrast to what has been observed in countries with floating exchange rates.

There must remain some doubt as to the interpretation of this improvement in performance also with respect to domestic interest rates. One contributing factor could be the improved credibility of monetary policy in the EMS. Another which might apply to France and Italy prior to 1985–6 is the existence of capital controls which has protected domestic financial markets against the defensive rise in interest rates which is normally required during a speculative attack on a currency. In the first half of the 1980s capital controls enabled France and Italy to divert such attacks to the external markets for francs and lire to which only non-residents had access. Rates in these markets did indeed become more volatile in periods of tension than previously observed, though this is not the case for the EMS period on average.

While the results are clear enough and offer a positive interpretation of important short-term features of the EMS as a 'zone of monetary stability'; their overall importance may be limited. The contribution that a reduction in the short-term variability of exchange rates can make to the creation of trade among the participants is probably in itself modest. A more significant concern centres on the capacity of the EMS to contain misalignments – i.e., the long-term departures from a structure of intra-EMS exchange rates consistent with macroeconomic equilibrium. The authors note that trendwise real depreciation of some currencies (DM, guilder and Belgian franc) has persisted along with real appreciation of the remaining currencies, though the speed of building up such misalignments has been reduced. While the standard of reference here is less clear, and the interpretation of what are sustainable imbalances is somewhat arbitrary, the residual lack of convergence is worrying.

The authors finally note that the progress achieved in the EMS has not yet been successful in rendering the participating currencies close substitutes. The simple uncovered interest rate parity condition is closer to being fulfilled between the DM and the dollar than between the DM and other EMS currencies. The risk premium has not been reduced to zero even for the guilder. This suggests that financial markets still question the credibility of the longer-run commitment of the EMS countries to develop into an area of more permanently fixed exchange rates.

The following two studies go deeper into the analytical foundations of the compatibility of a 'fixed but adjustable' exchange-rate system such as the EMS with perfect capital mobility and a high degree of foresight in financial markets. This extension of the analysis of the EMS is timely, because the removal of capital controls has already proceeded well beyond the stage typical for the estimation period for most of the empirical work reported in this volume; and further steps towards full liberalisation of capital movements and of trade in financial services have been proposed by the European Commission and are currently under debate in the Council of Ministers. Can the EMS reconcile stable exchange rates and perfect capital mobility?

John Driffill (Chapter 8) does not find the implications of removing capital controls in the EMS particularly severe for the macroeconomic policies of participants. Inflation differentials and other divergencies in performance have been reduced sufficiently to allow them to be accommodated by realignments, at roughly annual intervals, modest enough to avoid discontinuity of market exchange rates. Analogies with the experience of the final years of the Bretton Woods system, or reference to the literature on collapsing exchange-rate regimes inspired by Latin American experiments in currency stabilisation and financial liberalisation, are likely to be misleading, because the residual divergencies and the prospects of speculative gains are much more modest in the present EMS. But in order to preserve its reputation for relative robustness, admittedly achieved under conditions of less than perfect capital mobility, which rests on the notion that EMS governments have gradually precommitted themselves not to allow exchange rates to jump, realignments cannot become too infrequent. Their timing should continue to be uncertain as well.

Driffill's discussion of the rules of monetary management which could underpin an EMS without capital controls takes as its point of departure a two-country model by Buiter (1986), where the two central banks continuously react to incipient reserve flows by adjusting their domestic credit expansion to accommodate shifts in money demand; hence reserve flows are minimised. A less constraining mechanism can be envisaged for the EMS which has large reciprocal credit facilities for the participating central banks and in which reserves are sizeable. But it remains essential that there is an early feedback from reserve flows to the adjustment of domestic policy instruments.

As noted by Driffill, the EMS is in the process of enlarging the scope for financing temporary imbalances. By the so-called Nyborg Agreements of September 1987 the Committee of Central Bank Governors extended the duration of the very short-term financing facility (VSTF). They also recognised that intramarginal interventions in EMS currencies could, within certain limits, qualify for this source of finance. These provisions and the close coordination of intervention and interest-rate policies which they imply were tested a few weeks after the Perugia conference. The experience in early November 1987, when Germany and France, in a jointly announced statement, moved their short-term interest rates in opposite directions following large intramarginal interventions, is a good illustration of Driffill's point that feedback rules exist, even under perfect capital mobility, which can sustain the EMS. Such rules might do more than avert a short-term crisis; as has happened since early November, they may succeed in reversing the initial speculative flow without further fundamental adjustment. Within the time limit of the VSTF, France had regained through private inflows the amount spent in interventions in October–November.

Driffill's study leaves open the question whether the EMS can be sustained under perfect capital mobility as a symmetrical system. I return to this point in relation to the discussion of rules in the chapter by Russo and Tullio (Chapter 11).

Maurice Obstfeld (Chapter 9) takes a more sceptical view of the compatibility of free financial flows and an exchange-rate system in which parity changes can rationally be expected from time to time. More specifically he asks the question: What kinds of equilibria can arise when markets expect a loss of competitiveness of domestically-produced goods to lead to a realignment?

If such behaviour has been observed on the part of the authorities for some time and realignments have typically restored competitiveness – the type of constant real exchange rate maintained through a crawling peg, as suggested by Dornbusch – devaluation fears may force a collapse and an inflationary spiral. If, on the other hand, a practice is visibly developed, as appears to have been the case in the EMS over the post-1983 period, in which realignments typically give less than full compensation for cumulative excess inflation since the previous realignment – those of April 1986 and January 1987 between the DM and the French franc were only about half the size required fully to remove the real appreciation of the franc since 1983 – an inflation devaluation spiral cannot occur.

Multiple equilibria are also possible as shown in a second model by Obstfeld, if the expectation of a realignment is driven by expansionary fiscal policy in the home country. If past behaviour justifies the belief that the government will ultimately fully offset the initial real appreciation resulting from a fiscal expansion, an exchange-rate collapse will occur when the expansion is announced, but before any real appreciation has occurred. This line of analysis captures some features of experience in the early stage of the EMS; even though capital mobility was far from perfect, on occasion capital flight from France followed the announcement of a more expansionary fiscal policy in the 1981–3 period. It is in part this perceived risk of engaging in individual fiscal expansion that has paralysed fiscal policy in some European countries. The analysis provides arguments for either undertaking fiscal action only as part of a coordinated, though possibly differentiated, package in the EMS countries, or moving to a more tightly managed exchange-rate system and ultimately a fixed-rate union in which destabilising expectations of devaluation and inflation would be effectively curtailed.

Obstfeld's study raises important stability issues for an EMS that has proceeded to full removal of capital controls before the underlying convergence of inflation rates and the coordination of the macropolicies which are seen to influence convergence have been achieved. Whereas Dornbusch may be too optimistic as to the feasibility of a 'fixed but adjustable rates' EMS in such circumstances, Obstfeld's vision seems to put excessive emphasis on instability as a likely consequence. As noted in the discussion of Dornbusch's study, it is the assumption of a high degree of foresight on the part of economic agents as to the actions governments will take in the EMS and their consequences that creates the possibility of an inflationary spiral, rather than the assumption of high capital mobility. The uncertainty on the timing and size of EMS realignments and the practice of giving no assurance to 'inflationary' countries that they can restore competitiveness fully may well be enough in practice to stabilise the system.

The chapter by Cristina Mastropasqua, Stefano Micossi and Roberto Rinaldi (Chapter 10) offers detailed insights into the intervention rules and practices in the EMS and case studies of the interactions of domestic and external components in money creation in four countries (Belgium, France, Germany and Italy). Their empirical work clearly brings out that intervention burdens have so far not been equally shared between Germany and the other countries studied, particularly since the Bundesbank has not participated in intramarginal interventions until very recently. For a long period other central banks in the EMS, when they wanted to intervene in DM, changed their holdings of this currency in the external (euro) DM market.

Potentially more interesting than this observation is the authors' efforts to measure asymmetries between countries in the degree to which they have preserved monetary autonomy. One such indicator is the extent of sterilisation of intervention. Using quarterly data for 1979 through 1986 they find that whereas Belgium, France and Italy have on average sterilised 30–40 per cent of the net change in the foreign assets of their central banks, that proportion is 60–80 per cent in Germany. The findings confirm the image of an EMS which is asymmetric in the sense that Germany pursues a domestic monetary target and sterilises external flows that upset it in a major way, while the other EMS countries conduct policy in terms of domestic credit expansion, allowing external flows to influence domestic monetary conditions.

It is important to note, however, that the asymmetry is not complete. Germany has intervened, and substantially at times, and the Bundesbank has been influenced by external considerations in allowing departures from its monetary target, especially in 1986–7. There are traces in the empirical results of an influence from monetary growth in non-German EMS countries on the growth rate of the monetary base in Germany. More recently, the Bundesbank has engaged in much heavier intervention, and for the first time in intramarginal intervention following the Nyborg Agreement. Even more significantly, the Bundesbank Council towards the end of 1987 decided to lower German short-term interest rates at a time when the monetary target had already been significantly overshot – just the opposite prescription of that suggested by a narrow domestic focus.

The authors note these improvements in the short-term functioning of the EMS, and conclude that acceptance of a greater degree of symmetry in monetary management in present conditions should no longer be regarded as inconsistent with preservation of the system's stable nominal anchor. Greater symmetry will, however, 'require a degree of consensus on medium-term policy objectives that simply does not exist today'.

The main effort of the authors of the final chapter (Chapter 11) in this part, Massimo Russo and Giuseppe Tullio, is to discuss various procedures for decentralised or centralised monetary management in the EMS area which will force explicit consideration of how far such a consensus goes. Drawing on the history of the international monetary system they look at the explicit or implicit adjustment mechanisms under the gold standard and the Bretton Woods system, and examine how the proposals for international monetary reform by McKinnon and by Williamson and Miller could be implemented within a reformed EMS. This gives concreteness to the notion of symmetry.

The simplest idea – but also the most radical – would be to fix an aggregate monetary objective for the EMS countries combined. Preliminary research reported in the study suggests that an aggregate EMS money demand function could prove to be at least as stable as the money demand function in Germany which may begin to be blurred by currency substitution. But would it be possible for the EMS countries to agree explicitly on a common inflation objective, as would be required to set an *ex ante* collective monetary target, and how would the national components be assigned in the absence of a full-scale European central bank? This model, desirable as a long-term objective, would require a jump in economic and monetary integration which seems unlikely within the horizon of even 5 to 10 years.

A second, very interesting possibility is to try to replicate the desirable properties of the first proposal by a decentralised rule in which all participants including Germany set a national objective for the domestic component of monetary base creation, but agree to refrain from sterilising the interventions which would be required to sustain fixed exchange rates in such a system. This would remove the asymmetry documented empirically by Mastropasqua *et al.* and implicit in the functioning of the system in recent years. If there were no net interventions in dollars and other third currencies, aggregate domestic credit expansion (DCE) in the EMS countries would be equal to total money creation, and the participants might jointly consider whether monetary growth for the area as a whole were acceptable. They would also have a check through the performance of the average of the EMS currencies *vis-à-vis* the dollar.

Such a symmetrical, decentralised system has an apparent appeal. But it would require protracted discussions between some collective EMS body and national authorities in cases when the domestic credit expansion targets suggested by individual countries seemed excessive, or when they were subsequently transgressed. A system with no other discipline than that stemming from (non-sterilisation of) reserve flows might well prove insufficient in a situation where national currencies are still far from perfect substitutes. Individual countries would have an incentive to overreport expected real growth in justification of their credit targets. On the whole, the procedure could destabilise the EMS relative to recent performance as long as there were no joint authority to change relative interest rates so as to contain incipient reserve flows. A policy of non-sterilisation can hardly be monitored or even sustained on a current basis without some joint discretionary authority of this type.

The study also considers two other, partly decentralised, procedures inspired by the international monetary reform discussion: a nominal income target and a monetary rule for each EMS participant, subject to a common inflation target – e.g., stable wholesale or traded goods prices for the EMS as a whole. These proposals have the virtue of addressing the issue of the nominal anchor for the system explicitly. The second approach might be suitable as a medium-term objective for a European central bank and could be stated explicitly to reinforce the intended autonomy of such an institution *vis-à-vis* more cyclical views of monetary management and help to build its reputation. But there are operational problems in designing the feedback rules that are to link departures from stability to the changes in national money growth rates. Setting national nominal income targets may have desirable features in principle, but the lack of precision of the objective and the time lags involved in knowing how close particular countries are to a stated path, are considerable. The task of translating this type of rule into anything operational for shorter-term management in a decentralised system seems forbiddingly difficult.

The more one regards proposals for reforming the EMS into a more symmetrical system – and it would be difficult to improve intellectually on the sample presented and discussed by Russo and Tullio – the more one becomes aware of the attractive simplicity of the EMS as it has evolved through practice. As long as fairly smooth management can be reconciled with some degree of asymmetry to preserve the nominal anchor function of German monetary policy, modifying the system significantly and visibly in the interest of symmetry, prior to the existence of a European central bank with important powers of collective decision-making and autonomy, has to be defended and justified very carefully. The system has already modified itself somewhat in the direction of symmetry through the Nyborg Agreements and their application in some well-coordinated actions in interest-rate management.

4   The future of the EMS

Though the main contribution of the present volume is to review the past functioning of the EMS and its implicit or explicit rationale, the final part of the book, with a chapter by Tommaso Padoa-Schioppa (Chapter 12) and the concluding panel discussion, looks at how the EMS might evolve. In most respects my interpretation of the theoretical and empirical work presented in the ten chapters that I have surveyed is favourable to the present EMS, indeed so much so that one may ask why there is any need for major reform. This view is shared by the Bundesbank and some other monetary authorities in the EMS, but increasingly questioned by others.

The virtue of Tommaso Padoa-Schioppa's study is that it combines a positive assessment of the achievements of the present EMS with a clear perception that the system is likely – in the light of both economic analysis and historical experience – to prove inadequate as a mechanism for reconciling the contradictions that will arise from trying to push far towards the internal market for goods and full-scale financial integration by 1992, while increasing the degree of nominal exchange-rate fixity and maintaining some national monetary autonomy. In his view, and in mine, it is clearly the latter that will have to give among this potentially 'inconsistent quartet' of desiderata. He restates the case for ultimate monetary union and a common money but, more constructively, he shows how the EMS could evolve towards that long-run objective in the phase where national monies coexist more or less easily and the decisions of monetary management which have traditionally been national are gradually moved to the European level. The role of a parallel currency (the ECU) is seen as critical in building the foundations for European monetary control in the form of a joint monetary base for the participating central banks. Above all, his carefully reasoned study is a plea for exercise at the European level of the discretionary powers essential to good monetary management once a broad consensus on the basic rules of conduct is established. The volume as a whole suggests to me that we are nearer to that stage than most observers recognise, and Padoa-Schioppa explicitly says that further important institutional steps need not await political unification. I leave to the reader to assess whether this hopeful scenario is also, as I believe, realistic.

NOTE
* The author gratefully acknowledges many discussions with Dr Daniel Gros, CEPS Research Fellow.

REFERENCES
Buiter, Willem (1986). 'A Gold Standard Isn't Viable Unless Supported by Sufficiently Flexible Monetary and Fiscal Policy', CEPR Discussion Paper, No. 125.
Dornbusch, Rudiger (1982). 'PPP, Exchange-Rate Rules and Macroeconomic Stability', *Journal of Political Economy*, Vol. 90, No. 1 (February).

Giavazzi, Francesco and Marco Pagano (1986). 'The Advantage of Tying One's Hands: EMS Discipline and Central Bank Credibility', CEPR Discussion Paper, No. 135; (1988) *European Economic Review* (June).

I The International Environment

2   The European Monetary System, the Dollar and the Yen*

RUDIGER DORNBUSCH

This study discusses challenges to international monetary stability in the coming years. Are the current levels of exchange rates (with allowance for moderate trends due to divergent inflation) substantially sustainable and is the European Monetary System (EMS) sustainable with its current institutional structure? I will argue that a number of problems remain unresolved and are likely to bring about major exchange-rate problems in the coming years:

(a) The EMS is inefficient as an adjustable-peg, low-inflation system. It would be improved by an explicit shift to a crawling-peg or constant real exchange-rate model.
(b) The US is insufficiently competitive at the current exchange rate and therefore will opt for depreciation or protection.
(c) The world real interest rate needs to decline sharply, a situation more strongly accepted and recognised in the US than elsewhere.

But there is also a wave of renewed interest in reforming the international monetary system by a return to more nearly fixed exchange rates.

Such an idea has been advocated by McKinnon over the past few years and is strongly argued in a recent 'blueprint' by Williamson and Miller (1987). These proposals subordinate macroeconomic policies and policy coordination to the vagaries of capital flows. A preferable alternative, as I shall argue, is to segment the capital account by a dual exchange-rate system.

(d) If capital controls are unacceptable and policy coordination is considered undesirable it is worthwhile giving serious attention to dual exchange rates among industrialised countries. This would reinforce the partial dual exchange-rate system that Europe and the US in fact have.

23

We start our analysis with debt problems of the world economy and the implications for a desirable EMS structure and for lower world real interest rates. We then turn to the dollar overvaluation and to dual exchange rates.

1   Real interest rates, inflation and public finance

In the past decade the combination of high real interest rates and high (and rising) debt–GNP ratios have been critically weakening public finance throughout the world economy. We want to draw attention here, in particular, to three aspects of this problem. One, why have real interest rates been high? Second, what has been the role of financial liberalisation in undermining the fiscal position? Third, what is the implication of inflation policy for budget financing? The significance of these issues differs across countries, but the last is of outstanding importance for low-velocity countries such as Italy or the new entrants into the Common Market.

A convenient framework for the discussion of the fiscal issue is the dynamics of the ratio of debt to GDP, x, which is shown in equation (2.1)[1],

$$x=d+(r-y)x-(\pi+y)[\alpha-\beta(r+\pi)]; \quad \alpha>\beta(r+\pi) \tag{2.1}$$

where

x ratio of debt to GDP
r real interest rate
y real growth
d non-interest deficit as percent of GDP
π inflation
α, β parameters of the velocity equation

The equation is derived by assuming that the part of the budget deficit not financed by highpowered money creation is financed by debt. Debt accumulation, relative to GDP, is thus determined by the two traditional terms: the non-interest budget deficit (measured as a fraction of GDP) and the discrepancy between the real interest rate and the growth rate. The part of the deficit financed by money is subtracted. This part depends for a given velocity positively on growth and inflation, but the velocity of highpowered money itself depends negatively on inflation and the real interest rate.

Equation (2.1) highlights real growth, real interest rates and inflation as determinants of debt accumulation. The non-interest budget and the existing debt–income ratio serve as parameters for the accumulation process.

It is apparent from equation (2.1) that increased real interest rates increase the rate of debt accumulation via two channels. First they directly raise the growth of debt by increasing the interest burden. But they also undermine the potential for money creation and hence reinforce the debt accumulation process.

A reduction in the growth rate of output limits the room for seignorage at each rate of inflation. This effect is more important the higher is the ratio of money to income. In financially underdeveloped countries, this effect would be particularly important. Friedman (1971) has pointed out that in strongly growing economies the revenue-maximising inflation rate is reduced by the fact that 'growth seignorage' is positively related to the level of real balances. But if growth is only very moderate then the optimal inflation rate is certainly not zero.

The debt accumulation equation also draws attention to a range of problems centred on the demand for highpowered money. Two major influences on the growth of highpowered money demand stand out. One is the disinflation of the past six years. In countries where highpowered money velocity is very low there is scope to finance a relatively large budget deficit by relatively moderate rates of inflation. Shifting to a hard money stance (by slowing down the rate of depreciation and inflation) reduces the revenue from money creation and hence requires either an offsetting correction in the budget or else implies a more rapid growth of debt.

This problem is strikingly apparent in all of Southern Europe, where the quest for disinflation has been pursued without recognition of the long-term budget consequences. To put it simply, the public finance role of inflation was left out of sight. The difficulty, of course, is that budget correction via increased taxation is definitely bad supply-side economics. The difficulties are sharply accentuated by the fact that growth rates of real output are far lower than in the past, and hence reinforce the disappearance of zero interest budget finance.

The quantitative importance of this point is brought out in Table 2.1 where we show seignorage as a fraction of GDP for several countries.[2] These data show that a very significant fraction of GDP can be financed by money creation and that a reduction in inflation to negligible levels involves sacrificing this opportunity, more so if growth is low.

Financial intermediation has also affected the scope for money creation as a means of budget finance. The decline in real highpowered money relative to GDP which is associated with reductions in required reserves means that now a larger share of the deficit is financed by debt and that

	Italy	Spain	Portugal	Greece
Seignorage[1]	2.6	2.9	3.4	3.4
Inflation	15.0	15.0	23.0	18.0
Growth	2.4	1.5	3.2	2.4

Table 2.1 Seignorage, Growth and Inflation, 1976–85 (Per Cent, Period Average)

Note:
[1]Seignorage is measured as the December to December change in reserve money (Line 14 in *International Financial Statistics*) expressed as a fraction of GDP. For Portugal, all data refer to 1976–84.

accordingly debt grows more rapidly. The same is true to the extent that currency has been displaced by alternative means of payment.

We now draw out some implications of this debt equation for the EMS and for an appropriate world real interest-rate policy.

a.   A crawling-peg EMS

The debt equation in equation (2.1) above shows the inflation rate to be an important determinant of debt accumulation. For moderate rates of inflation an increase in the rate of inflation reduces the rate at which the ratio of debt to income rises.[3] If debt accumulation is a problem area, then choosing the appropriate rate of inflation is an issue whose importance is of the first order. Specifically, the case can be made that countries with a debt problem should most definitely not seek near-zero inflation.

The inflation issue has a bearing on optimum currency areas. The traditional argument has focused on the (menu cost) advantages of a single money. The argument advanced here is more consequential. Public finance imposes an important constraint on the possibility of monetary unions. Countries for whom the efficient tax structure implies the use of an inflation tax – because the marginal cost of an extra dollar of resources raised this way is significantly less than that of raising (say) social security tax rates – should not merge with others for whom zero inflation is the policy objective.

In the short run, this argument does not carry much force, but over time it cumulates into significance. The loss of a per cent or a per cent and a half in zero interest financing, when added to the load in growth seignorage, is a dramatic effect on public finance. Higher real interest rates and reduced growth presumably would have made a case for using a higher rate of inflation, not a lower one. Shifting in the opposite direction builds up debt relative to GDP in a manner that opens long-run questions of sustainability. Doubts about sustainability, in turn, misallocate resources.

Recognising the role of public finance leads one to argue for a crawling-peg EMS. Rather than the current mix of excessively low inflation (for example, in Italy) and recurrent realignments, real exchange rates should be maintained by continuous depreciation. This allows the EMS to separate two issues: one relevant real interest rate, the other the rate of inflation. At present, the confusion of the two issues allows Germany to say a firm 'no' to any alteration in the real interest-rate stance.

In 1970 Robert Mundell correctly predicted the end of a US-led world monetary system, as indeed had Triffin for quite a while. Mundell wrote:[4]

> In the long run, however, retention of the monetary leadership in the U.S. will depend on the quality of U.S. performance, with erratic or antisocial behavior ultimately forcing Europe into a currency coalition. The greater the departure from acceptable norms the more likely is the emergence of monetary leadership in Europe.

Much the same issue arises today in Europe where the benefits of German monetary leadership are called into question. The common denominator is either a change in the institutional structure, with crawling-peg constant real exchange rates, and two blocks of which one has German inflation and the other significantly higher rates. The alternative – not necessarily imminent but accordingly more dramatic when it happens – is financial disarray in the periphery countries. The accession of underdeveloped countries like Portugal, Spain and Greece to the Common Market makes it timely to explore a common denominator better suited for the exchange-rate system.

It might be argued that, in fact, the EMS has functioned so far much in the crawling-peg manner. But that would be misreading the fact that the system has been used as a corset to promote disinflation. Having reached moderate inflation – or gone even too far – it is now time to use a system of less erratic real exchange rates and a stable inflation.[5]

There is, of course, rightly a concern with the issue of inflation stability. Does a real crawling-peg involve inflationary instability because it is tantamount to indexation? This issue is discussed in Dornbusch (1980, Chapter 9) where it is shown that PPP rules with full indexation of the exchange rate and of money are, indeed, unstable in respect to the price level. This simply points to the need to defend with monetary and fiscal

Period	Real rate	Period	Real rate
1926–80	−0.1	1970–80	−1.1
1950–80	−0.1	1980–7	3.5
1960–70	1.3	1986–7	3.2

Table 2.2 US Real Interest Rates (Period Averages)

Note: *T*-bill rate adjusted for the rate of CPI inflation.

policy a stable, moderate rate of inflation. The argument that only a zero inflation rate can be defended is a myth. What cannot be defended is a rate of inflation that has no rationale.

b.   Real interest rates

All industrialised countries, and of course the LDC debtors, share the common problem of exceptionally high real interest rates. As a benchmark the real interest rate on US Treasury bills between 1928 and 1980 averaged zero. Today real interest rates in the US, on the basis of producers' prices, are still near 3 per cent. In Europe and Japan likewise, real interest rates remain exceptionally high. These high real rates (shown in Table 2.2) raise two issues. One, where do they come from? Second, what are their implications for the budget?

Five competing hypotheses can be offered for the high real rates that we observe today:

(a) They might reflect primarily high levels of capital productivity.
(b) They could be a reflection of low levels of world saving, in large part the result of budget deficits.
(c) They might be the consequence of financial innovation and liberalisation – in short, the result of financial engineering.
(d) They could be the consequence of disinflation without sufficient monetary accommodation.
(e) Finally there is the argument that in any relevant sense real interest rates are not really high; nominal rates may be high, but this is a reflection of high rates of anticipated inflation.

There is no need to place the explanation all in one category, except to say that there is definitely no evidence of a world capital spending boom. It is true that stock markets have been booming, but strictly without a commensurate accumulation of physical capital.

To focus the discussion, we next consider the short-term real interest rate. It is commonly agreed that short-term real rates are determined in the money market. We can therefore invert the money market equilibrium condition:

$$M/P = L(i, \pi, Y) \tag{2.2}$$

to yield:

$$i = h(M/P, Y, \pi) \tag{2.2a}$$

We have allowed in equation (2.2) for a role of inflation that immediately raises the following argument: an increase in expected inflation, *given output and real balances*, cannot explain a rise in real interest rates. Why? Because an increase in expected inflation, if it has any effect at all, reduces real money demand and hence must *lower* the nominal interest rate. It must therefore certainly reduce real rates.

More generally, inflationary expectations can be a reason for high real interest rates only if they raise the level of economic activity, typically via an investment spending boom. Here is the conventional theory of the transmission mechanism of inflationary expectations to short-term nominal interest rates. Increased inflation expectations, given real balances and output (and hence the equilibrium nominal interest rate that clears the money market), reduce expected real interest rates. This leads to an increase in investment and aggregate demand, and hence to an expansion in output. It is the output expansion which raises the demand for real balances and hence puts upward pressure on the nominal interest rate; there is no transmission from expectations to nominal interest rates, bypassing the goods market. Moreover, inflation expectations can certainly not explain the rise in real interest rates evident in Table 2.2.

Budget deficits and financial engineering do offer a plausible explanation for high real rates. We can ask how is it that *despite* high real short-term rates real aggregate demand remains strong. One reason, in the United States, is the low level of taxation and hence the high level of current real disposable income. Without Ricardian equivalence, or with finite lives, that is enough to sustain high demand even in the face of high real interest rates. Even though budget deficits are a plausible explanation for high levels of demand, budget data would not seem to support that view. Both IMF and OECD data of fiscal stance, measured by the fiscal impulse, show a cumulative restraint for the period 1981–6. This can be seen in Table 2.3.

Financial engineering and financial liberalisation that led to a removal of credit constraints on households is a very plausible source of increased aggregate demand. This would come in an indirect fashion: they raise the value of consumer wealth or remove credit constraints previously

	US	Germany	Japan	Major 7
IMF	−1.5	4.0	3.8	0.8
OECD	−0.8	4.3	4.7	0.1

Table 2.3 Stance of Fiscal Policy, 1981–6 (Fiscal Impulse, % of GDP)

applicable. Two examples make the point. One case is where accumulated capital gains on owner-occupied housing are liquified by home equity loans. Another example is the increasing tendency of firms to give stock holders untaxable earnings in the form of capital gains (through stock purchases or mergers) rather than taxable dividends. Both techniques rely crucially on the tax system and on the increasing use of debt. Financial engineering thus represents a self-administered tax cut. While these advances in finance have no productive counterpart, they do boost aggregate demand at each level of the real interest rate. As a result, for a given real money stock, they will tend to raise interest rates.

Disinflation is another reason for continued high real interest rates. In order to achieve a reduction in nominal interest rates commensurate with the slowdown in inflation the real money stock must rise. That means nominal money growth must exceed the rate of inflation on average by enough to make allowance for real income growth, for changes in velocity induced by structural changes *and* for the liquification that must accompany disinflation. This point is strikingly obvious in the stabilisation of very high inflation, but it is equally true for the case of moderate inflation. While it may be true that money growth has systematically exceeded inflation in the past few years, the point is that even so money growth has not been sufficient.

It is difficult to know what part of the high real interest rates to attribute to each of the three surviving explanations. But the implications are quite clear: the high real rates reduce the rate of investment and they directly undermine the budget. The reduction in investment, in turn, slows down the growth of potential output, which further weakens the budget. By raising the need for non-interest surpluses there is a tendency to resort to further taxation of factor incomes, and that in turn slows supply-side growth.

The high real interest-rate problem arises not only in respect to public sector budgets but applies to overindebtedness throughout the world economy. In part as a result of high real interest rates themselves, in part in response to declining real prices of commodities and oil, in part in response to fiscal incentives to incur debt, there has been an altogether excessive accumulation of debt. Debt burdens today are sufficiently large that (at least in the US) the possibility of a '1929' is discussed in almost a matter-of-fact manner. The possibility is certainly seen as sufficiently realistic to act as a constraint on monetary policy to *raise* real interest rates. The proper direction for real interest rates is, of course, downward. How can this be done?

One immediate means for reducing real interest rates is a firm move to stop financial engineering. This is desirable on any number of grounds, ranging from resource allocation to public finance. But the major move to cut real interest rates must certainly be to cut the US budget. Early and sustained deficit reduction now is once again a serious possibility. In any event, it has to be done. But a decisive question concerns monetary policy in the course of budget correction. A common view holds that fiscal correction, by itself, will reduce interest rates. But, as equation (2.2a) shows, nominal interest rates fall only if fiscal tightening leads to a decline in activity. For output to remain constant (or grow in trend) there needs to be an active monetary policy that allows real balances to grow. In practice, that means an acceleration of money growth. A period of accelerated money growth would bring down nominal interest rates and hence achieve the crowding in required for sustained growth. There is, of course, the alternative of a reduction in real interest rates via accelerating inflation. But that is unlikely in the course of a fiscal contraction unless it be accompanied by a particularly sharp dollar depreciation.

US budget correction and the correction of the external balance, if they are to be achieved under conditions of full employment, require lower real interest rates in the US and dollar depreciation. The less Europe and Japan are willing to follow the US into a low-interest rate strategy the more the US will adjust with depreciation and inflation, and the more the rest of the world will adjust with increased unemployment. It is clear that a worldwide cut in real interest rates is a preferable strategy.

It might be argued that real interest rates cannot be cut by faster money growth. That is certainly not the case at the relevant short end of the term structure. If exchange rates remain constant the only major impact on inflation comes from activity and possibly a recovery of commodity prices induced by lower carrying costs. It is more plausible to argue that they cannot be cut permanently by faster money growth, but even that may not be true if the reason for the currently high levels is an insufficient liquification in the process of disinflation. In fact, anyone who believes that real interest rates cannot be lowered by monetary policy *must* be arguing that US budget correction will lower real interest rates because it creates a recession. In that case, it is somewhat doubtful why there is so much enthusiasm about US budget cutting in the rest of the world.

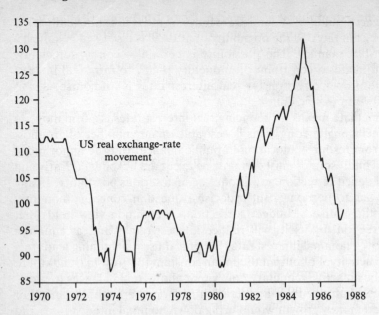

Figure 2.1   US real exchange rates, index 1980–2 = 100

But even if real interest-rate reduction were only transitory it would still achieve the important purpose of reducing (at least for a while) the pace of debt accumulation.

2   The need for further dollar depreciation[6]

The likely continuation of a large US external deficit poses another challenge to the stability of exchange rates at current levels. Figure 2.1 shows the real exchange rate of the dollar, using the Morgan Guaranty measure which includes developed and newly industrialised countries. It will be noted that the current level of the dollar has not returned to the level of 1980 and continues much above the average of the period 1973–80. That is a suitable starting point for evaluating whether the current level of the dollar is appropriate.

It may be useful at the outset to ask what factors explain the massive US deficit of 1986–7. There are basically five reasons:

(a) The extraordinary overvaluation of 1982–5.
(b) The sharp shift in trade with the NICs: the US has experienced a $60 billion shift in its manufactures trade with these countries since 1980.

(c) To the extent that it is a separate factor from point (b) above, the debt crisis has forced Latin America and other countries into becoming net exporters to the US.

(d) The 13 per cent gap in demand growth between the US and other OECD countries, which has meant a rapid growth of imports and only moderate export growth.

(e) Finally, as a result of the preceding factors, the emergence of a current account deficit has brought about a decumulation of external assets, and now a growing external debt which generates a worsening current account deficit by its own debt dynamics.

a.   Why the dollar might have depreciated enough

Most observers who feel that the dollar now is correctly valued place their confidence in one of two arguments. Either they argue that adjustment lags to the depreciation of the past two years are long, and that patience is required to await the full benefits. Or else they believe that there is basically no need for a US current account balance because deficits can be financed almost indefinitely.

The adjustment lag argument does not stand up to scrutiny. I have reported elsewhere a simulation of US net exports on the assumption that real exchange rates are maintained at the level of the early 1980s and that growth in the US and abroad proceeds at the same pace.[7] The conclusion is that the deficit will decline over the period to 1989, but that in the end a $100 billion (and growing) deficit remains. Only if the rest of the world experiences a major spurt in demand could the gap be closed. Of course, the prospect of such a spurt is quite unlikely.

The alternative is to say that the US does not really need to adjust because deficits can be financed for a very long period. This argument is most frequently supported by reference to an almost unlimited ability of the US to finance current account imbalances by selling off assets. It is correctly observed that the rest of the world holds as yet a small share of its portfolio in the form of US assets and that accordingly there are years' worth of saving from all industrialised countries available to finance a continuation of the deficit even at $100 billion levels. Just as a country with a terms of trade improvement can spend the extra real income without impairing its creditworthiness so can the US spend the rents that flow from the attractiveness of its assets.

It is certainly true that if the world economy had newly-discovered US assets, and if as a result there were massive capital gains, US residents could spend some of that increased wealth. The question is, however, what happens when the capital gains run out? If the exchange rate is allowed to stay overvalued this leads inevitably to disinvestment in the traded goods sector. If ultimately a cut in absorption and a reversal of the current account becomes necessary, that adjustment will have to be extra large because of the disappearance of capacity and other hysteresis effects.

The fact that in 1987 central banks rather than private savers have been financing the US current account calls into question this argument. The international capital flow argument is more validly an argument about two-way diversification rather than one about international one-way lending. There is certainly no life-cycle story of why the US should be running down assets.

There is an entirely different line of argument, which has been brought by McKinnon (1987a, 1987b). He has made the case that the dollar is *under*valued and the yen *over*valued. The argument is made on the basis of absolute purchasing power comparison.

It is difficult to understand what to make of the McKinnon discussion. Perhaps there is a belief that fiscal policy alone governs current account imbalances and that relative prices do not – or should not – play a role. But the entire history of PPP, starting with Cassel, emphasises that when real variables change so do equilibrium real exchange rates. This is most obviously true for the trend changes in real exchange rates brought about by Ricardo–Balassa–Kravis–Marston productivity growth differentials. But it is, of course, also true for fiscal changes, as we know from the transfer problem literature. The McKinnon contention must therefore be viewed as curious until further clarification is offered.

In the meantime, it is worth emphasising one factor which suggests a need for trend depreciation of the dollar arising from the special role played in the US market by the NICs. This argument was made in Dornbusch (1979) and has, since then, become dramatically more apparent. The emergence of NICs as suppliers of manufactures in world trade is largely acted out in the US market: the US market is wide open and large, thus inviting any infant industry to try itself. By contrast, Europe and Japan are heavily protected. This suggests that over the next decade the US will suffer an unusually large share of the exports of the NICs. Of course, these countries will also be importing, but there is nothing that singles out the US for a special supplier role. As a result the US is bound to suffer a widening trade deficit with the NICs. Moreover, political interests make it very difficult to try and close that gap by protection. Thus, unless the NICs can be pushed into real appreciation and inward-looking growth, there is a need for US depreciation relative to Europe and Japan to provide the room for increased net exports from the developing world.

b.   Why the dollar is not depreciating more rapidly

The preceding argument makes the case that the dollar is undoubtedly overvalued, by my estimate as much as 30 per cent. The interesting question then is, why have there not been more decisive speculative attacks? It is certainly a fact that there are no compensating interest differentials that would rationally support holding US assets. This is a hard question, which a more prudent writer might avoid. The probable answer lies not in irrationality but rather in the short horizon of speculation.

Asset markets are dominated by speculators who are limited in their ability to make short-term capital losses in their own currency. Regulatory reporting requirements prevent financial institutions engaging in long-term speculation if the short-term uncertainty is too high. Thus, even though there may be a consensus that over a two-year period the dollar will undergo a 30 per cent depreciation, few institutions take a long-term position and sit out that depreciation. The reason is that a short-run adverse trend is seen as much more costly than the ultimate – almost certain – profit. Of course, there is some long-term speculation. But there is also some central bank intervention, in fact an extraordinary amount. But more than the magnitude of intervention counts the willingness of central banks to stop one-way speculation by creating sufficient uncertainty about the near-term pace of depreciation. That means that depreciation occurs in chunks, with irregular intervals of stability (or even partial reversal) in between.

Looking back, we observe that a massive dollar depreciation has taken place without any significant influence on US interest rates or on inflationary expectations. Looking forward, it seems hard to believe that another 30 per cent is possible without speculators catching on. But small action on interest rates is enough to check speculation. Moreover, the further the depreciation is carried the more diffuse are expectations about the magnitude and timing of any remaining depreciation, and hence the easier the task of destabilising the speculators.

A further argument in this direction is frequently made: continuing dollar depreciation in the near term would imply that the *J*-curve is persistently at work. Further, depreciation – with its adverse effects on valuation – keeps dominating the quantity adjustments and hence current account improvement simply does not come into sight. The failure of current account improvement to emerge in time tests the patience of speculators, who take an excessively pessimistic view of the currency and might stage a run that affects control. Hence the need to space out depreciation to allow volume adjustments to become significant, and thus aid stabilising speculation.

This interpretation of foreign-exchange markets in the past half year assumes that central banks agree on the need for much further dollar depreciation, but choose to bring it about in a controlled fashion. If so, there must presumably also be an idea of how Europe and Japan absorb the gain in US competitiveness. The alternative explanation is that the US accepts that the dollar has gone far enough – on whatever basis – and is simply helping to demonstrate to the market the new equilibrium rate – if necessary, with increased interest rates. Of course, it might also be a much more shortsighted policy pursued for the convenience of an election year and motivated by concern about increasing US inflation in the next twelve months. Whichever the motivation, defending an over-valued exchange rate is a dead-end street. The costs in terms of disruptive high interest rates and ultimate collapse are extremely high. There is no conceivable merit for the US (or the trading partners) in perpetuating the overvaluation, other than as a policy of a controlled dollar decline.

3   Dual exchange rates

The preceding discussion has tried to put in question the theory that current exchange rates, real interest rates and institutional structures are likely to persist undisturbed for a long time. It would certainly be inappropriate, if this view is correct, to go in the direction of fixing exchange rates or of adopting target zones, except if they were to recognise explicitly the objectives of a lower world real interest rate and a major dollar depreciation.

But even if cooperation were sufficient to allow a level of real exchange rates that sustains US full employment (after budget cuts) with a sharply improved external competitiveness or much lower world interest rate, there is a question of how a system of more nearly fixed exchange rates might be designed. I shall argue that dual exchange rates have received insufficient attention so far.

James Tobin and others have identified international short-term capital flows as a distinct nuisance to an efficient performance of the world economy. Tobin (1978) argues:

> There are two ways to go. One is toward a common currency, common monetary and fiscal policy, and economic integration. The other is toward greater financial segmentation between nations or currency areas, permitting their central banks and governments greater autonomy.

Tobin's proposal is to impose a worldwide, moderate transactions tax on foreign-exchange purchases so as to reduce the profitability of short-term hot money trips. Other proposals involve variable, transitory interest equalisation taxes. A different way of handling the interference of undesirable capital flows with macroeconomic stability is a dual exchange-rate system. Under such a dual exchange-rate system there would be a fixed commercial rate and a flexible capital account rate. The fixed commercial rate would avoid the interference of portfolio shifts with the stability of trade flows and the stability of price levels. The flexible capital account rate would serve as a shock absorber for asset market disturbances, fads and other motives for portfolio shifts which may be reflected in excessively large or persistent exchange-rate movements.

A dual exchange-rate system has been applied in many countries, often with very mixed success – at least, that is the common argument. Three questions must be asked. First, can it be applied in practice among industrial countries? Second, what are the principal institutional features? Third, supposing these issues are settled, what are the merits? There is an extensive literature on the theory of an experience with dual rates.[8] The common criticism is that dual rates are impractical because either the premium is very small (and hence they do not serve much of a purpose) or the premium is large, and leakages from one market to another become an important source of misallocation.

The evidence on dual exchange rates in developing countries does, indeed, suggest these conclusions, but that also makes them much less relevant to industrial countries. The best analogy is presumably with income taxes. When they were first introduced exactly the same arguments were made – namely, that there would be pervasive evasion. Clearly that is not the case today. Moreover since most international transactions are carried out by audited institutions a comprehensive system of dual rates among industrial countries, with appropriate legal sanctions, should minimise evasion to lower levels than are experienced in income tax collection. In other words, most of the undesirable traffic can be stopped.

There will, of course, be a need for bureaucracy and red tape. But it is difficult to believe that the resource cost is at all comparable to the vast costs experienced in the course of say the UK or the US real appreciation.

As to the details of implementation there are questions such as this. Do all capital account transactions go into the flexible-rate market? The answer is that long-term direct and portfolio investment can certainly go into the fixed-rate market. Where do interest earnings go? The answer here is that they should go into the flexible-rate market. But these issues cannot be discussed in isolation since the main point will be to have a

	US	Germany	UK	Japan
1975–87: 1				
Real effective rate	10.6	5.1	15.8	10.4
Dollar rate	–	15.6	19.9	16.1
1979–87: 1				
Real effective rate	12.0	4.9	8.2	9.2
Dollar rate	–	17.9	21.0	12.8

Table 2.4 Variability of Real Effective and Dollar Exchange Rates, 1985–87: 1

Note: Variability is measured by 100× ratio of the standard deviation to the mean – i.e., the coefficient of variation. The real effective exchange rate is the IMF series of relative value added deflators in manufacturing.

Source: IMF.

consistent blueprint that avoids the possibility of speculative runs on the fixed rate. A third question concerns rules for the fixed rate. Here the correct answer is to use a crawling-peg real exchange rate, possibly with some drift to offset trend changes in the current account balance.

Now to the advantages of such a system. The principal advantage of a dual exchange-rate system is to remove from the goods markets the vagaries of exchange-rate fluctuations provoked by asset market disturbances.[9] Of course, this does not come free. All the problems of a fixed current account exchange rate remain: there is a need for enough flexibility to adjust to persistent real changes and also to allow for divergent inflation trends. Moreover, there is also the fact that once the capital account rate is detached from the anchor of trade flows it might take off on its own for much further trips. In fact, except for the valuation effects of foreign assets in wealth there would be little impact on the real economy. The gain lies in monetary policy being potentially freed for domestic objectives – and, more importantly, the removal of asset market disturbances from interference with goods flows. A dollar overvaluation, as occurred in 1982–5 as a result of the monetary fiscal mix, would not have occurred.

There is a sense in which Europe (and to a much more limited extent the US) have in fact practised such a dual exchange-rate system. The fact that Europe is relatively closed and operates fixed exchange rates within it has worked almost like a fixed current account rate. By contrast, the capital account rate – the $/DM rate – has been flexible. Indeed, because

Figure 2.2 Real exchange rates, index 1980 = 100

the rate mattered so little it could fluctuate so much. Table 2.4 shows the coefficient of variation of nominal and real effective exchange rates, using quarterly data, for several key currencies.

Table 2.4 demonstrates that the German real effective exchange rate shows less than half the variability of the US real rate. The DM/$ rate is three times more variable than the trade exchange rate. In this sense, Germany has more nearly a dual exchange-rate system. Figure 2.2 makes the same point by highlighting the much larger fluctuations in the US real exchange rate.

This dual exchange-rate argument does not, however, apply to Japan except to the extent that Japan and Europe floated jointly relative to the dollar, thus dampening the impact on the effective real exchange rate of Japan's large $/yen movements. But there may be a compensating element in the flexibility of Japan's wage level, which dampened the real effects of large nominal rate movements.

This discussion suggests that in fact we are already part of the way to a dual-rate system, and the only question remaining is what the merits are of making current account rates more closely tied. On balance, there appears little merit in fixing rates between the US and Europe: trade flows are limited and the uncertainty about policies and the need for real exchange-rate adjustment makes market solutions preferable, even if they contain excess noise introduced by the capital account.

The same is probably not true for the US–Japan case. Misalignments of the dollar/yen rate carry increasingly the threat of protection. Moreover, $/yen exchange-rate movements have important spillover effects on countries like Korea. Given the importance of trade flows and of political relations, there may be a case here for moving toward stable real exchange rates for commercial transactions and toward the accompanying policy coordination. Unlike Europe, Japan may be small enough to prefer US macroeconomic leadership to the threat of protection.

NOTES

* I am indebted to Ralph Bryant, Dale Henderson, Stefano Micossi, Robert Triffin and Charles Wyplosz for helpful suggestions.
1 See Dornbusch (1978) where this framework is used in the context of a neoclassical growth model to show that a shift from money to debt finance raises inflation and lowers capital intensity.
2 A very helpful comprehensive evaluation of the seignorage question is offered in Fischer (1982).
3 The rate of debt accumulation declines if

$$\pi < [\alpha/\beta - (r+y)]/2$$

Since $\pi > y$ for high inflation countries our functional form yields an increase in seignorage for all rates of inflation. This would not be the case for example for the Cagan function which yields a Laffer curve.
4 'European and American Monetary Policy', in Mundell (1971, p. 169).
5 I recognise that rates are significantly more stable than prior to the EMS, but I doubt that anyone would seriously argue that there would be a misallocation of resources involved in eliminating the real appreciation prior to realignment and the accompanying crises.
6 This section draws on Dornbusch (1987, 1988).
7 See Dornbusch (1987). The basic equation is as follows:

$$\text{Net} = 90 \quad -5.9\log(P/eP^*) - 12.3\log(D/D^*) - 0.04 \text{ Time}$$
$$(7.9) \quad (-3.8) \qquad\qquad (-3.7) \qquad\qquad (-6.2)$$

$R^2 = 0.96$ Rho $= 0.43$ where t-statistics are given in parenthesis.

The term P/eP^* represents the real exchange rate and D/D^* relative levels of demand in the US and abroad. The equation is estimated with quarterly data, allowing for lags.
8 See Dornbusch (1986) for references and a model of dual exchange rates for a small country.
9 See Hogarth and Reder (1986) on the debate regarding less than perfect rationality of economic agents, especially as reflected in asset markets.

REFERENCES

Dornbusch, R. (1978). 'Inflation, Capital and Deficit Finance', *Journal of Money Credit and Banking* (February).

(1979). 'Issues in International Finance: Who or What Controls the Dollar?' Data Resources, Inc., *World Economic Bulletin* (Spring).

(1980). *Open Economy Macroeconomics*, New York, Basic Books.

(1986). 'Special Exchange for Capital Account Transactions', *World Bank Economic Review*, Vol. 1, No. 1.

(1987). 'External Balance Correction: Depreciation or Protection?' Brookings Papers on Economic Activity, No. 1.

(1988). 'Some Doubts About the McKinnon Standard', *Economic Perspectives*, 1 (Winter).

Fischer, S.S. (1982). 'Seignorage and the Case for a National Money', *Journal of Political Economy*, Vol. 90, No.2 (April), pp. 295–313.

Friedman, M. (1971). 'Government Revenue from Inflation', *Journal of Political Economy*, Vol. 79, No.4 (July–August), pp. 846–56.

Hogarth, R. and M. Reder (eds) (1986). *Rational Choice*, Chicago, University of Chicago Press.

McKinnon, R. (1987a). 'Currency Protectionism: Parity Lost', *Wall Street Journal* (2 February).

(1987b). 'A Gold Standard Without Gold. Putting a Stop to Rapid Currency Swings', *New York Times* (12 April).

(1987c). 'A Model for Currency Cooperation', *Wall Street Journal* (21 September).

Marston, R. (1986). 'Real Exchange Rates and Productivity Growth in the United States and in Japan', NBER Working Paper, No.1922.

Mundell, R. A. (1971). *Monetary Theory*, Pacific Palisades, Goodyear.

Nurkse, R. (1946). *International Currency Experience in the Interwar Period*, Geneva, League of Nations (reprinted by Arno Press).

Spaventa, L. (1987). 'The Growth of Public Debt: Sustainability, Fiscal Rules and Monetary Rules', IMF Staff Papers (June).

Tobin, J. (1978). 'A Proposal for International Monetary Reform', *Eastern Economic Journal*, 3 (July/October). Reprinted in J. Tobin, *Essays in Economics. Theory and Policy*, Cambridge, Mass., MIT Press.

Williamson, J. and M. Miller (1987). 'Targets and Indicators: A Blueprint for the International Co-ordination of Economic Policy,' Washington, DC, Institute for International Economics, Policy Analyses in International Economics, No. 22 (September).

Discussion

ROBERT TRIFFIN

You will be relieved to hear that my comments will be relatively brief – and pleasing to our friend Rudiger – since I agree fully with most of his arguments, and particularly with his imaginative, but *second-best* proposal for a dual exchange-rate system such as has long applied in Belgium.[1] Rudiger agrees himself, on p. 23 of his study, that this proposal would be desirable only 'if capital controls are unacceptable and policy coordination is considered undesirable', and Belgium has indicated its willingness to abandon its dual rates in favour of the 'first-best' proposals of the Delors EEC plan. I shall come back to this in my concluding remarks.

Let me first raise a few minor questions or points of dissent:

(a) P. 27: Is inflation really low in Italy? I invite comments from our Italian friends.

(b) P. 27: Intra-EMS *real* rates have *not* – I repeat *not* – been erratic. They have, on the contrary, preserved their stability at competitive levels, both by offsetting promptly *current* inflation differentials by the realignment of nominal rates, and by correcting the *initial* overvaluation of the Belgian franc and undervaluation of the Italian lira.

(c) P. 32: The dollar exchange rate has depreciated vastly *vis-à-vis* strong currencies, but *not vis-à-vis* the weaker currencies of important US export markets, such as Latin America, Canada, etc.

(d) P. 34: Is it clear that Europe and Japan are more heavily protected than the United States?

(e) P. 35: 'overvalued . . . as much as 30 per cent' – as of when, or what level? My estimate would be less as of now, but likely to grow over future months and years if the US does not succeed in correcting its internal budgetary deficits and its external balance of payments deficits.

My own conclusion is that the fantastic US deficits and capital imports are *unsustainable* as well as *unacceptable* – humanely and economically – for the US as well as for the rest of the world, but that it will take years to correct them. In the meantime, the EEC countries should strengthen the EMS and offer the US 'swap substitution accounts' denominated in their own currencies, or in ECUs, and without imperative amortisation ('*consols*' or '*rentes perpétuelles*' in French). They should also resort to exchange controls if necessary to avoid unnecessary realignments of their mutual exchange rates, such as that of January 1987 which may be a feeble forecast of similar (and worse) future crises.

In answer to those who argue that such controls would be impossible to enforce in practice, I would point out:

(a) That they could certainly be applied by central banks and other official agencies to their own investments in the US market (now totalling about $240 billion), and to the even larger investment of their commercial banks.

(b) That enforcement would be far easier if applied *jointly* by deficit *and* surplus countries, since deterring speculative capital movements should be as desirable for the latter as for the former.

NOTE
1 And in Switzerland in the early post-war years.

Discussion

CHARLES WYPLOSZ

This is a traditional Dornbusch study: it is broad-ranging, provocative and sure to have ripple effects on policy discussions. It includes his favourite themes (the dollar overvaluation, excessively high real interest rates, the disruptive effects of capital mobility) and presents his favourite arguments with customary forcefulness. While I agree with several conclusions I do have a number of objections, in particular about the proposal to move the EMS towards a crawling peg.

The study has a taste of history. It was presented on Friday 16 October 1987, the day when the release of new US trade figures initiated the Great Crash of 1987. It is hard, then, to disagree with Dornbusch's diagnosis that the US current account and budget deficits were on an unstable path, with serious threats hanging over stock prices and the dollar! If he is to be right again, we should realise that none of the factors of instability identified by Dornbusch has been eliminated since the crash: too little progress on the US budget deficit, no serious attempt at expanding in Europe (outside of the UK), no depreciation in the NICs despite their mammoth surpluses. The only good move is the (moderate) Japanese expansion. As for the dollar, its fall at the end of 1987 means that some tensions have eased up, but Dornbusch's calculations suggest that more is to come. Thus the core of the message of the study has already been proven right.

I have problems with the explanation of the high real interest rates. Dornbusch comes up with five potential culprits. Out of these, he rules out an investment boom, the budget deficits and inflationary expectations. This leaves two possibilities which he endorses: financial engineering and insufficient liquification in the wake of the disinflation of the mid-1980s. I have no disagreement about the characterisation of monetary policies. I have some doubts about the size of the effects of financial engineering. But I feel uneasy with his views on the interest-rate effects of inflationary expectations and budget deficits.

Starting with the budget deficits, Dornbusch correctly remarks that, overall, the budgetary stance has been restrictive among the seven large OECD countries, with the (sharp) expansion in the US matched by a (sharp) contraction elsewhere. But why should we explain interest rates by flows rather than stocks? The ratio of public debt to GNP among the seven large countries has risen from 21.2 per cent in 1979 to 33.3 per cent in 1987. The stock and flow views thus send conflicting signals, and Dornbusch does not tell us why he dismisses one of them.

Regarding frequently-heard suggestions that the currently high levels of nominal interest rates simply reflect high inflationary expectations, Dornbusch takes a rather extreme position. He asserts that inflationary expectations, if anything, lead to lower real *and* nominal rates. That real rates should decrease is reasonably well accepted and since this is what he is mainly driving up to, we could stop here. But the notion that nominal rates should fall is too much at odds with conventional wisdom to be simply overlooked. To be sure, this result comes straight out of his equation (2.2) if, as is reasonable, he assumes $\partial L/\partial i < 0$ and $\partial L/\partial \pi < 0$ with M/P and Y constant. But what of the rest of the model? He seems to have in mind a sluggish *IS* curve, and that too is acceptable in the short run (but over five years, as in Table 2.3?). Yet the whole implicit model seems unrealistically restrictive for the purpose at hand. It concerns an economy with only nominal assets and no trade in assets. In the tradition of Tobin, allow for the existence of capital and re-write the portfolio model as:

$$\frac{M}{P} = L(i, \pi, Y). W \tag{D2.1}$$

$$K = f(i - \pi, Y). W \tag{D2.2}$$

with K the (fixed) stock of capital and W total financial wealth, including nominal bonds (omitted thanks to Walras's law).

Then the model can be represented as in Figure D2.1. The *KK* curve represents equation (D2.2). The *MM* curve represents equation (D2.1). An exogenous increase in inflationary expectations π shifts *KK* to *K'K'*

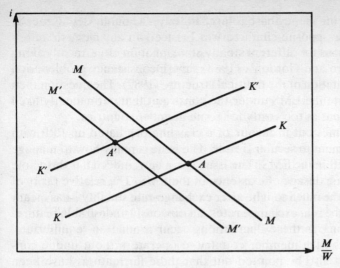

Figure D2.1 The portfolio model

and MM to $M'M'$ (holding Y and M/P constant as Dornbusch does). Dornbusch's result is simply the vertical downward shift of the MM schedule. But the KK schedule shifts upward one for one with π. The overall effect is theoretically ambiguous and is positive when $|df/\partial\ (i-\pi)|df/\partial(i-\pi)|>|\partial L/\partial\pi|$.

The omission of trade in assets is also problematic. Openness makes the assumption that M/P is constant, untenable over more than the very short run. Indeed, an increase in inflationary expectations should trigger a capital outflow. Either the exchange rate is left free to float and its depreciation raises the price level, or there is a central bank intervention and M falls – unless sterilised, which cannot last much. In both cases, M/P falls and the nominal interest rate must rise.

Leaving these technical details aside, I find Dornbusch's remark about the need for EMS countries to maintain different inflation rates most important. His fundamental argument is that the optimal inflation tax is not zero. When combined with the fact that the debt service and the relative size of the money base taxable through inflation differs considerably from country to country, we indeed reach the conclusion that individual countries have a strong incentive to settle on different steady-state inflation rates. Two remarks, however, are called for on this issue. First, optimal tax rates are likely to be reasonably close, even with widely different money bases. Second, the inflation tax also operates on the nominal non-indexed portion of the public debt and global data would be needed to come to a full assessment of what is at stake. (For example, while the money base is large in Italy, the public debt is mostly short term. The opposite characterises France.) In any case, there are other good reasons for different steady-state inflation rates, mostly along the line of Barro and Gordon's (1983) time inconsistency problem and Alesina's exploitation of the political structure (1987). The question then is how to operate the EMS under the constraint that permanently fixed rates are ruled out as too costly for some member countries.

Dornbusch comes out in favour of a crawling peg based on PPP with possible adjustment to secular trends. The issue is really how to manage realignments within the EMS. The issue is not new, indeed it is the whole history of the first decade of existence of the EMS. The relative rarity of realignments – the much sought-after exchange-rate stability – has meant fluctuations of the real exchange rates, an obviously undesirable feature. However, as long as these fluctuations occur around an 'equilibrium' level this allows each member country to operate without undue constraints. It must also be pointed out that these fluctuations have been contained within a narrow band of about 10 per cent, a major improvement over free floating outside the EMS area. There also were capital controls in devaluation-prone countries which undoubtedly helped get through the apparently inevitable spells of speculative attacks.

In the end, the choice on how to continue operating the EMS boils down to either the status quo (including the maintenance of capital controls), or a modification of the system so as to avoid discrete jumps at the time of realignments and therefore speculative attacks and the need for capital controls, or better intervention agreements. The no-jump solution, of which the crawling peg is one example, is a respectable solution but one which gives up much of the soul of the EMS, so that other options should also be considered. One possibility could be a much enlarged pooling of central bank reserves as recently proposed by Grilli and Alesina (1987). Yet another, more ambitious, possibility is to opt for a monetary union, but here the public-finance aspects emphasised by Dornbusch represent a major hurdle: those who advocate a monetary union should also explain how highly-indebted countries such as Belgium, Italy or Ireland will operate.

While this discussion is interesting – and quite relevant in view of the plan wholly to liberalise capital flows within the European Community by 1992 – it fails to address what is in my view the central weakness of the EMS, namely its evolution into a Deutsche mark zone. This evolution is often explained by the overriding importance of inflation as a policy target; if that were true, the apparently long-lasting decline of inflation would signal a weakening of the German influence. However, Dornbusch's observation about the inevitability of different steady-state inflation rates may provide another explanation. The idea is that there exists a fundamental asymmetry between devaluation and revaluation-prone countries in their ability to resist speculative attacks. This asymmetry, although at work only at the time of crises, may well in fact tilt the whole balance of power within the EMS in favour of the country with the strongest currency (Wyplosz, 1987). The practical result is that Germany's emphasis on sound money and budgetary orthodoxy works as a contractionary restraint on the policy choices open to the other EMS countries. The only possibility for them to expand (should they wish so) would be by first depreciating their currencies *vis-à-vis* the DM which, given the unanimity rule, Germany successfully vetoes. The experience of the last two or three years indeed shows that most other countries have maintained, on average, a current account balance under conditions of weak internal demand and slow growth. A resumption of faster growth, of the kind required to deliver some relief from mass unemployment, would either lead to unsustainable current account deficits or require a sustained real devaluation. The first option is not acceptable as a policy option, the second is ruled out by the current rules of the game within the EMS. The overall picture is one of a lack of policy coordination within the EMS, a by-product of which is a lack of coordination between the EMS countries and the US.

REFERENCES
Alesina, Alberto (1987). 'Macroeconomic Policy in a Two-Party System as a Repeated Game', *Quarterly Journal of Economics*, Vol. 102, No. 3 (August), pp. 651–78.
Barro, Robert and David Gordon (1983). 'Rules, Discretion and Reputation in a Model of Monetary Policy', *Journal of Monetary Economics*, Vol. 12 (July), pp. 101–21.
Grilli, Vittorio U. and Alberto Alesina (1987). 'Avoiding Speculative Attacks on EMS Currencies: A Proposal', Yale University (mimeo).
Wyplosz, Charles (1987). 'The Swinging Dollar: Is Europe Out of Step', INSEAD, Working Paper, No. 88–05.

II   Disinflation, External Adjustment and Cooperation

3   Monetary Discipline and Cooperation in the European Monetary System: A Synthesis*

JACQUES MELITZ

Efforts to understand the European Monetary System (EMS) as a strategic game sometimes emphasise monetary discipline, sometimes the gains of exchange-rate cooperation.[1] This study attempts to combine the two approaches in order to benefit from the respective merits of each. The monetary discipline hypothesis is especially helpful in understanding the interest of the inflation-prone members in the system, while the issue of strategic cooperation is essential in explaining the German presence. The German benefits are also more secure than those to the rest. The argument further implies that tighter monetary policy will result in the EMS not only from the behaviour of the others, but from that of Germany itself.

The first part of the study will be devoted to the proposition that neither cooperation nor monetary discipline alone provides an adequate basis for the EMS. The second part will contain the proposed theoretical framework for analysing monetary discipline, in which we will admit cooperation later on in the third part. The cooperative element, in this next part, will revolve around the competitiveness of traded goods. A short concluding section will follow.

1.   The shortcomings of either cooperation or monetary discipline as the sole basis for the EMS

Standard application of game theory shows that the EMS can benefit everybody by avoiding competitive exchange-rate appreciation or depreciation. The cooperative interpretation of the EMS has two empirical drawbacks, however. In the first place, it cannot explain the dominant position of Germany. This country may be the largest in the EMS, but it is not exceptionally large in relation to the next biggest, and it is not easy to explain its dominant position on the basis of any particular structural characteristics, at least in the context of game theory. Indeed, the

51

tendency in modelling the EMS has been to assume two identical members, but simply to consider the one which disposes of the monetary instrument as Germany.[2] However, this way of admitting the special reserve-currency status of the country is inadequate. As soon as a shock affecting all of the members enters the analysis, the allocation of the instruments between them can make a difference. But if all of them are really identical, the difference is difficult to comprehend. The difficulty comes out most clearly in Giavazzi and Giovannini (1984), who show, with particular reference to the EMS, that in case of an oil shock affecting two identical members of an exchange-rate union identically, the one with control over the exchange rate can take advantage of its twin which controls the stock of money.[3] But in a game-theoretical context, there is no reason for the disadvantaged twin to go along with the arrangement.

Another possibility is to interpret Germany as a Stackelberg leader. It is well known that Stackelberg leadership may benefit both players in a strategic game, follower as well as leader.[4] But the application of this next approach to the EMS poses even greater difficulties. As a Stackelberg leader with reserve-currency status, Germany moves first, and does so in anticipation of the responses of the other member(s). The approach thus is inconsistent with any notion of German indifference to the others, or any 'benign neglect' by the Germans. But, quite independently, the weakness of the others is then radical, since in practice they do not even retain control over their exchange rate. The Federal Republic is very much a party to all realignments. Furthermore, the record of the EMS will not brook the idea that the non-German members basically get the exchange rate they want.[5] The Stackelberg interpretation therefore puts the non-Germans in a particularly weak position. What makes them so weak and what advantage do they get from the system notwithstanding?

The second empirical drawback of the cooperative interpretation of the EMS relates to the anti-inflationary tendency of the system in the 1980s. An anti-inflationary stance prevailed throughout most of the Western world during the period. This might suggest that the members would have disinflated as much had they been outside the system. But the evidence goes the other way. Since 1972, the pressure in the fixed-rate arrangements that have existed in continental Europe has always been on the weak-currency countries to adjust. Under the 'snake', members in difficulty often moved out of the system, and any disinflationary effect can therefore be easily discounted, if not dismissed. But there have been no similar exits from the EMS, and realignments have provided the countries with the weaker currencies incomplete relief, as the adjustments in exchange rates have failed to offset the excess in their inflation rates.[6] Hence the pressure on the weaker currencies has been felt. More specific evidence is available too. The French decision to stay in the EMS in the summer of 1981 was instrumental in the reversal of the expansionary fiscal policy of the Socialist government of Mitterand. Italian membership in the EMS has strengthened the Bank of Italy's hand in dealing with political pressures to inflate at home. The view that entry into the EMS would hook Great Britain to tighter monetary policy has been a regular feature in the British parliamentary debates about entry since 1983.[7] Hence the indications of the disinflationary tendency of the system are impressive.

Unfortunately, the strategic interpretation of the EMS has a great deal of difficulty in coming to terms with this tendency. If we assume that Italy and France followed an anti-inflationary course by choice in recent years, the game-theoretical interpretation would say that had the two been outside the system, they would have gone further in this direction, since they would then have been prodded by the resistance of the others to their effort to appreciate their currency. On this view, therefore, the EMS calmed the French and Italian proclivity to disinflate. In other words, if either France or Italy had moved out of the system, there would have been more disinflation by the departing country. But it looks very much the opposite, as if such an exit by either one would have been associated with easier monetary policy.[8]

The 'monetary discipline' hypothesis has the merit of meeting both of the previous difficulties. The hypothesis would certainly explain why the other members would expect Germany to retain its monetary independence in the system, since it effectively says that the others would like to have German monetary policy for themselves but are unable to get it. The hypothesis must also say, if it is to make sense, that the non-German members would generate less inflation once inside the system. The basic problem with the hypothesis, however, is that it will not explain the German participation, at least not in any simple way.

Admittedly, the Germans suffer no disadvantage from the ability of others to benefit from their own central bank's policies. At worst, the others' gain should leave them indifferent. But this simply means that the Germans should have no objection if the others tied their currency to theirs like the Austrians do with their schilling. But why should the Germans offer anything in exchange? Yet this is exactly what they do in the EMS. According to the rules of the system, Germany must automatically lend support to any member currency that hits the bottom of the band. This automatic-support provision has even necessitated heavy purchases of other currencies by the Bundesbank on occasion, as it did prior to the realignment of January 1987. Further, the Bundesbank has often emphasised the importance of the provision for support at the limits in its annual reports.[9] Of course, German interventions at the limits can be sterilised. In addition, any German interventions inside the system can be countered by pressure for immediate realignment, thereby limiting the German support. But this does not answer the question why the Germans should even have agreed to such a commitment in the first place. However moderate the true importance of the automatic-support provision may be, it would be difficult to argue that the Germans are in the same position relative to France, Belgium, Denmark, and Italy as they are relative to everybody else.

Over and above this, the simple fact is that the EMS was never imposed upon the Germans, but was sought by them. The system emerged out of an agreement between the German Chancellor Helmut Schmidt and the French President Giscard d'Estaing. When German interest in forming the EMS arose in 1977–8, it was under the impact of current account deficits combined with an appreciating mark. Presumably the Germans were not interested in aiding anyone to get more monetary discipline at the time. Any model design failing to bring out the German interest in the system hence cannot be sufficient.

It is also possible that those who benefit from monetary discipline in the system could find better ways of reaping the same advantage, and this might be seen as another objection to the hypothesis. But it should not be. Countries often act in their self-interest without doing what is *best* for them. If we insist on limiting ourselves to the domain of the best, we will probably never explain the EMS, and little else perhaps. The possibility of superior alternatives to the EMS for getting monetary discipline, I think, pertains not to the origins and motives of the system, but its future prospects. This is the connection in which I propose to come back to the issue later.

2.   Monetary discipline and the EMS

a.   Monetary discipline outside the EMS

Kydland and Prescott (1977) offer a tractable means of dealing with the issue of monetary discipline. The source of such discipline, in their example, is the temptation to inflate by surprise. Surprise inflation may raise output if nominal wages are fixed over a contract period. In addition, normal output may be below optimum because of market imperfections, like governmental interferences with laying off or firing labour or payroll taxes. It follows that a well-meaning government may be tempted to inflate by surprise. Still, to resist the temptation is better, and therefore a matter of discipline, because the private sector will adjust its expectations to any such temptation as may exist, and the result will thus be positive inflation without any corresponding benefit (see Barro and Gordon, 1983a, 1983b).

To apply these ideas to the EMS means putting the problem in an international setting. Let there be two countries producing a separate good, consuming both of them, but each with a preference for its own good in consumption. We shall use asterisks to denote the foreign country, 'Germany', and regard the home one as 'France'. The equations are:

$$\begin{cases} y = c(p - p_e) + \bar{y} \\ y^* = c(p^* - p_e^*) + \bar{y}^* \end{cases} \tag{3.1}$$

$$\begin{cases} i = \psi p + (1 - \psi)(p^* + e) = p + (1 - \psi)q \\ i^* = \psi p^* + (1 - \psi)(p - e) = p^* - (1 - \psi)q \end{cases} \quad 0.5 < \psi < 1 \tag{3.2}$$

$$q = p^* + e - p = 0 \tag{3.3}$$

$$L = \sum_{j=0}^{\infty} \left(\frac{1}{1+\delta}\right)^j \{(y - k\bar{y})^2 + ai^2\} \tag{3.4}$$

$$L^* = \sum_{j=0}^{\infty} \left(\frac{1}{1+\delta^*}\right)^j \{(y^* - k\bar{y}^*)^2 + ai^{*2}\}$$

$$0 < \delta^* \ll \delta \quad k > 1$$

Equation (3.1) is the ordinary Phillips curve in 'news' form. p is the growth rate of the price of the home produced good and p_e the expected value of p. $\bar{y}$ is the logarithm of normal output. Equation (3.2) gives the growth rate of the consumer price level. q is the rate of change of the commodity terms of trade, and e therefore the rate of appreciation of the mark relative to the franc. Equation (3.3) expresses the assumption of purchasing power parity. From (3.2) and (3.3) combined, we infer:

$$\begin{cases} i = p \\ i^* = p^* \end{cases} \tag{3.5}$$

There is thus no difference between producer and consumer price inflation.

Equation (3.4) defines the utility losses resulting from deviations from optimal levels of y and i, the two target variables. As regards y, $k\bar{y}$ is optimal, $k>1$: for i, 0 is so. The target values $k\bar{y}$ and 0, and the weight attached to inflation, a, reflect the preferences of everybody, government and private individuals alike. There is only one difference between France and Germany in the system: it relates to the rate of discount of the future. δ^* is the private rate of discount of the future in both countries, and is also the socially optimal discount rate. But whereas the German monetary authorities actually use δ^* in setting their monetary instrument, the French do not, but use the much higher rate δ. Therefrom follows the monetary discipline of the Germans and the lack of it of the French.[10]

No issue of discipline can arise, though, as long as we suppose that the monetary authorities, in direct control of p or p^*, as the case may be, cannot affect private expectations. In this case, the French solution must be:

$$p_d = \frac{c\{(k-1)\bar{y}+cp_e\}}{a+c^2} = i_d \tag{3.6}$$

(where the subscript 'd' stands for discretionary) and the German solution is the corresponding one with asterisks. If the private sector sets its expectations accordingly, equation (3.6) gives us:

$$p_d = \frac{c(k-1)\bar{y}}{a} = i_d \tag{3.7}$$

This last equation exhibits the aforementioned dilemma of a positive rate of inflation of no value to anyone. The corresponding welfare loss is:

$$L_d = \frac{a+c^2}{a}(k-1)^2\,\bar{y}^2 \tag{3.8}$$

This loss is to be compared with $(k-1)^2\,\bar{y}^2$, or the loss under zero inflation, which is necessarily lower.[11]

Things change once we allow the possibility of an official influence on popular expectations through promises. In this case, a so-called 'reputational equilibrium' arises, wherein the authorities will make advantageous promises that everyone believes because the officials have every reason to keep them. As long as there is a penalty for lying, some reputational equilibrium below p_d is possible. Moreover, such a penalty is logical since the private sector must respond to false promises of low ps by losing confidence, and therefore expecting higher p values in the future.

Barro and Gordon show how such an equilibrium can be derived. It is a matter of equating temptation to cheat, at any given anticipated rate of inflation below p_d, with the discounted present value of the future penalty for cheating. In fact, the exact equilibrium is somewhat arbitrary, depending upon the postulated revision of popular expectations following lies, and even the uniqueness of the equilibrium can be questioned.[12] But the basic principle of credible promises of inflation below p_d suffices at present. On this principle, we shall make the simplest possible assumptions, that we will borrow from Barro–Gordon (which they in turn found in James Friedman, 1971). These assumptions are that as long as the authorities behave as they were expected to in the previous period, any promise they make that would be advantageously kept will be believed; otherwise, whatever the officials may say, the short-run discretionary solution p_d will be expected.

On these assumptions, we may take two extreme examples, one of which we shall associate with Germany, the other with France. The first is that the discount of the future is so low as to admit a zero-inflation reputational equilibrium; the other is that it is so high as to yield a reputational equilibrium only negligibly below p_d. Both possibilities are clear. The zero-inflation reputational equilibrium follows on Barro–Gordon's assumptions so long as $\delta^* a \leq c^2$, and thus exists for low enough values of δ^*.[13] The possibility of a reputational equilibrium close to the short-run discretionary one is nearly obvious since the penalty for cheating disappears as δ^* goes toward infinity, which gets us closer to the p_d solution. The basic problem is to explain the difference between the postulated German and French behaviour.

On this matter, we shall rely entirely on a question of central bank independence. The Bundesbank supposedly enjoys total political independence, while the Banque de France does not, but is under the thumb of elected officials. Consequently, the German monetary authorities can discount the future in the ordinary way, or like the man in the street, while the French ones cannot, but must assign unusual priority to all events prior to the next elections. The assumption of a French reputational equilibrium verging on the short-run discretionary solution i_d of equation (3.7) is a mere simplification without basic importance. Any reputational solution with a positive p would do as well.

b. Monetary discipline inside the EMS

The EMS is an arrangement fixing the franc–mark between realignments, at which time, we will suppose, the terms of trade are brought back to their initial position. The frequency of realignments is very important in the arrangement, as we will see. Two cases may be distinguished: that of realignments every period; and that of less frequent realignments, which we will take to mean realignments every other period.

(*i*)   *Realignments every period*. In case of realignments every period, nothing changes in the analysis unless we provide for it. But we will, since new costs of inflating arise for France in the EMS for two reasons. First, there is the new burden of stemming the induced capital outflows between realignments. These costs may take the form of capital controls, official reserve losses, or the compromise of another policy instrument besides p (like fiscal policy), in order to keep the interest rate as high as required. The simplest factor to admit would be capital controls. The second source of the costs is the political unpopularity of devaluations. Under flexible rates, voters are likely to view exchange rates as determined essentially by the market, while in case of a political agreement about the exchange rate, they hold their political leaders responsible for devaluations. Devaluations cost votes.[14]

We will model these costs as follows:

$$C_1 = \alpha_0 + \alpha_1(i - i^*) \tag{3.9}$$

$$\alpha_0, \ \alpha_1 \begin{cases} = 0 \text{ if } i \leqslant i^* \\ > 0 \text{ if } i > i^* \end{cases}$$

This formulation says that the costs of the EMS are borne entirely by the high-inflation country. If so, Germany remains completely unaffected. The hypothesis also posits some fixed costs and some variable ones. The distinction between the two sorts of costs turns out to be vital since a different solution emerges depending on the level of the fixed ones.

According to equation (3.9), there is a discontinuity in the cost function at the point where French inflation passes above the zero German level to any positive number. At this point, the costs C_1 jump up by α_0. If sufficiently high, therefore, α_0 will induce France to opt for a zero-inflation solution in the EMS. Moreover, in this case, France will bear no costs C_1, any more than Germany does. This EMS solution then would seem to reflect the highest ambitions of the system for France. Examples of fixed costs would be the installation and/or maintenance of capital controls, and the lost votes resulting from any devaluation, no matter how small.

Working against the previous solution, of course, is the temptation to inflate if people expect $p=0$. This temptation will evidently incline France toward the other EMS solution, at a positive p, though one which is lower than that in equation (3.7), applying outside the system. The evidence would show that the EMS has failed to induce the high-inflation members to reduce their inflation rates all the way down to the German level. Hence we may take this second EMS solution as the relevant one.[15] The derivation is as follows.

To find the solution, we must minimise:

$$L = \sum_{j=0}^{\infty} \left(\frac{1}{1+\delta}\right)^j \{(y - k\bar{y})^2 + ai^2 + C_1\} \tag{3.10}$$

with respect to p, given equations (3.1)–(3.3) and (3.9). This yields:

$$p_{ems}(= i_{ems}) = \frac{2c(k-1)\bar{y} - \alpha_1}{2a} = p_d - \frac{\alpha_1}{2a} \tag{3.11}$$

As this solution holds only for positive values of p_{ems}, it is useful to define

$$\eta = \frac{\alpha_1}{2c(k-1)\bar{y}} \qquad\qquad 0 < \eta < 1 \tag{3.12}$$

and then restate (3.11) as:

$$p_{ems}(= i_{ems}) = \frac{(1-\eta)c(k-1)\bar{y}}{a} \qquad\qquad 0 < \eta < 1 \tag{3.13}$$

We then see at once the necessary positive value of p_{ems}. According to (3.13), monetary discipline also springs exclusively from the variable-cost coefficient η (or α_1). The fixed-cost coefficient, α_0, does not even come in. This coefficient is nevertheless a factor in defining the conditions for the previous solution to hold, as α_0 reduces welfare in the EMS, and obviously α_0 must be low enough for L_{ems} to be less than L_d.

There is a further requirement for the previous EMS solution to hold, since we know from previous reasoning that for any p below p_d, there is a temptation to inflate, or at least there would be one outside the system. Since $p_{ems} < p_d$, based on (3.13), this means the presence of a temptation to make a surprise move out of the EMS if nothing prevents it. Some interference with such a surprise move makes sense, as the move would be highly conspicuous, and presumably would be interpreted by voters as breaking an international engagement. But the costs of moving out, C_2, must also be high enough.

Figure 3.1 will clarify matters. Along the horizontal axis, we measure alternative price rules or price promises, p_r. The $L_r - L_d$ schedule is the temptation-to-cheat outside the EMS, which is built along Barro–Gordon principles. For every price promise, L_r is the loss if the promise is kept while L_d is the minimised loss if the promise is disregarded and p is simply set optimally on a current basis without any regard for the future. The difference between the two is therefore the current gain from cheating if people expect the promise to be held. This gain is positive for

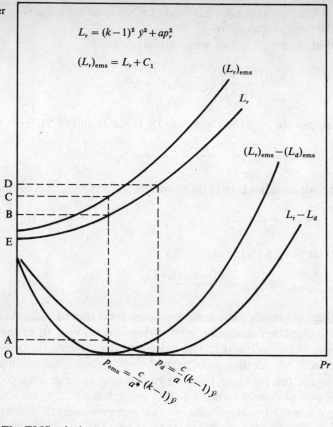

Losses under price rules, gains from cheating

$$L_r = (k-1)^2 \, \bar{y}^2 + a p_r^2$$

$$(L_r)_{ems} = L_r + C_1$$

$(L_r)_{ems}$

L_r

$(L_r)_{ems} - (L_d)_{ems}$

$L_r - L_d$

D
C
B
E

A
O

$p_{ems} = \dfrac{c}{a^*} (k-1) \bar{y}$ $p_d = \dfrac{c}{a} (k-1) \bar{y}$ Pr

Figure 3.1 The EMS solution

all price rules p_r below p_d. By definition, at $p_r = p_d$, $L_r - L_d$ is nil: there is no temptation to cheat. For clarity, therefore, the value of p_r at the meeting point with p_d is shown in Figure 3.1 as the right-hand side of equation (3.7). The exact reputational solution is not shown. It hinges on a punishment schedule regarding the present value of future losses from cheating. But since in any case the reputational solution is supposedly so close to p_d as almost to merge with it (i.e., the lower intersection of the punishment curve with the temptation-to-cheat is negligibly below p_d), we can simply identify the punishment schedule with the horizontal axis.

The $(L_r)_{ems} - (L_d)_{ems}$ schedule is the corresponding temptation-to-cheat inside the EMS. This schedule necessarily attains tangency with the horizontal axis below p_d, since $p_{ems} < p_d$. At this point of tangency p_r also corresponds exactly to equation (3.13). But we represent the point $p_r = p_{ems}$ in Figure 3.1, not as equation (3.13), but as:

$$p_r = p_{ems} = \frac{c}{a^*}(k-1)\bar{y} \tag{3.14}$$

This simply introduces a new hypothetical weight on the inflation objective, a^*, such that equations (3.14) and (3.13) are equivalent, implying

$$a^* = \frac{a}{1-\eta} \tag{3.15}$$

Therefore a^* is necessarily greater than a.

The required conditions for the p_{ems} solution can now be explained as follows. The loss associated with the adherence to any given price rule outside the EMS is provided by the schedule L_r.[16] The corresponding loss schedule inside the EMS, $(L_r)_{ems}$, is L_r plus C_1, or it is so everywhere except at $p_r=0$ where C_1 is nil and L_r and $(L_r)_{ems}$ therefore coincide. Outside the EMS, accordingly, welfare losses would be OD, whereas inside of it, they are only OC. The required condition $L_{ems}<L_d$ is thus met. But as can be seen from Figure 3.1, it need not have been, and would not have if α_0, affecting the vertical distance between $(L_r)_{ems}$ and L_r without touching p_{ems}, had been sufficiently high. Next, the temptation to cheat outside the EMS at $p_r = p_{ems}$ is OA. Hence, the required condition for the previous solution concerning C_2 – i.e., that it be greater than the gains of a surprise move out of the EMS – is C_2 greater than OA. There is another requirement for the solution to hold, since it must be the right one as opposed to $p_{ems} = 0$. But this last condition must be left in the background.[17]

In a related work dealing with the problem of excessive inflation in a closed economy, Rogoff (1985a) proposes the introduction of a 'conservative' central banker. The coefficient a^* facilitates the interpretation of his suggestion. Any central banker placing the weight a^* on the inflation objective would obviously deliver the same rate of inflation to France as the EMS does. But the result would be higher welfare since the cost C_1 would be eliminated. The merit of Rogoff's suggestion is thus clear. However, the hold of the conservative central banker on office would remain a problem in case of this suggestion, since OA would be the gain of suddenly dismissing the conservative central banker. The political cost of this action, in turn, might be lower than that of a lightning move out of the EMS. The EMS may therefore be a superior alternative after all. We shall return to this issue in the final section.

(ii) *Realignments every other period.* If realignments occur only every other period, a new factor enters the analysis, since right after every realignment the relation between p and i is upset. A percentage-point increase in the price of the home-produced good (p) at this time has a distributed-lag effect on the growth of the cost-of-living index (i). Part of the effect comes in the current period, but part takes place only in the next one, when the devaluation finally raises the purchase price of the imported good. Since the next-period effect is discounted by the authorities, the sum-effect on i is less than one. Surprise inflation (meaning surprise p) thus is less costly (in utility terms), and the result is pro-inflationary. This point is essentially the same as Rogoff's in another study arguing that exchange-rate cooperation can be counter-productive (Rogoff, 1985b).

Quite specifically, in case of realignments every other period, the rate of inflation in the EMS following every realignment will be:

$$i = \frac{(\theta - \eta)c(k-1)\bar{y}}{a} \quad \theta > 1 \tag{3.16}$$

where the crucial coefficient θ is greater than one and therefore the solution is higher than before, in equation (3.13).[18] (The excess of θ over one also naturally rises with δ, the rate of discount of the future.) Thus, for the EMS to work as a disciplinary device, the variable political costs of realignments, η, must now be greater than before. For low enough values of η, $\theta - \eta > 1$, and the EMS will not even reduce inflation at all. Moreover, since in any event the equilibrium i_{ems} is higher based on (3.16), L_{ems} is also larger, and the required condition $L_{\text{ems}} < L_d$ is more stringent. Correspondingly, though, the required level of C_2, or for lack of an incentive to make a surprise move out of the system is lower.

Of course, all this is true in the period immediately following a realignment. Every next period, or every one preceding a realignment, i_{ems} is exactly the same as before. There is a difference in this period regarding p, which is lower because it must be short of i to the right extent for i_{ems} to stay the same as previously despite the adjustment of the exchange rate at the end of the period to the excess of p over p^* in the previous period as well as the current one. But this has no welfare consequence.

Germany, on its part, keeps $i^* = 0$ in all periods. To do so now simply requires some manipulation of p^*. Whereas previously we had $p^* = i^* = 0$ at all times, in the period right after realignment or when $e = 0$, $i^* = 0$ now says:

$$i^* = \psi p^* + (1 - \psi)p = 0 \tag{3.17}$$

and thus requires

$$p^* = -\frac{1-\psi}{\psi} p \tag{3.18}$$

while in the period preceding a realignment, when

$$e_{+1} = (p_{+1} + p) - (p^*_{+1} + p^*),$$

the condition $i^*_{+1} = 0$ says:

$$i^*_{+1} = \psi_{\not{p}} 1 + (1 - \psi)(p_{+1} - e_{+1}) = 0 \tag{3.19}$$

and requires

$$p^*_{+1} = \frac{1-\psi}{\psi} p \tag{3.20}$$

By continually adjusting p^*, therefore, Germany can maintain its welfare always unchanged.

The idea that less frequent realignments *weaken* the disciplinary effect of exchange-rate cooperation – which is the basic conclusion of this sub-section – will be familiar from the literature, since it parallels Rogoff's well-known reasoning (1985b). This reasoning, for example, underlies Taylor's conclusion (1985), in his simulations of the Seven Summit countries, that cooperation leads to more accommodation of inflation. The reasoning is also intimately connected to the verdict of dynamic game analysis that, in the absence of 'pre-commitment' – or, in our case, monetary discipline – international cooperation can lead to worse outcomes than non-cooperation.[19] All the same, the conclusion is not really satisfactory here. If the EMS encourages monetary discipline, it is counter-intuitive to argue that the shortest possible time between realignments, and thus the highest possible frequency of realignments, heightens the disciplinary effect. Informed opinion about the EMS is that the commitment not to realign over significant stretches of time supports discipline, not the contrary. But we shall be able to come to grips with this problem only in the next section, when we finally inject an element of international cooperation.

3.   The cooperative feature of the EMS

Up to now, movements of the terms of trade have affected nothing but inflation. Since one of the countries in the analysis is perfectly able to cope with inflation, questions of international conflict or cooperation could not arise. Another typical effect of movements in the terms of trade, however, is to alter the competitiveness of the traded goods industry. If both countries in the analysis are concerned with this effect as well as inflation, but lack separate tools to deal with both of them, an issue of cooperation will emerge. A period of falling competitiveness of German industry is indeed precisely what awakened German interest in the EMS in the first place, as we have already mentioned. Consequently, introducing competitiveness seems right.

In order to allow for this influence, the basic step will be to admit a sector of non-traded goods. The traded-goods industry will thus be able to raise output by attracting factors from elsewhere in the economy. Still, total output need not rise in the process, since there can be constant returns to scale everywhere. We will assume so in order to keep the analysis simple; this will enable us also to continue to argue that policy affects total output strictly through price surprises. But if so, the welfare significance of international competitiveness must depend on its effect in changing the composition of output.

In this connection, we shall argue, in analogy with the previous section, that there are market imperfections (besides the earlier ones reducing total output) keeping traded goods too low relative to non-traded ones. These next imperfections are trade-protection measures. The best examples would not be ordinary tariffs and subsidies, since we are dealing with members of the European Community, but licensing, uniformity requirements, quotas on foreign plants and foreign ownership of home industries, and excessive government purchases at home based on national defence and infant-industry arguments.[20] These last protective measures, like all the rest, raise the relative price of traded goods above the efficiency level, thereby lowering the relative size of the traded-goods sector below optimum, and they do so everywhere. As a result, both Germany and France would like higher ratios of traded goods than they get outside the EMS. For this reason, they would prefer higher competitiveness.

The revised model is:

$$\begin{cases} p = \zeta p_h + (1 - \zeta)p_t \\ p^* = \zeta p_h^* + (1 - \zeta)p_t^* \end{cases} \qquad 0<\zeta<1 \quad (3.21)$$

$$\begin{cases} y = c(p - p_e) + \bar{y} \\ y^* = c(p^* - p_e^*) + \bar{y}^* \end{cases} \qquad (3.22)$$

$$\begin{cases} i = \psi p + (1 - \psi)(p_t^* + e) \\ i^* = \psi p^* + (1 - \psi)(p_t - e) \end{cases} \qquad 0.5<\psi<1 \quad (3.23)$$

$$q = p_t^* + e - p_t \qquad (3.24)$$

$$t_n = d \sum_{i=0}^{n} q_i + f \sum_{i=0}^{n} (p_h - p_t)_i$$
$$\{$$
$$\quad\quad\quad\quad\quad\quad\quad\quad\quad\quad\quad\quad (3.25)$$
$$t_n^* = -d \sum_{i=0}^{n} q_i + f \sum_{i=0}^{n} (p_h^* - p_t^*)_i$$

$$L_0 = \sum_{j=0}^{\infty} \left(\frac{1}{1+\delta}\right)^j \{(y_j - k\bar{y})^2 + ai_j^2 + b(t_j - \bar{t})^2\}$$
$$\{ \quad\quad\quad\quad\quad\quad\quad\quad\quad \bar{t}, \bar{t}^* > 0 \quad (3.26)$$
$$L_0^* = \sum_{j=0}^{\infty} \left(\frac{1}{1+\delta^*}\right)^j \{(y_j^* - k\bar{y}^*)^2 + ai_j^{*2} + b(t_j^* - \bar{t}^*)^2\}$$

The p subscripts, t and h, refer here to traded and home goods respectively. Equation (3.22) is obviously identical to the previous (3.1), except for the interpretation of p. If we further assume:

$$p_h = p_t$$
$$\{ \quad\quad\quad\quad\quad\quad\quad\quad\quad\quad\quad\quad\quad (3.27)$$
$$p_h^* = p_t^*$$

or constant relative prices of home-produced goods in both countries, we can also equate (3.23) with (3.2) and (3.24) with (3.3).

Equations (3.25) and (3.26) contain the basic changes. t in (3.25) is the log of the ratio of traded to non-traded goods. Since q is always zero outside the EMS, and there is no constant term in the equation, t must be zero outside the EMS as well. This implicitly fixes the ratio of traded to non-traded goods outside the system as one. But what matters is that with t zero and $\bar{t}$, or optimal t, positive, t is less than $\bar{t}$ outside the EMS, as we require.

In the case of realignments every period, the new system of equations (3.21)–(3.27) – or alternatively (3.1)–(3.3) plus (3.25)–(3.26) – yields no difference between the German situation in or out of the EMS, and in the French case, the differences it does yield are exactly the same as before. Even in the case of realignments every other period, there are no notable differences in the period immediately preceding a realignment. But important differences arise in the one right after a realignment, on which attention therefore must focus. For this essential period – hence when a realignment is not about to come – the results may be set forward in a series of propositions for which the proofs will be relegated to an Appendix (containing all of the solutions for p and i of Part 2 as well).

Proposition 1 As long as French inflation raises no German concern over excessive traded goods. Germany is necessarily better off in the EMS.

Any French inflation evidently raises t^* inside the EMS under the new conditions. Hence, as long as French inflation is such as to keep t^* below $\bar{t}^*$, Germany is necessarily better off inside the EMS. This is clear since the Germans could cut p^* sufficiently to keep $i^*=0$ and yet enjoy an improvement in t^*. In this case, the fall in p^* would even add to the improvement in t^*.

If France inflated enough, though, the Germans could be made worse off. For sufficiently large values of p, keeping $i^*=0$ would imply $t^*>\bar{t}$. At such large values of p, the best the Germans could do would be to accept excessive inflation and excessive t^*, as any deflation would only aggravate their problem of excessive traded goods. Hence, as p rises indefinitely, there must come a point where the Germans' best alternative is a combination of excessive i^* and excessive t^* which is worse for them than the optimal combination $i^*=t^*=0$ outside the EMS.

Proposition 2   There is an optimal level of French inflation for the Germans, which permits them to get both zero inflation and their desired ratio of traded goods. As p rises, keeping $i^*=0$ means $t^*<\bar{t}^*$ at first and $t^*>\bar{t}^*$ later. Hence there must come a cut-off point as p rises where the Germans can have both $i^*=0$ and $t^*=\bar{t}^*$ simultaneously. At this point, evidently, Germany gets the most it can out of the EMS, its only unsolved macroeconomic problem remaining that $y^*<k\bar{y}^*$.

Proposition 3   If the French do not inflate enough to suit Germany perfectly, the Germans will deflate. This basic proposition corroborates the frequent suspicion in Europe that the EMS encourages the Germans to disinflate more than they would outside. The logic is simple: if the German opportunity set is such that fixing inflation at zero would mean too low a t^* level, the Germans' best opportunity will be to deviate from their inflation objective slightly in the direction of improving competitiveness and t^*, and this will mean deflating. The obverse of the proposition is also true: if the French inflate too much from the German perspective, the Germans will inflate. In the latter case, the Germans might simply reduce p^* too little to prevent i^* from rising, and need not actually raise p^*.

Proposition 4   The traded-goods objectives of both countries foster monetary discipline in France. The contribution of the French traded-goods objective to monetary discipline in France is obvious. Any producer-price inflation, p, worsens the shortfall of t below $\bar{t}$, and thus encourages monetary restraint. The contribution of the German objective $\bar{t}^*$ to French inflation is less obvious, but depends on p in the lower range of the previous proposition. In this case, p^* falls. The extra German disinflation is then bound to lower i, but its effect on p is ambiguous. More specifically, the damaging effect of the p^* fall on French competitivety will induce France to lower p, while its beneficial effect on French consumer inflation, i, will tend the opposite way. But in any case, as regards i, the direct effect of the lower p^* through French import prices will prevail. The unambiguous effect of the German behaviour on French 'discipline', therefore, depends on the choice of measure of discipline in terms of i, not p.

Proposition 5   Lengthening the interval between realignments can enhance rather than diminish monetary discipline in France. Longer intervals between realignments induce monetary laxness or lack of discipline for the previous reasons, that is, by reducing the efficiency of a fall in p in cutting i. But now there is a countervailing influence. The longer e stays fixed at zero, the greater the effect of a fall in p in raising q, therefore t. This last effect may then dominate.

Proposition 6   The welfare advantage of the EMS in France remains an ambiguous proposition. We saw before that the EMS may benefit France under special conditions, which are not necessarily intuitive. Analysis shows that this welfare benefit now remains as vague as before. While France's traded-goods objective must bring the country closer to zero inflation, it must also lead it to a lower ratio of traded goods. Germany contributes to both good and bad effect, the good one on inflation and the bad one on competitiveness.

From the strategic perspective, of course, the survival of the EMS could be said to imply that the conditions for a beneficial outcome in France are met. But the previous ambiguity of the theoretical result is still important since it means that the balance one day could tip the other way.

Basically, the ambiguity of the welfare outcome for France can be traced back to the sub-optimal French behaviour with respect to the future. As a result, while Germany is sure to obtain cooperative benefits, France is not.[21]

Proposition 7   The traded-goods objective does not provide a basis for eliminating the political costs of the EMS from the analysis. Since the traded-goods target fosters monetary discipline, there might be an impulse now to go back and remove the political costs of the EMS from the analysis. Upon closer examination, this is not possible, if only because the costs C_2 retain all of their importance. The incentive to make a surprise move out of the system in France remains as much an issue now as before. Indeed, the worsening of competitiveness between realignments may add to the tendency. Furthermore, eliminating C_1 would not necessarily be wise, because doing so would make a sufficiently long time between realignments become a critical issue. We can see, empirically, that if realignments come quickly enough, the terms-of-trade effect on discipline must be small. The C_1 factor avoids this problem entirely, and does so in a convincing way: namely, by pointing to costs of realigning as such. Furthermore, the political costs C_1 correspond to reality. The devaluations of the franc and the lira since 1979 have generally been a political embarrassment. Capital controls raise separate issues that are difficult to relate neatly to timing of realignments. But the practical relevance of costs of such controls is clear. The occasional tightening of capital controls in France and Italy have been unpopular, and the relaxation of the controls a political advantage. The political costs of type C_1 thus belong in the argument.

4. Conclusion

We have presented a certain combination of political and economic considerations that explain a variety of features of the EMS that are not necessarily easy to fit together otherwise. These features include the benefits to Germany and the others, the German predominance, the contractionary monetary tendency of the system, both for the Germans and the rest, and the disciplinary influence of longer waiting periods between realignments outside of Germany.

One element of the system that receives special emphasis here is its oft-noted asymmetry. Not only does Germany retain a certain monetary independence that the others lack, but it also gets totally different benefits than the rest. Furthermore, the German benefits are more secure. The Germans are able to get better terms of trade in return for something the others value, but which costs the Germans nothing. On the other hand, the benefits to the rest depend on a balance of considerations that can be upset.[22]

This naturally brings us to the question of the robustness of the arrangement. The basic institutional flaw in the other member countries besides Germany, which explains why they subscribe in the first place, is their lack of central bank independence. The seeming remedy would be to allow their central banks independence. Rogoff's proposal of placing a conservative central banker at the helm has a certain appeal. But as we indicated, the proposal does not avoid the issue of central bank independence since it leaves open the question of the ease of removing the conservative head from office. Over and above this the proposal of central bank independence must dominate Rogoff's reform in any model, like ours, where a reputational equilibrium is attainable at zero inflation, since in this type of model any central banker with preferences that do not reflect the views of the community would introduce unnecessary distortions as soon as we admit possible shock requiring some inflation for optimal policy during a transition. This last argument applies as well to the idea of raising the fixed political costs of inflating (relative to the Germans) enough to attain the zero-inflation EMS solution. Even if this plan were feasible, the objection would be that, once adopted, the enacting country would be strapped if new circumstances made a little inflation desirable (since the costs of moving out would need to be raised as well, or else the reform very likely would do nothing but harm).

But if central bank independence is the answer, maybe it will come. There is already a movement afoot in France toward the independence of the Bank of France. Indeed, this movement got its start only since the country managed to narrow the gap between its inflation rate and the German level in recent years. Hence, the EMS may have paved the way for the change. What if the movement should reach its final objective? Evidently the only parts of our analysis of the EMS that would remain intact are those pertaining to cooperation. But if France is to get cooperative benefits from the EMS, the system will need to change, since such benefits are not very likely so long as the Germans retain their monetary independence while they share control over the franc–mark with France.

This entire reasoning, of course, hinges on the strategic approach. Another possibly would be to see the EMS as a budding common-currency area.[23] This is indeed the preferred vision in the European Commission in Brussels. Admittedly, in this case, France might benefit, even under preceding conditions of German dominance, and even if monetary discipline ceases to be a problem, because of the advantages of a single currency. However, this alternative basis for mutual benefits of the EMS also requires major institutional changes. It would mean eliminating possible realignments, the bands around the parities, the existing costs of currency conversions, and the large vestiges of capital controls. From any perspective, therefore, should the non-German members ever resolve their problems of monetary discipline, the EMS will need to evolve if it is to remain viable.

APPENDIX: PROOFS OF THE PROPOSITIONS OF SECTION 3

1. Proofs of propositions 1, 2, and 3

With regard to the German situation, if we use equation (3.26) to calculate German losses at time 0 following a realignment, and consider the relevant two-period horizon $(0, +1)$, we get:

$$L^* + \varrho^* L^*_{+1} = (y^* - k\bar{y}^*)^2 + ai^{*2} + b(t^* - \bar{t}^*)^2$$
$$+ \varrho^*(y^*_{+1} - k\bar{y}^*)^2 + \varrho^* ai^{*\,2}_{+1}$$
$$+ \varrho^* b(t^*_{+1} - \bar{t}^*)^2 \quad \varrho^* = \frac{1}{1+\delta^*} \tag{A3.1}$$

It is necessary first to substitute for y^*, y^*_{+1}, i^*, i^*_{+1}, t^* and t^*_{+1} in this equation. Since $e = 0$, $q = p^* - p$, and $q + q_{+1} = 0$, from (3.2), we have:

$$\begin{cases} i &= \psi p^* + (1 - \psi)(p - e) = \psi p^* + (1 - \psi)p \\ i^*_{+1} &= p^*_{+1} - (1 - \psi)q_{+1} = p^*_{+1} + (1 - \psi)(p^* - p) \end{cases} \tag{A3.2}$$

Equation (3.25), together with (3.27), says:

$$\begin{cases} t^* &= - dq = d(p - p^*) \\ t^*_{+1} &= 0 \end{cases} \tag{A3.3}$$

By assumption, ϱ^* is sufficiently close to one so that the zero-inflation reputational equilibrium holds for the Germans ($\delta^* \leqslant c^2 a$),[24] and the German authorities hence equate p^* and p^*_e and p^*_{+1} and $(p^*_{+1})_e$ in their optimisation programme. Putting all of these things together, and additionally using (3.1), we get from (A3.1):

$$L^* + \varrho^* L^*_{+1} = (1 + \varrho^*)(k - 1)^2 \bar{y}^{*2} + a\{\psi p^* + (1 - \psi)p\}^2$$
$$+ a\varrho^*\{p^*_{+1} + (1 - \psi)(p^* - p)\}^2$$
$$+ b\{d(p^* - p) - \bar{t}^*\}^2 + \varrho^* b\bar{t}^{*2} \tag{A3.4}$$

After differentiating with respect to p^* and solving, this yields:

$$p^* = \frac{\{bd^2 - a(1 - \psi)[\psi + \varrho^*(\psi - 1)]\}p - a\varrho^*(1 - \psi)p^*_{+1} - bd\bar{t}^*}{a\psi^2 + a\varrho^*(1 - \psi)^2 + bd^2} \tag{A3.5}$$

In order to eliminate p^*_{+1}, we must next consider L^*_{+1} where:

$$L^*_{+1} = (k - 1)^2 \bar{y}^{*2} + a\{p^*_{+1} + (1 - \psi)(p^* - p)\}^2 + b\bar{t}^{*2} \tag{A3.6}$$

Minimising L^*_{+1} with respect to p^*_{+1} yields:

$$p^*_{+1} = (1 - \psi)(p - p^*) \tag{A3.7}$$

(Minimising $L^* + \varrho^* L^*_{+1}$ with respect to p^*_{+1} yields the same result.) Notice, in passing, that (A3.2), together with (A3.7), says $i^*_{+1} = 0$. If we now use (A3.7) to eliminate p^*_{+1} in (A3.5), we get:

$$p^* = \frac{- \{a\psi(1 - \psi)p + bd(\bar{t}^* - dp)\}}{a\psi^2 + bd^2} \tag{A3.8}$$

From (A3.2), defining i^*, we then obtain:

$$i^* = \frac{- db(\psi\bar{t}^* - dp)}{a\psi^2 + bd^2} \tag{A3.9}$$

Thus, if dp equalled $\psi \bar{\imath}^*$ (in other words, if $(\partial t^*/\partial p)p$ equalled $\psi \bar{\imath}^*$), i^* would equal zero. Further, for this special case, p^* in (A3.8) reduces to:

$$p^* = -\frac{1-\psi}{\psi} p \qquad (A3.10)$$

which is, of course, exactly equation (3.18) regarding p^* in the EMS in this period. In addition, for this special case, equation (A3.3) says:

$$t^* = d\left(p + \frac{1-\psi}{\psi} p\right) = \frac{dp}{\psi} = \bar{\imath}^* \qquad (A3.11)$$

$p = \psi \bar{\imath}^*/d$ is then the critical French inflation rate mentioned in proposition 2 that makes it possible for Germany to have both $i^* = 0$ and $t^* = \bar{\imath}^*$. Proposition 3 follows directly. Based on (A3.8) and (A3.9), if France inflates less than $p = \psi \bar{\imath}^*/d$, p^* will be smaller and i^* will be negative. By implication, t^* will also be less than shown in equation (A3.11), hence less than $\bar{\imath}^*$.

It will simplify matters if we next define a variable π such that:

$$\pi = \psi \bar{\imath}^* - dp \qquad (A3.12)$$

In this case, from (A3.8), p^* becomes:

$$p^* = -\frac{1-\psi}{\psi} p - \frac{\nabla}{\psi} \qquad (A3.13)$$

where

$$\nabla = \frac{bd\pi}{a\psi^2 + bd^2}$$

After eliminating p^* from (A3.2), we have, quite simply:

$$i^* = -\nabla \qquad (A3.14)$$

Both π and ∇ can be seen as measures of German ambitions about t^* that the French will not permit the Germans to satisfy without deviating from their inflation objective.

Next let us calculate German welfare. For the period $+1$, we find the same level in or out of the EMS, namely:

$$L^*_{+1} = (k-1)^2 \bar{y}^{*2} + b\bar{\imath}^{*2} \qquad (A3.15)$$

But for the period 0, the German loss function:

$$L^* = (y^* - k\bar{y}^*)^2 + ai^{*2} + b(t^* - \bar{\imath}^*)^2$$

gives different results depending on the presence or absence of the EMS. Inside the EMS, it yields:

$$L^*_{ems} = (k-1)^2 \bar{y}^{*2} + a\nabla^2 + b\{d(p_{ems} - p^*_{ems}) - \bar{\imath}^*\}^2 \qquad (A3.16)$$

Since:

$$p_{ems} - p^*_{ems} = p_{ems} + \frac{(1-\psi)p_{ems} + \nabla}{\psi} = \frac{p_{ems} + \nabla}{\psi} \qquad (A3.17)$$

and

$$\tilde{\iota}^* = \frac{\pi + dp_{\mathrm{ems}}}{\psi} = \frac{dp_{\mathrm{ems}}}{\psi} + \frac{(a\psi^2 + bd^2)\nabla}{bd\psi}$$

$$= \frac{d(p_{\mathrm{ems}} + \nabla)}{\psi} + \frac{a\psi}{bd}\nabla \tag{A3.18}$$

equation (A3.16) reduces to:

$$L^*_{\mathrm{ems}} = (k-1)^2\bar{y}^{*2} + a\nabla^2 + b\left(\frac{a\psi}{bd}\nabla\right)^2 \tag{A3.19}$$

It follows directly that L^*_{ems} will be minimised for $\nabla = 0$ (or $p_{\mathrm{ems}} = \psi\tilde{\iota}^*/d$). At this point, the shortfall of L^*_{ems} below L^* – thus the benefit of the EMS to Germany – will be exactly $b\tilde{\iota}^{*2}$. Equation (A3.19) also gives us, as a general expression for the difference between L^* in and out of the EMS:

$$L^* - L^*_{\mathrm{ems}} = b\tilde{\iota}^{*2} - a\nabla^2 - b\left(\frac{a\psi}{bd}\nabla\right)^2 \tag{A3.20}$$

From this last expression, we get, after substituting (A3.18) for $\tilde{\iota}^*$:

$$L^* - L^*_{\mathrm{ems}} = \frac{\{bd^2 p_{\mathrm{ems}} + (a\psi^2 + bd^2)\nabla\}^2}{bd^2\psi^2}$$

$$- a\psi^2\left(\frac{a\psi^2 + bd^2}{bd^2\psi^2}\right)\nabla^2 \tag{A3.21}$$

As we see by examining (A3.21), the entire negative $a\psi^2(\ )\nabla^2$ term at the end cancels while a positive ∇^2 value remains. Hence proposition 1 follows: the EMS benefits Germany for all positive values of ∇. It can also be shown, by carrying the calculation further, that $L^* - L^*_{\mathrm{ems}}$ will not turn negative before p_{ems} is sufficiently high to bring about large negative ∇ values (requiring p_{ems} more than twice the size of $\psi\tilde{\iota}^*/d$).

2   Proofs of propositions 4, 5 and 6

The next three propositions concern France. Starting with the French loss function over the relevant future, we have:

$$\begin{aligned}
L + \varrho L_{+1} &= (y - k\bar{y})^2 + ai^2 + b(t - \tilde{\iota})^2 + \alpha_0 + \alpha_1(i - i^*) \\
&+ \varrho(y_{+1} - k\bar{y})^2 + \varrho ai^2_{+1} + \varrho b(t_{+1} - \tilde{\iota})^2 + \varrho\alpha_0 \\
&+ \varrho\alpha_1(i_{+1} - i^*_{+1}) \quad \varrho = \frac{1}{1 + \delta}
\end{aligned} \tag{A3.22}$$

For all practical purposes, the French authorities take p_e as given in their optimisation programme. From (A3.2), (A3.7), and (A3.13), we have:

$$\left\{\begin{aligned}
i &= \psi p + (1 - \psi)p^* = \frac{2\psi - 1}{\psi}p - \frac{1 - \psi}{\psi}\nabla \\
i_{+1} &= p_{+1} + (1 - \psi)q_{+1} = p_{+1} + (1 + \psi)(p - p^*)
\end{aligned}\right. \tag{A3.23}$$

$$= p_{+1} + \frac{1 - \psi}{\psi} (p + \nabla)$$

Keeping in mind $i^* = - \nabla$ and $i^*_{+1} = 0$, we thus have:

$$L + \varrho L_{+1} = \{c(p - p_e) + (1 - k)\bar{y}\}^2$$

$$+ a \left\{ \frac{2\psi - 1}{\psi} p^* - \frac{1 - \psi}{\psi} \nabla \right\}^2$$

$$+ b \left\{ - \frac{d}{\psi} (p + \nabla) - \bar{i} \right\}^2$$

$$+ \alpha_1 \left\{ \frac{2\psi - 1}{\psi} (p + \nabla) \right\} + (1 + \varrho)\alpha_0$$

$$+ \varrho\{c(p_{+1} - (p_{+1})_e) + (1 - k)\bar{y}\}^2$$

$$+ \varrho a \left\{ p_{+1} + \frac{1 - \psi}{\psi} (p + \nabla) \right\}^2$$

$$+ \varrho b \bar{i}^2 + \varrho \alpha_1 \left\{ p_{+1} + \frac{1 - \psi}{\psi} (p + \nabla) \right\} \tag{A3.24}$$

After differentiating with respect to p, solving, and only subsequently setting $p = p_e$ and $p_{+1} = (p_{+1})_e$, we further get (using (3.12) to eliminate α_1):

$$p = \frac{\psi\{\psi - \eta((2\psi - 1) + \varrho\, (1 - \psi))\}c(k - 1)\bar{y} - \varrho a\psi(1 - \psi)p_{+1}}{a\{(2\psi - 1)^2 + \varrho(1 - \psi)^2\} + bd^2}$$

$$+ \frac{-\psi b d\bar{i} + \{a(1 - \psi)((2\psi - 1) - \varrho(1 - \psi)) - bd^2\}\nabla}{a\{(2\psi - 1)^2 + \varrho(1 - \psi)^2\} + bd^2} \tag{A3.25}$$

Next, in order to solve for p_{+1}, we need L_{+1} where:

$$L_{+1} = \{c(p_{+1} - (p_{+1})_e) + (1 - k)\bar{y}\}^2$$

$$+ a \left\{ p_{+1} + \frac{1 - \psi}{\psi} (p + \nabla) \right\}^2$$

$$+ b\bar{i}^2 + \alpha_0 + \alpha_1 \left\{ p_{+1} + \frac{1 - \psi}{\psi} (p + \nabla) \right\} \tag{A3.26}$$

Consequently, we get:

$$p_{+1} = \frac{\psi(1 - \eta)c(k - 1)\bar{y} - a(1 - \psi)(p + \nabla)}{a\psi} \tag{A3.27}$$

From (A3.23), therefore, we immediately obtain:

$$i_{+1} = \frac{(1 - \eta)c(k - 1)\bar{y}}{a} \tag{A3.28}$$

which is the exact formula in the text for i in the case of realignments every period, or equation (3.13), and also for i_{+1} in the case of realignments every other period. We can then proceed to eliminate p_{+1} from equation (A3.25) using (A3.27), which gives:

$$p = \frac{\psi\{\psi - \eta(2\psi - 1) + \varrho(1 - \psi)\}c(k - 1)\bar{y} - \psi b d\bar{\imath}}{a(2\psi - 1)^2 + bd^2}$$

$$+ \frac{\{a(1 - \psi)(2\psi - 1) - bd^2\}\nabla}{a(2\psi - 1)^2 + bd^2} \tag{A3.29}$$

From (A3.23) it follows:

$$i = \frac{(2\psi - 1)\{\psi - \eta(2\psi - 1) + \varrho(1 - \psi)\}c(k - 1)\bar{y} - bd\{d\nabla + (2\psi - 1)\bar{\imath}\}}{a(2\psi - 1)^2 + bd^2}$$

$$\tag{A3.30}$$

Proposition 4 (p. 66) results directly. The ∇ term, containing $\bar{\imath}^*$, evidently reflects the German deflationary response to insufficient French inflation from the German point of view. We observe from (A3.29) the ambiguous effect of this term on p. The deflationary effect of ∇ through import prices encourages the Bank of France to raise p, while the damaging effect of ∇ on French competitiveness induces the Bank of France to do the opposite. But in any case, the effect of ∇, thus $\bar{\imath}^*$, on i is negative. $\bar{\imath}$ has a negative effect on i as well. Both French and German traded-good objectives therefore intensify monetary discipline in France.

A little manipulation suffices now to establish proposition 5 (p. 67). We easily find, as a start, that if we remove everything concerned with traded goods from consideration, and therefore set all the bd terms in (A3.30) at zero, then a larger interval between realignments *lowers* monetary discipline, just as argued in the section on monetary discipline in the EMS. This equation becomes:

$$i = \frac{\{\psi - \eta(2\psi - 1) - \varrho(1 - \psi)\}c(k - 1)\bar{y}}{a(2\psi - 1)} \tag{A3.31}$$

and defining θ as

$$\theta = \frac{\psi - \varrho(1 - \psi)}{2\psi - 1} \tag{A3.32}$$

we immediately find equation (3.16):

$$i = \frac{(\theta - \eta)c(k-1)\bar{y}}{a} \tag{A3.33}$$

θ is indeed greater than one, as stated in the text, since

$$\psi - \varrho(1 - \psi) > 2\psi - 1 \text{ (or } 1 - \psi > \varrho(1 - \psi)) \text{ if only } \varrho < 1.$$

Hence i of equation (A3.33) is necessarily *greater than* i of equation (3.12). But the bd term lowers the numerator and raises the denominator of equation (A3.30). Thus, the terms-of-trade considerations necessarily reinforce monetary discipline.

In case of realignments every third period instead of every second, all of the conclusions would be strengthened. We would then need to solve for i subject to the minimisation of

$$L + \varrho L_{+1} + \varrho^2 L_{+2}$$

As long as ϱ is positive, the additional $\varrho^2 L_{+2}$ term would necessarily reinforce the positive or negative wedge between i in and out of the EMS, whichever it may be. If ϱ is low for France, however, too much should not be made of this.

Turning our attention to proposition 6 there is no difference between L_{+1} in and out of the EMS, since i_{+1}, i_{+1}^*, and t_{+1} are the same, and the issue turns entirely around the difference between welfare in and out in the period immediately following a realignment. If we compare L of (A3.22) (ignoring ϱL_{+1}) with L outside the EMS, that is, with:

$$L = (k-1)^2 \bar{y}^{*2} + ai^2 + b\bar{t}^2 \tag{A3.34}$$

we find:

$$L - L_{\text{cms}} = a(i^2 - i_{\text{cms}}^2) - b\frac{d}{\psi}(p_{\text{cms}} + \nabla)\left\{\frac{d}{\psi}(p_{\text{cms}} + \nabla) + 2\bar{t}\right\}$$

$$- \alpha_0 - \alpha_1 \left(\frac{2\psi - 1}{\psi}\right)(p_{\text{cms}} + \nabla) \tag{A3.35}$$

The $i^2 - i_{\text{cms}}^2$ term favours the EMS, but all of the other terms go against it. This establishes proposition 6.

NOTES

* This study received financial assistance from the French Commissariat au Plan and is part of the Centre for Economic Policy Research's research programme in International Macroeconomics. The author wishes to thank Matthew Canzoneri and Guy Laroque for valuable comments.
1 As regards monetary discipline and the EMS, see Giavazzi and Pagano (1986)

and Melitz (1987a, 1987b). As regards exchange-rate cooperation, see Cooper (1985), Sachs (1983), Oudiz and Sachs (1984), and Bean (1985), and with direct application to the EMS, Melitz (1985), (1988), and Oudiz (1985a, 1985b).

2 See, for example, Marston (1980, 1982), and Giavazzi and Giovannini (1984) and compare Canzoneri and Henderson (1985).

3 See also Giavazzi and Giovannini (1986a, 1986b).

4 For an interesting historical application, see Eichengreen (1986).

5 See House of Commons Treasury and Civil Service Committee. Report (1985), p. xviii, para. 36.

6 This is mostly so for the Italians and the Irish. See Ungerer *et al.* (1986), Tables 11 and 13.

7 See the House of Lords Select Committee (1983); and the House of Commons Treasury and Civil Committee (1985).

8 There is a way of avoiding this conclusion in our discussion, but it does not fit. This would be to suppose a positive supply shock in Europe that raised output above target levels during the period. In this case, France and Italy would have wished to contract in order to limit output, and would have regarded the disinflationary consequences of this action as unfortunate repercussions. Therefore, the EMS would have allowed both countries to go further in a contractionary direction by eliminating their fear of currency appreciation. An exit from the system by either one in these circumstances would indeed have been associated with expansionary monetary policy. I need hardly insist on the inapplicability of this example.

9 See the sections of the annual reports of 1983 and 1984 of the Deutsche Bundesbank dealing with the EMS, and compare Thygesen (1984) and Vaubel (1985).

10 One might object that, in fact, perhaps because of the scarring experience of the 1920s, the Germans really place a higher weight on no inflation than the French. Introducing this factor into the analysis, however, would only complicate matters, since in so far as French inflation proceeds from popular preferences, the lack of French monetary discipline is less of an issue in the first place. Correspondingly, the EMS is less important from this perspective.

11 Compare the exposition in Fischer (1986), containing the same equations.

12 Cf. Rogoff (1987).

13 For the proof, see Melitz (1987a or 1987b). Barro–Gordon actually obtain this result only for $\delta^* = 0$. But this limitation of their argument hinges entirely on their use of the utility function

$$L = k\bar{y} - y + ai^2$$

rather than the more evenly quadratic form

$$L = (k\bar{y} - y)^2 + ai^2$$

14 Earlier emphasis on this point may be found in Johnson (1972).

15 In Melitz (1987a), I ignored the zero-inflation EMS solution, which is then developed in (1987b), containing a broad discussion of the choice between the two alternative solutions.

16 The formula for L_r is $(k-1)^2\bar{y}^2 + ap_r^2$.

17 The orders of magnitude in the figure, however, are entirely consistent with the satisfaction of the condition. Basically, α_0 must be moderate enough. The required condition amounts to:

$$\alpha_0 < \{p_d^2 - (p_d - p_{ems})^2\} \frac{a}{a+c^2}$$

or α_0 sufficiently low relative to the distance between p_d and p_{ems}. See Melitz (1987b).
18 The proof is in the Appendix, where θ is given by equation (A3.32).
19 See Currie, Levine, and Vidalis (1987) and Miller and Salmon (1986).
20 Compare De Grauwe and Verfaille (1988).
21 Once again, the work of Currie–Levine and Miller–Salmon is relevant here. See note 19 above and the further citations in the references therein.
22 For similar emphasis, compare Cohen, Melitz, and Oudiz (1988).
23 Compare Cohen (1986).
24 See note 13 and the surrounding text.

REFERENCES

Barro, R. and D. Gordon (1983a). 'A Positive Theory of Monetary Policy in a Natural-Rate Model', *Journal of Political Economy*, Vol. 91 (August), pp. 589–610.
    (1983b). 'Rules, Discretion and Reputation in a Model of Monetary Policy', *Journal of Monetary Economics*, Vol. 12 (July), pp. 101–21.
Bean, C. (1985). 'Macroeconomic Policy Coordination: Theory and Evidence', *Recherches Economiques de Louvain*, Vol. 51, pp. 267–83.
Canzoneri, M. and D. Henderson (1985). 'Strategic Aspects of Macroeconomic Policy-making in Interdependent Economies: Three Countries and Coalitions', Chapter 2 of a book to be published by the Brookings Institution (forthcoming) (mimeo, 1985).
Cohen, D. (1986). '*Imaginer la monnaie unique*', in Michel Aglietta (ed.), *L'Ecu et la Vielle Dame*, Paris, CEPII, Economica, Chapter 5.
Cohen, D., J. Melitz and G. Oudiz (1988). '*Le Système Monétaire Européen et l'assymétrie Franc–Mark*', *Revue Economique* (forthcoming).
Cooper, R. (1985). 'Economic Interdependence and Coordination of Economic Policies', in Richard Jones and Peter Kenen (eds), *Handbook of International Economics*, Vol. II, Amsterdam, North-Holland.
Currie, D., P. Levine and N. Vidalis (1987). 'Cooperative and Non-cooperative Rules for Monetary and Fiscal Policy in an Empirical Two-Bloc Model', in R. Bryant and R. Portes (eds), *Global Macroeconomics: Policy Conflict and Cooperation*, London, Macmillan.
De Grauwe, P. and G. Verfaille (1988). 'Exchange Rate Variability, Misalignment and the European Monetary System', in R. Marston (ed.), *Misalignment of Exchange Rates: Effects on Trade and Industry*, NBER (forthcoming).
Eichengreen, B. (1986). 'Conducting the International Orchestra: The Bank of England and Strategic Interdependence under the Classical Gold Standard', Brookings Discussion Papers in International Economics, No. 43.
Fischer, S. (1986). 'Time-Consistent Monetary and Fiscal Policies: A Survey', prepared for Bellagio Seminar on Economic Policy in Closed and Open Economies (January) (mimeo).
Friedman, J. (1971). 'A Non-Cooperative Equilibrium for Supergames', *Review of Economic Studies*, Vol. 38, pp. 861–74.
Giavazzi, F. and A. Giovannini (1984). 'The Dollar and the European Monetary

System', prepared for the University of Manchester Conference on *The EMS: Policy Coordination and Exchange Rate Systems* (26–28 September) (mimeo).

(1986a). 'The EMS and the Dollar', *Economic Policy*, Vol. 2 (April), pp. 456–85.

(1986b). 'Monetary Policy Interactions Under Managed Exchange Rates', CEPR Discussion Paper, No. 123; (1988) *Economica* (forthcoming).

Giavazzi, F., A. Giovannini and M. Pagano (1986). 'The Advantage of Tying One's Hands: EMS Discipline and Central Bank Credibility', University of Venice and University of Naples (mimeo); (1988) *European Economic Review* (June).

House of Commons, Treasury and Civil Service Committee (1985). 'The Financial and Economic Consequences of UK Membership of the European Communities, The European Monetary System', London, HMSO.

House of Lords, Select Committee (1983). 'European Monetary System', London, HMSO.

Johnson, H. (1972). 'The Case for Flexible Exchange Rates, 1969', in Harry Johnson, *Further Essays in Monetary Economics*, London, George Allen & Unwin, Chapter 8.

Kydland, F. E. and E. C. Prescott (1977). 'Rules Rather than Discretion: The Inconsistency of Optimal Plans', *Journal of Political Economy*, Vol. 85, pp. 473–910.

Marston, R. (1980). 'Exchange-Rate Unions and the Volatility of the Dollar', NBER Working Paper, No.492.

(1982). 'Exchange-Rate Unions as an Alternative to Flexible Exchange Rates', NBER Working Paper, No. 992; also in J. F. O. Bilson and R. Marston (eds) (1984), *Exchange Rate Theory and Practice*, Cambridge, Mass., MIT Press.

Melitz, Jacques (1985). 'The Welfare Case for the European Monetary System', *Journal of International Money and Finance*, Vol. 4, pp. 485–506.

(1987a). 'Monetary Discipline, Germany, and the European Monetary System', CEPR Discussion Paper, No. 178.

(1987b). *'Discipline Monétaire, la République Fédérale, et le Système Monétaire Européen'*, *Annales d'Economie et de Statistique*, No. 8 (October–December).

(1988). 'The Prospect of a Depreciating Dollar and Possible Tension inside the European Monetary System', *Schweizerische Zeitschrift für Volkswirtschaft und Statistik*, No. 1.

Miller, M. and M. Salmon (1986). 'When Does Coordination Pay?', University of Warwick (mimeo).

Oudiz, G. (1985a). *'Stratégies économiques européennes: Coordination ou confrontation?'*, *Cahiers de l'Institut de Sciences Mathématiques et Economiques Appliquées*, pp. 265–96.

(1985b). 'European Policy Coordination: An Evaluation', *Recherches Economiques de Louvain*, Vol. 51 (December), pp. 301–39.

Oudiz, G. and J. Sachs (1984). 'Macroeconomic Policy Coordination among the Industrial Economies', Brookings Papers on Economic Activity, No. 1, pp. 1–64.

Rogoff, K. (1985a). 'The Optimal Degree of Commitment to an Intermediate Monetary Target', *Quarterly Journal of Economics*, Vol. 100, pp. 1169–89.

(1985b). 'Can International Monetary Policy Cooperation be Counter-productive?', *Journal of International Economics*, Vol. 18, pp. 199–217.

(1987). 'Reputational Constraints on Monetary Policy', Carnegie–Rochester Conference Series on Public Policy, Vol. 26 (Spring), pp. 141–81.

Sachs, J. (1983). 'International Policy Coordination in a Dynamic Macroeconomic Model', NBER Working Paper, No. 1166.

Taylor, J. (1985). 'International Coordination in the Design of Macroeconomic Policy Rules', European Economic Review, Vol. 28, pp. 53–81.

Thygesen, N. (1984). 'Exchange-Rate Policies and Monetary Targets in the EMS Countries', in Rainer Masera and Robert Triffin (eds), Europe's Money: Problems in European Monetary Co-ordination and Integration, Oxford, Clarendon Press.

Ungerer, H., O. Evans, T. Mayer and P. Young (1986). 'The European Monetary System: Recent Developments', IMF Occasional Papers, No. 48 (December).

Vaubel, R. (1988). Evidence to the House of Commons, Treasury and Civil Service Committee.

Discussion

JOSÉ VIÑALS

Jacques Melitz's study performs two useful roles: on the one hand, it helps us understand more clearly the basic economic forces underlying the actual workings of the EMS. On the other, it provides us with a useful benchmark model in order that we can think about the implications of several hypothetical scenarios regarding the future configuration of the system. I will divide my comments into four parts: (1) main policy issues addressed in the study, (2) results obtained, (3) validity and generality of the results, and (4) implications for the EMS of the removal of capital controls in the EEC by 1992.

1   Main policy issues

Melitz's study seeks to explain why it is in the interest of both Germany and non-German EMS members to participate in the system. As the author himself indicates, while the monetary discipline hypothesis can account for the disinflationary tendency observed in the EMS – and for the special position of Germany in the system – it cannot explain why it is in the interest of Germany to be part of it. At the same time, while strategic cooperation considerations can provide an explanation for the interest of all present members to be in the EMS, they cannot justify the asymmetric features of the system and the leading role of Germany.

Melitz's strategy consists in integrating the monetary discipline and cooperative reasons to explain the asymmetric behaviour of the EMS, its disinflationary properties, and German participation.

2   The basic model and results

The basic framework used by the author is an open-economy, two-country version of the well-known Barro and Gordon (1983a, 1983b) model of monetary policy. With the help of this simple model, Melitz compares the solutions resulting for the price level and the loss function of the authorities in two situations: (a) in a flexible exchange-rate regime where prices and exchange rates adjust proportionally; and (b) in the EMS.

As is typical in the kind of model employed by Melitz, in the context of flexible exchange rates the price level turns out to be inefficiently high as a result of the (unsuccessful) attempt by the authorities to increase output by expanding demand. However, things are different in the case of Germany and France (representing non-German European countries) because it is assumed that German authorities are far-sighted and have a low discount rate, while French authorities are short-sighted and have a high discount rate. As a result, a reputational equilibrium occurs where inflation is higher in France than in Germany. Against the benchmark provided by the flexible exchange-rate case, Melitz builds three alternative models of the EMS, which I will term Models 1, 2 and 3.

In *Model 1* (Section 2(*b*)(*i*) of the study), it is assumed that exchange-rate realignments happen every period to keep competitiveness unchanged, and that France incurs certain costs as a result of being an EMS member. These costs are those associated with the use of capital controls, with the losses of official reserves between realignments (within each period), as well as the political costs of provoking realignments. However, the key characteristics of those costs is that they are modelled as the sum of two components: a lump-sum cost (α_0), and a variable cost that *increases* with the French inflation rate (α_1). Consequently, France's entrance into the EMS implies an extra weight attached to the cost of inflation in the loss function of the French authorities. This, in turn, results in a lower inflation rate for France in the EMS than with flexible exchange rates.

However, France need not be necessarily better off inside than outside the EMS, since the gains experienced by reducing inflation have to be weighed against the capital controls cost associated with EMS membership. Still, if all the current EMS members have chosen to remain in the system it must have been the case – so far – that the net gains from staying have been larger than the gains obtained outside the system *minus* the costs of leaving the system.

In *Model 2* (Section 2(*b*)(*ii*) of the study), the assumption of realignments every period is dropped, allowing instead for realignments every other period. Nevertheless, international competitiveness still does not enter into any behavioural equation in the system, which remains an unsatisfactory feature of the model. Within this framework, it is still the case that the French authorities have an incentive to lower inflation inside the EMS as a result of the inflation-dependent costs imposed by capital controls. But, at the same time, the French authorities have also an incentive to increase inflation, since now an increase in domestic prices does not translate immediately into a proportional increase in the consumer price index – which enters the authorities' loss function – due to the delayed response of the exchange rate.

Therefore, Model 2 has two surprising implications: first, if the incentive to increase inflation dominates over the incentive to reduce inflation it may be the case that EMS membership increases – rather than lowers – French inflation. Second, as realignments become less frequent the inflationary discipline of the EMS is relaxed. Obviously, the implications of Model 2 seem to be quite at variance with the existing general consensus about the performance of the EMS.

Model 3 (Section 3 of the study) tries to get rid of the above counterintuitive results by introducing cooperative features. In the model – the most realistic of the three – it is still the case that realignments occur every other period (letting competitiveness vary) and that France incurs the cost of having capital controls, but now competitiveness *does* have an effect on the economy.

In principle, one would expect competitiveness to affect total output, making policymakers care about the worsening of the international competitiveness of the country. However, the way Melitz models the real effects of competitiveness is rather peculiar. Indeed, changes in competitiveness are assumed to leave output unaffected but influence the mix between traded and non-traded goods – which according to the author has welfare costs. Through this indirect and cumbersome channel, competitiveness enters into the loss function of the authorities, helping restore price discipline in France. At the same time, it turns out that less frequent realignments can again enhance monetary discipline in France by increasing the overall losses derived from having high inflation.

Another interesting result obtained with this last model is that it shows Germany benefiting from the EMS by having low inflation without having to suffer the international competitiveness losses that would exist with a flexible exchange-rate system in Europe – where other countries may pursue policies of competitive depreciation. Consequently, both France and Germany can gain from EMS membership. In the case of France, the benefits come mainly as a result of the reduction in inflation, while in the case of Germany they come as a result of having better competitiveness than otherwise. Still, it is important to notice that the asymmetric functioning of the EMS is also reflected in the net benefits that France and Germany get: German benefits are not only different qualitatively from those obtained by France, but seem also more secure.

3   Validity and generality of the results

The main results obtained in the study suggest that although both Germany and France are presently gaining from EMS membership, the erosion of competitiveness suffered by France may come to a point where membership becomes too high a price to pay, therefore leading to tensions inside the system. In turn, this conclusion is based on the asymmetric nature of the benefits derived by Germany and the other members of the EMS.

While I agree with the above conclusion, it is not clear that those benefits are as asymmetric as shown in the study. Specifically, although the author mentions that Germany also bears some costs from being in the EMS, these costs are not modelled explicitly. In this regard, it should be recognised that the costs of capital controls do not fall entirely on the country imposing them (France) but also on other countries (Germany) whose residents are prevented from carrying out financial transactions. At the same time, Germany also experiences the cost of having its money supply go up when the Bundesbank is forced to help weaker EMS currencies – a cost that is likely to rise with the weaker-currency inflation rate.

Consequently, Germany will benefit from the EMS only when the gains in terms of competitiveness exceed the costs described above. And, in turn, although it must have been the case so far that Germany has made net gains in the EMS, these are no longer secure – as is the case with non–German members – and can potentially be reversed. The kind of net benefits derived by Germany are therefore now more symmetric relative to those derived by non-German EMS members, in the sense of having a common cost component.

Another important modelling issue in Melitz's study is the assumption that high-inflation EMS countries reset their exchange rate at realignment time to go back to the initial level of competitiveness of the previous period. This is relevant because it means that – between realignments – the competitiveness of the high-inflation country will be below the level required to keep the current account balance in equilibrium. Therefore, the higher-inflation non-German country will experience most of the time a current account deficit and deplete its foreign reserves, making the EMS an unsustainable system in the long run. This important point, addressed recently by Giavazzi and Pagano (1986), is not tackled by Melitz.

Another unsatisfactory aspect of Melitz's study is the way competitiveness is introduced in Model 3. Rather than forcing output to be unaffected in the presence of changes in international competitiveness, a more sensible and natural route to take would be to let output vary with changes in competitiveness through the typical supply and demand channels. Although I am aware that this may complicate the mathematical complexities of the solution to Model 3, I think it ought to be done to increase the plausibility and practical appeal of the conclusions.

4   The removal of capital controls

The achievement by 1992 of complete freedom of capital flows in the European Economic Community raises serious doubts about the viability of the EMS. On the pessimistic side, it is often mentioned that the removal of capital controls without a sufficient coordination of monetary policies in Europe will lead to exchange-rate pressures and to larger and more frequent realignments which will, in turn, weaken the discipline and stability of the system. In this regard, it is advised that the EMS be softened with wider bands and more frequent realignments. On the optimistic side, it is argued that the removal of capital controls may provide just the necessary incentive for EMS countries fully to coordinate monetary policies by making extremely high – in terms of exchange-rate pressures and reserve changes – the costs of pursuing non-coordinated policies.

Melitz's model can actually be used to examine some of the implications for the EMS of removing capital controls. Although it would have been desirable for the model to allow for an endogenous timing of realignments depending on the costs of capital controls (α_0, α_1), Model 3 can still be used to do a simple comparative statics exercise. Specifically, a reduction of capital controls leads to a decrease of fixed costs (α_0) and to an increase of variable costs (α_1). Intuitively, there will be a reduction in the administrative costs associated with the existence of capital controls, and an increase in the costs suffered by the higher-inflation country in terms of reserve losses – and, perhaps, also in terms of interest-rate volatility. As the fixed costs decrease there will therefore be an increase in the net benefit of non-German (and I think also of German) members of the EMS, and as the variable costs increase there will be a further convergence of inflation rates and economic policies. In sum, the model seems to justify the optimistic rather than the pessimistic view.

  While recognising the disciplinary virtues of free capital mobility, it is not clear that the full coordination of economic policies which is needed to preserve the stability of the EMS will be so easily obtained in practice without changing the structure of the EMS itself. Perhaps the new situation calls for a more symmetric behaviour inside the EMS, where the inflation target is defined jointly by Germany and the other member countries in the system, and where monetary and fiscal policy share more equally the burden of preserving exchange-rate stability.

REFERENCES

Barro, R. and D. Gordon (1983a). 'A Positive Theory of Monetary Policy in a Natural Rate Model', *Journal of Political Economy*, Vol. 91 (August), pp. 589–610.

——— (1983b). 'Rules, Discretion and Reputation in a Model of Monetary Policy', *Journal of Monetary Economics*, Vol. 12 (July), pp. 101–12.

Giavazzi, F. and M. Pagano (1986). 'The Advantage of Tying One's Hands: EMS Discipline and Central Bank Credibility', CEPR Discussion Paper, No. 135; (1988) *European Economic Review* (June).

4   The Role of the Exchange-rate Regime in a Disinflation: Empirical Evidence on the European Monetary System*

FRANCESCO GIAVAZZI and ALBERTO GIOVANNINI

1   Introduction

Since the beginning of the 1980s, countries belonging to the European Monetary System (EMS) have experienced a large fall in inflation: Table 4.1 reports the evolution of inflation rates in Germany, France, Italy and Denmark, as well as – for the purpose of comparison – in the United Kingdom.[1] This study illustrates what role the exchange-rate regime could have played in the disinflation, and empirically measures the effects predicted by the theoretical models.

The professional views about the role of the exchange-rate regime in a disinflation, as well as the actual experiences, differ widely. At one end of the spectrum, the negative experiences include the Southern-Cone 'new style' IMF plans where the exchange rate was used to stop very high inflation rates. These experiments were criticised, among others, by Dornbusch (1982): critics pointed to the disruptive effects of the large real exchange-rate appreciations, their ultimate unsustainability, and the lack of credibility of the exchange-rate targets. At the other end, Bruno (1986) suggests that the exchange-rate policy might have had an important role in the successful Israeli stabilisation. The positive role of the exchange-rate policy in the Bolivian stabilisation is also stressed by Sachs (1986).

In the case of the EMS experience, most observers tend to conclude that the exchange-rate regime helped the high-inflation economies. Fischer (1987) describes the EMS as 'an arrangement for France and Italy to purchase a committment to low inflation by accepting German monetary policy'. Even in countries considering EMS membership the main advantages of membership are associated with Germany's reputation. *The Economist* (21 September 1985) writes: 'If sterling does join the biggest change will be the transfer of responsibility for Britain's monetary policy from the Bank of England to the Bundesbank which, as the central bank

Year	Germany	France	Italy	Denmark	UK
1979	4.17	10.67	14.90	9.61	13.4
1983	3.31	9.62	14.58	6.91	5.2
1986	−0.25	2.53	5.86	3.62	4.0

Table 4.1 The Disinflation of the 1980s (CPI Inflation Rates in Selected European Countries)

Note: Data are in per cent per annum.

Source: IMF, *International Financial Statistics*.

keenest on sound money, sets the pace for others to follow. This would be a blessing: tory governments may like appointing City gents as governors of the Bank, but Mr Karl Otto Poehl would do a better job'. *The Financial Times* (28 September 1987) writes: 'In place of money supply targetry, long since discredited, we would have that unflinching guardian of monetary rectitude, the Bundesbank, standing as guarantor against Britain's endemic propensity to generate double-figure rates of inflation'.

Section 2 of this study describes the channels through which credible exchange-rate pegging can help monetary authorities in a disinflation. To this end, we use a family of models that emphasise both the interactions between price setters and the monetary authority (as analysed by Barro and Gordon, 1983a, 1983b), and the interaction between different countries' monetary authorities (studied, among others, by Canzoneri and Gray, 1985 and Rogoff, 1985).

Section 3 provides empirical evidence to highlight the shifts in inflationary expectations after the start of the EMS. There seems to be weak evidence suggesting that, some time after the start of the EMS, inflationary expectations have fallen in the 'high-inflation' countries. This shift in expectations, however, could be caused by dramatic (and endogenous) shifts in domestic policies.

2   Expectations and disinflation: domestic and international aspects

The stubbornness of inflation is here modelled in the manner of Barro and Gordon (1983a, 1983b), by considering an economy where prices are predetermined, and are set in the expectation of monetary policies. With predetermined prices, the monetary authority has an incentive to generate surprise inflation whenever its target level of activity exceeds the economy's natural rate. In equilibrium, inflation is high enough to eliminate any incentive of the monetary authority to surprise the public with excessive monetary growth. To illustrate the effects of alternative exchange-rate regimes on equilibrium inflation, we use the now-standard Canzoneri and Henderson (1987) two-country model. The model is described by the following equations:

$$y = - (w - p)(1 - \alpha)/\alpha \tag{4.1}$$

$$y^* = - (w^* - p^*)(1 - \alpha)/\alpha \tag{4.1'}$$

$$y - y^* = \delta(e + p^* - p) \tag{4.2}$$

$$m - p = y \tag{4.3}$$

$$m^* - p^* = y^* \tag{4.3'}$$

$$\Omega = - \sigma(n - k)^2 - (q)^2 \tag{4.4}$$

$$\Omega^* = - \sigma(n^* - k^*)^2 - (q^*)^2 \tag{4.4'}$$

$$q = p + \beta(e + p^* - p) \tag{4.5}$$

$$q^* = p^* + \beta(p - e - p^*) \tag{4.5'}$$

Equations (4.1) and (4.1′) are output supply equations, where the (log of) output in the domestic and foreign (*) country is a decreasing function of the (log of the) real product wage. Employment in the two countries, n and n^*, equals $-1/\alpha$ times the product wage. Equation (4.2) shows that the relative demand for output in the two countries depends on the real exchange rate. Equations (4.3) and (4.3′) are money demand functions, while (4.4) and (4.4′) describe the central bankers' objectives. The central bankers' employment targets, k and k^*, exceed the natural rates of employment (normalised to zero).[2] Equations (4.5) and (4.5′) are simply the definitions of the consumer price indices. To close the model we need to specify how wages are set. We assume that unions set wages trying to minimise the conditional variance of employment. Since the conditional variance of employment depends on the exchange-rate regime, wages depend on the exchange-rate regime.

We consider three regimes. The first is flexible exchange rates. The other two regimes are asymmetric: in one case (managed exchange rates) one country sets the money supply, assuming that, given the exchange rate, the other country accommodates changes in its money supply one-for-one; in the other case (fixed exchange rates), one country gives up the option of using monetary policy strategically, and passively pegs the exchange rate to the foreign country. In each regime we study only time-consistent Nash equilibria – i.e., we assume that each central bank sets monetary policy taking as given price expectations in the domestic labour market, as well as the foreign country's policy variable – be it the exchange rate or the stock of money.

a.   Flexible exchange rates

In the flexible exchange-rate regime each central bank sets its own money supply taking the partner's money supply as given. The exchange rate is endogenous. Minimisation of the unions' loss function implies the following wage-setting rule:

$$w = m^e \tag{4.6}$$

$$w^* = m^{*e} \tag{4.6'}$$

Solution of the model under perfect foresight leads to the following expressions:

$$n = n^* = 0 \tag{4.7}$$

$$q = m = \frac{\sigma}{\epsilon + \alpha} k \tag{4.8}$$

$$q^* = m^* = \frac{\sigma}{\epsilon + \alpha} k^* \tag{4.8'}$$

where

$$\epsilon = (1 - \alpha)\beta/\delta$$

Equilibrium inflation under flexible exchange rates is the result of two offsetting effects. On one side, the interactions between the central banks and the public, as in the Barro–Gordon closed-economy model, give rise to excessive inflation.[3] Notice that the closed-country case corresponds to the case where β (and therefore ϵ) equals zero. In the closed economy inflation is too high relative to the first-best solution (zero inflation) by a factor proportional to the central bank's incentive to surprise the public.

The interaction between the two central banks, however, is associated with the second externality, which offsets the first. Central banks could decrease inflation at a relatively low output cost through a surprise monetary contraction, which generates a real exchange-rate appreciation, and export high prices abroad. When both central banks attempt to do this, the equilibrium is characterised by a deflationary bias, as Canzoneri and Gray pointed out. This is the interpretation of the term ϵ in the denominator of equations (4.8) and (4.8'). Given that the inefficiency associated with the lack of international cooperation offsets the domestic credibility problem of central banks, international cooperation in this model actually produces an inferior outcome.[4]

b.   Managed exchange rates

In the flexible exchange-rate regime studied above, each central bank takes the other country's money supply as given: each central bank believes that a change in its own money stock can affect the exchange rate. Because the exchange rate feeds back into domestic prices, monetary policy can improve the output–price level trade-off. In a regime of managed exchange rates, in contrast, the two countries perceive different trade-offs. One country sets its own money stock taking the exchange rate as given, and assuming that (given the exchange rate) the foreign country will perfectly accommodate. The other country, on the contrary, believes – as in the case of flexible rates – that it can affect the price level with a smaller output loss by changing the exchange rate.

Under managed rates, optimal wage setting implies:

$$w = (m^{*e} + e^e) \tag{4.9}$$

$$w^* = (m^*)^e \tag{4.9'}$$

where a^* now denotes the country that controls the money supply. Proceeding as in the case of flexible rates, the Nash equilibrium in the managed exchange-rate regime is:

$$n^* = n = 0 \tag{4.7}$$

$$q^* = \frac{\sigma}{\alpha} k^* \tag{4.10}$$

$$q = \frac{\sigma}{\epsilon + \alpha} k \tag{4.10'}$$

Under managed rates, the benefit from inflation exporting accrues only to the country that sets the exchange rate. There, equilibrium inflation equals that prevailing under flexible rates. The 'centre' country, however, faces the world output–inflation trade-off, ending up with an inflation rate equal to that in the closed economy.

c.   Fixed exchange rates

The lesson from the analysis of flexible and managed rates is that the strategic interaction among countries gives rise to a contractionary bias that partly offsets the 'domestic' inflationary bias associated with the central banks' incentive to affect real wages when nominal wages are preset. This is just an example of the general theorem of the second best.

From the viewpoint of a central bank in search of an exchange-rate regime that would stabilise expectations – and thus help it to disinflate – there is no difference between flexible rates and a managed-rates regime in which it retains the ability to affect the exchange rate. In what ways can exchange-rate pegging help to bring down inflation? A central bank can bring down inflationary expectations only by pegging to a low-inflation country, and convincing the public that it has given up its monetary independence. This is the case of credibly and irrevocably fixed exchange rates. Under fixed exchange rates, we assume that the $*$ country sets monetary policy, and the other country accommodates any change in m^* by changing m accordingly. The perfect-foresight equilibrium is:

$$n^* = n = 0 \tag{4.7}$$

$$q = q^* = \frac{\sigma}{\alpha} k^* \tag{4.11}$$

A comparison of equations (4.10$'$) and (4.11) clearly points to the conditions for fixed exchange rates to be an attractive option for a central bank facing a credibility problem. Under flexible (or managed) rates, the equilibrium price level in the domestic country is $[\sigma/(\epsilon+\alpha)]k$. Under fixed exchange rates, the equilibrium price level equals that prevailing in the foreign country. If the foreign central bank does not suffer from a credibility problem (so that $k^*=0$) fixed rates remove the domestic inefficiency. The domestic central bank acquires the reputation of the foreign central bank, and price expectations are automatically stabilised. The attractiveness of fixed exchange rates is reduced the more similar is the foreign to the domestic country. Pegging to a country whose central bank faces a credibility problem similar to that faced at home clearly does not help. Furthermore, for pegging to be an attractive option the 'credibility gap' must be sufficiently large: the reason is that fixed exchange rates remove all strategic interactions, and (as we have seen above) strategic interactions dampen the domestic inflationary bias. The condition for fixed rates to be superior to flexible rates is:

$$\frac{k-k^*}{k^*} > \frac{\epsilon}{\alpha} \tag{4.12}$$

Fixed exchange rates are superior to flexible rates if the 'credibility gap' is large relative to the incentive to affect the exchange rate under flexible rates.

3 Empirical evidence

In Section 2 we have shown that pegging the exchange rate to a low-inflation country can help break the inertia associated with inflation expectations if the central bank gives up completely its own monetary independence – and, in particular, if it gives up the right to change the exchange rate at will. Under these conditions, price-setters' expectations adjust endogenously, and the equilibrium rate of inflation for the country pegging the exchange rate is lower than in a regime of flexible rates. On the other hand, the 'centre' country faces a higher inflation rate than in the flexible-rates regime.

Whether or not the exchange-rate targets of the EMS are perceived by member central banks (and by the public) to be binding, remains largely an empirical question. In particular, the model we used is silent on the question of credibility of the exchange-rate targets. The purpose of this section is to measure the shifts in expectations associated with the institution of the EMS, and their impact on inflation rates.

We concentrate on the joint dynamics of wages, prices and output, and identify the role of the EMS in the European disinflation by exploiting the empirical implications of the Lucas 'critique'. In his celebrated Carnegie–Rochester study,[5] Lucas pointed out that statistical relationships between macroeconomic time series are affected by policy regimes, and therefore cannot be used to predict the effects of changes in policy. This proposition implies that – if we can clearly identify changes in policy regimes – empirical shifts of the statistical relations among economic time series provide evidence on the effects of the new regimes.

How can we use the Lucas critique to assess the effects of the EMS in the European disinflation?[6] We specify a reduced-form system of equations for the dynamics of prices, wages and output. This reduced form is consistent with general models of wage and price setting characterised by short-run nominal rigidities and forward-looking behaviour, as in the models we used in Section 2. In these reduced forms, we control for shifts in price and wage inflation caused by monetary policy, and by changes in aggregate demand and costs originating from fluctuations of foreign final goods prices and imported commodities' prices. The parameters of the reduced forms, as well as their lag structure, depend on stochastic properties of exogenous variables and the policy regime of the economy, both of which affect expectations and the behaviour of price setters. If we can control for all variables that influence the joint dynamics of prices and wages, a change in the policy regime would generate an adjustment in expectations, a change in behaviour of price setters – and, as a consequence, a shift in the parameters of the reduced-form equations.

Therefore, any systematic failure of our statistical model – estimated over the period preceding the EMS – to predict price and wage inflation during the EMS is an estimate of the quantitative role of the exchange-rate regime in the disinflation. If our reduced-form equations, estimated over the period preceding the EMS, overpredict inflation in the EMS period, we tend to conclude that the EMS has had a positive effect on the disinflation by shifting inflation expectations downward, and therefore decreasing the output cost of the inflation reduction.

Our statistical model of wage–price dynamics is specified as follows:[7]

$$Y_t = A(L)Y_{t-1} + B(L)Z_{t-1} + u_t \qquad (4.13)$$

where $A(L)$ and $B(L)$ are polynominals in the lag operator, and

$$Y_t = [p_t, \ w_t, \ y_t]'$$

is the vector of the endogenous variables: price inflation, wage inflation, and output growth.[8] The vector Z_t contains a constant, a linear time trend, seasonal dummies and other dummies (specified below), money growth, the relative price of imported raw materials, and the relative price of imported finished goods (in rates of change). These two last variables capture demand and supply effects in the international transmission of price disturbances.[9]

The most important feature of (4.13) is that the variables in Z other than the trend and the dummies are assumed to be determined outside of the system.[10] This limits the number of parameters to be estimated, and as a result contains the sampling error in the dynamic simulations we perform below. The assumption that the variables in Z can be left out of the vector-autoregression is warranted if the variables in Z_t that are correlated with u_t affect Y only with a lag. Plausibly, money growth and the relative price of imported intermediate and final goods (which are affected by movements in the nominal exchange rate) are correlated with innovations in output growth and wage and price inflation. On the other hand, the assumption that the Z variables affect Y with at least a one-quarter lag is consistent with the view that prices and wages are predetermined with respect to money growth and relative prices of imported intermediate and final goods, and that output responds slowly to changes in those variables.

Here we do not make any attempt to provide 'structural' interpretations of the system (4.13). In particular, we do not use our reduced-form equations to address the questions about the peculiar behaviour of the European Phillips curves raised, for example, by Blanchard and Summers (1986) and Bean, Layard and Nickell (1986). According to Blanchard and Summers, the nature of wage bargaining in Europe produces hysteresis in employment: in their view, European countries have faced high and persistent unemployment in the 1980s because of negative aggregate demand shocks (accommodation to the monetary contraction in the US coupled with fiscal conservatism) coupled with increases in real wages, that have validated the increase in unemployment. The statistical model of wage–price inflation and output growth that we use appears ill-suited to capture the effects discussed by Blanchard and Summers. The model is instead designed to capture the formation of expectations in wage and price setting.

Our basic strategy is to estimate the system (4.13) over the period preceding the EMS, and to use the estimates to forecast the endogenous variables during the EMS. Table 4.2 contains summary statistics of the model, estimated with quarterly data for Germany, Denmark, France, Italy and the United Kingdom. The choice of these countries is mainly dictated by the availability of the data.[11] We include the United Kingdom to allow a comparison with a country which experienced a fall in inflation outside of the EMS. The equations were estimated with ordinary least squares using four lags for all variables. In addition to seasonals and the time trend, we included dummy variables to capture the fall of the Bretton Woods regime and country-specific experiences that the model cannot explain.[12]

Long-run neutrality imposes restrictions on the coefficients of the equations in (4.13). The sum of the coefficients of lagged p and w and lagged money growth should be 1 in the p and w equations, and should equal zero in the y equation. These restrictions are tested, equation by equation, and are imposed when the test does not reject them. Tests of long-run neutrality are in some sense specification tests for the lag length: Table 4.2 also reports tests of zero autocorrelation of the residuals, which can also provide evidence of misspecification. Table 4.2 contains, country-by-country and equation-by-equation, the corrected R-square, the marginal significance level for the hypothesis of zero autocorrelation of residuals,[13] the marginal significance level for the F-test of the neutrality restrictions, and the marginal significance levels for tests of sub-sample stability. We test the null hypothesis of no shift in the parameters of the equation after the EMS, and the hypothesis of no shift in the parameters in the mid-1980s.[14]

Table 4.2 shows that the neutrality restrictions are not rejected, at the 5 per cent level, in all cases. Similarly, the hypothesis of zero autocorrelation of the output equation in France. The hypothesis of no change in the parameters of the equations after the beginning of the EMS is also not rejected, in all cases, except for the price equation in France. This result might suggest that the EMS has not brought about any of the

Germany: 1960:2 1979:1 (Sample ends 1987:2)

Equation	d.o.f.	$\bar{R}^2$	Q	Neutrality test	Shift: (79:2)	(81:4)
p	38	0.642	0.126	0.811	0.633	0.528
w	38	0.187	0.820	0.186	0.962	0.893
y	38	0.238	0.517	0.700	0.770	0.697

Denmark: 1968:2 1979:1 (Sample ends 1984:4)

Equation	d.o.f.	$\bar{R}^2$	Q	Neutrality test	Shift: (79:2)	(82:4)
p	10	0.490	0.074	0.462	0.521	0.636
w	10	0.257	0.423	0.554	0.899	0.901
y	10	0.193	0.154	0.636	0.400	0.976

France: 1960:2 1979:1 (Sample ends 1987:2)

Equation	d.o.f.	$\bar{R}^2$	Q	Neutrality test	Shift: (79:2)	(83:1)
p	40	0.743	0.897	0.120	0.010	0.027
w	40	0.690	0.171	0.545	0.057	0.112
y	40	0.455	0.013	0.929	0.846	0.918

Italy: 1960:2 1979:1 (Sample ends 1986:4)

Equation	d.o.f.	$\bar{R}^2$	Q	Neutrality test	Shift: (79:2)	(82:1)
p	41	0.667	0.405	0.604	0.891	0.995
w	41	0.612	0.952	0.591	0.879	0.872
y	41	0.117	0.051	0.718	0.922	0.911

UK: 1963:2 1979:1 (Sample ends 1987:1)

Equation	d.o.f.	$\bar{R}^2$	Q	Neutrality test	Shift: (79:2)	(82:4)
p	28	0.779	0.907	0.200	0.208	0.982
w	28	0.419	0.981	0.491	0.951	0.993
y	28	0.861	0.772	0.939	0.671	0.976

Table 4.2 Summary Statistics for the Inflation–Output Model

changes in expectations that we describe in the sections above, with the possible exception of France. The result should be interpreted with caution, however: as pointed out by Maddala (1977), the F-tests for shifts in the parameters constructed for the case where the second sub-sample does not contain enough degrees of freedom, has much less power than the standard Chow test. Tests of shifts of parameters thus tend to be inconclusive.

We provide additional evidence on shifts of wage–price dynamics by simulating the estimated model after 1979. The results of the simulations are reported in Figures 4.1–4.15. For each country, we report actual and forecast values of wage inflation, price inflation, and output growth during the EMS period. The forecasts are produced by estimating the model up to the first quarter of 1979, and using the estimates to obtain predictions on the vector Y, given the *actual* realisations of the variables in Z. An interesting result from Figures 4.1–4.15 is the asymmetry between Germany and the other countries in the EMS. In the case of Germany, the model underpredicts wage and price inflation, but over-predicts output growth. In the case of Denmark, exactly the opposite happens: the model overpredicts inflation but underpredicts output growth. The results of the simulations for France and Italy are slightly more difficult to describe. In France, actual inflation starts clearly diverging from the model's predictions from the third quarter of 1982. In the case of Italy, the model estimated up to 1979 underpredicts the inflation of the early 1980s, but overpredicts it in the recent past. Output growth also seems higher than predicted by the model after 1984.[15]

What is the interpretation of these experiments? Since the F-tests for parameter stability do not reject the null hypothesis, the wide divergences between actual and predicted values of the endogenous variables should not be taken to provide strong support to the hypothesis that the EMS has helped countries other than Germany in the disinflation of the 1980s, and (if anything) has hindered the Deutsche Bundesbank's monetary restraint. We are prevented from reaching this conclusion also because we do not compute the standard errors of the forecasts, and cannot perform a formal test of the difference between the model's predictions and actual experience. We do, however, find the results in Figures 4.1–4.15 suggestive. The results of the simulations are consistent with a shift in expectations. This shift in expectations is consistent with the theories discussed above.

Figures 4.1–4.15 also seem to suggest that, if an adjustment of expectations similar to those described above has taken place, it has (except possibly in the case of Denmark) occurred well after the start of the EMS. This result is consistent with informal accounts of the EMS experience, and the generally sceptical reactions of the public after its institution in 1979. Similarly, the figures for the United Kingdom would indicate a shift in expectations well after the change in regime. What could give rise to lagged adjustment of expectations? Two factors might

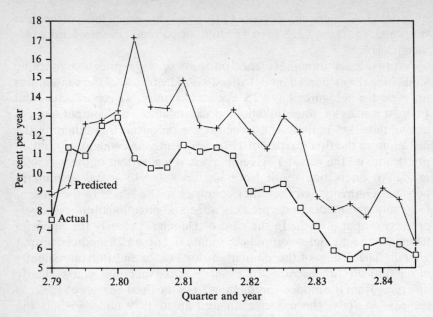

Figure 4.1 Denmark in the EMS, CPI inflation

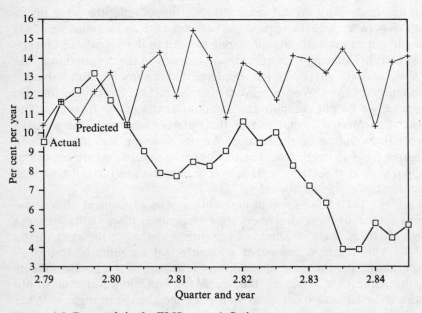

Figure 4.2 Denmark in the EMS, wage inflation

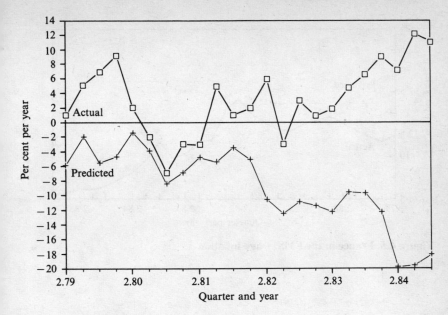

Figure 4.3 Denmark in the EMS, output growth

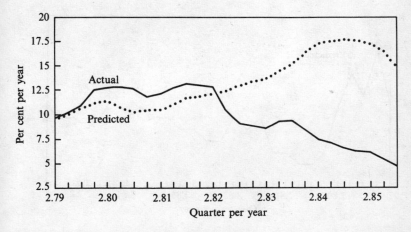

Figure 4.4 France in the EMS, CPI inflation

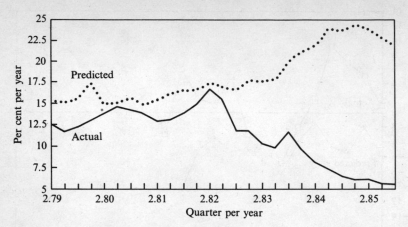

Figure 4.5 France in the EMS, wage inflation

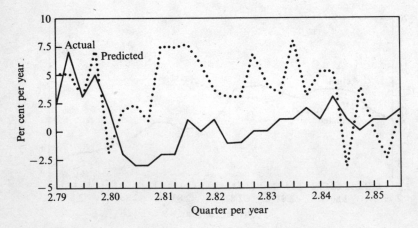

Figure 4.6 France in the EMS, output growth

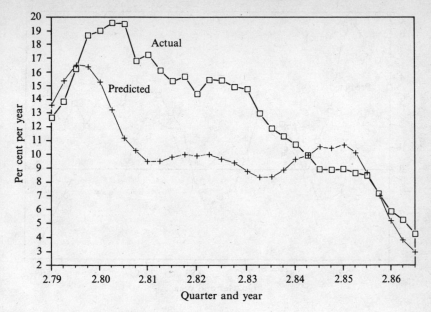

Figure 4.7 Italy in the EMS, CPI inflation

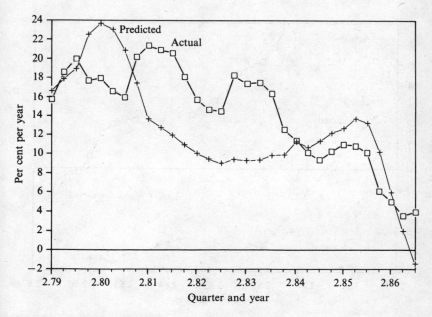

Figure 4.8 Italy in the EMS, wage inflation

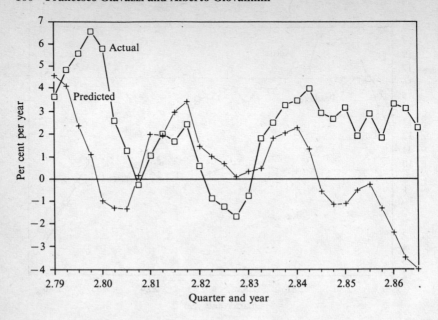

Figure 4.9 Italy in the EMS, output growth

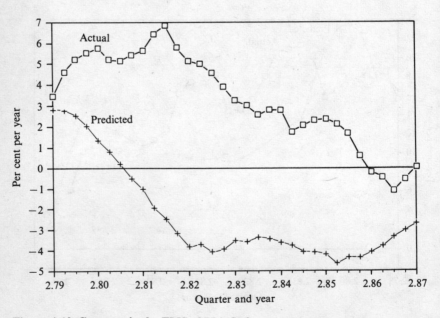

Figure 4.10 Germany in the EMS, CPI inflation

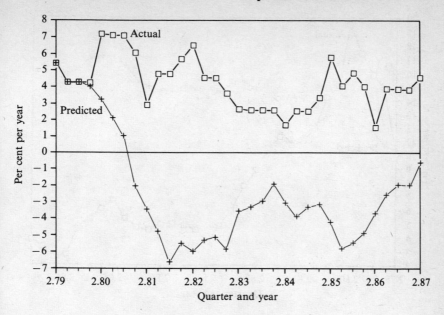

Figure 4.11 Germany in the EMS, wage inflation

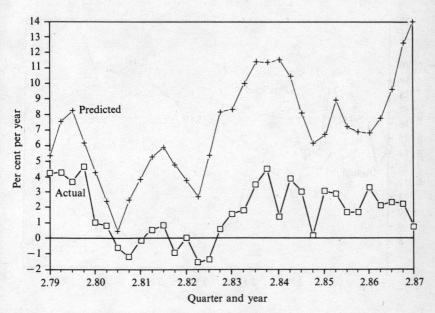

Figure 4.12 Germany in the EMS, output growth

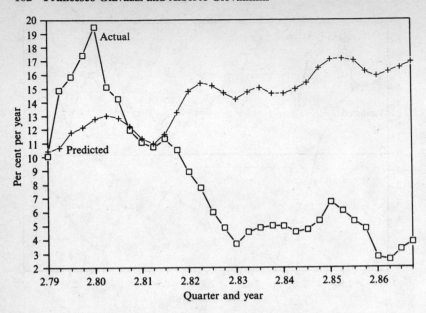

Figure 4.13 The UK during the EMS, CPI inflation

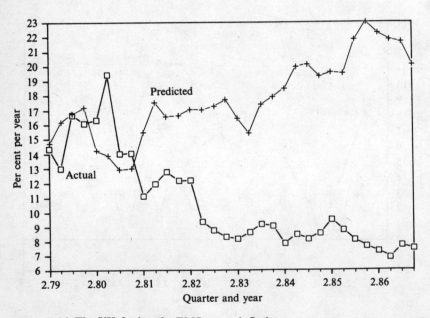

Figure 4.14 The UK during the EMS, wage inflation

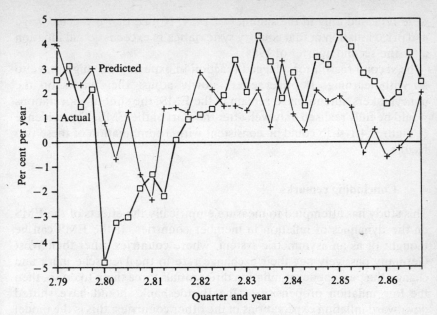

Figure 4.15 The UK during the EMS, output growth

explain it. The first is the large real depreciation of the lira and the French franc in 1978: this might have made the EMS rules less 'binding' for these countries, at least during the first months. Sachs and Wyplosz (1986, pp. 294–5), describing the events of 1981 and 1983, suggest that French authorities clearly signalled their intentions to abide to the EMS 'discipline' well after the start of the system:

> The role of external pressure was extremely important, since there is good reason to believe that French committments to the EMS tipped the balance towards austerity. Unlike the much looser committments under the European Snake in the 1970s, which France abandoned on two occasions, membership of the EMS has been invested with enormous political importance at the very highest levels of the government. That is why the debate over leaving the EMS was treated as synonymous with the debate over abandoning other spheres of cooperation in Europe, including participation in the Common Market . . .
>   Economists have long debated whether international exchange rate agreements can really bind national policies, since the sanctions for breaking agreements are so small and diffuse. The example of the Socialist turnaround in March 1983 suggests that an international agreement can help to tip the balance towards domestic restraint.

Similarly, in the case of Italy the government signalled its strong stance against inflation well after the start of the EMS. Wage-indexation laws

were repealed only in the summer of 1984. Notice that predicted wage
and price inflation in that country systematically exceeds actual inflation
after the second quarter of 1984.

The second reason for a lagged reaction in expectations might have to
do with learning. If price setters slowly adjust their views on the
policymakers' intentions to remain in the EMS, the shift in expectations
would be fully realised only well after the start of the EMS. The evidence
of Figures 4.1–4.15 could be consistent with a combination of these two
factors.

4   Concluding remarks

This study has attempted to measure empirically the effects of the EMS
on the dynamics of inflation in member countries. If the EMS can be
thought of as an asymmetric system, where countries other than West
Germany passively peg their exchange rate to the Deutsche mark and
change the peg whenever inflation differentials force them to do so, then
the low inflation propensity of the Bundesbank should have shifted
downward inflation expectations in the other countries: this is the model
of 'imported credibility' discussed by Giavazzi and Giovannini (1987),
Giavazzi and Pagano (1988), among others. The model of imported
credibility was illustrated in the case of a one-shot game in Section 2.

To measure the effects of the EMS we exploit the predictions of the
Lucas critique. In correspondence to a shift in regime, the public's
expectations change, as well as their behavioural rules. As a consequence, the observed shifts in well-specified reduced-form equations
provide a measure of the effects of the shifts in expectations.

Our empirical results appear broadly in agreement with our theoretical
presumptions. There are, however, a number of important caveats. The
first regards the lack of statistical significance of the point estimates.
Statistical tests indicate that the shifts in structural equations – although
in the direction predicted by the theory – are not significant in the
majority of cases. This is a well-known problem encountered by most
empirical researchers applying vector autoregressions to macroeconomic
time series. The second caveat concerns the timing, and the interpretation, of the shifts in structural equations. In Italy and France a downward
adjustment of the inflation process – consistent with a downward
adjustment of inflation expectations – occurs at least three years after the
inception of the EMS. In both countries, the shift in the inflation process
takes place in correspondence to an important reversal in government
policies. This result could be the effect of two phenomena. First,
immediately after the beginning of the EMS economic agents might have

spent some time learning how the system works, and monetary authorities might have needed some time to convince the public of their intentions to stick to the rules of the new regime. Second, the 1982–3 policy turnaround in France, as well as the tough stance of the Italian government towards wage indexation in 1984, could both be motivated by the desire of the governments in the two countries to remain in the EMS, and by their willingness to appeal to the EMS rules as an external justification for unpopular domestic policies.

APPENDIX: DATA FOR FIGURES 4.1–4.15

The two main sources are OECD *Main Economic Indicators* (OECD), and IMF *International Financial Statistics* (IFS).

Price Levels Consumer price indices (OECD).

Wage Rates Denmark – Index of hourly earnings in industry (OECD).
France – Index of hourly wage rates in manufacturing (OECD).
Germany – Index of hourly earnings in manufacturing (OECD).
Italy – Index of hourly wages in manufacturing (OECD).
UK – Index of weekly wages in manufacturing (OECD).

Imported Materials Denmark – WPI Industrial raw materials (OECD).
France – WPI Raw materials (OECD).
Germany – 1960–7 WPI Raw material prices (OECD).
1967–87 Basic material goods prices (OECD).
Italy – 1960–70 US WPI Raw materials (OECD) × lira/$ exchange rate (IFS); 1971–87 *Indice Confindustria Materie Prime Non-alimentari*.
UK – WPI Inputs of basic materials and fuels (OECD).

Exchange Rates IFS line rf (quarterly averages).

Money Stocks IFS line 34 (M1).

Output IFS lines 99 (real GNP or GDP).
Denmark – *IFS* line 66c (Industrial Production).
France – *IFS* line 66c (Industrial Production).

All variables are first differences of logs. Imported materials are relative to the CPI; imported final goods are obtained as a weighted average of the domestic-currency value of foreign CPIs, including all six countries plus the United States, and are relative to the domestic CPI. The weights for the indices, as well as the computer programs and the data sets used in the programs, are available from the authors on request.

NOTES

* We are indebted to Sabine Miltner for able research assistance and discussions, and to Bill Branson for several useful suggestions. Alberto Giovannini's research is funded by a grant from the John M. Olin Foundation. Francesco Giavazzi was supported by grants from Consiglio Nazionale delle Ricerche, Progetto Finalizzato Economica and CEPR.

1 The United Kingdom has never been formally linked to its European partners with any exchange-rate arrangement, but has experienced a drastic change in economic policies, starting roughly at the same time as the EMS.

2 These parameters represent the central bankers' inclinations to inflate. It is presumably related to the presence of distortions, as a result of which the natural rate of output lies within the country's production possibility frontier.

3 Since we are studying one-shot games, there is no distinction between the price level and the rate of inflation.

4 See Rogoff (1985). The result that international cooperation may be counter-productive is questioned in Carraro and Giavazzi (1988).

5 Lucas (1976).

6 Blanchard (1984) studies shifts in the Phillips curve and the term structure equation in the US during the new monetary policy 'regime' after 1979.

7 See also Branson (1984) for an analysis of vector-autoregressive models of the open economy. Branson's focus, unlike ours, is the structural interpretation of the estimated coefficients, and covariance matrix of residuals.

8 The variables are (quarterly) changes in the logs of prices, wages, and real GDP.

9 See the Appendix for a description of the data we used.

10 Blanchard (1986) uses similar models to study wage and price inflation in the US.

11 We could not estimate the model for Belgium, since the wage series in that country follows a markedly different pattern before and after 1972. The real GNP series in Italy has been updated with the new national income accounts figures. The growth rate of real GNP from 1979:4 to 1980:1 has been computed using the old data. GNP numbers are available for France only after 1965. For this reason, we used industrial production. The results with the GNP data (and a smaller sample) are very similar to the ones we report, and, of course, are available on request.

12 The precise list of dummy variables is as follows. All countries: from 1971:3 to end of sample fall of Bretton Woods. Italy: 1969:2–1970:1 *Autunno Caldo*. France: 1968:2–1968:3 'May '68'; 1964–5, 1974, 1976, 1982:3 to 1983:4 wage and price controls. UK: 1967:4 sterling devaluation, 1973:4–1974:4 wage controls.

13 This is the probability that the Q-statistic exceeds the computed value, under the null hypothesis. The Q-statistic is distributed as a chi-square, with degrees of freedom that depend on the size of the sample.

14 This test statistic differs from the usual Chow test because the number of observations in the second sub-sample is smaller than the number of para-meters in the equations. See Maddala (1977).

15 We have also found that, if the model is estimated for Italy up to the last quarter of 1981, inflation in the following years is systematically overpredic-ted and output growth is underpredicted. These results are not reported.

REFERENCES

Barro, R. J. and D. Gordon (1983a). 'Rules, Discretion, and Reputation in a Model of Monetary Policy', *Journal of Monetary Economics*, Vol. 12 (July), pp. 101–21.

(1983b). 'A Positive Theory of Monetary Policy in a Natural-Rate Model', *Journal of Political Economy*, Vol. 91 (August), pp. 589–610.

Bean, C. R., P. R. G. Layard and S. J. Nickell (1986). 'The Rise in Unemployment: A Multi-Country Study', *Economica*, Vol. 53, pp. S1–S22.

Blanchard, O. J. (1984). 'The Lucas Critique and The Volker Deflation', *American Economic Review–Papers and Proceedings*, Vol. 74 (May), pp. 211–15.

(1986). 'Empirical Structural Evidence on Wages, Prices and Employment in the United States', NBER, Working Paper, No. 2044.

Blanchard, O. J. and L. H. Summers (1986). 'Hysteresis and the European Unemployment', *NBER Macroeconomics Annual*, pp. 15–90.

Branson, W. H. (1984). 'Exchange Rate Policy After a Decade of "Floating"', in J. F. O. Bilson and R. C. Marston (eds), *Exchange Rate Theory and Practice*, Chicago, University of Chicago Press, pp. 79–120.

Bruno, M. (1986). 'Sharp Disinflation Strategy: Israel 1985', *Economic Policy*, Vol. 2 (April), pp. 379–408.

Canzoneri, M. B. and J. Gray (1985). 'Monetary Policy Games and the Consequences of Non-Cooperative Behavior', *International Economic Review*, Vol. 26, pp. 547–64.

Canzoneri, M. B. and D. W. Henderson (1987). 'Is Sovereign Policymaking Bad?' (August) Harvard University; Carnegie–Rochester Conference Series on Public Policy (forthcoming).

Carraro, C. and F. Giavazzi (1988). 'Can International Policy Coordination Really be Counterproductive?' (mimeo).

Dornbusch, R. (1982). 'Stabilization Policies in Developing Countries: What Have We Learned?', *World Development*, Vol. 10, No. 9, pp. 701–8.

Fischer, S. (1987). 'British Monetary Policy', in R. Dornbusch and R. Layard (eds), *The Performance of the British Economy*, Oxford, Oxford University Press.

Giavazzi, F. and A. Giovannini (1987). 'Models of the EMS: Is Europe a Greater Deutschmark Area?', in R. Bryant and R. Portes (eds), *Global Macroeconomics: Policy Conflict and Cooperation*, London, Macmillan, pp. 237–76.

Giavazzi, F. and M. Pagano (1988). 'The Advantage of Tying One's Hands: EMS Discipline and Central Bank Credibility', *European Economic Review* (June).

Lucas, R. E., Jr (1976). 'Econometric Policy Evaluation: A Critique', in K. Brunner and A. Meltzer (eds), *The Phillips Curve and Labor Markets*, Carnegie–Rochester Conference Series on Public Policy, Vol. 1, pp. 19–46.

Maddala, G. S. (1977). *Econometrics*, New York, McGraw-Hill.

Rogoff, K. (1985). 'Can International Monetary Cooperation be Counterproductive?', *Journal of International Economics*, Vol. 18, pp. 199–217.

Sachs, J. (1986). 'The Bolivian Hyperinflation and Stabilization', NBER Working Paper, No. 2073.

Sachs, J. and C. Wyplosz (1986). 'The Economic Consequences of President Mitterrand', *Economic Policy*, Vol. 2 (April), pp. 261–313.

Discussion

WILLIAM BRANSON

It is a great pleasure to be once again in the Bank of Italy's facility in Perugia, and an honour to be asked to discuss this interesting study by Francesco Giavazzi and Alberto Giovannini. Using the current language of international monetary discussions, I will refer to the authors as the G2. They provide a very nice illustration of the strategic problems in exchange-rate policy in their theoretical Section 2, and some intriguing empirical results in Section 3. The two sections are not very well integrated, however, and the G2 do not provide a model of the operation of the EMS here, although they have done so elsewhere. The models of Section 2 assume flexible, managed, or fixed rates, with no reference to potential problems with EMS-style bands, and the dynamic output and inflation equations of Section 3 are not particularly EMS-specific. I will first provide a summary and analysis of the results, and then discuss some issues of modelling that are raised by the study.

The fundamental message from the G2 is in the first paragraph of Section 3: 'pegging the exchange rate to a low-inflation country can help break the inertia associated with inflation expectations . . . price-setters' expectations adjust endogenously, and the equilibrium rate of inflation for the country pegging the exchange rate is lower than in a regime of flexible rates. On the other hand, the "centre" country faces a higher inflation rate than in the flexible-rates regime'. This message is generated by the theoretical analysis of the interaction of two strategic games facing policy-makers – one internal and one external – and the empirical results support it. Let us discuss first the two games.

The first is the internal game of wage-setters against the central bank. The setting is an economy with nominal wages set at the beginning of the period by agents with rational expectations who care about the real consumption wage. Due to an unspecified inefficiency in the economy, the central bank would like the unemployment rate to be below the natural rate. This is specified by assuming that k and k^* in equations (4.4) and (4.4') are positive. In this setting, the central bank has an incentive to inflate to achieve an increase in output; this undermines its credibility. The rational wage-setters are aware of this inflationary incentive for the central bank, so they increase their wage accordingly. This, in turn, requires monetary validation, resulting in a positive equilibrium inflation rate with no gain in output. This would be represented by the terms $\alpha k/\alpha$

and $\sigma k^*/\alpha$ in the G2 equations (4.8) and (4.8'). These terms give the inflationary bias due to the domestic game between wage-setters and the central bank.

The second game is between the two central banks in a flexible-rate system trying to use exchange-rate appreciation to disinflate. Each has an incentive to tighten monetary policy to appreciate its currency to reduce inflation. If both tighten, there is no effect on the exchange rate, but an increase in interest rates and excessive deflation in both countries. The international game with flexible rates thus imparts a deflationary bias. When the two games are put together, the result is the equilibrium inflation shown in equations (4.8) and (4.8'). The international game adds the ϵ term in the denominator, offsetting partially the effects of the domestic game.

G2 analyse the three cases of flexible, managed, and fixed rates in this framework. With no cooperation and flexible rates, the result is the inflation bias in equations (4.8) and (4.8'). In this case, cooperation would make things worse by removing the international offset to the domestic bias. Managed rates are modelled by assuming that a centre country sets monetary policy taking the exchange rate as given, while the other country sets the exchange rate to reduce inflation. Again, the result is worse than the flexible, non-cooperative case. In equation (4.10) the centre country has the higher closed-economy inflation rate, while the other obtains the same result as with flexible rates.

In their analysis of the fixed-rate case, G2 assume that the peripheral central bank can solve its credibility problem by pegging to the central country. In this case, the latter sets monetary policy, and the peripheral country accommodates to hold the fixed rate. The result is that both have the closed-economy inflation of the centre country in equation (4.11). If the inflation tendency in the centre is sufficiently lower than in the periphery, the latter can gain by credibly pegging, as is shown in equation (4.12). In this case the centre country loses from the arrangement, since q^* is larger in (4.11) than in (4.8'), and the peripheral country gains. G2 do not explain what special feature of the pegging policy makes it credible when other policies executed by the same authorities are not.

The empirical work in Section 3 of the study reports tests of sets of vector autoregressions (VARs) for the growth rate of output and wage and price inflation for four EMS countries – Denmark, France, Germany, and Italy – and the UK. The G2 test for structural change in the parameters of the VARs before and after the establishment of the EMS; this is interpreted as a test for changed expectations or credibility due to the existence of the EMS. The statistical test for existence of a structural shift turns out to be insignificant in Table 4.2. The G2 then plot the predicted values of the variables from the pre-EMS equations against the actual EMS outcomes. These plots are interesting, if insignificant.

From the plots, we see that Germany's performance during the EMS period has been markedly worse than the performance predicted from the pre-EMS regressions, with higher inflation and slower output growth than predicted. Denmark and France (lower inflation and more stable output growth) have fared better in the EMS than predicted by the pre-EMS regressions, as has Italy since 1983. The UK has also done better than predicted, even though it remained outside the EMS. Does this mean that the UK was able to achieve the same degree of credibility as Denmark, France, and Italy without any formal commitment to the EMS?

One interpretation of the evidence in the plots is that all participants thought the formation of the EMS would lead to convergence of inflation rates. This raised inflationary expectations in Germany and reduced them elsewhere, giving the performance results. This evidence is consistent with the implication of the theoretical model that the centre country loses and the peripheral ones gain from an EMS-type arrangement.

The evidence also raises the obvious question that occupied much time at the conference: why is Germany in the EMS? Perhaps the answer is not to be found within the limited sphere of economic policy, but rather in the international politics of Europe. The EMS is one part of a system of unifying structures in Western Europe; presumably Germany gains from this system of unification overall, even if it does not benefit from the EMS in particular.

This observation also suggests that the gains from policy coordination may not be evident if the search for them is confined to too narrow a set of policy instruments. In the study of macroeconomic policy coordination, we may not observe important exchanges across policy issue areas – for example, the 1978 Bonn summit results can be interpreted as an attempt to trade between macro policy in Europe and energy-pricing policy in the US. The domain of policies to be coordinated is too frequently taken as already defined by the models that are used to quantify the problem in existing studies of economic policy coordination. The present G2 study may be an example.

Three problems in modelling the EMS are assumed away or avoided in the G2 study. The first is the possibility of indeterminacy of the exchange rate within the EMS bands. If the only clear and credible statement of policy is that the rate will not be allowed to move outside the band, the rationale for selection of the stable 'saddlepath' as the rational expectations solution for the model disappears. All values of the rate within the band are equal candidates for the equilibrium, since the market knows the authorities will not let the rate go outside the band. This result is described in detail in Choe (1987). G2 avoid the problem by characterising the EMS as a fixed-rate system.

A second important (but limiting) assumption is that of price stability in the centre country. This permits the periphery countries to achieve price stability by pegging the exchange rate and following an accommodating monetary policy. If the price level in the centre were not so stable – for example, if it were stochastic – then a policy of offsetting exchange-rate changes would be required for stability in the periphery.

Finally, the theory in Section 2 of the G2 study deals with levels of output and the price level, while the empirical work is done on rates of change. The difference is dismissed in footnote 3 by reference to one-shot games. But if the actual setting is one of growth and inflation, might this not influence expectations and credibility? This is probably not a serious problem, but it is rather troubling in a study that focusses on these issues.

These remarks should not be interpreted as being very critical of the G2 paper: the job of a discussant is not to praise the study, but to bury it. The study provides an accessible discussion of the two policy games and their relevance for an evaluation of the EMS; it shows clearly the problem in understanding the interest of Germany in the system, both theoretically and empirically. It is a study well worth reading.

REFERENCES
Choe, Yoonjae (1987). 'The Indeterminacy of Short-run Exchange Rates in a Managed Float Regime', Woodrow Wilson School Discussion Papers in Economics, No. 128, Princeton University (May).

5 Inflation and the European Monetary System*

SUSAN M. COLLINS

1 Introduction

In 1978, the year before the European Monetary System (EMS) was instituted, (CPI) inflation among the prospective members averaged 7.2 per cent. The rates ranged from 2.7 per cent in Germany to 12.0 per cent in Italy. Inflation rates rose even further during 1979–80, as a result of the second oil shock. By the end of 1986, average EMS inflation had fallen to 2.4 per cent, and the range had narrowed considerably: − 0.2 per cent in Germany and 5.9 per cent in Italy. The timing of these developments suggests what I will call the 'EMS-Inflation Hypothesis' – that the EMS itself may have been responsible for the inflation reduction and convergence which member countries have experienced.

There seems to be growing consensus that the EMS-inflation hypothesis is true. To give two examples, the *Wall Street Journal* recently stated without qualification that 'the EMS has had its successes, such as helping to bring inflation in the other countries down toward the low level prevailing in West Germany' (8 September 1987). Giavazzi and Pagano (1986) assert that 'the central issue is not whether the EMS is an effective disciplinary device for inflation-prone countries . . . It is obvious that their inflation will be lower inside than outside the EMS'.

In contrast, early studies of the EMS found little evidence supporting the hypothesis. Rogoff (1985a) analyses data through March 1984. He concludes (p. 96) that:

> the formation of the EMS did not produce a rapid convergence of inflation rates . . . there is no evidence whatsoever of any convergence between France's, Germany's and Italy's inflation rates . . . any convergence that took place was between the inflation rates of Germany, Japan and the United Kingdom . . . Even if French, German and Italian inflation do ultimately converge at a low level, one should be cautious in attributing this success to the existence of the EMS.

112

Padoa-Schioppa (1985) and Ungerer *et al.* (1983) are more optimistic, but also find little evidence for the hypothesis.

The purpose of this study is to ask whether existing theoretical and empirical evidence supports the current consensus that the EMS-inflation hypothesis is true. It is difficult to test the proposition conclusively because to do so would require comparison of the actual inflation experiences of member countries to a counterfactual – the inflation that these countries would have experienced if they had not joined the EMS. A simple comparison of pre- and post-EMS experiences is inadequate for a number of reasons, in particular, because external shocks were quite different in the two periods. Similarly, a simple comparison of member and non-member country experiences is inadequate because the economic structures of the two groups of countries is likely to be quite different. Nonetheless, it would seem sensible to believe the hypothesis only if the evidence (both theoretical and empirical) consistently supports an affirmative conclusion.

Why should the EMS help to reduce inflation? The usual argument is that membership in the EMS provides additional 'discipline' to monetary authorities in inflation-prone countries. The key channels of this 'discipline' are perhaps best illustrated in the theoretical model developed by Giavazzi and Pagano (1986). In their framework, joining the EMS forces policymakers to accept a higher cost to expansionary policy through real appreciation. Realignments are assumed to devalue the currencies of above-average inflation members by at most enough to restore purchasing power parity (PPP).[1] Therefore, monetary expansion causes inflation which leads to a real appreciation (until the next realignment), and the loss in competitiveness reduces output. It is not surprising that inflation will be lower in this regime than in a flexible exchange-rate regime which maintains PPP throughout, regardless of the domestic inflation rate.

The model very intuitively illustrates two key channels for 'discipline'. First, it provides the central bank with added incentives to remain tough and to stick to an austerity programme. Second, it increases central bank credibility when austerity is announced. A familiar theme in theoretical macroeconomic literature is precisely that the costs of disinflation will be smaller when domestic residents believe that the programme will actually be followed.[2]

However, the study can *not* tell us whether joining the EMS is likely to reduce inflation, because the theoretical framework begins with this as an assumption. Taking the EMS-inflation hypothesis as given, the authors' interest is when inflation-prone countries would gain from tying their hands.

In fact, there are many reasons to doubt that the simple announcement of joining the EMS has been viewed by either monetary authorities or domestic residents as tying the hands of the central bank. I have already mentioned that virtually no evidence of monetary or inflation convergence emerged during 1979–82. Sachs and Wyplosz (1986) show that 'stock prices, capital outflows and the forward discount' during parts of 1981, 1982 and early 1983 'all point to a significant worsening in confidence' in French macroeconomic and exchange rate policy (p. 294). Expectations of disinflation emerged, not when France joined the EMS in 1979, but after domestic policies turned sharply restrictive in 1982–3. Many authors have discussed also the role of capital controls in enabling France (and Italy) to conduct independent monetary policies.[3] It is not at all clear what role the EMS played in the reversal. In particular, if France had opted for austerity, and had stuck to a consistent programme of restraints, the disinflation may well have occurred even if France had still belonged to the snake.

This study applies work on international policy coordination to the EMS to ask whether joining the EMS should have helped to reduce inflation rates after the second oil shock.[4] Other studies which examine policy coordination in the EMS include Canzoneri and Gray (1985), Melitz (1985), Oudiz (1985), Giavazzi and Giovannini (1986b), Canzoneri and Henderson (1987) and Roubini (1987); these are discussed further in Section 2.

This approach does allow us to ask whether, *ceteris paribus*, joining the EMS is likely to reduce inflation. It is also useful because it focuses on how the rules defining the interaction between countries affect the outcomes.

Three interrelated issues are involved: the impact on expectations and on wage-setting behaviour, the effect on central bank resolve and/or objectives and the implications of 'changing the rules of the game'. While it is possible to subsume all three under 'changing the rules of the game' and to derive the implications theoretically, I believe that the issues are separate in the real world, and that it is useful to distinguish among them. As discussed above, joining the EMS need not have tied the hands of the French central bank, and need not have influenced expectations about future prices and exchange rates. However, the EMS is an unusual multilateral exchange arrangement with different 'rules' than alternative exchange arrangements.

Section 2 of this study applies the international policy coordination approach to the EMS under alternative interaction rules. It has two objectives. The first is to examine the implications of alternative exchange regimes (including cooperative and non-cooperative regimes) on average inflation and on the divergence of inflation rates under the assumption that wage formation and exchange-rate expectations are unaffected. If being in the EMS has no effect on central bank credibility, what effect will it have on inflation? The second is to compare the inflationary implications of shifts in expectations under the alternative exchange-rate regimes. If a central bank manages to convince domestic residents that it will carry through a disinflation, does it matter what the exchange regime is?

To anticipate one of the key issues from the theoretical analysis: how inflation within the EMS differs from inflation in a non-EMS regime depends critically on how the EMS exchange regime is specified. This point is also stressed by Canzoneri and Henderson (1987), however, they use a different framework, and do not attempt to separate the effects of different rules from the effects of a change in credibility.

In fact, there is widespread disagreement about how to model the system. (The various approaches are discussed in Section 2.) The study shows that, depending on one's view, one could expect that the EMS regime would either raise or lower the mean and variance of inflation among members. Thus, theoretical analysis alone cannot support or refute the EMS-inflation hypothesis. Many of the questions are empirical ones.

There is relatively little empirical analysis of the impact of the EMS on inflation. While a detailed empirical analysis is not the focus of this study, it is informative to explore some of the evidence. Proponents of the hypothesis often point to empirical findings in Ungerer et al. (1986). Their study estimates inflation equations across a large sample of industrial countries from 1974 to 1984, and finds that the coefficient on an EMS 'dummy' variable is consistently negative and significant. However, in addition to some econometric problems, there are alternative explanations for their findings. In particular, many non-EMS countries also underwent deflations after 1979.

This study is composed of three further sections. Section 2 as we have stated develops a theoretical model, and identifies a number of ways to specify the EMS exchange regime. It then examines the inflationary implications of various regimes. Section 3 reviews and extends the empirical evidence. Section 4 provides a summary and discussion of the EMS-inflation hypothesis in light of the theoretical and empirical findings.

2   A theoretical framework

This section theoretically examines the implications of different exchange regimes for the mean and the variance of intra-EMS inflation. To highlight the view that the announcement of a change in government policy is not enough to change perceptions about the future, I choose a version of the two-country Mundell–Flemming model in which expectations are backward-looking. Oudiz (1985) uses a similar framework to simulate the welfare gains under alternative regimes for EMS countries.

It is important to note that the framework considers deflation from an initial inflationary position – a realistic depiction of the post-1979 oil shock situation. It does not analyse inflation arising from a game played by labour unions and policymakers, which is the approach taken by Giavazzi and Giovannini (1986b) and Canzoneri and Henderson (1987) among others.

a.   A simple model

There are two countries, called France and Germany (denoted by *). They produce aggregate outputs, y and y^*, at prices p and p^*. The nominal exchange rate, e, is the price of Deutsche marks in terms of francs. All variables (with the exception of interest rates) are measured in logs and output is measured as deviations from full employment. The subscript t will denote time.

Output is demand-determined, as described by equations (5.1a) and (5.1b). Demand increases as a result of a real depreciation, a rise in foreign output or a decline in real interest rates:

$$y_t = a \cdot s_t + b \cdot y_t^* - cr_t \tag{5.1a}$$

$$y_t^* = - a \cdot s_t + b \cdot y_t - cr_t^* \tag{5.1b}$$

where $s_t \equiv e_t + p_t^* - p_t$ is the real exchange rate, $r_t \equiv i_t - p_{t+1}^e + p_t$ and $r_t^* \equiv i_t^* - p_{t+1}^{*e} + p_t^*$ are real interest rates. The superscript e denotes the expectation at time t.

Capital is assumed to be freely mobile[5] (equation 5.2). Equation (5.3) describes real exchange-rate expectations as static, but allows for shift, u. This specification captures the idea that different regimes need not alter market beliefs about the future, but allows for changes in perceptions independent of the regime. The assumption also simplifies the analysis because it implies that the problem for policymakers is time-separable. Equations (5.2) and (5.3) imply that real interest rates differ only by u.

$$i_t - i_t^* \equiv e_{t+1}^e - e_t \tag{5.2}$$

$$e_{t+1}^e + p_{t+1}^{*e} - p_{t+1}^e = e_t + p_t^* - p_t + u \tag{5.3}$$

$$r_t = r_t^* + u \tag{5.4}$$

For most of the discussion, u will be assumed equal to zero. The consequences of a non-zero u are examined at the end of the section.

The evolution of domestic prices is given by equations (5.5a) and (5.5b). This depends on lagged (CPI) inflation and deviations from full employment output.[6] Consumer prices, ϱ and ϱ^*, are a weighted average of prices in each country (equations 5.6a and 5.6b) and inflation is $\pi_t \equiv \varrho_t - \varrho_{t-1}$:

$$p_t - p_{t-1} = \pi_{t-1} + \gamma y_t \tag{5.5a}$$

$$p_t^* - p_{t-1}^* = \pi_{t-1}^* + \gamma y_t^* \tag{5.5b}$$

$$\varrho_t = \lambda p_t + (1 - \lambda)(e_t + p_t^*) = p_t + (1 - \lambda)s_t \tag{5.6a}$$

$$\varrho_t^* = \lambda p_t^* + (1 - \lambda)(p_t - e_t) = p_t^* - (1 - \lambda)s_t \tag{5.6b}$$

Equations (5.7a) and (5.7b) relate real balances to income in each country:

$$m_t - p_t = y_t \tag{5.7a}$$

$$m_t^* - p_t^* = y_t^* \tag{5.7b}$$

Substituting from (5.5) into (5.7), it is clear that authorities in each country can directly control their own output level through monetary policy. To simplify the notation, output is taken as the instrument of the monetary authorities.

Finally, French and German authorities wish to minimise a loss function that is *quadratic* in inflation and output.[7] As already mentioned, it is not necessary to consider the entire intertemporal problem, because utility is separable over time periods. The remainder of the section will drop the time subscripts, except where it is confusing to do so:

$$L = (y^2 + \phi\pi^2)/2 \tag{5.8a}$$

$$L^* = (y^{*2} + \phi\pi^{*2})/2 \tag{5.8b}$$

To solve the model, each country's inflation must be solved for in terms of outputs. This is easily done in two steps. First, equations (5.1) and (5.4) give the following expressions for real exchange rates and real interest rates:

$$s = \left(\frac{1+b}{2a}\right)(y - y^*) + \frac{c}{2a}u \tag{5.9}$$

$$r = -\left(\frac{1-b}{2c}\right)(y + y^*) + \tfrac{1}{2}u \tag{5.10a}$$

$$r^* = - \left(\frac{1-b}{2a}\right)(y + y^*) - \tfrac{1}{2}u \tag{5.10b}$$

As usual, the real exchange rate depends on differences in the policies of the two countries, while the real interest rates depend on combined policies.

The second step is to solve for inflation using equations (5.5), (5.6) and (5.9). Notice that changes in expectations formation (u) are equivalent to shifts in the predetermined portion of inflation (π_0). France is assumed to have a higher base inflation rate than Germany $\pi_0 > \pi_0^*$. So far, this is the first asymmetry between the two countries:

$$\pi = \pi_0 + \gamma y + \alpha(y - y^*) \tag{5.11a}$$
$$\pi^* = \pi_0^* + \gamma y^* - \alpha(y - y^*) \tag{5.11b}$$

where

$$\pi_0 \equiv \pi_{t-1} + (1 - \lambda)(s_{t-1} + cu/2a),\ \pi_0 > \pi_0^*$$
$$\pi_0^* \equiv \pi_{t-1}^* - (1 - \lambda)(s_{t-1} + cu^*/2a)$$

and $\alpha \equiv (1 - \lambda)(1 + b)/2a$

Our primary interest is in the average inflation rate and in the divergence between the two countries' inflation rates. These are simple functions of average outputs and of the divergence between outputs respectively:

$$\pi^a = \pi_0^a + \gamma y^a \tag{5.12a}$$
$$\pi^d = \pi_0^d + (\gamma + 2a) y^d \tag{5.12b}$$

where for any variable x $x^a = (x + x^*)/2$ and $x^d = (x - x^*)/2$.

We also solve for French output as a function of the nominal exchange rates, which will be useful for examining policy regimes in which the exchange rate, not the money supply, is the policy instrument. Using equations (5.1), (5.5) and (5.10), we get:

$$y = y^* + \tau(e + \kappa) \tag{5.13}$$

where $\tau \equiv 2a/(1 + b + 2a\gamma)$ and $\kappa \equiv p_{t-1}^* - p_{t-1} + \pi_{t-1}^* - \pi_{t-1} \dfrac{-cu}{2a}$.

Equation (5.13) also points out that if France uses monetary policy (sets output) so as to maintain a fixed nominal exchange rate, France must essentially follow German leadership by adjusting domestic policy one-for-one with German policy. In the fixed exchange-rate regimes, it is convenient to assume that the nominal exchange rate is set equal to κ.

b. The EMS: alternatives

The next step is to specify alternative exchange regimes. Ideally, we would like to compare the EMS to the most likely non-EMS regime. However not only is it difficult to identify the latter, there is also considerable disagreement over how to best model the EMS itself. The many views can be grouped according to whether policies are chosen cooperatively or non-cooperatively, and whether Germany and other members are treated symmetrically or asymmetrically.

Many authors assume both non-cooperative behaviour and asymmetry by depicting Germany as the 'leader'. For example, Fischer (1987, p. 41) says that 'the EMS can be viewed as an agreement by France and Italy to accept German leadership in monetary policy, imposing constraints on domestic monetary and fiscal policies.'

There are two different formulations of German leadership. The first assumes that Germany sets monetary policy while the other members subordinate their monetary (and fiscal) policies to maintain fixed exchange rates.[8] This regime has been used to model the EMS by Canzoneri and Gray (1985) and by Roubini (1987), while Oudiz (1985) uses it to model the snake. An alternative assumption, adopted by Giavazzi and Giovannini (1986b), is that Germany sets its monetary policy while the other members set their exchange rates relative to the Deutsche mark. One obvious problem with the first approach is that it rules out the possibility of exchange-rate adjustments through realignment. On the other hand, the second probably goes too far in allowing exchange-rate adjustment each 'period'. (The appropriateness of the alternative approaches is discussed further below.)

Canzoneri and Henderson (1987) discuss both cases. They point out that it makes a difference which approach is taken. The first is a game in which both countries select quantities (of money), while the second is a game in which one player (Germany) selects a quantity while the other selects a price (the exchange rate). It is a well-known result from game theory that, in most cases, the outcome of a game depends on whether the instruments are prices or quantities.

Melitz (1985) takes the opposite tack. He assumes that EMS policymaking is cooperative and treats the members symmetrically. Roubini (1987) and Oudiz (1985) both consider cooperation as one of many alternative views of the EMS.

Finally, countries may act symmetrically, but non-cooperatively. If

Regime	Average (y^a)	Divergence (y^d)
Non-cooperative		
Cournot–Nash	$-\dfrac{\phi(\gamma+\alpha)}{1+\phi\gamma(\gamma+\alpha)}\pi_0^a$	$\dfrac{\phi\alpha(\gamma+\alpha)}{1+\phi(\gamma+\alpha)(\gamma+2\alpha)}\pi_0^d$
German leader	$-\dfrac{\phi\gamma}{1+\phi\gamma^2}\pi_0^*$	0
Money exchange	$-\dfrac{1}{\sigma}\left\{\phi\gamma[1+\phi(\gamma+\alpha)(\gamma+2\alpha)]\pi_0^a\right\}$	$-\dfrac{\phi}{\sigma}\left\{\gamma(1+\phi\gamma(\gamma+\alpha)]\pi_0^d-\dfrac{\alpha}{2}\pi_0^*\right\}$
Cooperative		
Fixed rates	$-\dfrac{\phi\gamma}{1+\phi\gamma^2}\pi_0^a$	0
Realignment	$-\dfrac{\phi\gamma}{1+\phi\gamma^2}\pi_0^a$	$-\dfrac{\phi(\gamma+2\alpha)}{1+\phi(\gamma+2\alpha)^2}\pi_0^d$

where $\sigma \equiv 1 + \phi(\gamma+\alpha)[\alpha + 2\gamma + \phi\gamma^2(\gamma+2\alpha)]$

Table 5.1 Policy Under Alternative Regimes

both policymakers use monetary policy as an instrument, and set their own policy under the assumption that the other country's instrument is given, this scenario is the familiar Cournot–Nash game which is often used as a benchmark against which to compare the EMS.

A total of five alternatives will thus be considered. Three are non-cooperative and assume that each policymaker sets its own instrument to minimise domestic loss, taking the other country's policy as given. In the remaining two, policies are set cooperatively based on an equally-weighted function of losses in the two countries. In each case, policymakers are assumed to expect that real exchange-rate expectations are static ($u = 0$).

To facilitate the comparisons, outcomes under each regime are depicted graphically. From equation (5.12), it is clear that, given π_0 and π_0^*, y^a and y^d determine average inflation and the inflation differential. The expressions for y^a, y^d, π^a and π^d in each of the five regimes are given in Tables 5.1 and 5.2. These variables are the focus of the regime comparisons.

Regime	Average (π^a)	Divergence (π^d)
Non-cooperative		
Cournot–Nash	$\dfrac{\pi_0^a}{1 + \phi\gamma(\gamma + \alpha)}$	$\dfrac{\pi_0^d}{1 + \phi(\gamma + \alpha)(\gamma + 2\alpha)}$
German leader	$\pi_0^a - \left(\dfrac{\phi\gamma^2}{1 + \phi\gamma^2}\right)\pi_0^*$	π_0^d
Money exchange		
$\dfrac{1}{\sigma}\left\{[1 + \phi(\gamma^2 + \alpha^2 + 3\gamma\alpha)]\pi_0^a - \dfrac{\alpha\gamma}{2}\pi_0^*\right\}$		$\dfrac{1}{\sigma}\left\{[1 + \phi\alpha(\gamma + 2\alpha)]\pi_0^d + \dfrac{\alpha\phi}{2}\pi_0^*\right\}$
Cooperative		
Fixed rates	$\dfrac{\pi_0^a}{1 + \phi\gamma^2}$	π_0^d
Realignment	$\dfrac{\phi\gamma}{1 + \phi\gamma^2}\pi_0^a$	$\dfrac{\pi_0^d}{1 + \phi(\gamma + 2\alpha)^2}$

where $\sigma \equiv 1 + \phi(\gamma + \alpha)[\alpha + 2\gamma + \phi\gamma^2(\gamma + 2\alpha)]$

Table 5.2 Inflation Under Alternative Regimes

(*i*) *Cournot–Nash (C)* Policymakers in each country choose output to minimise losses, as shown in equation (5.14):

$$\underset{y}{\text{Min}}\ (y^2 + \phi\pi^2)/2 \qquad (5.14a)$$
$$\pi = \pi_0 + \gamma y + \alpha(y - y^*)$$

$$\underset{y^*}{\text{Min}}\ (y^{*2} + \phi\pi^{*2})/2 \qquad (5.14b)$$
$$\pi^* = \pi_0^* + \gamma y^* - \alpha(y - y^*)$$

The first-order conditions imply the following reaction functions:

$$y = -_N(\alpha y^* - \pi_0) \qquad (5.15a)$$
$$\Delta_N \equiv \phi(\gamma + \alpha)/[1 + \phi(\gamma + \alpha)^2]$$
$$y^* = \Delta_N(\alpha y - \pi_0^*) \qquad (5.15b)$$

The equilibrium is shown in Figure 5.1, at point C. The French and German reaction functions are labelled NN and N^*N^* respectively. The bliss points are denoted by B and B^*. The result is a familiar one. The countries engage in a competitive deflation. France (the country which

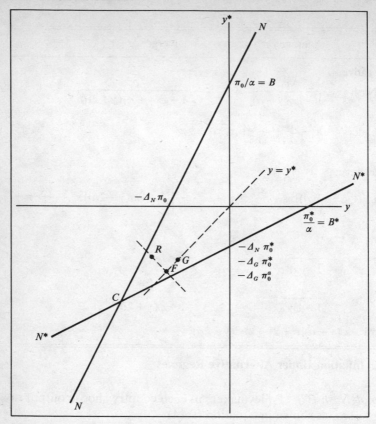

Figure 5.1 Policy under alternative regimes

inherited a higher inflation rate) pursues the more restrictive policy: $y < y^*$ and $y^d < 0$ (Table 5.1). The French real exchange rate appreciates (see equation 5.9), and (as shown in Table 5.2) there is some convergence in inflation rates ($\pi^d < \pi_0^d$).

(*ii*) *German leadership (G)*   Germany sets output (monetary policy) independently while France maintains a fixed nominal exchange rate. German authorities minimise equation (5.16) while France simply follows, setting $y = y^*$:

$$\underset{y^*}{\text{Min}} \ (y^{*2} + \phi\pi^{*2})/2 \tag{5.16}$$

$$\pi^* = \pi_0^* + \gamma y^* + \alpha(y - y^*)$$

$$y \ = y^*$$

The first-order conditions imply the following solution:

$$y^* = -\Delta_G \pi_0^* = y, \qquad \Delta_G \equiv \phi\gamma/[1 + \phi\gamma^2] \qquad (5.17)$$

Graphically, Germany chooses the point along $y - y^*$ which gives highest German utility. This is denoted by point G in Figure 5.1.

Because Germany knows that France will follow its policy lead, there is no competitive deflation. Policies are less restrictive in both countries than in the Cournot–Nash equilibrium discussed above. Average inflation is higher than in the Nash outcome, and there is no move towards convergence $\pi^d = \pi_0^d$.

(iii) Cooperation with fixed exchange rates (F) France and Germany set outputs cooperatively and maintain a fixed exchange rate. A common policy is thus chosen to minimise the (equally-weighted) loss function in (5.18):

$$\text{Min}_{y,y^*} (y^2 + \phi\pi^2)/2 + (y^{*2} + \phi\pi^{*2})/2 \qquad (5.18)$$
$$\pi = \pi_0 + \gamma y + \alpha(y - y^*)$$
$$\pi^* = \pi_0^* + \gamma y^* + \alpha(y - y^*)$$
$$y = y^*$$

The first-order conditions imply:

$$y = -\Delta_g \pi_0^* = y^* \qquad (5.19)$$

The outcome (denoted by F in Figure 5.1) is more deflationary than the non-cooperative German leadership with fixed exchange rates because it takes into account France's higher base inflation (Table 5.2). German welfare is lower than it was at G, but French welfare is higher.

(iv) Cooperation with realignment (R) France and Germany set outputs and the nominal exchange rate cooperatively:[9]

$$\text{Min}_{y,y^*} (y^2 + \phi\pi^2)/2 + (y^{*2} + \phi\pi^{*2})/2 \qquad (5.20)$$
$$\pi = \pi_0 + \gamma y + \alpha(y - y^*)$$
$$\pi^* = \pi_0^* + \gamma y^* + \alpha(y - y^*)$$

Noticing that $(y^2 + y^{*2})/2 = y^{a2} + y^{d2}$ and that $(\pi^2 + \pi^{*2})/2 = \pi^{a2} + \pi^{d2}$, equation (5.20) is equivalent to equation (5.21). The problem can be separated into selecting average outputs and the divergence between outputs:

$$\text{Min}_{y^a,y^d} (y^{a2} + \phi\pi^{a2})/2 + (y^{d2} + \phi\pi^{d2})/2 \qquad (5.21)$$

$$\pi^a = \pi_0^a + \gamma y^a$$

$$\pi^d = \pi_0^d + (\gamma + 2a) y^d$$

In the solution (Tables 5.1 and 5.2), average inflation is the same in the two cooperative regimes. The only difference is that when realignment is allowed, the high-inflation country (France) will follow more deflationary policy, and will experience a real appreciation. Table 5.1 also shows that output divergence, y^d, is larger under the cooperative regime with realignment than it was in the non-cooperative Nash. Therefore, there is greater convergence of inflation rates.

Graphically, the outcome is denoted by R in Figure 5.1. It is along the constant average inflation line that passes through G. The larger output divergence relative to Cournot–Nash implies that the ray from R to the origin is flatter than the ray from C to the origin, as drawn.

(v) Money exchange-rate (M)   The final regime is the most complex. Germany sets output (monetary policy) taking the nominal exchange rate as given while France controls the exchange rate, taking German output as given:

$$\underset{e}{\text{Min}} \ (y^2 + \phi\pi^2)/2 \tag{5.22a}$$

$$\pi = \pi_0 + \gamma y + \alpha(y - y^*)$$

$$y = \tau(e + \kappa) + y^*$$

$$\underset{y^*}{\text{Min}} \ (y^{*2} + \phi\pi^{*2})/2 \tag{5.22b}$$

$$\pi^* = \pi_0^* + \gamma y^* + \alpha(y - y^*)$$

$$y = \tau(e + \kappa) + y^*$$

To simplify notation, we take $x \equiv \tau (e + \kappa)$ as the French policy instrument. As shown in equation (5.23a), the first-order condition for France parallels the one from the Nash game. Even though the policy instrument has changed, France would like the same change in domestic output in response to changes in foreign output as in the Nash game:

$$y = x + y^* = \Delta_N(\alpha y^* - \pi_0) \tag{5.23a}$$

$$x = -\Delta_N \pi_0 + (\gamma\Delta_N - 1)y^* \tag{5.23a$'$}$$

Equation (5.23a$'$) gives the French reaction function. An appreciation partially offsets the German expansion so that France responds to a German expansion with a smaller domestic expansion.

Solving the German first-order conditions, we get Germany's reaction function in equation (5.24). Notice that, given the nominal exchange rate, Germany expects French output to move one-for-one with its own. Not surprisingly, the German reaction here parallels the German leadership game.

$$y^* = - \Delta_G(\pi_0^* - \alpha x) \tag{5.24}$$

To facilitate comparison of the outcome under this regime with the outcomes under the other four regimes, we focus on the equilibrium values of y and y^*. As before, the averages and divergences of output and inflation are given in Tables 5.1 and 5.2.

It is also useful to depict the outcomes graphically. Figure 5.2 shows the equilibria for the four regimes discussed above together with the equilibrium from the money-exchange regime. Equation (5.23a) shows the value of y that will result from the French selection of x given each y^*. As noted above, this relationship is simply NN.

Equation (5.24) shows the y^* Germany will select given x. The relationship between y^* and the implied value of y is given by equation (5.25). The trade-off for Germany is flatter than it was in the Cournot–Nash game.[10] Taking x as given, Germany now expects y to move one-for-one with y^*. Therefore, y^* is less responsive to different values of y than if German policymakers took y as given:

$$y^* = \Delta_M(\alpha y - \pi_0^*), \qquad \Delta_M \equiv \phi\gamma/[1 + \phi\gamma(\gamma + \alpha)] < \Delta_N \tag{5.25}$$

Equation (5.25) is shown as M^*M^* in Figure 5.2. It crosses N^*N^* at $y^* = 0$. It also passes through the point GL. The equilibrium for the money-exchange regime is denoted by M.

Although less deflationary than the Nash, this regime is more deflationary than any of the other formulations of the EMS. This can be shown by noting from Table 5.2 that average output under the M, C, F and R regimes can be rewritten as:

$$M: \qquad y_a = - \omega_1 \pi_0 - \omega_2 \pi_0^*$$
$$C: \qquad y_a = - \omega_N \pi_0^a$$
$$F \text{ and } R: y_a = - \omega_G \pi_0^a \tag{5.26}$$

where ω_i, $i = 1, 2, N, G$ are defined in Table 5.1 and $\pi_0 > \pi_0^*$.

It is straightforward to show that

$$\omega_G < \omega_1 < \omega_2 < \omega_N,$$

so that C is the most deflationary, followed by M and then by the two cooperative regimes. The intuition is that France engages in the same competitive deflation here as in the Nash game. But because Germany

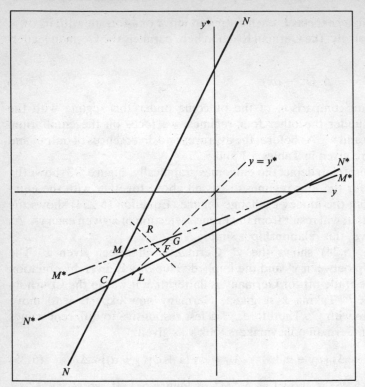

Figure 5.2 The money-exchange regime

expects y and y^* to move together, policymakers engage in less competitive deflation.

Figure 5.2 also shows clearly that the two types of 'German leadership'
are very different. If leadership means that high-inflation EMS members
must use their policies to peg the exchange rate (G), the outcome is less
deflationary than a cooperative policy would be. The opposite is true if
German leadership means that Germany sets monetary policy independently, and the other members select the exchange rate (M).

A final issue is the extent of policy divergence. While it is clear that
there is more output divergence (and therefore inflation convergence) in
the M than in the C regime, the comparison between the M and R
regimes is ambiguous. Manipulating the expressions for π^d in Table 5.2,
it is possible to show that policies diverge more in the R than in the
M regime as long as α is not too small relative to γ.[11] The smaller α, the
less sensitive domestic inflation rates are to foreign output, and the
smaller the scope for EMS members to manage policy differentials
cooperatively so as to foster inflation convergence.

c.   Inflation under alternate regimes

Using Figures 5.1 and 5.2, and Tables 5.1 and 5.2, it is straightforward to compare the average and the divergence of inflation rates across regimes. The results are summarised below:

> *Average inflation* (π^a):
>
> Cournot–<Money- < German < Cooperation
> Nash   exchange leader   (both)
>
> *Inflation divergence* (π^d):
>
> Cooperation < Cournot– < Fixed rates
> (realignment) Nash   (German leader
>   and cooperation)

As discussed above, the ranking of the money-exchange regimes in terms of inflation divergence is ambiguous. There is clearly less divergence than in a Nash game, but there may be either more or less than in the cooperative regime with realignment.

At the beginning of the EMS, all members had relatively high inflation as a result of the 1979 oil price increases. Inflation rates would have fallen under any of the five regimes; however, they would have fallen less under any of the four approaches to modelling the EMS than under a Cournot–Nash game. Of course this very deflationary regime also produces the lowest welfare. Rapid deflation is not an achievement to be proud of here.

The second point is that inflationary behaviour in the EMS depends on how the system is formulated. The analysis above shows that the EMS will be deflationary if exchange rates are fixed, especially when Germany acts as the leader. The EMS is most deflationary if the high-inflation countries use exchange rates as instruments while the low-inflation ones set monetary policy.

Third, reductions in average inflation need not coincide with convergence of inflation rates. The most convergence is likely to occur when members cooperatively set both the exchange rate and monetary policies. In general, there is no convergence when the exchange rate is fixed between member countries.

Which of these regimes most accurately describes the EMS? A complete answer is beyond the scope of this study. Instead, I make two observations. First, some evidence does suggest an asymmetric role for Germany. Giavazzi and Giovannini (1987) and Roubini (1987) argue that Germany has continued to sterilise the impact of foreign-exchange interventions on the domestic money supply. As they point out, asymmetric sterilisation can turn a system with symmetric rules for intervention into an asymmetric system.

The second is that none of these regimes is likely to do a good job over the entire 1979–87 period because none of these approaches accurately captures the exchange-rate management issue. Exchange rates have remained fixed over long periods of time. Adjustments have come at irregular intervals, and have been of various magnitudes. With only a few adjustments, it is difficult to tell whether or not the timing and magnitude has been a cooperative decision.[12]

One possibility is that Germany acts as the leader between realignments by setting monetary policy. The extent to which other EMS members must follow depends on the width of their exchange-rate band and the importance of capital controls. However, this scenario is still consistent with cooperation – or bargaining – when the exchange-rate bands are adjusted.

d.   Changes in expectations

One of the most frequently cited reasons for why the EMS should help to bring down inflation is that it might alter expectations. Our analysis so far has ruled out this channel. In fact, there is little evidence of shifts when the EMS was first instituted. For example, Sachs and Wyplosz (1986) argue that expectations did not change until 1982–3.

We now suppose that after a series of restrictive measures, for in the high-inflation country there is a decline in the inertial part of inflation (π_0 falls). In the current formulation, the shift comes about through an expected real appreciation (a fall in u). Alternatively, the shift could be introduced through the domestic pricing equation (5.5).

The impact on the average and the divergence of inflation rates can be found by differentiating the expressions in Table 5.2 with respect to π_0. Since our primary interest is in the relative sizes of the effects, the ranking is shown below:

Impact of a change in π_0 on π^a:

Cournot– <Money- < Cooperative < German
Nash   exchange   (both)   leader

Impact of a change in π_0 on π^d:

Cooperative? < Money < Cournot– < Cooperative German
(realign)   exchange Nash   (fixed)   leader

Although the Cournot–Nash regime was the most deflationary, a fall in the inertial French inflation has the smallest effect on average inflation of EMS members because both will engage in less competitive deflation. In fact, the largest payoffs, in terms of lower average inflation, come in the German leadership regime. Since policy depends only on inertial inflation in Germany, there is no offsetting change in equilibrium policies.

Similarly, the fall in π_0 has the largest effect on inflation differentials under the two fixed exchange-rate regimes. As discussed above, the ranking of the Cooperative-realignment and the Money-exchange regimes is ambiguous. In both of these regimes, a reduction in the initial inflation differential will result in an offsetting reduction in the extent to which policies contribute towards inflation convergence.

This discussion provides one explanation for the original doubts about, but recent popularity of, the EMS-inflation hypothesis. During the first few years of the EMS, there was little empirical evidence supporting the view that joining had fostered convergence. It was not until perceptions of government policies changed some years later that observers noted the rapid deflation and attributed it to the EMS.

3   Empirical evidence

This section assesses some empirical evidence for the inflation convergence hypothesis. The results are not conclusive; they should be viewed as a first step to a detailed analysis of the data, which is beyond the scope of this study. It is useful to begin with an overview of the inflation experiences for EMS and non-EMS countries. I consider seven EMS countries and fifteen non-EMS countries from 1974 to 1986.[13]

a.   Overview of the inflation experience

Table 5.3 shows the mean and standard deviation inflation rates for the two country groups over different time periods. As shown, the group of non-EMS countries had larger average and more variable inflation rates than the EMS countries both before (1974–8) and after (1979–86) the EMS was instituted. Table 5.3 also shows that, while the average inflation rates declined in both country groups between 1974–8 and 1979–86, the decline was larger with the EMS (22 per cent) than outside the EMS (14 per cent). Furthermore, the standard deviation of inflation rates increased only marginally within the EMS but increased substantially outside of the system. These facts provide some support for the EMS-inflation hypothesis.

	1974–8	1979–86	1979–82	1983–6
EMS				
average	10.52	8.18	10.93	5.43
std. dev.	5.11	5.22	5.25	3.51
Non-EMS				
average	14.20	12.26	14.31	10.21
std. dev.	9.19	12.10	11.32	12.59

Table 5.3 Inflation Rates

However, Table 5.3 shows no evidence of any average reduction or convergence of inflation among EMS members during the first three years (1979–82). These indicators rose for both country groups in the years following the second oil shock.

It is also important to point out that the comparisons are sensitive to which countries are included in the non-EMS group. The broad sample included in Table 5.3 provides the 'best case' for the hypothesis. EMS members would more closely resemble a comparator group which excluded Portugal, Spain, and especially Iceland. (Inflation in Iceland ranged from 22 per cent to 86 per cent during 1974–86.)

b.   *Results from panel data*

A second approach is econometrically to examine the differences between the two-country groups using pooled cross-section, time-series data. This is the approach followed by Ungerer *et al.* (1986). They conclude that the EMS did help to reduce inflation because they find a significant and negative coefficient on an EMS dummy variable. This section explores their conclusions.

For each country, real money demand is assumed to be an increasing function of real income, and a decreasing function of expected inflation. As shown in equation (5.27), a simple log linear structure is assumed:

$$\log(M) - \log(P) = \beta_0 + \beta_1 \log(Y) - \beta_2 \pi^e \tag{5.27}$$

Expressing the relationship in terms of growth rates and solving for inflation gives equation (5.28):

$$\pi = \hat{m} - \beta_1 \hat{y} + \beta_2(\pi^e - \pi^e_{t-1}) \tag{5.28}$$

A variety of options are available at this point. Following Ungerer *et al.*, we assume that the slope coefficients are identical across countries and

	Dependent variable: inflation (π_t)				
	1	2	3[1]	4	5[1]
Constant	0.055 (0.006)[2]	0.064 (0.008)	0.085 (0.007)	0.064 (0.009)	0.081 (0.007)
$\hat{M}$	0.514 (0.033)	0.238 (0.033)	0.484 (0.040)	0.202 (0.036)	(0.040)
$\hat{Y}$	−0.074 (0.082)	−0.083 (0.082)	−0.030 (0.065)	−0.076 (0.091)	0.011 (0.067)
$(\pi_t - \pi_{t-1})$	0.691 (0.079)	0.684 (0.078)	0.651 (0.087)		
$(\pi_{t-1} - \pi_{t-2})$				0.407 (0.086)	0.606 (0.088)
Pre-EMS (1974–8)		−0.022 (0.011)	−0.010 (0.008)	−0.022 (0.012)	−0.008 (0.008)
EMS (1979–85)	−0.009 (0.008)	−0.007 (0.009)	−0.001 (0.007)	−0.008 (0.010)	−0.002 (0.007)
1979–85		−0.011 (0.008)	−0.016 (0.006)	−0.008 (0.009)	−0.008 (0.006)
R-Bar^2	0.552	0.556	0.280	0.447	0.278
Std. error	0.483	0.480	0.420	0.527	0.361
# Obs.	252	252	240	252	240

Table 5.4 OLS Results

Notes:
[1] Excluding Iceland.
[2] Standing errors in parentheses.

estimate equations using the pooled data set. They substitute the actual change in inflation for the difference in expected inflation rates, and include a dummy variable (EMS) which is one for EMS members after 1979 and zero otherwise. We begin with this approach, and then include additional dummy variables, and consider an alternative proxy for expected inflation.

The first column from Table 5.4 reports the results following the approach in Ungerer *et al.*[14] As shown, the EMS shift term is negative, although not significant. The magnitude implies that, other things equal, inflation in EMS members was 0.9 per cent smaller during the EMS period than either before 1979 or for non-EMS members.

However, there are many possible explanations for this finding. In particular, all countries may have experienced shifts in the behaviour of inflation after 1979. Alternatively, the EMS countries could have had lower average inflation before the EMS was instituted.

The second column of Table 5.4 presents the results of a regression which includes two additional shift parameters. One allows the EMS period (post-1979) to differ from the pre-EMS period for all countries in the sample. The other allows a separate constant term for the EMS member countries in the pre-EMS period.

As shown in column 2 of Table 5.4, the additional variables have little effect on the estimated relationships between money and income growth and inflation. But the original EMS shift parameter decreases in magnitude and in significance. The post-1979 dummy and the earlier EMS dummy both have larger negative coefficients. The latter is significantly different from zero. These results provide no support for the EMS-inflation hypothesis.

In fact, if Iceland is excluded from the country list, the point comes through even more strongly. These estimates are reported in column 3 of Table 5.4. First, the fit of this simple regression equation deteriorates significantly. Most of the deterioration can be attributed to the decreased importance of money growth. Second, the post-1979 dummy variable is now strongly significant, while both EMS dummies decline in magnitude and in significance. Whatever shift occurred after 1979 occurred among both EMS and non-EMS countries.

Table 5.4 does not support the inflation convergence hypothesis. But neither does it refute the hypothesis, because the equations are seriously misspecified. Perhaps the most important problem is the usage of the actual inflation differential as a proxy for expected inflation.[15] Since this variable includes the current inflation rate, it is clearly endogenous. The fourth and fifth columns of Table 5.4 address this problem by using lagged inflational differentials as a proxy for expectations. Columns 4 and 5 of Table 5.4 report regressions which respectively include and exclude Iceland. In both cases, the explanatory power of the estimated equation declines, and the post-1979 dummy becomes less significant.

There is thus evidence of a shift in inflation behaviour after 1979 among industrialised countries as a whole. There is little or no evidence of any special shifts among EMS members. However, these results should be viewed as suggestive only. They are very sensitive to which countries are included in the sample. (They are also sensitive to the period of estimation.) Furthermore, the equations explain only a fraction of the inflationary behaviour of these countries. A conclusive analysis will require more carefully specified structures which allow for differences among countries. This is an interesting area for future research.

4 Concluding remarks

Between 1979 and 1986 there was an impressive reduction and convergence of inflation rates among EMS members. However coincidence alone is not enough to determine causality. The fact that little convergence occurred during the first half of the system's existence makes the claims especially suspect.

This study has argued that changing the policy regime can affect the inflationary outcome in at least two ways. First, it can change market perceptions and increase credibility in a disinflationary programme. Second, it alters the rules of the game – the instruments available to policymakers and the trade-offs they perceive from changing instruments. In the real world, these two need not occur simultaneously. Evidence suggests that they did not, at least for France. While joining the EMS may have altered the rules of the game, it had little initial impact on expectations or on the credibility of the high-inflation governments. Changes in credibility, price-setting behaviour and expectations came a few years later.

The study has developed a theoretical model in which changes in the rules of the game could be distinguished from changes in expectation formation. There are three basic points. First, if expectations are backward-looking, an EMS is likely to be less deflationary than a non-cooperative Cournot–Nash alternative. However, more deflation is not necessarily a good thing. In fact, welfare is higher under less deflationary EMS regimes than under the most deflationary non-cooperative regime.

Second, it makes a difference how the EMS works. If Germany leads with the other members maintaining fixed exchange rates, then a move to more cooperation would tend to be deflationary. However, if German leadership implies that the followers select the exchange rate, a more cooperative regime would be more expansionary.

Third, if a change in expectations comes about – perhaps because of persistent and consistent policymakers – average inflation rates will fall more under EMS regimes than under the Cournot–Nash alternative. Again, the particular outcome depends critically on how the EMS functions. This result may help to explain why many observers are now convinced that the EMS itself helped to reduce inflation, even though there were few believers until recently.

Finally, simple cross-section time-series analysis does not show evidence of any shift in EMS inflation behaviour after 1979. Instead, there is some evidence that all countries underwent a shift after 1979 and that inflation rates were lower and less divergent within EMS countries even before they joined the system.

NOTES

* I would like to thank Dale Henderson for pointing out an error in an earlier draft of this study. Participants in the Banca d'Italia, STEP and CEPR Conference on the EMS and the NBER Conference on the EMS also provided helpful comments and suggestions. Ana Revenga provided able research assistance. Generous financial support from the John M. Olin Foundation is gratefully acknowledged.

1 An alternative would have been to assume that realignments not only compensated for cumulative inflation differentials since the last realignment, but also adjusted for expected future inflation differentials so that the PPP was maintained on average over the duration of each fixed exchange rate. See Giavazzi and Pagano (1985) and Collins (1987b).

2 McCallum (1984) discusses and evaluates the links between credibility and disinflation, focusing on the United States.

3 Giavazzi and Pagano (1985) provide one discussion of capital controls.

4 Useful references to the policy coordination literature include Buiter and Marston (1985), Canzoneri and Henderson (1987) and Fischer (1987).

5 Roubini (1987) simulates the effects of capital controls in an EMS without realignment.

6 Equation (5.5) can be derived under the assumptions that the price of domestic output is a mark-up over wages ($w_t - p_t$) and that wage inflation depends on lagged CPI inflation and current output

$$(w_{t+1} = w_t + \pi_t + \gamma y_{t+1}).$$

The same specification is assumed in Germany.

7 Oudiz (1985) estimates a higher weight on inflation in Germany's objective function than for any of the other EMS countries. Incorporating this asymmetry would provide an additional channel for inflationary bias in France.

8 For simplicity, I model the EMS as establishing fixed rates among members between realignments. This is potentially problematic for Italy, which maintains bands of ± 6.0 per cent.

9 Roubini (1987) points out that whether or not countries sterilise intervention in foreign-exchange markets determines whether a cooperative system in name operates symmetrically in practice.

10 Canzoneri and Henderson (1987) provide additional discussion of the choice of policy instrument and reaction functions in the EMS.

11 The algebraic condition is quite complex. A sufficient (but not necessary) condition for greater inflation convergence with cooperative realignment than with the money-exchange regime is that $\alpha > \gamma/2$.

12 Some recent studies apply models with fixed costs to exchange-rate adjustment to examine the timing and magnitude of exchange-rate adjustments in the EMS. Giavazzi and Pagano (1985) assume that France is a small country which can select the exchange rate. Collins (1987b) assumes that France and Germany act cooperatively.

13 The EMS countries are Belgium, Denmark, France, Germany, Ireland, Italy and the Netherlands. The non-EMS countries are Australia, Austria, Canada, Finland, Greece, Iceland, Japan, New Zealand, Norway, Portugal, Spain, Sweden, Switzerland, the United Kingdom and the United States.

14 The results in Table 5.4 differ from those reported in Ungerer *et al.* because of

differences in the time period and in the group of non-EMS countries. Ungerer *et al.* reports statistically significant EMS shift parameters. The study also presents estimates using alternative measures of inflation and money growth.

15 Another problem is that the money supplies will be endogenous for countries with fixed exchange rates and that coefficients are likely to differ across countries. There are also difficulties of interpretation if the money demand functions are unstable.

REFERENCES

Buiter, W. H. and R. C. Marston (1985). *International Economic Policy Coordination*, New York, Cambridge University Press.

Canzoneri, M. and J. Gray (1985). 'Monetary Policy Games and the Consequences of Non-Cooperative Behavior', *International Economic Review*, Vol. 26, pp. 547–64.

Canzoneri, M. and D. Henderson (1987). 'Is Sovereign Policymaking Bad?' (August) (Harvard University). Carnegie–Rochester Conference Series on Public Policy (forthcoming).

Collins, S. M. (1986). 'The Expected Timing of Devaluation: A Model of Realignment in the European Monetary System' (Harvard University).

(1987a). 'PPP and the Peso Problem', paper presented at the Conference on the IMS, EMS, ECU and Plans for World Monetary Reform, European University Institute, Florence, Italy (2–3 April).

(1987b). 'Realignments and Misalignments: Exchange Rate Management in the European Monetary System' (Harvard University).

Fischer, S. (1987). 'International Macroeconomic Policy Coordination', NBER Working Paper, No. 2244 (May).

Giavazzi, F. and A. Giovannini (1986a). 'The EMS and the Dollar', *Economic Policy*, Vol. 2 (April), pp. 456–85.

(1986b). 'Monetary Policy Interactions Under Managed Exchange Rates', CEPR Discussion Paper, No. 123; (1988) *Economica* (forthcoming).

(1987). 'Models of the EMS: Is Europe a Greater Deutschmark Area?', in Ralph Bryant and Richard Portes (eds), *Global Macroeconomics: Policy Conflict and Cooperation*, London, Macmillan, pp. 237–76.

Giavazzi, F. and M. Pagano (1985). 'Capital Controls and the European Monetary System', in F. Giavazzi (ed.), *Capital Controls and Foreign Exchange Legislation*, Euromobiliare Occasional Papers, No. 1 (June).

(1987). 'The Advantage of Tying One's Hands: EMS Discipline and Central Bank Credibility, CEPR Discussion Paper, No. 135; (1988) *European Economic Review* (June).

Marston, R. C. (1985). 'Exchange-Rate Unions as an Alternative to Flexible Rates: The Effects of Real and Monetary Disturbances', in J. F. O. Bilson and R. C. Marston (eds), *Exchange Rate Theory and Practice*, Chicago, Chicago University Press.

McCallum, B. T. (1984). 'Credibility and Monetary Policy', NBER Working Paper, No. 1490.

Melitz, J. (1985). 'The Welfare Case for the European Monetary System', *Journal of International Money and Finance*, Vol. 14 (December), pp. 485–506.

Oudiz, G. (1985). 'European Policy Coordination: An Evaluation', *Recherches Economiques de Louvain*, Vol. 51 (December), pp. 301–39.

Padoa-Schioppa, T. (1985). 'Policy Coordination and the EMS Experience', in W. Buiter and R. Marston (eds), *International Policy Coordination*, New York, Cambridge University Press.

Rogoff, K. (1985a). 'Can Exchange Rate Predictability be Achieved Without Monetary Convergence? Evidence from the EMS', *European Economic Review*, Vol. 28, No. 1–2 (June–July), pp. 93–115.

   (1985b). 'The Optimal Degree of Commitment to an Intermediate Monetary Target', *Quarterly Journal of Economics*, Vol. 100, pp. 1169–89.

Roubini, N. (1987). 'Leadership and Policy Coordination in the EMS', Harvard University (August) (Harvard University).

Sachs, J. and C. Wyplosz (1986). 'The Economic Consequences of President Mitterrand', *Economic Policy*, Vol. 2 (April), pp. 261–313.

Ungerer, H., O. Evans and P. Nyberg (1983). 'The European Monetary System: The Experience, 1979–82', IMF Occasional Papers, No. 19 (May).

Ungerer, H., O. Evans, T. Mayer and P. Young (1986). 'The European Monetary System: Recent Developments', IMF Occasional Papers, No. 48 (December).

Discussion

JEAN-JACQUES REY

Has the European Monetary System (EMS) been helpful in bringing down inflation in those countries which participate in its exchange-rate mechanism (ERM)? Professor Collins should be praised for throwing light on the issues involved in answering this controversial question. Even if the case remains empirically unsettled, the reasons why it is so are clearly spelled out.

One problem is fairly familiar: it consists in disentangling the role of the EMS from the role of other factors – such as external shocks – in setting in motion a powerful disinflationary process during the period under review. However, Professor Collins identifies two further issues and provides ways to tackle them. First, it is important to explain the transmission process through which joining the EMS may conceivably help in reducing the rate of inflation. Two channels are suggested and separately explored: the alternation of the rules of the game, and a change in expectations. Second, Professor Collins rightly observes that the working of the EMS is itself highly ambiguous, and needs to be specified if one is to evaluate its inflationary–deflationary potential. Different specifications yield different outcomes. Professor Collins's findings strike a note of caution about the validity of recent evidence showing that the EMS apparently did matter in bringing down inflation.

From the point of view of a practitioner, relying on his own intuitive experience, it is not difficult to side with Professor Collins's conclusions. The new rules provided by the EMS did not by themselves produce the set of policies and developments which led to greater price stability. Rather, the reverse is true. The decision to adopt more stringent policies in inflation-prone countries in the late 1970s or early 1980s was by no means confined to EMS countries, and was instrumental in bringing about both a generalised disinflationary trend and more realistic prospects for exchange-rate stabilisation, if felt desirable; the added value flowing from participation in ERM was to be greater exchange-rate stability. Admittedly, participation was also seen to entail feedback effects in the form of incentives towards price stability, but the first-round sequence goes from the basic policy reversal to ERM sustainability, not the other way round. Unless the feedback effects are found to be very powerful, it is not surprising that the ERM countries did not outperform the others in their disinflationary record.

So what is at stake is precisely to measure these feedback effects apart from external shocks and the general policy reversal. There remains the difficult problem of identifying what kind of change the mere fact of joining the ERM brings about. If the aim is to link the theoretical approach to empirical findings, it is not evident that the Cournot–Nash alternative is the appropriate benchmark against which to compare various interpretations of the EMS. Indeed, more emphasis should be given to the fact that several ERM members were linked together in the snake arrangement when the EMS was first set up. Looking at the 'rules of the game' channel, the snake involved far tighter rules than the EMS was perceived to provide. The former was under clear German leadership, and the obligation to peg to the Deutsche mark was felt much more strongly. When governments were unwilling to adjust their domestic policies in line with the requirements of the German-led exchange-rate regime, they simply had to opt out – which indeed happened in several instances.

The new EMS appeared, at the time – at least for some of its members – as a soft option – or, in terms of the author's scheme, as a more cooperative model than the one they previously belonged to. The well-publicised reluctance with which the Bundesbank rallied to the EMS proposal illustrates this. Using Professor Collins's ranking of the alternative exchange-rate regimes, the transition to EMS would therefore normally result in higher inflation, at least for those members that were snake participants.

What about the second channel through which the EMS could influence the rate of inflation – i.e., its impact on expectations? There again, a close look at the sequence of events seems relevant in explaining why inflation rates at first did not come down faster within the EMS group than in the non-EMS countries. The history of the attempts at monetary integration in Europe over the previous decade had been chaotic, so that most observers reacted sceptically when it was announced that the EMS would provide the framework for monetary stability that had been persistently failing in Europe. Moreover, the participation of countries like France and Italy – which had previously dropped out of the snake – was sometimes interpreted as a sign that the system would on average allow higher inflation than the snake had.

It may be argued that the decisive change of mood came about after 1982, when countries like Belgium, Denmark and France decided to operate major economic policy adjustments, involving a clear shift towards a Deutsche mark exchange-rate target. This change in policy orientation did not occur because of EMS, but for other reasons suggested below: however it did restore the credibility of the EMS as an arrangement for exchange-rate stabilisation and it did engineer a shift in expectations. In terms of Professor Collins's theoretical model, the episode may be looked at as a change in the exchange-rate regime, back from a cooperative towards a German-led model.

This is not the place to provide a thorough explanation of the revised policy stance adopted by several EMS countries around 1982. Clearly, by then, the costs of economic divergence within the ERM had become obvious, and they were unlikely to disappear simply by opting out of the system. Several factors account for this, such as the degree of openness of the countries concerned, the various facets of their linkages within the EEC, or the previous experience of opting out of the exchange arrangement.

To summarise, given the channels through which an arrangement like the EMS could influence the inflationary outcome, and given the pre-1979 experience of the various ERM participants, it would be fair to consider that the potential impact of the system on the reduction of inflation was given a chance only after 1982. The empirical results obtained in Table 5.3 would seem to be consistent with this particular time-profile (see the last two columns). On that basis, one might conclude that the feedback effects of participation in the ERM were indeed not negligible.

One footnote may be added on a minor point. Professor Collins stresses that the results obtained for the non-EMS group of countries are sensitive to which countries are included in this group; she points to the influence of Iceland on the outcome. One may also argue that countries like Austria and Switzerland – which largely peg their exchange rate to the Deutsche mark – substantially if not formally belong to the EMS rather than to the non-EMS sample.

6   Economic Growth and Exchange Rates in the European Monetary System: Their Trade Effects in a Changing External Environment*

STEFANO VONA and LORENZO BINI SMAGHI

1   Introduction

This study intends to examine the effects of external economic developments on the trade relations and inflation performance of the countries participating in the Exchange-Rate Mechanism (ERM) of the European Monetary System (EMS). The direction of the overall impact on the system of the external factors considered is difficult to assess. On the one hand, the oil shock of 1979–80 and the subsequent dollar appreciation increased inflation in the ERM countries and probably accentuated inflation differentials,[1] thus undermining exchange-rate cohesion. On the other hand, the large real appreciation of most non-ERM currencies *vis-à-vis* those of the ERM, and the strong recovery of the US economy in the period 1983–5 sustained the growth of economic activity in Europe and may also have contributed to the stability of the exchange-rate system. In this study, we concentrate on this latter aspect, which has not received sufficient attention in the literature on the EMS,[2] and is becoming even more important now since the direction of its development has dramatically reversed.

The study formulates a quantitative framework for the assessment of the effects produced by some of the external factors mentioned above on the trade relations of the three major ERM countries (Germany, France and Italy), with the rest of the ERM area and the other industrial countries. The model outlined in the study is also used to evaluate the implications for trade and inflation of alternative exchange-rate policies and different patterns of aggregate demand growth. However, since the model refers only to the manufacturing sector and is based on a partial equilibrium approach, the findings should be interpreted with caution.

The study is organised as follows. Section 2 examines some issues

140

concerning the trade performances of the ERM countries and describes the development of some economic variables which are crucial in the explanation of trade flows. Section 3 briefly outlines the trade and price model developed to assess the quantitative impact of the external factors mentioned above. Section 4 reviews the results obtained in the estimation of the model. Section 5 presents the results of some policy-relevant simulations. Finally, in Section 6 we discuss the main conclusions of our work.

2   ERM countries' trade: the role of external factors

a.   An overview of the problem

The EMS has achieved remarkable results in stabilising intra-ERM exchange rates and in promoting convergence of member countries' inflation towards low levels. However, persistent divergence of growth rates, especially those of domestic demand, led to large trade imbalances among the member countries (Figure 6.1).

This phenomenon has received little attention from either academic circles or policymakers, and exchange-rate policy within the area aimed primarily at avoiding major medium-term changes in price competitiveness.[3] There are two possible explanations for this approach. The first is that the priority given to inflation reduction and convergence implied that real exchange rates were not managed with the objective of equilibrating trade flows among member countries. The second explanation is that attention was put on countries' overall trade balance, rather than on bilateral trade with particular area or countries.

With respect to the first explanation, we have shown in a previous work (Bini Smaghi and Vona, 1988) that while some appreciation of real exchange rates in high-inflation countries has been tolerated as part of or as the result of the disinflation strategy, the emergence of large trade imbalances within the ERM area in the 1979–85 period has been mostly due to the divergence in the growth rates of aggregate demand of member countries. The increasing imbalances have rendered more costly the disinflation process in high-inflation countries; had trade imbalances been given greater attention, we claimed, a better allocation of the adjustment costs could have been made, with the result of speeding up the process and enhancing exchange-rate stability.

As far as the second aspect is concerned – i.e., that only overall trade balance matters in the conduct of exchange-rate policy – it is acceptable only in the hypothesis that the latter is conducted uniformly *vis-à-vis* all the other major currencies. This is clearly not the case for the ERM

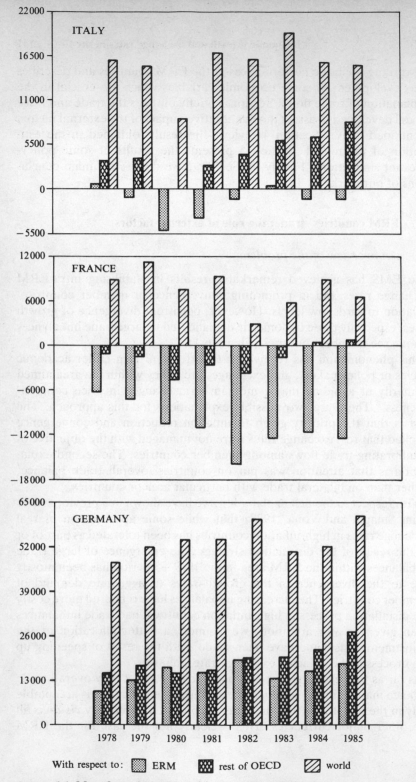

Figure 6.1 Manufacturing trade balances, million dollars

Note: The definition of manufacturing sector is based on NACE classification.
Source: EEC, Volimex data.

countries, who have explicit commitments only with respect to intra-ERM rates. In order to evaluate the performance of an exchange-rate agreement like that of the EMS within the wider international monetary system, it is therefore necessary to look at appropriate indicators that allow to take into account the influence of outside factors. If the assessment of the performance of the system is based, among other indicators, on the trade balances, we claim that intra-ERM balances have a significant role to play.[4] Figure 6.1 reveals that their behaviour was strikingly different from that of the global trade balance of the countries concerned.

A number of special factors determined this divergent pattern. As mentioned in the introduction, the real appreciation of the dollar, the fast growth in the US, and (in 1986) the oil counter-shock all reinforced the external position of the ERM countries. On the other hand, they contributed to hiding the emergence of large intra-ERM imbalances. The effects of these factors are now vanishing (oil shock) or even reversing (the dollar is depreciating, the US economy growth is slowing down). Consequently, intra-ERM trade imbalances may emerge as a very acute problem for the stability of the system, which could require corrective policy actions.

b.   Germany, France and Italy: relative growth and competitiveness

In this study, we restrict the analysis to the manufacturing trade flows of the three largest ERM economies – Germany, France and Italy – with respect to two areas – the ERM area and the rest of the OECD – so as to evaluate the effects of exchange rate and growth developments in this latter area on intra-ERM exchange-rate cohesion. For the three countries considered, we provide a brief description of the development of the variables which are most important for the explanation of the trade flows. A particular feature of the present work is that indicators of real exchange rates have been calculated by using indices of bilateral unit values, obtained from the Volimex data bank of the EEC Commission Services. This data bank made it possible to construct, for each of the three countries considered, indicators of price competitiveness (real exchange rates) *vis-à-vis* any desired country or group of countries, using the 'true' unit value (uv) indices of their bilateral trade. This represents a significant improvement on the standard procedure of using, for lack of statistical information, the overall uv of exports as a proxy for the uv of exports towards a specific area or country, since export prices may vary significantly depending on the market of destination, as a consequence both of differences in the product composition of trade flows and/or of

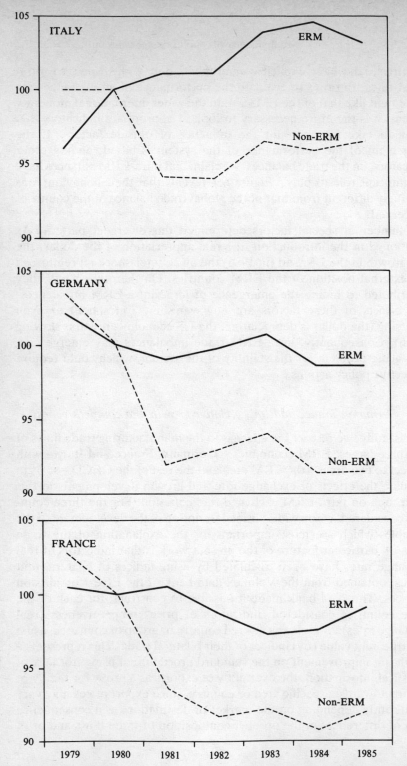

Figure 6.2 Indicators of price competitiveness, indices 1980 = 100
Note: Ratio between the domestic and foreign unit values of exports, expressed in common currency, towards the area considered. An increase indicates a loss in competitiveness.

of specific 'pricing to market' strategies which may have been adopted in a period of floating exchange rates.[5]

The results of our calculations are presented in Figure 6.2. They concern real effective exchange rates with both the ERM partners and the other OECD countries. With respect to the ERM area, the data show a loss of competitiveness for the Italian industry and a small gain for that of Germany, which confirms the result of other real exchange-rate indicators. For France, our indicators give the impression of a more positive performance in the period 1984–6 than that expected on the basis of other existing indicators. With respect to the rest of the OECD, all three countries scored substantial gains – as a consequence of the sharp appreciation of the dollar, and (to a lesser extent) the yen and the pound sterling.

The evaluation of the aggregate demand performance of the three countries differs widely depending on whether it is measured with respect to the ERM or the non-ERM area (Figure 6.3), since the latter has on average grown much faster than the former. Within the ERM area the growth rate of domestic demand has been well below average in Germany and significantly faster in Italy and France (Figure 6.4).

Developments in real exchange rates and relative growth rates have combined to determine wide differences in the trade performances of the three countries considered, *vis-à-vis* both the ERM and non-ERM industrial countries (Figure 6.1).

Italy's trade performance with the ERM area has been distinctly worse than that with the rest of the OECD and the rest of the world. In particular, the trade balance with the non-ERM industrial countries has improved continuously and significantly since 1980, while in 1984 and 1985 that with the ERM countries still recorded deficits, although for smaller amounts.

France's trade deficit with the ERM countries has markedly deteriorated during the EMS period. Its trade balance with the other OECD industrial countries has performed better than that with ERM countries, but not sufficiently to prevent the overall manufacturing trade surplus from remaining smaller than Italy's (and especially Germany's).

For the latter country, the manufacturing trade balance confirms the good performance of German industry in trade with the other industrial countries: the trade balance improved with both non-ERM industrial countries and the ERM ones (comparing the EMS period with the 1977–8 average). However, by contrast with Italy and France, Germany performed somewhat worse in its trade with the non-industrial area.

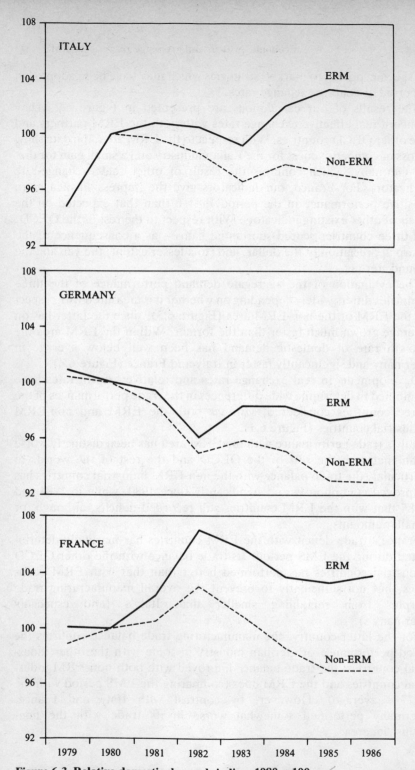

Figure 6.3 Relative domestic demand, indices 1980 = 100
Note: Ratio between the domestic and the competitors' aggregate demand in the two areas. A rise in the variable indicates that the domestic demand grows at a faster rate than the foreign demand.

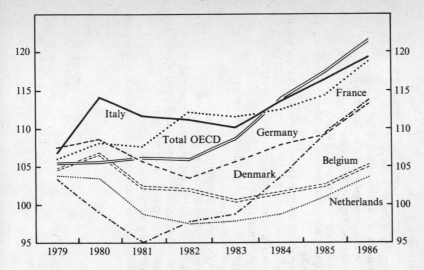

Figure 6.4 Domestic aggregate demand, indices 1977–8 = 100

3   The trade and inflation model

The analysis of the manufacturing trade flows of the three ERM countries considered is based on a model which assumes product differentiation and therefore imperfect substitutability (Goldstein and Kahn, 1985). Its structure is similar to the World Trade Model of the IMF (Spencer, 1984), which considers the effects of changes in major countries' exchange rates on their domestic prices and on trade prices and volumes. In contrast with this model, however, its fundamental characteristic is that it is a model of trade flows with two separate areas rather than with the whole world, and therefore allows for distinct parameter estimates according to the area considered – i.e., the ERM area or the non-ERM OECD area. The underlying microeconomic structure is one in which the representative producer is a discriminating monopolist selling differentiated products in the segregated home and foreign markets (Stevens, 1984). Supply elasticities are assumed to be infinite and the representative firm follows a mark-up over prime-cost pricing strategy.[6] In this model, therefore, quantities and prices are not determined simultaneously, given that the marginal cost curve is infinitely elastic.

The model is presented in Table 6.1, and has four behavioural equations and six identities for each country and area of destination. The trade volume equations are functions of total domestic demand and price competitiveness.[7] In equation (6.1) the volume of exports (X) of country

Model		Variables
$X_i^A = X(DA_i, CX_i^A \ldots)$	(6.1)	X_i^A = Exports of country i to A
$M_i^A = M(D_i, CM^A \ldots)$	(6.2)	M_i^A = Imports of country i from A
$PX_i^A = PX(PAX_i^A, PI_i \ldots)$	(6.3)	DA_i = Domestic demand of A calculated as in (6.10)
$PI_i = PI(CL_i, MAT_i, PM_i, GAP_i \ldots)$	(6.4)	D_i = Domestic demand of country i
$CX_i^A = PX_i^A/PAX_i^A$	(6.5)	PX_i^A = Export prices of country i to A
$CM_i^A = (PI_i^A + PM_i^{NA1-\lambda})/PM_i^A$	(6.6)	CX_i^A = Export competitiveness, calculated as shown in (6.5)
$B_i^A = PX_i^A \cdot X_i^A - PM_i^A \cdot M_i^A$	(6.7)	CM^A = Import competitiveness, calculated as shown in (6.6)
$PM_i = PM_i^{A\alpha} + PM_i^{NA1-\alpha}$	(6.8)	PAX_i^A = Prices of competitors of country i in A, calculated as shown in (6.9)
$PAX_i^A = \sum_{j\neq i} w_j PX_j^A + \sum_{j\neq i} z_j PI_j + \sum_{k\neq i\neq j} v_k PX_k$	(6.9)	PI_i = Prices of domestic producer of country i
		CL_i = Unit labour costs of country i
$DA_i = \sum_{j\neq i} z_j D_i$	(6.10)	PM_i^A = Import prices of country i from A
		PM_i^{NA} = Import prices of country i from NA
		MAT_i = Raw materials import prices of country i
		GAP_i = Domestic demand deviation from trend of country i
$0<\alpha, \lambda<1; \quad j \in A; \quad k \in NA; \quad \Sigma w_j + \Sigma z_j + \Sigma v_k = 1$		w = Multilateral competitive weights
		z = Bilateral export weights

Table 6.1 Model for Analysis of Manufacturing Trade Flows

Note: A, NA = ERM or non-ERM, respectively.

i towards area *A* (the ERM or the non-ERM OECD area) is a function of the aggregate demand (*DA*) of the area considered, calculated as shown in equation (6.10), and the export price competitiveness (*CX*) defined in equation (6.5) as the ratio of the export prices of domestic exporters and those of their competitors in that market. These are, specifically (equation 6.9), the exporters and the domestic producers of the other countries of area *A* and the exporters of the other area considered (*NA*). Because *CX* is defined as a ratio of the relevant prices, the own and cross-price elasticities of export volumes are assumed to be equal.

Equation (6.2) defines the demand for imports (*M*) of country *i* from area *A* as a function of its domestic demand (*D*) and the import price competitiveness (*CM*). The latter is the inverse of the ratio of the prices of imports from area *A* (PM^A) and those of their competitors on the domestic market, which is a weighted average of domestic producer prices (*PI*) and the import price of the other area (PM^{NA}). Equal own and cross-price elasticities are also assumed for import volumes.

Because the macroeconomic structure of the model is not one of pure competition, the export prices of each country (equation (6.3)) towards area *A* are expressed as a function of the prices of its competitors (PAX^A) in that market and of the producer prices on the domestic market (*PI*), which are used here as a proxy for overall costs. Consequently, the representative exporter is not assumed to be a price taker in the international market but adopts a pricing strategy which takes account of the behaviour of domestic costs. In this specification, the weight of foreign competitors' prices in relation to that of costs in the determination of the export prices of the three countries considered depends on the degree of substitutability between domestic and foreign goods and on the degree of competitiveness of the market structure. The greater the market power of exporters, the less they take competitors' prices into consideration in setting their export prices (Deppler and Ripley, 1978), and consequently the smaller the value of the relative coefficient.

Domestic producer prices are determined through a mark-up over unit labour costs (*CL*), imported raw materials (*MAT*) and imported manufactures (*PM*); the mark-up is cyclically flexible, depending on the deviations of domestic demand with respect to its trend (*GAP*).

The data utilised in this analysis permits separate considerations of the prices of the three countries' exports to each of the other two areas.[8] The different pricing behaviour in the two markets depends on several factors, including product composition, the degree of industry competition and interaction among producers (Dornbusch, 1987).

The model makes it possible to examine the effects of changes in the pattern of the exogenous variables (exchange rates and total domestic demand) on inflation and trade with the two areas considered. These effects operate through: (a) the export price competition between countries of the two areas, and (b) the pass-through from the export prices of countries belonging to one of the two areas to the import prices – and hence the producer prices – of the countries of the other area.

Considering the simplified structure of the model and its partial equilibrium nature, the results obtained from simulating shocks to the exogenous variables should be interpreted with caution. Following Branson (1972, p. 17), they can be considered as impact effects that occur 'before any compensating effects working through income or the general price level set in. On one interpretation, these estimates give the final results if governments act to prevent a net effect on income and price levels'.

Other types of interrelations are omitted in the formulation of the model as a consequence of the assumptions of exogeneity of individual countries' domestic demand and exchange rates. These hypotheses are traditional ones in this class of models. It is obvious, however, that intra-ERM exchange rates are not in fact independent of exchange-rate movements outside the area – in particular, those of the dollar. Furthermore, the medium-term behaviour of the exchange rates within the ERM is based on overall balance of payments developments, in particular the current account balance, which is strongly influenced by developments outside the EMS area. While not considering these two latter effects in the specification of the model, we have tried to take them into account in discussing the results of some of the simulations presented in Section 5.

4   Empirical results

a.   Regression estimates

The results of the empirical estimation of the 21 behavioural equations of the model are synthetically presented in Tables 6.2–6.4 below, while the full description of the regression results for each equation, with all the relevant statistics and the lag structure of the independent variables, are shown in Tables A6.1–A6.7 of the Appendix.[9]

The price elasticities of intra-ERM trade are all smaller than one, fairly similar for the imports and the exports of each country and considerably below the average value in the case of France (Table 6.2). This is consistent with the hypothesis of imperfect substitution between domestic and foreign goods. It also appears that the degree of substitutability is smaller for France, as a result of a difference in the quality of domestic vis-à-vis foreign goods and/or a mismatching between the baskets of home-produced and foreign-produced manufactures.

Exports to	ERM countries		Non-ERM OECD countries	
From	Price	Expenditure	Price	Expenditure
Italy	−0.82	2.21	−1.04	2.40
Germany	−0.97	1.88	−0.68	1.66
France	−0.57	1.90	−0.57	1.71

Imports from	ERM countries		Non-ERM OECD countries	
To	Price	Expenditure	Price	Expenditure
Italy	0.98	2.16	1.23	2.32
Germany	0.89	1.64	1.23	1.89
France	0.58	2.74	0.95	2.73

Table 6.2 Price and Expenditure 'Equilibrium' Elasticities of Manufacturing Export and Import Volumes

The price elasticities of imports from the non-ERM OECD countries are generally higher than those from the ERM countries, while the price elasticities of exports are diversified: only Italy's exports to non-ERM OECD countries are more responsive to changes in price competitiveness than its exports to the ERM area. This means that an equal gain in the price competitiveness of Italian goods in the two markets would cause a much larger improvement in Italy's real trade balance of manufactures with the rest of the OECD than with the ERM countries. This also holds for France, while in the case of Germany the effects of a change in price competitiveness would be more or less the same in the two markets in terms of real trade balances. It is also worth noting that the sum of export and import price elasticities is larger than one for every country and for both intra-ERM and extra-ERM trade. Hence, under the condition of initial trade balance equilibrium, the traditional Marshall–Lerner conditions hold.

Italy has the highest export expenditure elasticities, which are coupled, however, with nearly equal import expenditure elasticities. Italian manufacturing industry seems therefore to have benefitted from a growing demand for its exports from the other industrial countries. Another implication is that, for any fixed level of price competitiveness, Italy is able to maintain the same rate of growth of domestic demand as that of the other ERM and non-ERM industrial countries without any deterioration in its trade balance.

In the case of Germany, the elasticities are much smaller, but (as for Italy) the average value of export elasticities is roughly similar to that of imports. The values indicate that German industry is in a relatively favourable position within the ERM area.

The expenditure elasticities of France are rather surprising. While those of exports are fairly similar to those of Germany – ranging between 1.7 for extra-ERM trade and 1.9 for intra-ERM trade – those of imports considerably exceed those of the other two countries, amounting to about 2.7. Although the lack of a truly appropriate index of domestic prices of manufactures[10] may have affected the estimated import elasticities of France, these high values probably contributed to the strong import penetration in the French market for manufactures in the last ten years.[11] These results indicate that the French economy is not able to sustain a growth rate similar to that of the other industrial countries without incurring a sharp deterioration in its manufacturing trade balance, unless significant gains of price competitiveness can be achieved.

In the model, the prices of ERM countries' exports towards the two areas considered are determined endogenously. While the prices of imports from the rest of the OECD are assumed to be exogenous, those of imports from ERM countries are linked to endogenous export prices through a technical equation that relates the former to import 'shadow prices', calculated as the weighted average of the prices of the exports of the other ERM countries to the whole ERM area. The estimate of the unconstrained coefficient of the independent variable (the shadow price) is close to one for every country. Consequently, in all the following exercises it is assumed – as in other multicountry models (see in particular Spencer, 1984)[12] – that exchange-rate changes are entirely translated into import prices.

The export price equations (Table 6.3) show that the role of competitors' prices and domestic costs in determining the price behaviour of exporters in intra-ERM trade is of similar importance in Germany, France and Italy. The values of the coefficients for all three countries are respectively close to 0.4 and 0.6. As regards exports to the other OECD countries, the importance of foreign competitors is smaller for German exporters (and, to a lesser extent, for the French ones), while Italian exporters still take considerable account of the pricing strategy of competitors. Overall, these findings tend to confirm that German firms have a higher degree of market power in international trade, in particular outside the ERM area. More precisely, German firms may have adopted an aggressive price strategy to gain market shares in a period in which the exchange rate of the DM was rapidly depreciating with respect to

	ERM countries		Non-ERM OECD countries	
	*PI**	*PAX***	*PI**	*PAX***
Italy	0.58	0.42	0.57	0.43
Germany	0.63	0.37	0.87	0.13
France	0.61	0.39	0.69	0.31

Table 6.3 Domestic and Competitors' Price Elasticities of Manufacturing Export Prices

Notes:
*Domestic producer prices.
**Competitors' prices.

	Italy	Germany	France
Raw materials import prices	0.17	0.06	0.08
Manufacturing import prices	0.50	0.60	0.56
Unit labour costs	0.33	0.34	0.36
Domestic demand gap	0.30	0.13	0.28

Table 6.4 Elasticities of Manufacturing Producer Prices' Determinants

non-ERM currencies. The opposite holds for Italian exporters, who have been obliged to squeeze their profit margins in their trade with the ERM area, given the severe exchange-rate policy the Italian authorities have pursued. Accordingly they may have compensated for this loss by increasing their profit margins in trade with the rest of the OECD.

Finally, the estimates of the domestic price equations reveal some interesting differences between the three countries (Table 6.4). While the elasticities of the producer prices of manufactures with respect to unit labour costs are similar for the three countries, there is a substantial difference in the values of the price elasticities of imported raw materials; Italian prices are much more responsive to changes in raw material import prices. Since the sum of the three coefficients of the cost variables is constrained to one, these differences are inversely reflected in those of the manufacturing import price elasticities of producer prices. The latter approximates three different effects: (a) a 'cost effect' that reflects the behaviour of the prices of the intermediate goods included in the basket

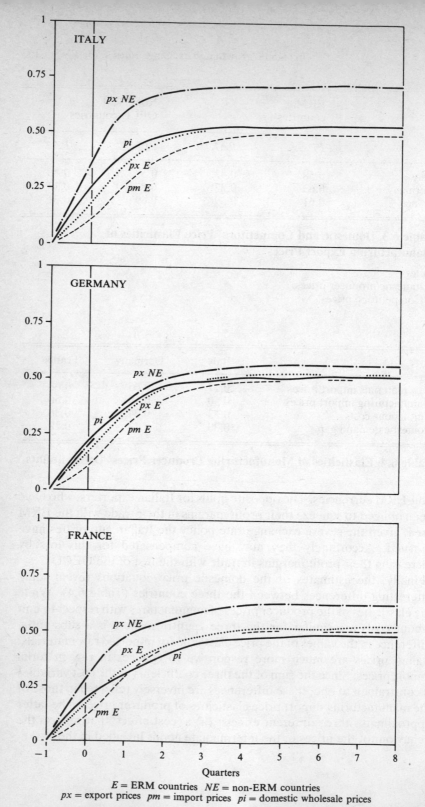

Quarters

E = ERM countries *NE* = non-ERM countries
px = export prices *pm* = import prices *pi* = domestic wholesale prices

Figure 6.5 Effect on prices of a joint devaluation of ERM currencies
Note: Devaluation with respect to all the currencies external to the ERM area.

of imported manufactures; (b) a 'composition effect', which derives from the inclusion of imported manufactures in the set of goods that make up the producer price index basket; (c) a 'competition effect', that derives from the fact that imports of both intermediate and finished goods compete with domestically-produced substitutes.

b.   Dynamic properties of the model

The dynamic behaviour of the endogenous variables of the model can be evaluated by examining the adjustment to shocks imparted to the exogenous variables. In a previous work (Bini Smaghi and Vona, 1988) we considered the effects of changes in intra-ERM exchange rates and relative demand growth on the pattern of trade between member countries, for given unchanged conditions outside the area. In this study we concentrate on the effects on trade, both within the ERM and with the rest of the OECD, of a simultaneous change in the exchange rates and demand growth of all the ERM countries with respect to the rest of the OECD.

Figure 6.5 shows the effects that a joint devaluation of ERM currencies with respect to the rest of the OECD has on the prices of exports to the ERM area and the rest of the OECD, on domestic producer prices and on the prices of imports from ERM countries.

First, it is worth noting that the joint devaluation of ERM currencies does not produce a significantly different effect on the domestic producer prices of the three countries considered; they all rise by about 50 per cent of the amount of the devaluation. Had the devaluation been only with respect to the US dollar, and not with respect to all the other non-ERM currencies, the inflationary effect would, however, have been greatest for Italy, followed by France, given the larger coefficient of imported raw material prices in the producer price equations of these two countries.

The effect of the depreciation of the ERM currencies on the prices of exports towards non-ERM countries is largest in Italy (70 per cent of the devaluation), as a result of the greater importance that Italian exporters give to competitors' prices in the non-ERM market. Germany registers the lowest effect (55 per cent), while France is in an intermediate position (60 per cent). Hence, a joint devaluation of the ERM currencies determines an improvement in German exporters' price competitiveness towards the rest of the OECD market, compared not only with local producers but also with the exporters of Italy and France. On the other hand, intra-ERM export price competitiveness is not significantly altered, as the prices of exports to the ERM area tend to rise by similar amounts (45 per cent). On the import side, intra-ERM price competi-

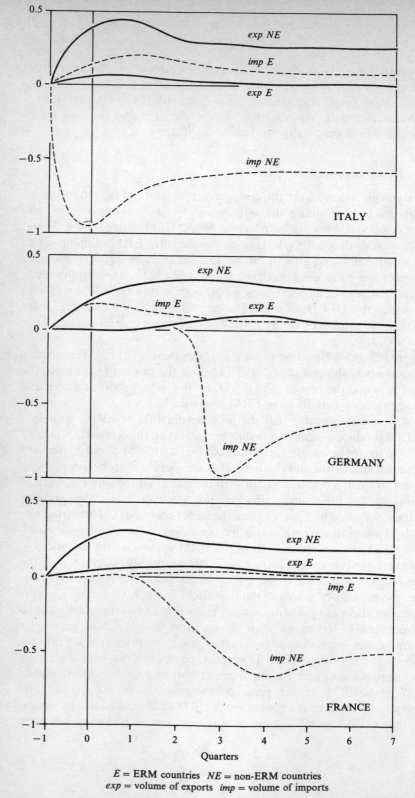

E = ERM countries NE = non-ERM countries
exp = volume of exports imp = volume of imports

Figure 6.6 Effect on trade volumes of a joint devaluation of ERM currencies

tiveness deteriorates to a small extent in Italy (3 per cent) since domestic producer prices rise by a greater amount than the prices of imports from the ERM area. There is a small gain for France, while Germany's competitiveness remains practically unchanged.

In summary, following a devaluation of the ERM currencies the three countries considered gain competitiveness, both on the import and on the export side, with respect to the non-ERM OECD countries. There is, however, also a redistributive effect among ERM producers: on the non-ERM market German exporters tend to be advantaged, while French producers benefit from a small gain in intra-ERM competitiveness, and Italian manufacturers suffer losses in both areas. However, these differences appear to be small.

Figure 6.6 shows the effects of the joint devaluation of ERM currencies on trade volumes, with respect to the two areas considered. Exports to the non-ERM area increase in all three countries; France records the smallest effect in view of its lower export price elasticity. Imports from the rest of the OECD fall in all three countries, although with a lag of three-quarters in Germany and France. Intra-ERM trade flows tend to increase, as expected, since ERM producers gain competitiveness. Imports rise more than exports in Italy and (initially) in Germany, owing to the gap between domestic producer prices and the prices in imports from the ERM. In France, by contrast, exports to the ERM area increase more than imports.

The combined influence on the manufacturing trade balances of all the price and quantity effects described above can be assessed by looking at the result of the first of the following four exercises, which are intended to analyse the effects of changes in the exogenous variables outside the ERM on the trade balances of the three countries concerned (Figure 6.7). Several shocks have been considered: (a) a 1 per cent devaluation of the ERM currencies with respect to all other currencies; (b) a 1 per cent devaluation of the ERM currencies with respect to the US dollar only; (c) a 1 per cent increase of domestic demand in the non-ERM countries; (d) a 1 per cent increase of domestic demand in the US alone. We obtain the following results:

(a) In the long run, the devaluation of the ERM currencies with respect to all the other OECD currencies improves the trade balances of all three countries. For each 1 per cent depreciation, France gains about 150 million dollars, Italy and Germany about 100 million dollars each.

(b) A 1 per cent devaluation of the ERM currencies with respect to the US dollar improves the trade balance of Italy only in the short run (60 million dollars in the first two quarters), since in the longer run any advantage tends to fade as the increase in domestic prices reduces

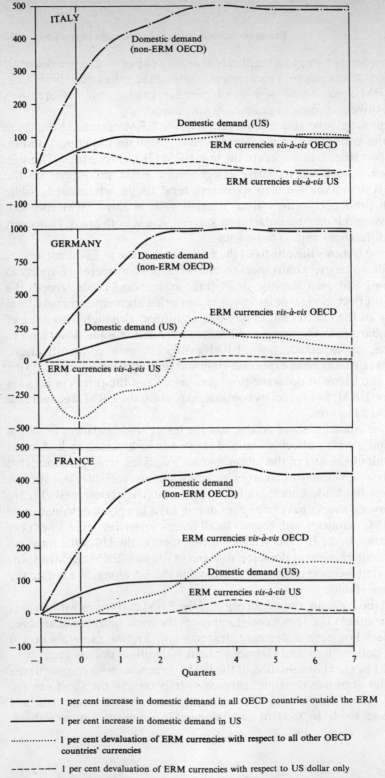

Figure 6.7 Effect on the overall trade balance of changes in the exchange rates and domestic demands outside the ERM area

competitiveness. The gain produced by the devaluation with respect to the dollar is also small for Germany and France (less than 20 million dollars).

(c) A one percentage point rise in domestic demand in the non-ERM OECD countries determines a large improvement in the trade balances of all three countries. Germany records the largest gain (about 1 billion dollars), while the trade balances of France and Italy improve by more than 400 million dollars.[13] The effect on the trade balance is greater than in the previous exercise, since the increase in foreign demand is entirely transmitted to the exports of the country.

(d) An increase in domestic demand in the US improves the manufacturing trade balance of Germany by about 200 million dollars and that of Italy and France by about 100 million.

In summary, the trade balances of the three countries considered seem to be significantly sensitive to changes occurring outside the ERM area, especially with regards to aggregate demand. Exchange-rate changes have a somewhat smaller impact, because of the domestic price reaction that attenuates their effect on price competitiveness, especially in Italy.

5 Simulation of alternative scenarios

To make a broader evaluation of the effects of external developments on the trade relations of the three countries considered, we have simulated alternative scenarios in which the pattern of both exchange rates and aggregate demand outside the ERM are modified during the period 1979–85. In these exercises, exchange rates and aggregate demand continue to be considered as exogenous and therefore the results should be considered as a benchmark rather than counterfactual.

a. Simulation 1

We first analyse the effect of the actual depreciation of the ERM currencies in the period examined, in particular with respect to the dollar, the yen and the pound sterling. We simulate a scenario in which the exchange rate of the ERM currencies does not depreciate as much as in the 1981–5 period with respect to the non-ERM currencies. For simplicity it is assumed that the DM–dollar rate is the pivot rate for the simulation, and is modified as shown in Figure 6.8, while the exchange rates within the two single areas remain unchanged with respect to their historical pattern.

In this scenario, the inflation rates and the trade balances of the three ERM countries considered change significantly in comparison with the baseline historical values (Table 6.5). The anti-inflationary effect – which

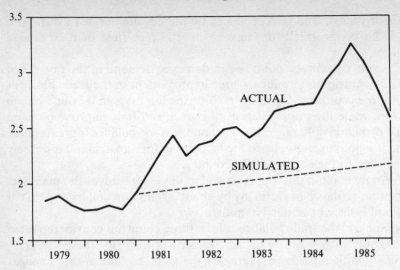

Figure 6.8 Simulation 1: hypothesis on the DM–US dollar exchange rate

comes from lower import prices – is quite strong: in 1981 the rate of inflation is about six percentage points lower in all three countries, and remains at a lower level in the subsequent years.[14] The inflation rate differential is altered in favour of Germany by 1.4 percentage points, on a yearly average, with respect to Italy, and 1.7 points with respect to France. The smaller depreciation of the ERM currencies with respect to those of the non-ERM area (in comparison to historical values) nonetheless implies a loss of competitiveness that tends to worsen their trade balances. The deterioration of the Italian trade account amounts to around 1.5 billion dollars in 1981 and rises to 3 billion in 1984. The French trade deficit deteriorates by 3.3 billion dollars in 1982 and over 6 billion in 1985. The worsening of the trade balance in the 1981–5 period totals about 11 billion dollars in Italy and 15 billion in France. The effect is greater for that latter country because of its worse starting situation (Table 6.5). It is surprising to find that an appreciation of the DM with respect to the non-ERM countries would have caused little change in the German trade balance. This is due to the 'persistent' *J*-curve effect, whereby changes in trade volume are obscured by offsetting price changes. These results refer, of course, only to manufacturing trade and can therefore not be used as a precise indicator of the overall effect of the alternative exchange-rate simulation on the trade balances of the three countries. They nonetheless provide a benchmark for policy evaluation.[15]

The evolution of manufacturing trade can be related to that of domestic production to evaluate the impact on the growth of that specific sector. In the scenario described above, the deterioration of the manufacturing trade balance amounts to a loss of 1 per cent of domestic production on average in the 1981–5 period for France and Italy, and of 3 per cent for Germany. At the same time, industrial output in Germany and France in 1985 would have been lower than the historical level by respectively 3.5 and 1.3 percentage points. That of Italy would have been about the same.

b.   Simulation 2

Another important development outside the ERM has been the particularly sustained growth of aggregate demand, especially in North America. To evaluate its effect on the trade relations of the three countries considered, we have simulated an alternative scenario with the non-ERM area growing at the same rate as the ERM area between 1981 and 1985. Table 6.5 shows that the trade balance of all three countries would deteriorate, especially after 1983 when the US upturn started. The trade balance of France and Italy worsened by about 1.3 and 1.1 billion dollars, respectively; on average for the 1981–5 period, Germany records a slightly larger deterioration (2.3 billions).

If the two simulations above are considered jointly, the worsening of the trade balance of France becomes particularly large, and practically cancels the adjustment of the trade balance registered since 1983. In Italy, in spite of the deterioration with respect to the historical pattern, there is still a small improvement in the trade balance after 1980. Examining these effects in terms of contribution to growth, the deterioration of the manufacturing trade balance in volume terms would have compressed domestic production through 1985 by 3.5 percentage points in Germany and about two points in France and Italy.

Considering the already depressed development of domestic production in the ERM countries (especially in Italy and France), a less favourable external environment would have seriously undermined the efforts made to reduce their inflation rate. Further, in the latter two countries the further aggravation of the trade deficits (especially between 1981 and 1982) could have hardly been sustained. In particular, the deterioration of the French trade account resulting from the above scenario (about 11 billion dollars in 1984–5) would have probably jeopardised the external adjustment process under way since 1983.

If policy authorities consider these effects unacceptable and unsustainable, especially for those ERM countries with the largest trade imbalances and the slowest-growing domestic production, a series of alternative scenarios can be examined. The question we ask is the following: had there not been a gain in competitiveness with respect to

Historical data	1981	1982	1983	1984	1985	Average 1981–5
Italy						
Inflation[1]	17.2	13.7	10.1	10.4	7.3	11.7
Balance of trade[2]	−630	2,910	6,470	5,160	6,940	4,170
Industrial production[3]	98.4	95.1	91.9	95.1	96.1	95.3
Germany						
Inflation[1]	6.0	4.8	1.5	2.8	2.0	3.4
Balance of trade[2]	31,490	38,980	33,830	38,270	45,815	37,677
Industrial production[3]	98.3	95.3	96.3	99.5	105.0	98.9
France						
Inflation[1]	11.2	11.4	9.1	8.9	4.4	9.0
Balance of trade[2]	−13,710	−19,670	−14,090	−11,040	−11,660	−14,052
Industrial production[3]	98.3	97.8	97.5	97.0	97.0	97.5

Effects of different scenarios (deviations from historical data)

Scenario 1 Different exchange-rate pattern *vis-à-vis* non-ERM countries[4]

	1981	1982	1983	1984	1985	Average 1981–5
Italy						
Inflation[5]	−7.1	−3.5	−1.4	−3.9	−2.9	−3.8
Balance of trade[2]	−1,500	−1,630	−1,750	−3,000	−3,125	−2,200
Industrial production[3]	−0.9	−0.9	−1.3	−3.1	−0.3	−1.3
Germany						
Inflation[5]	−6.1	−3.9	−1.4	−3.3	−3.0	−3.5
Balance of trade[2]	3,260	−1,300	−1,090	50	−6,520	−1,120
Industrial production[3]	−0.8	−3.1	−3.3	−2.7	−3.5	−2.7
France						
Inflation[5]	−5.7	−3.1	−1.6	−3.5	−3.1	−3.4
Balance of trade[2]	−690	−3,310	−2,760	−3,450	−5,170	−3,070
Industrial production[3]	−0.4	−1.0	−1.1	−1.4	−1.3	−1.0

Notes:
[1] Percentage change in manufacturing producer prices.
[2] Manufacturing trade with respect to total OECD area in million current dollars.
[3] Level of industrial production in manufacturing (index 1980 = 100).
[4] The DM–dollar exchange rate is simulated as in Figure 6.8. The exchange rates of other non-ERM currencies with respect to the dollar and those of ERM currencies with respect to the DM are kept at historical level.
[5] Difference in percentage points from historical data.
[6] Difference in million dollars from historical data.
[7] Difference in percentage from historical data.

Scenario 2 Different domestic demand pattern in non-ERM countries[8]

Italy

Balance of trade[6]	−170	−470	−1,180	−1,650	−2,820	−1,260
Industrial production[7]	−0.2	−0.4	−0.8	−0.3	−1.5	−0.8

Germany

Balance of trade[6]	−420	−1,460	−2,290	−2,500	−4,790	−2,290
Industrial production[7]	−0.2	−0.6	−0.8	−1.1	−1.3	−0.8

France

Balance of trade[6]	−240	−590	−1,030	−1,380	−2,070	−1,060
Industrial production[7]	−0.1	−0.3	−0.4	−0.6	−0.8	−0.4

Scenario 3 Different domestic demand pattern in ERM countries[9]

Italy

Balance of trade[6]	2,100	1,500	1,060	2,880	4,390	2,390

Germany

Balance of trade[6]	−2,000	−6,800	−5,200	−4,200	−6,400	−4,920

France

Balance of trade[6]	1,000	4,170	4,670	2,800	1,500	2,830

Table 6.5 Effects of Alternative Policy Simulations

[8] Non-ERM countries' domestic demand grow at the same rate as that of the ERM average.

[9] ERM countries' domestic demand grow at the same rate as the average of non-ERM area.

the non-ERM area in the 1981–5 period (Simulation 1), what alternative policy actions could the ERM countries have undertaken to avoid a further deterioration in domestic manufacturing production – and, in some of these countries, the worsening of their external imbalances? Two different answers can be envisaged: one based on a framework of aggregate demand policies coordinated among member countries, the other based on changes in intra-ERM exchange rates.

c.   Simulation 3

Consider first a coordinated policy action by the ERM countries based on a common objective for the growth of aggregate demand. We shall assume that all the ERM countries set a common target for their domestic demand growth similar to that recorded during the period by non-ERM countries (Table 6.5). Manufacturing output in the three countries would have performed better. It is difficult to evaluate the overall effect since the model does not specify a relationship between domestic demand and manufacturing production. Assuming unitary elasticity, the level of the latter, in 1985 would be more than 6 per cent above the historical level in Germany, and more than 3 per cent above in Italy and France.

Further, the two latter countries' trade balances would have significantly improved, thereby offsetting the negative effects of the appreciation of the ERM currencies *vis-à-vis* the rest of the OECD. Moreover, the better performance in the earlier part of the EMS period might even have enabled the French and Italians to sustain a further appreciation of their currencies in real terms with respect to the other ERM countries, with an acceleration in the reduction in their inflation rates.

With this strategy, the trade account of Germany would have worsened by nearly 7 billion dollars in 1982, and by somewhat less in the subsequent years. In spite of this deterioration, the trade surplus of Germany with the OECD would have remained constant until 1983, and even slightly increased in the last two years. The overall German trade performance seems to indicate that such a loss (due only to an increase in imports) would have been acceptable, given that Germany doubled its trade surplus from 1981 to 1983 and that the current account balance moved into surplus in the same period.

d.   Simulation 4

If such a strategy of demand coordination among the ERM countries had not been feasible, the two countries seeking to make large reductions in their inflation rates (France and Italy) could have countered their output losses and trade balance deteriorations only through modifications of intra-ERM exchange rates. The exercise performed with this simulation calculates, for a given DM–dollar exchange rate set as in Simulation 1 (Figure 6.8), the exchange rates of the French franc and the lira with respect to the other ERM countries that would have permitted their trade accounts to remain at the historical level. This exercise is conducted jointly for France and Italy. The results are shown in Figure 6.9. The lira would have had to depreciate by 11 per cent in 1981 with respect to the baseline, and by about seven more percentage points in the following two years. At the end of 1985 it would have reached 908 lire per DM, 33 per cent higher than its historical value. The French franc would have had to depreciate against the DM by fifteen percentage points in 1981 and 1982. It would have reached 4.65 francs at the end of 1985, about 50 per cent higher than its historical level. Only through this joint exchange-rate adjustment could the trade balance of France and Italy have been maintained at the baseline 'acceptable' level, at the expense of that of Germany and of the other ERM countries.

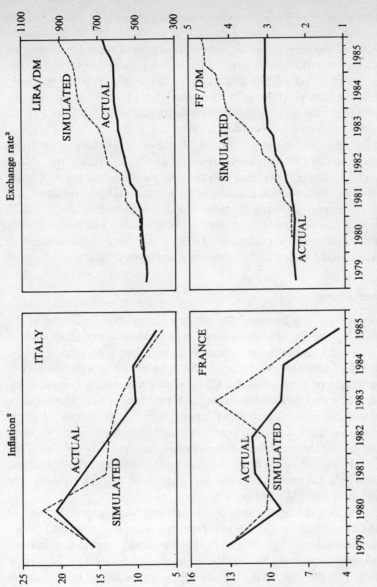

Figure 6.9 Simulation 4: Alternative exchange rate for Italy and France[1]

Notes:

1 Exchange rates *vis-à-vis* the DM which determine a change in the trade balance that compensates for the effects resulting from Simulation 1

2 Producer prices of manufactures

3 Domestic currency per DM

The size of the intra-ERM exchange-rate adjustment is due in part to the fact that it occurs simultaneously in France and Italy, thereby neutralising a sizeable part of the competitive gain of these two countries in view of the importance of bilateral trade flows. Another reason is that the inflationary effect of this alternative exchange-rate strategy partly attenuates the competitive gain produced by the depreciation. The Italian inflation rate returns close to its historical level, and the French rate actually exceeds that recorded in 1983.

On the other hand, the depreciation of the lira and the French franc with respect to the DM can be considered as an underestimate of that which would have been necessary to restore the historical level of trade balances since the exchange rates of the other ERM countries are assumed to remain unchanged, with a loss of competitiveness and a deterioration of their trade account that might not have been entirely sustainable, especially for countries like Belgium, Denmark and Ireland, which experienced balance of payments difficulties in that period.

6   Conclusions

This study is part of a broader project to examine the evolution of the EMS, focusing on the development of real economic variables such as growth rates and real exchange rates and their role with respect to the stability of the exchange-rate system. This approach is complementary to the main stream of analysis of the EMS, which has mostly been centred upon monetary and financial aspects. In a previous article,[16] we examined the effects on trade relations among member countries of intra-ERM exchange rate and aggregate demand developments and their consequences for the cohesion of the system. In this study we assess the contribution of external factors (the real appreciation of the dollar and other non-ERM currencies and the fast growth of the US economy) to the cohesion of the EMS during 1981–5.

Notwithstanding the limitations of the methodology adopted, some of the results deserve attention. Developments external to the EMS area – and in particular those regarding exchange rates and aggregate demand – have had important effects on the evolution of member countries' economies. On the one hand, the relative appreciation of currencies outside the area helped to increase the inflation rates of Germany, France and Italy. These effects have been distributed more or less uniformly across countries, so that, in general, differential effects have not been very important. On the other hand, the loss of competitiveness of countries outside the area and their faster growth of domestic demand have eased the adjustment of external imbalances of the three ERM countries considered. These gains were especially important for France and Italy, since they came in a period in which these countries were pursuing rigorous anti-inflationary policies that caused their real exchange rates to appreciate with respect to the other ERM currencies. Since no support was provided during the period by the rather sluggish growth of aggregate expenditure in the low-inflation countries of the ERM, it is doubtful whether France and Italy would have been able to follow the same exchange rate and domestic demand policies in the absence of the positive contribution to growth coming from outside the area. We thus contend that some of the celebrated disciplinary effects of the EMS were made possible by the favourable conditions prevailing outside the area. In particular, France's trade performance would have been substantially worse in view of the structural weakness of its manufacturing sector, which also emerges from the values of the parameter estimates of the trade model.

The analysis conducted in this study seems to be relevant also for the discussion of the main problems that the EMS is currently facing. The international environment has radically changed and the external factors we are considering are now working against the EMS countries owing to the persistent weakness of the dollar and the slowdown of the US economy. The reason why these developments have not yet attracted sufficient attention is that their negative influence has been compensated by the positive one deriving from the 1986 oil counter-shock. Since this is waning, the divergence in the current account performances of the ERM countries is becoming a threat to the exchange-rate stability of the ERM area. In particular, the deterioration in the current account balance of Italy and France is now coming to light, while Germany is still running a large surplus. These different performances may well become the driving force for the formation of exchange-rate expectations. In such circumstances, it would become rather difficult to manage the exchange-rate system smoothly, by reducing the size and the frequency of the realignments and taking full advantage of the reduction of inflation-rate differentials. Nonetheless, our results point to the dangers of competitive devaluations, which would have strongly adverse effects on inflation.

In view of the recent developments in the external economic variables, the results of this study reinforce the conclusions of our earlier research – i.e., that the ERM countries should now try to progress toward the harmonisation of their growth patterns. Such a strategy seems to be essential if intra-ERM exchange-rate cohesion is to be maintained as a first step towards the final goal of the EMS: the creation of an area of monetary stability in Europe.

APPENDIX: REGRESSION RESULTS

A Italy

$$\Delta X_t = 0.003 + ci_1 \Delta CX_t + ci_2 \Delta DA_t$$
$$(0.47)$$
$$+ 0.084\ D812$$
$$(2.77)$$

$R_c^2 = 0.940$; DW = 2.16
SSR = 0.026; SE = 0.028

ci_1	Lag	Coeff.	t-Stat.
	0	−0.552	−2.15
	1	−0.278	−2.14
	2	0.000	Rest
		−0.829	−2.15

ci_2			
	0	1.47	3.17
	1	0.74	3.16
	2	0.00	Rest
		2.21	3.17

B Germany

$$\Delta X_t = 0.003 + cg_1 \Delta CX_t + cg_2 \Delta DA_t$$
$$(0.80)$$
$$- 0.047\ D781 - 0.050\ D804$$
$$(-2.18)(-2.27)$$

$R_c^2 = 0.965$; DW = 1.78
SSR = 0.017; SE = 0.021

cg_1	Lag	Coeff.	t-Stat.
	2	−0.292	−1.94
	3	−0.389	−1.94
	4	−0.292	−1.94
	5	0.000	Rest
		−0.973	−1.94

cg_2			
	0	1.26	5.68
	1	0.63	5.66
	2	0.00	Rest
		1.89	5.68

C France

$$\Delta X_t = -0.003 + cf_1 \Delta CX_t + cf_2 \Delta DA_t$$
$$(-1.11)$$
$$+ 0.027\ D791$$
$$(1.65)$$

$R_c^2 = 0.971$; DW = 1.85
SSR = 0.010; SE = 0.016

cf_1	Lag	Coeff.	t-Stat.
	0	−0.229	−2.33
	1	−0.171	−2.31
	2	−0.113	−2.20
	3	−0.056	−2.03
	4	0.000	Rest
		−0.569	−2.32

cf_2			
	0	0.949	7.42
	1	0.633	7.40
	2	0.317	7.24
	3	0.000	Rest
		1.90	7.42

Table A6.1 Manufacturing Exports Towards ERM Countries

Notes:
X = Manufacturing exports towards ERM countries.
CX = Export competitiveness.
DA = Domestic demand of other ERM countries.
DX = Dummy seasonal.
DYYZ = Dummy for quarter Z of year YY.
Δ = Percentage change.

A Italy

$$\Delta X_t = 0.011 + ci_1\, \Delta CX_t + ci_2\, \Delta DA_t$$
$$(1.31)$$

$R_c^2 = 0.955$; DW = 1.80
SSR = 0.061; SE = 0.042

	Lag	Coeff.	t-Stat.
ci_1	0	-0.695	-1.75
	1	-0.347	-1.75
	2	0.000	Rest
		-1.04	-1.75
ci_2	0	1.60	2.07
	1	0.79	2.07
	2	0.00	Rest
		2.40	2.07

B Germany

$$\Delta X_t = 0.009 + cg_1\, \Delta CX_t + cg_2\, \Delta DA_t$$
$$(1.45)$$
$$-0.047\ D8423$$
$$(-2.44)$$

$R_c^2 = 0.978$; DW = 1.84
SSR = 0.027; SE = 0.027

	Lag	Coeff.	t-Stat.
cg_1	0	-0.271	-2.28
	1	-0.206	-2.36
	2	-0.138	-2.26
	3	-0.070	-1.99
	4	0.000	Rest
		-0.686	-2.14
cg_2	0	0.831	2.13
	1	0.553	2.13
	2	0.276	2.11
	3	0.000	Rest
		1.66	2.14

C France

$$\Delta X_t = 0.010 + cf_1\, \Delta CX_t + cf_2\, \Delta DA_t$$
$$(1.63)$$
$$-0.083\ D842$$
$$(-2.68)$$

$R_c^2 = 0.973$; DW = 1.76
SSR = 0.034; SE = 0.030

	Lag	Coeff.	t-Stat.
cf_1	0	-0.378	-1.91
	1	-0.190	-1.91
	2	-0.000	Rest
		-0.568	-1.91
cf_2	0	1.14	2.23
	1	0.57	2.23
	2	0.00	Rest
		1.71	2.23

Table A6.2 Manufacturing Exports Towards Non-ERM OECD Countries

Notes:
X = Manufacturing exports towards non-ERM OECD countries.
CX = Export competitiveness.
DA = Domestic demand of other non-ERM countries.
DX = Dummy seasonal.
$DYYZ$ = Dummy for quarter Z of year YY.
Δ = Percentage change.
R^2 refers to the level of the dependent variable.

A Italy

$$\Delta M_t = -0.005 + ci_1 \, \Delta CM_t + ci_2 \, \Delta DI_t$$
$$ (-1.05)$$
$$-0.096 \, D761 + 0.075 \, D774$$
$$ (-2.45) \qquad\;\; (1.85)$$

$$u_t = -0.49 \, u_{t-1}$$
$$ (-3.71)$$

$R_c^2 = 0.941$; DW = 1.96
SSR = 0.066; SE = 0.041

	Lag	Coeff.	t-Stat.
ci_1	0	0.657	2.70
	1	0.327	2.70
	2	0.000	Rest
		0.984	2.70
ci_2	0	1.14	5.80
	1	0.72	5.80
	2	0.00	Rest
		2.16	5.80

B Germany

$$\Delta M_t = 0.001 + 0.890 \, \Delta CM_t + cg_1 \, \Delta DI_t$$
$$ (0.42) \quad\; (2.11)$$
$$-0.031 \, D771$$
$$(-1.91)$$

$R_c^2 = 0.948$; DW = 2.34
SSR = 0.009; SE = 0.016

	Lag	Coeff.	t-Stat.
cg_1	0	0.822	5.20
	1	0.548	5.19
	2	0.273	5.11
	3	0.000	Rest
		1.64	5.11

C France

$$\Delta M_t = -0.007 + cf_1 \, \Delta CM_t + cf_2 \, \Delta DI_t$$
$$ (-1.64)$$
$$+0.032 \, D841$$
$$ (1.75)$$

$R_c^2 = 0.965$; DW = 1.93
SSR = 0.012; SE = 0.018

	Lag	Coeff.	t-Stat.
cf_1	1	0.114	1.79
	2	0.171	1.81
	3	0.170	1.80
	4	0.113	1.77
	5	0.000	Rest
		0.568	1.81
cf_2	0	1.37	5.87
	1	0.912	5.86
	3	0.455	5.80
	4	0.000	Rest
		2.74	5.87

Table A6.3   Manufacturing Imports From ERM Countries

Notes:

M = Manufacturing imports from ERM countries.
CM = Import competitiveness.
DI = Domestic demand.
DX = Dummy seasonal.
$DYYZ$ = Dummy for quarter Z of year YY.
Δ = Percentage change.
R^2 refers to the level of the dependent variable

A Italy

$$\Delta M_t = 0.001 + 1.23 \, \Delta CM_t + ci_1 \Delta DI_t$$
$$ (1.71) \quad (2.32)$$
$$+ 0.083 \; D774 + 0.081 \; D793$$
$$ (1.85) \quad\quad (1.90)$$

$$u_t = -0.590 \, u_{t-1}$$
$$ (-4.40)$$

$R_c^2 = 0.940$; DW = 1.87
SSR = 0.071; SE = 0.047

	Lag	Coeff.	t-Stat.
ci_1	0	1.54	3.77
	1	0.77	3.77
	2	0.000	Rest
		2.31	3.78

B Germany

$$\Delta M_t = 0.006 + 1.23 \, \Delta CM_{t-3} + cg_1 \Delta DI_t$$
$$ (1.86) \quad (2.52)$$
$$- 0.070 \; D7823 + 0.055 \; D784$$
$$ (-5.48) \quad\quad (2.88)$$
$$- 0.45 \; D804$$
$$ (-2.44)$$

$R_c^2 = 0.971$; DW = 2.04
SSR = 0.009; SE = 0.018

	Lag	Coeff.	t-Stat.
cg_1	0	1.26	5.33
	1	0.63	5.32
	2	0.00	Rest
		1.89	5.33

C France

$$\Delta M_t = 0.132 + cf_1 \Delta CM_t + cf_2 \Delta DI_t$$
$$ (19.22)$$
$$- 0.126 \; D1 - 0.113 \; D2 - 0.277 \; D3$$
$$ (-13.59) \quad (-12.09) \quad (-29.62)$$
$$+ 0.053 \; D801 - 0.048 \; D823$$
$$ (2.61) \quad\quad (-2.35)$$

$R_c^2 = 0.979$; DW = 2.64
SSR = 0.010; SE = 0.019

	Lag	Coeff.	t-Stat.
cf_1	2	0.283	2.84
	3	0.378	2.85
	4	0.284	2.84
	5	0.000	Rest
		0.946	2.85
cf_2	0	1.82	5.84
	1	0.91	5.84
	2	0.00	Rest
		2.73	5.84

Table A6.4 Manufacturing Imports From Non-ERM OECD Countries

Notes:

M = Manufacturing imports from non-ERM OECD countries.

CM = Import competitiveness.

DI = Domestic demand.

DX = Dummy seasonal.

$DYYZ$ = Dummy for quarter Z of year YY.

Δ = Percentage change.

R^2 refers to the level of the dependent variable.

A Italy

$$\Delta PX_t = 0.000 + ci_1 \Delta PI_t + ci_2 \Delta PAX_t$$
$$(0.16)$$
$$-0.23\ \text{D761}$$
$$(-1.72)$$

$R_c^2 = 0.999$; DW = 2.30
SSR = 0.006; SE = 0.013

	Lag	Coeff.	t-Stat.
ci_1	0	0.390	4.14
	1	0.195	4.13
	2	0.000	Rest
		0.585	4.15
ci_2	0	0.278	2.95
	1	0.138	2.92
	2	0.000	Rest
		0.415	2.95

B Germany

$$\Delta PX_t = 0.000 + cg_1 \Delta PI_t + cg_2 \Delta PAX_t$$
$$(-0.09)$$

$R_c^2 = 0.995$; DW = 2.07
SSR = 0.003; SE = 0.009

	Lag	Coeff.	t-Stat.
cg_1	0	0.417	4.54
	1	0.209	4.53
	2	0.000	Rest
		0.626	4.54
cg_2	0	0.249	2.71
	1	0.125	2.71
	2	0.000	Rest
		0.374	2.71

C France

$$\Delta PX_t = 0.003 + cf_1 \Delta PI_t + cf_2 \Delta PAX_t$$
$$(1.72)$$
$$-0.029\ \text{D814}$$
$$(-2.53)$$

$R_c^2 = 0.998$; DW = 2.22
SSR = 0.004; SE = 0.011

	Lag	Coeff.	t-Stat.
cf_1	0	0.405	4.62
	1	0.203	4.62
	2	0.000	Rest
		0.673	4.63
cf_2	0	0.261	2.98
	1	0.131	2.99
	2	0.000	Rest
		0.392	2.99

Table A6.5 Unit Values of Exports of Manufacturing Products Towards ERM Countries

Notes:

PX = Unit values of export to ERM countries.
PI = Wholesale prices of manufacturing products.
PAX = Price of competitors.
DX = Dummy seasonal.
DYYZ = Dummy for quarter Z of year YY.
Δ = Percentage change.

A Italy

$$\Delta PX_t = 0.002 + ci_1 \Delta PI_t + ci_2 \Delta PAX_t$$
$$(0.85)$$

$R_c^2 = 0.999$; DW = 2.17
SSR = 0.004; SE = 0.011

	Lag	Coeff.	t-Stat.
ci_1	0	0.383	5.45
	1	0.191	5.42
	2	0.000	Rest
		0.574	5.45
ci_2	0	0.284	4.05
	1	0.142	4.01
	2	0.000	Rest
		0.426	4.05

B Germany

$$\Delta PX_t = 0.000 + cg_1 \Delta PI_t + cg_2 \Delta PAX_t$$
$$(-0.316)$$
$$+ 0.021\ D774 - 0.021\ D792$$
$$(2.49) \qquad (-2.37)$$

$R_c^2 = 0.995$; DW = 1.87
SSR = 0.0025; SE = 0.008

	Lag	Coeff.	t-Stat.
cg_1	0	0.582	13.31
	1	0.290	13.31
	2	0.000	Rest
		0.872	13.31
cg_2	0	0.085	1.95
	1	0.042	1.93
	2	0.000	Rest
		0.127	1.95

C France

$$\Delta PX_t = 0.004 + cf_1 \Delta PI_t + cf_2 \Delta PAX_t$$
$$(1.84)$$
$$- 0.028\ D814$$
$$(-2.34)$$

$R_c^2 = 0.999$; DW = 2.25
SSR = 0.0044; SE = 0.012

	Lag	Coeff.	t-Stat.
cf_1	0	0.462	7.95
	1	0.231	7.91
	2	0.000	Rest
		0.692	7.98
cf_2	0	0.205	3.54
	1	0.103	3.51
	2	0.000	Rest
		0.308	3.55

Table A6.6 Unit Values of Exports of Manufacturing Products Towards Non-ERM OECD Countries

Notes:
PX = Unit values of export to non-ERM OECD countries.
PI = Wholesale prices of manufacturing products.
PAX = Price of competitors.
DX = Dummy seasonal.
$DYYZ$ = Dummy for quarter Z of year YY.
Δ = Percentage change.
R^2 refers to the level of the dependent variable.

A Italy

$$\Delta PI_t = -0.003 + ci_1 \Delta MAT_t + ci_2 \Delta MP_t$$
$$(-1.76)$$
$$+ ci_3 \Delta CL_t + 0.303 \Delta GAP_t$$
$$(2.65)$$
$$+ 0.020\, D771 - 0.025\, D781$$
$$(2.24) \qquad (-2.76)$$

$R_c^2 = 0.999$; DW = 1.60
SSR = 0.0025; SE = 0.0086

ci_1	Lag	Coeff.	t-Stat.
	0	0.088	3.34
	1	0.058	3.33
	2	0.029	2.99
	3	0.000	Rest
		0.176	3.40

ci_2	Lag	Coeff.	t-Stat.
	0	0.331	5.93
	1	0.166	5.90
	2	0.000	Rest
		0.497	5.93

B Germany

$$\Delta PI_t = -0.002 + cg_1 \Delta MAT_t + cg_2 \Delta MP_t$$
$$(-3.65)$$
$$+ cg_3 \Delta CL_t + 0.133 \Delta GAP_t$$
$$(2.73)$$
$$+ 0.009\, D791 + 0.009\, D854$$
$$(2.53) \qquad (2.64)$$

$R_c^2 = 0.999$; DW = 2.15
SSR = 0.0002; SE = 0.0031

cg_1	Lag	Coeff.	t-Stat.
	0	0.038	4.53
	1	0.019	4.26
	2	0.000	Rest
		0.056	4.50

cg_2	Lag	Coeff.	t-Stat.
	0	0.300	8.44
	1	0.200	8.45
	2	0.100	8.38
	3	0.000	Rest
		0.600	8.46

C France

$$\Delta PI_t = -0.004 + 0.076 \Delta MAT_t + cf_1 \Delta MP_t$$
$$(-0.61) \quad (1.87)$$
$$+ cf_2 \Delta CL_t + 0.278 \Delta GAP_t$$
$$(1.36)$$
$$- 0.018\, D8234 + 0.021\, D831$$
$$(-2.62) \qquad (1.73)$$

$$u_t = 0.69\, u_{t-1}$$

$R_c^2 = 0.998$; DW = 2.01
SSR = 0.0065; SE = 0.013

cf_1	Lag	Coeff.	t-Stat.
	0	0.229	3.61
	1	0.170	3.64
	2	0.112	3.44
	3	0.055	3.01
	4	0.000	Rest
		0.565	3.64

cf_2	Lag	Coeff.	t-Stat.
	0	0.239	2.56
	1	0.119	2.54
	2	0.000	Rest
		0.358	2.56

ci_3		
3	0.164	6.23
4	0.109	6.22
5	0.055	5.49
6	0.000	Rest
	0.327	6.33

cg_3		
3	0.049	5.20
4	0.078	5.35
5	0.088	5.39
6	0.078	5.33
7	0.049	5.17
8	0.000	Rest
	0.343	5.40

Table A6.7 Manufacturing Producer Prices

Notes:

PI = Wholesale prices of manufacturing products.

MAT = Primary products import prices, expressed in domestic currency.

MP = Unit values of import of manufacturing products.

GAP = Deviation of domestic demand from trend.

CL = Unit labour cost.

DX = Dummy seasonal.

$DYYZ$ = Dummy for quarter Z of year YY.

Δ = Percentage change.

R^2 refers to the level of the dependent variable.

NOTES
* We wish to thank for useful comments the participants to the EMS conference held in Perugia and to the seminar on Application of Quantitative Methods to Trade Analysis held at Bocconi University, and in particular, G. Basevi, D. Begg, W. Branson, S. Micossi and F. Onida. D. Porciani provided valuable research assistance, and L. Dell'Armi and E. Genito edited the text and prepared the Tables and Figures. We also thank J. Smith for kindly reviewing the English version of the study. We are, of course, solely responsible for the opinions expressed in the study and for any remaining error.

1 See Giavazzi and Giovannini (1987).

2 Exceptions are Masera (1981), Melitz (1986).

3 Putting aside, for the moment, the initial phase of the EMS (1979–81), which can be considered as a running-in period affected by oil shock and characterised by large inflation differentials, intra-ERM real exchange rates in the 1982–6 period showed remarkable stability, which contrasted sharply with what occurred outside the area.

4 This phenomenon is considered with increasing attention by economists: 'From 1983 to the first half of 1987, DM 55 billion – or 80 per cent – of the rise in Germany's overall trade surplus was *vis-à-vis* other West European countries. In part this is why, despite the emergence of a massive US current account deficit, the current account positions of most other European countries, including France, Italy, and the United Kingdom, are now close to balance or in deficit' (Institute for International Economics, 1987).

5 On this issue see Krugman (1986) and Dornbusch (1987).

6 See note 12 below on the appropriateness of this assumption.

7 We have used the first variable because expenditure on manufactured goods (in real terms) was not available for the three countries, and because total expenditure has some advantages from the point of view of policy simulations.

8 Owing to the lack of complete data for Ireland (among the ERM countries) and Turkey (among the other OECD countries), these two were not considered in the econometric analysis.

9 We calculated quarterly data from the annual ones of the Volimex data bank by using the best available quarterly indicators for each country. The estimation period was generally from 1976 to 1985. The model was estimated, equation by equation, using OLS.

10 We have used the price indexes published by the OECD, Main Economic Indicators, tables on producer prices of manufactures. However, in the case of France the price index refers to a basket of products based especially on intermediate products, whose price tends to be highly volatile.

11 The import penetration rate, for the manufacturing sector, calculated by the INSEE in constant prices, increased from 23 per cent in 1978 to 30 per cent in 1985.

12 In a previous work on intra-ERM trade (Bini Smaghi and Vona, 1988) we estimated preliminary import price equations that allowed the elasticity of the import prices of the three countries considered to be calculated with respect to their exchange-rate changes. Applying the formula derived by Branson (1972), this elasticity can be related to the export supply and demand elasticities:

$$\epsilon_{p_m,\,e} = \frac{1}{1 - \epsilon_{d,x}/\epsilon_{s,x}}$$

Since the estimated values of ϵ_p, ϵ_m were quite near to one for the three countries, and the estimated values of $\epsilon_{d,x}$ in the range of 2–2.5, we interpreted these results as suggesting that supply elasticities of intra-ERM exports are infinite. This confirms the appropriateness of the hypothesis on supply elasticities adopted in the model.

13 The differential impact is, of course, due to the different level of exports to the non-ERM area. Germany has the largest effect since its exports to the non-ERM area are much larger than those of the other two countries.

14 As regards Italy, these findings are consistent with those obtained by simulating the new macro-model of the Banca d'Italia (see Gressani, Guiso and Visco, 1987).

15 Changes of the dollar exchange rate may also affect trade balances of primary commodities (including oil), since the dollar prices of these commodities react to dollar movements and domestic consumers also react to changes in prices (in national currencies). In the case of a depreciation of the dollar, as in the simulation considered, both of these effects tend to reinforce the deterioration of the global trade balance. An evaluation of these effects is made difficult by the lack of a full set of consistent estimates of the values of the relevant elasticities for the three countries considered.

16 See Bini Smaghi and Vona (1988).

REFERENCES

Bini Smaghi, L. and S. Vona (1988). 'The Effects of Economic Convergence and Competitiveness on Trade among EMS Countries', in D. Hodgman and G. Woods (eds), *Macroeconomic Policy and Economic Interdependence*, London, Macmillan.

Branson, W. (1972). 'The Trade Effects of the 1971 Currency Realignments', Brookings Papers on Economic Activity, No. 1, pp. 15–69.

Deppler, M. and D. Ripley (1978). 'The World Trade Model: Merchandise Trade', IMF Staff Papers, Vol. 25 (March), pp. 147–206.

Dornbusch, R. (1987). 'Exchange Rates and Prices', *American Economic Review*, Vol. 77, pp. 93–106.

Giavazzi, F. and A. Giovannini (1987). 'Exchange Rates and Prices in Europe' (mimeo).

Goldstein, M. and M. Kahn (1985). 'Income and Price Effects in Foreign Trade', in R. W. Jones and P. B. Kenen (eds), *Handbook of International Economics*, Amsterdam, North-Holland.

Gressani, D., L. Guiso and I. Visco (1987). '*Il rientro dall'inflazione: un'analisi con il modello econometrico della Banca d'Italia*', *Temi di Discussione* del Servizio Studi della Banca d'Italia, No. 90.

Institute for International Economics (1987). 'Resolving the Global Economic Crisis: After Wall Street', Washington DC (December).

Krugman, P. (1986). 'Pricing to Markets when the Exchange Rate Changes', NBER Working Paper, No. 1926.

Masera, R. (1981). 'The First Two Years of the EMS: The Exchange Rate Experience', Banca Nazionale del Lavoro, *Quarterly Review*, pp. 271–95.

Melitz, J. (1986). 'The Prospect of a Depreciating Dollar and Possible Tensions inside the EMS', CEPR Discussion Paper, No. 97.

Spencer, G. (1984). 'The World Trade Model: Revised Estimates', IMF Staff Papers, Vol. 31, pp. 469–98.

Stevens, G. *et al.* (1984). 'The US Economy in an Interdependent World', Washington, DC, Board of Governors of the Federal Reserve System.

Discussion

DAVID BEGG

The European Monetary System (EMS) is widely held to have played an important role in providing the credibility and discipline which the high-inflation countries required to undertake a successful programme of disinflation. Yet if this seems all too obvious when viewed from the perspective of the late 1980s, it should also be remembered that when the EMS was first established many economists were sceptical that it would survive, let alone succeed.

Vona and Bini Smaghi set out to explain why the EMS has had such an easy ride, and to evaluate whether trouble is just around the corner. They focus on behaviour outside the three largest members of the Exchange-Rate Mechanism (ERM) and examine its impact on trade patterns and inflation rates within Germany, France and Italy. Specifically, they are interested in differential impacts on these three countries which might give rise to tensions within the EMS.

In essence, their argument is as follows. During the first half of the 1980s, ERM countries faced a significant joint exchange-rate depreciation which added to their overall inflation rate but had little differential impact on different member countries; domestic austerity was able to cope with the overall inflation problem and external exchange-rate developments posed no special problems for nominal relativities of ERM members. Together, the additional competitiveness of the ERM countries and strong demand in non-ERM countries (notably the United States) significantly alleviated concerns of ERM members about their trade balances, greatly facilitating the disinflation process. However, the late 1980s have produced a dramatic turnaround: foreign growth has slowed down and ERM members have experienced a strong exchange-rate appreciation. These adverse effects, masked initially by a favourable fall in oil prices, will cause severe trade deficits, most notably in France. The differential impact will create strong tensions within the ERM which might be resolved by large realignments but are better handled by coordination of domestic demand policies. Effectively this would require a sizeable fiscal expansion in Germany.

I should say immediately that I think the authors have focused on a crucial policy issue, and I am in sympathy with their diagnosis of the problem and their recommendation for its solution. In short this is an important study. Like all such studies, it raises as many questions as it answers, and my comments are as much a plea for more research as a detailed critique of the particular methods employed by the authors.

One aspect in which the argument can be strengthened is by closer reference to the blossoming literature on policy coordination, a second relates to a fuller general equilibrium treatment, and a third to the Lucas critique. These three aspects are not independent.

The early literature on policy coordination sought on the one hand to quantify the extent of spillovers across countries which would give rise to externalities which non-cooperative policymaking would fail to take into account. It then sought to model policymaking within this framework. In terms of positive economics, the authors tend to collapse these two into one. The econometric model which they build to quantify the interdependence is partial equilibrium in the sense that key variables (notably the exchange rate, unit labour costs, and aggregate demand) are treated as exogenous. Similarly, the behavioural equations which are estimated assume that behaviour is independent on the policy regime in force. Future work should explore these issues more fully; I shall return to this point below.

The analysis concentrates exclusively on manufacturing trade. In part this is because the authors have a data series for manufacturing in fine detail, and they are keen to make use of it. Manufacturing trade is the most important single item of the current account of ERM countries, but it would have been nice to see this set in context. This point seems especially important to a UK discussant: in the UK, trade in services and primary commodities is far too important to be ignored.

Even if attention is confined to manufacturing, it is surely each country's overall multilateral trade balance which is of interest. The authors seem unwilling to grasp this nettle completely. On occasion they concede the point but elsewhere they come dangerously close to arguing that it is bilateral trade imbalances which give rise to potential tensions. To argue that, because (say) France and Germany are committed to a bilateral exchange rate they must consequently care *per se* about their bilateral trade position is surely fallacious.

Let me next discuss the econometric model on which the subsequent analysis is based. The model is one of imperfect competition, in which volumes of trade flows depend on a demand or income term and a relative price or competitiveness term; in which traded goods prices reflect domestic producer prices and competitors' prices; and in which domestic prices are a mark-up on domestic costs. I have a problem with the measure of competitiveness which utilises the data series on export prices. It is implicit in the economic logic that greater competition will force firms to trim prices and profit margins in the traded goods sector. This being so, competitiveness requires not merely a measure of relative export prices in a common currency but also a measure of profitability. This latter measure should be in the volume equations, but is not. Pricing to market is at the heart of the Dornbusch (1987) study to which the authors refer, but their analysis does not capture its full implications.

I turn now to the econometric methodology. First, the authors contend that prices and volumes are set independently, whence OLS estimation of volume equations can treat competitiveness as an exogenous right-hand side variable. This seems dubious to me. A full general equilibrium model would recognise that prices and quantities are simultaneously chosen by imperfect competitors, and that both will be affected by exchange-rate movements which are endogenous in the real world but viewed as exogenous within the partial equilibrium model. Second, I remain unhappy about the specification of all equations in first difference form, which rules out any levels effect necessary to determine a long-run or steady-state relationship. The first difference formulation may be a convenient starting point, partialling out all the relevant variables not explicitly addressed within the stripped down model; but if this is the interpretation it alerts us to the need to get some of these effects back into the story again.

A related point refers not to the estimation but to the subsequent interpretation. Exchange rates and unit labour costs are viewed as exogenous in the analysis. The authors then proceed to conduct simulations which exogenously change exchange rates, foreign demand, and so on. Since their equations have dynamics, they refer to 'equilibrium' solutions after these dynamics have worked their way through. In such a time horizon, it is surely unrealistic to maintain that unit labour costs (in nominal terms) will remain unaltered. On one occasion the authors recognise this, and properly describe their work as measuring 'impact effects' or effects on the assumption that induced changes in policy succeed in knocking out changes in wages and incomes which would otherwise have taken place. But this important caveat tends to be ignored later in the study, where the authors' conclusions read as if their results have robustly established that particular economies would get into trouble under particular scenarios. This observation also explains why changes in nominal exchange rates have permanent and powerful effects in the authors' analysis.

Greater emphasis on endogenising variables currently assumed to be exogenous to the analysis would also sidestep a second potential problem. When it comes to simulations, the authors exogenously alter exchange rates in one simulation and demand in the United States in a second. Moreover, these are presented very much as feasible counterfactuals for the early 1980s. However, it is surely more reasonable to argue that both the dollar appreciation and the American boom can be attributed to US fiscal policy. It is unclear what exogenous changes in the policy fundamentals might have produced the alternative path for particular endogenous variables which form the basis for separate simulations.

Let me turn finally to the authors' results. The story is basically that a deterioration in ERM competitiveness would cause France the gravest problem with its trade deficit; that a US recession hits all the ERM countries' trade balances; and that the two together will make the French position untenable on current policies. What is appealing about the authors' model is that it can trace through the consequences of such shocks for trade volumes, pricing behaviour, and hence for the trade balance. But it would be helpful to see such a decomposition spelled out more fully. In particular, we are told repeatedly that a joint appreciation by ERM countries hits the French trade position harder than that of Germany or Italy. Yet inspection of Table 6.2 indicates that French trade volumes are less elastic with respect to competitiveness than are those of Germany or Italy. From what I remember of the Marshall–Lerner literature this direct effect should tend to favour France; an appreciation should cause it fewer trade balance problems than its ERM partners. So the answer comes either from other asymmetries in pricing behaviour or in induced income effects. Spelling all this out would be enlightening.

The authors conclude by arguing that a collective demand expansion within the ERM will be the best way to cope with external conditions which are turning sour. Although earlier I have downplayed the significance of bilateral trade positions, if attention to these helped bring pressure for greater coordination of demand policies within the ERM – which given the targeting of monetary policy on exchange-rate considerations basically means greater fiscal coordination – I would be strongly in favour of such 'coordination by the back door'.

REFERENCE

Dornbusch, R. (1987). 'Exchange Rates and Prices', *American Economic Review*, Vol. 77, pp. 93–106.

III   Exchange Rates, Capital Mobility and Monetary Coordination

7 Exchange Rates, Interest Rates, Capital Controls and the European Monetary System: Assessing the Track Record*

MICHAEL J. ARTIS and
MARK P. TAYLOR

1 Introduction

The formal objective of the Exchange-Rate Mechanism (ERM) of the European Monetary System (EMS) is the stabilisation, within generally narrow pre-agreed bounds, of member countries' nominal exchange rates. Since the EMS is an exchange-rate mechanism of a customs union, however, it must be expected (if it is to survive in the long run) to ensure that member countries' competitiveness is protected; otherwise, the protection-reducing achievements of the customs union must be called into question as countries seek to restore their terms of trade. This is to suggest that, at the same time as the immediate and formal objective of the system is to stabilise *nominal* rates of exchange, its inner long-run rationale involves a requirement on *real* rates of exchange. This fundamental ambiguity accounts for what Goodhart (1986) has termed an 'unholy alliance' among those advocating British participation in the ERM – between those who seek to consolidate the counter-inflation gains of recent years and those who wish to protect the competitiveness of sterling from any repetition of the devastating overappreciation of the 1980–1 period. The two objectives are clearly not compatible without a convergence of inflation, at equilibrium levels of activity and external balance, between the member countries. In the period of the system's functioning so far, progress towards this objective has been provided in the historical context of the second OPEC oil shock, which induced among countries generally – and members of the EMS in particular – a strong desire to reduce inflation. Given Germany's low inflation rate and (recent) historical reputation for counter-inflationary policy, this has implied to a degree convergence on the German standard.

Given the number of realignments which have taken place within the

185

ERM of the EMS since its inception in 1979, and the fact that variations are permitted within the parity grid margins, it remains in principle questionable whether the provisions of the system have actually induced a greater degree of stability in either the real or the nominal exchange rate. One aim of this study is to present the results of a number of statistically rigorous tests for shifts in volatility and predictability of participating countries' exchange rates since March 1979, using data on a wide range of real and nominal, bilateral and effective exchange rates.

In the second place, however, we also examine the question of whether any reductions in exchange-rate volatility that may have occurred as a result of the operation of the ERM have been bought at the expense of increased interest-rate volatility. Finally, we examine the issue concerning the importance of capital controls in maintaining the ERM. This is clearly an important issue, given the prospect of liberalisation of capital controls in France and Italy and the possibility of full participation in the ERM by the UK, with its liberal payments regime.

The likelihood of the ERM achieving even its formal and immediate objective of stabilisation of nominal exchange rates was initially greeted with scepticism from a number of quarters. Moreover, starting from a position of high and divergent rates of inflation amongst member countries, the prospect of achieving this seemed difficult to imagine without imposing intolerable losses of competitiveness on at least some members. Yet the sceptics have largely been confounded by an unforeseen display of flexibility which has ensured the system's survival. This in turn has required that full advantage be taken of the provisions for flexibility contained in the system. We now turn to a brief account of what these are.

Provisions of the EMS

The provisions of the ERM of the EMS provide for participating countries to maintain their exchange rates within bilateral limits of $\pm 2\frac{1}{4}$ per cent. Exceptionally, Italy negotiated a wider margin of ± 6 per cent at the outset of the system. In addition to the provisions for a margin of fluctuation, realignments are permitted: and in all eleven such realignments have been undertaken to date. Their timing and amounts are shown in Table 7.1.

The system is formally organised around a composite currency, the ECU, with central rates for participating currencies being expressed in terms of it. Whilst this is purely formal, the ECU gave the opportunity for the introduction of an interesting technical innovation of the EMS, the divergence indicator and threshold positions. According to these

	Dates of realignments										
	24/9 1979	30/11 1979	22/3 1981	5/10 1981	22/2 1982	14/6 1982	21/3 1983	21/7 1985	7/4 1986	4/8 1986	12/1 1987
Belgian franc	0.0	0.0	0.0	0.0	−8.5	0.0	+1.5	+2.0	+1.0	0.0	+2.0
Danish kroner	−2.9	−4.8	0.0	0.0	−3.0	0.0	+2.5	+2.0	+1.0	0.0	0.0
German mark	+2.0	0.0	0.0	+5.5	0.0	+4.25	+5.5	+2.0	+3.0	0.0	+3.0
French franc	0.0	0.0	0.0	−3.0	0.0	−5.75	−2.5	+2.0	−3.0	0.0	0.0
Irish punt	0.0	0.0	0.0	0.0	0.0	0.0	−3.5	+2.0	0.0	−8.0	0.0
Italian lira	0.0	0.0	−6.0	−3.0	0.0	−2.75	−2.5	−6.0	0.0	0.0	0.0
Dutch guilder	0.0	0.0	0.0	+5.5	0.0	+4.25	+3.5	+2.0	+3.0	0.0	+3.0

Table 7.1 Changes in EMS Central Rates

provisions, when a currency triggered its divergence indicator threshold (calculated as the ECU value of a 75 per cent departure of its bilateral rates against all the other countries), a presumption was created that the country concerned should take corrective action. This technical provision was designed both to provide an early warning of bilateral limit infringements – and, more important, to isolate an errant currency, the one standing out against all the others. There was little doubt that in the minds of those who constructed these provisions the errant currency was going to be the strong DM.[1] It is one of the curiosities of the history of the system that in fact the DM has not often been at the upper end of its permitted range – and, more important, that the inflation-policy priority has been so strong that in practice it was not desired to single out the DM as an 'errant' currency (see Padoa-Schioppa, 1983). Some observers do believe, though, that the divergence indicator provisions have assisted convergence and stabilisation because a country does not like to attract the presumption of action which follows the public triggering of a threshold: it would prefer to undertake action on its own initiative and at its own discretion (see Melitz, 1985).

In addition to the formal provisions of the ERM it is important to note that the introduction of the system did not require the abolition of exchange controls, and significant controls over capital movements were retained, notably by France and Italy. These controls may have been helpful in fostering system stability, both by giving the authorities of the country concerned the whip-hand in negotiating realignments and by avoiding the immediate convergence of monetary policy which freedom from control, coupled with the obligation to defend central bilateral parities, would have implied.[2]

3   Exchange-rate volatility and the EMS

In this section, we present some new evidence on the effect of the ERM on exchange-rate volatility by an examination of a number of nominal and real, bilateral and effective exchange-rate changes.

a.   Previous volatility studies

There have been eleven realignments of the currencies participating in the EMS; this, together with the fact that quite wide variations are allowed by the parity grid margins, leaves it an open question in principle whether the provisions of the system actually do induce a greater degree of stability in either the nominal or the real exchange rate.

The difference, stressed by John Williamson (1985), between the concepts of exchange-rate *volatility* and *misalignment*, is important here. Volatility is a 'high-frequency' concept referring to movements in the exchange rate over comparatively short periods of time. Misalignment, on the other hand, refers to the capacity for an exchange rate to depart from its fundamental equilibrium value over a protracted period of time. It is known, without reference to statistical detail, that the two major currencies which have exhibited most marked misalignments in recent history are the US dollar and the pound sterling. No EMS currency has exhibited medium-term misalignment on a comparable scale. For the reasons given by Williamson it seems fair to argue that the greater welfare significance attaches to the diminution of misalignment than to the reduction of volatility where there is (perhaps surprisingly) little evidence to support the view that volatility is welfare-reducing. To be more precise, what has been tested is whether exchange-rate volatility appears to be trade-reducing. While a study by Akhtar and Hilton (1984) found that it was so for US–German trade, comparable studies by the Bank of England (1984) and the International Monetary Fund (1983) failed to confirm this finding for alternative trade flows, time period and volatility measures. Recent work by Cushman (1986) has, however, discovered evidence of volatility effects on trade when 'third-country' effects are controlled for (e.g., dollar–mark volatility may affect US–UK trade).

Nevertheless, a number of studies have concentrated on the evidence that the EMS has reduced exchange-rate volatility, most notably those by Ungerer *et al.* (1983), the European Commission (1982), Padoa-Schioppa (1983), Rogoff (1985) and, most recently, Ungerer *et al.* (1987). There are a large number of possible variations in the statistical approach to this question – the choice of exchange rates (bilateral, effective, nominal, real); data frequency (daily, weekly, monthly, quarterly); the standard against which stability is to be judged (the level or change in exchange rates, conditional or unconditional); the precise statistical measure chosen (standard deviation, etc.). Then there is the question of the counterfactual – supplied in these studies and others like them by the behaviour in the pre- and post-EMS period of a control group of non-EMS currencies. Without exception, however, the EMS in these studies has been judged as having contributed to improving the stability of intra-EMS bilateral exchange rates; the improvement is less marked for effective rates, and it has been argued in qualification that (with the lengthier data period over which it is now possible to run these tests) it is possible to show, in certain cases, that the earlier claims to stability of the EMS have weakened with the passage of time (see House of Commons Select Committee, 1985, p. xiii).

b.   Some new exchange-rate volatility tests

All of the studies cited above – which have tested for a downward shift in exchange-rate volatility for members of the EMS post-March 1979 – have generally relied on purely descriptive statistics. As such, they can be at most suggestive, and it is perhaps difficult to assess scientifically the performance of the EMS in this respect in the light of this evidence. The most straightforward approach to the problem – namely, estimating a specific parameterisation of the volatility and testing for a structural shift after March 1979 – is fraught with pitfalls. This is because economists are far from certain concerning the correct statistical distribution of exchange-rate changes. It is by now a stylised fact that percentage exchange-rate changes tend to follow leptokurtic (fat-tailed, highly-peaked) distributions. Westerfield (1977), for example, finds that the stable Paretian distribution with characteristic exponent less than two provides a superior fit to the change in the logarithm of spot exchange rates than the normal distribution. In a similar vein, Rogalski and Vinso (1977) suggest Student's *t*-distribution as a good approximation. It may well be that the distribution of exchange-rate changes is normal, but that the variance shifts through time – perhaps according to the amount of 'news'; this would give the appearance of a stable, leptokurtic distribution. Some evidence for such behaviour is provided by Boothe and Glassman (1987), who find that mixtures of normal distributions provide some of the best fits to their data. The possibility of a heteroscedastic conditional variance is pursued in Sub-section 3d below.

We wish to stress the importance of attempting to capture the correct distributional properties of exchange-rate changes in any volatility study. By relying on simple variance measures, the studies cited above are implicitly invoking a normality assumption, the legitimacy of which a growing number of studies are, at the very least, bringing into question (see Boothe and Glassman, 1987 for additional citations). For example, it might conceivably be the case that exchange-rate changes at a certain frequency have a Cauchy distribution, for which no finite moments of any order exist.

In order to try and circumvent some of these problems, we decided to apply non-parametric tests for volatility shifts which do not require actual estimation of the distributional parameters. Instead, exchange-rate changes are ranked in order of size and inferences are drawn with respect to the shape of the ranking. Intuitively, if a significant number of lower-ranked percentage changes were recorded in the latter half of the sample, a reduction in volatility would be indicated. The exact procedure is as follows. Let Δe_t be the change in the (logarithm of the) exchange rate at time t, then the maintained hypothesis is:

$$\Delta e_t = \mu + \sigma_t \epsilon_t \tag{7.1}$$

$$\sigma_t = \exp\{\alpha + \beta z_t\}$$

where μ, α and β are unknown, constant scalars, ϵ_t is independently and identically distributed with distribution function F and density function f, and z_t is a binary variable reflecting the hypothesised change in volatility.

In other words:

$$z_t = \begin{cases} 1, & t \leq \text{March 1979} \\ 0, & \text{otherwise} \end{cases}$$

Given (7.1), the null hypothesis of no shift in volatility is then:

$$H_0: \beta = 0 \tag{7.2}$$

Hajèk and Sidak (1967) (henceforth HS) develop a number of non-parametric rank tests for dealing with problems involving this kind of framework, which, under appropriate regularity conditions, are locally most powerful (HS, pp. 70–1). The test statistics take the form:

$$\zeta = \sum_{t=1}^{T} (z_t - \bar{z}) \, \alpha(u_t) \tag{7.3}$$

where $\bar{z}$ is the arithmetic mean of the z_t sequence of T observations

$$\bar{z} = T^{-1} \sum_{t=1}^{T} z_t$$

and u_t is defined as follows. Let $r(\Delta e_i)$ be the rank of Δe_i – i.e., Δe_i is the $r(\Delta e_i)$th smallest change in the total sequence considered; then

$$u_t = r(\Delta e_t)/(T+1).$$

Clearly, u_t must lie in the closed interval $[1/(T+1), T/(T+1)]$ (for no ties in rank). The function $\alpha(\cdot)$ in (7.3) is a score function defined in HS (p. 70), depending upon the assumed density of ϵ_t – i.e., f. HS define a class of functions which can be used in place of the score function in large samples, since $\alpha(\cdot)$ may in practice be difficult to evaluate. If F is the assumed distribution function of ϵ_t

$$F(x) = \int_{-\infty}^{x} f(y) \, dy$$

and $F^{-1}(u)$ is the inverse of F:

$$F^{-1}(u) = \inf\{x \,|\, F(x) \geq u\}$$

then the asymptotic score function, $\psi(\cdot)$, is defined (HS, p. 19):

$$\psi: (0, 1) \rightarrow \mathbb{R}$$

$$\psi(u) = -F^{-1}(u) \left[\frac{f'\{F^{-1}(u)\}}{f\{F^{-1}(u)\}} \right]^{-1}. \tag{7.4}$$

Under the maintained hypothesis (7.1), the statistic

$$\eta = \sum_{t=1}^{T} (z_t - \bar{z}) \, \psi(u_t) \tag{7.5}$$

(i.e., as in (7.3) with $\alpha(\cdot)$ replaced by $\psi(\cdot)$) will be asymptotically normally distributed. Under the null hypothesis (7.2), η will have mean zero and variance ϱ^2 given by (HS, pp. 159–60):

$$\varrho^2 = \left\{ \sum_{t=1}^{T} (z_t - \bar{z})^2 \right\} \int_{0}^{1} \{\psi(u) - \bar{\psi}\}^2 \, du \tag{7.6}$$

(a) German Mark Real Rates

Exchange rate	Normal	Logistic	Double exponential	Cauchy
DMK–DKR	3.21	2.72	2.71	2.88
	(0.65 E–3)	(0.32 E–2)	(0.34 E–2)	(0.20 E–2)
DMK–BFR	1.39	1.14	1.17	1.08
	(0.08)	(0.12)	(0.12)	(0.14)
DMK–FFR	4.53	3.75	3.68	3.67
	(0.30 E–5)	(0.90 E–4)	(0.12 E–3)	(0.12 E–3)
DMK–ITL	6.03	5.08	5.04	5.52
	(0.80 E–9)	(0.18 E–6)	(0.24 E–6)	(0.17 E–7)
DMK–NGL	3.45	2.86	2.98	3.28
	(0.23 E–3)	(0.20 E–2)	(0.14 E–2)	(0.50 E–3)
DMK–US$	0.17	−0.05	−0.10	−0.88
	(0.43)	(0.48)	(0.46)	(0.19)
DMK–CN$	1.01	0.55	0.58	−0.50
	(0.15)	(0.29)	(0.28)	(0.31)
DMK–JPY	0.96	0.55	0.47	−0.62
	(0.17)	(0.29)	(0.32)	(0.26)
DMK–UK£	−0.16	−0.33	−0.25	−1.00
	(0.43)	(0.37)	(0.40)	(0.16)

Table 7.2 Test Statistics for a Shift in Exchange-rate Volatility After March 1979[1]

Note: [1] All statistics are standard normal variates under the null hypothesis of no shift in volatility. Figures in parentheses are marginal (two-sided) significance levels. Significantly positive statistics indicate a reduction in volatility post-March 1979; significantly negative statistics indicate an increase in volatility.

where

$$\bar{\psi} = \int_0^1 \psi(u)\,du$$

The test is now as follows. For a given choice of f, η can be calculated as in (7.5) and referred to the normal distribution, to construct a test of any given nominal size, of the null hypothesis (7.2) (no change in volatility). Significantly negative values of η reflect a negative value for β in (7.1) – i.e., an increase in volatility post-March 1979 – whilst significantly positive values of η imply a reduction in volatility post-March 1979. The statistic η in (7.5) provides the locally most powerful test among the class of all possible tests (HS, p. 249).

Note that although the test procedure just outlined is non-parametric in

(b) Nominal Effective Rates

Exchange rate	Normal	Logistic	Double exponential	Cauchy
Danish kroner	−0.59	−0.48	−0.60	−0.95
	(0.28)	(0.31)	(0.27)	(0.17)
Belgian franc	1.59	1.28	1.26	1.01
	(0.06)	(0.10)	(0.10)	(0.16)
French franc	1.33	0.99	0.88	0.23
	(0.09)	(0.16)	(0.19)	(0.41)
Italian lira	3.35	2.51	2.45	1.32
	(0.4 E–3)	(0.60 E–2)	(0.71 E–2)	(0.09)
Dutch guilder	0.66	0.39	0.33	−0.40
	(0.25)	(0.34)	(0.37)	(0.34)
German mark	2.09	1.55	1.46	0.57
	(0.02)	(0.06)	(0.07)	(0.28)
US dollar	−2.62	−2.25	−2.31	−2.92
	(0.43 E–2)	(0.01)	(0.01)	(0.17 E–2)
Canadian dollar	2.03	1.74	1.76	2.05
	(0.02)	(0.04)	(0.04)	(0.02)
Japanese yen	−0.94	−0.62	−0.66	−0.12
	(0.17)	(0.27)	(0.25)	(0.49)
UK sterling	−1.84	−1.62	−1.66	−2.06
	(0.03)	(0.05)	(0.05)	(0.02)

the sense that no volatility measures are actually estimated, in implementing the procedure we cannot avoid choosing an appropriate distribution for changes in the exchange rate. In order to try and minimise the damage due to choosing an inappropriate distribution we selected four well-known ones – hopefully, the true distribution of exchange-rate changes is close to one of them. The densities used correspond to the normal, logistic, double exponential and Cauchy distributions. The density and asymptotic score functions (as defined in (7.4)) for these distributions are given in the Appendix. All of the chosen distributions are symmetric and both the double exponential and Cauchy distributions have fat tails.[3]

c.   *Exchange-rate volatility tests: empirical results*

Monthly (end month) data on bilateral US dollar exchange rates were taken from the *IFS* data tape for the period January 1973 to December 1986. Bilateral rates against the German mark and UK sterling were also

(c) Real Effective Rates

Exchange rate	Normal	Logistic	Double exponential	Cauchy
Danish kroner	4.36	3.61	3.57	3.45
	(0.65 E–5)	(0.15 E–3)	(0.18 E–3)	(0.27 E–3)
Belgian franc	1.92	1.61	1.62	1.95
	(0.03)	(0.05)	(0.05)	(0.03)
French franc	2.17	1.78	1.81	1.72
	(0.01)	(0.03)	(0.03)	(0.04)
Italian lira	3.14	2.45	2.49	2.09
	(0.85 E–3)	(0.71 E–2)	(0.63 E–2)	(0.02)
Dutch guilder	1.78	1.45	1.41	1.81
	(0.03)	(0.07)	(0.08)	(0.12)
German mark	3.35	2.54	2.49	1.32
	(0.41 E–3)	(0.50 E–2)	(0.63 E–2)	(0.09)
US dollar	−1.31	−1.32	−1.36	−2.48
	(0.09)	(0.09)	(0.08)	(0.65 E–2)
Canadian dollar	1.39	1.17	1.11	1.11
	(0.08)	(0.12)	(0.13)	(0.13)
Japanese yen	0.10	0.11	0.11	0.22
	(0.46)	(0.45)	(0.45)	(0.41)
UK sterling	−1.44	−1.12	−1.10	−0.91
	(0.07)	(0.13)	(0.13)	(0.18)

constructed by assuming a triangular arbitrage condition. Real exchange rates were constructed by deflating by the wholesale price index (also from the *IFS* tape). The currencies used included six ERM members – German mark, Danish kroner, Belgian franc, French franc, Italian lira and Dutch guilder – and four non-ERM members – US dollar, UK sterling, Japanese yen and Canadian dollar. All results reported are for shifts in the volatility of monthly exchange-rate changes. In each case, the test statistics were converted to standard normal variates under the null hypothesis by dividing through by the standard deviation ϱ (see (7.6)).

As would be expected, the results of applying these tests to nominal bilateral rates (not reported) indicated a significant reduction in volatility for ERM currencies against the mark, whilst dollar rates generally showed a significant *rise* in volatility post-1979. Perhaps a little more interesting is that these results are largely echoed by those in Table 7.2a, which gives results of the tests applied to *real* mark bilateral exchange rates. There is strong evidence of a significant reduction in volatility in the real mark exchange rate against most of the ERM currencies, which is in marked contrast for all the real mark exchange rates against the non-ERM currencies. With the exception of the dollar–lira real rate, there are no significant shifts in volatility recorded for either the dollar or the sterling real rates (not reported).

Table 7.2b reports results of the tests applied to nominal effective rates, using the standard IMF (multilateral exchange rate model or MERM) effective indices. This appears to weaken the volatility reduction effect for the EMS currencies – only the Italian lira and (to a lesser extent) the German mark, show a significant post-March 1979 volatility reduction. For the non-ERM currencies, both the US dollar and UK sterling effective indices show a significant post-ERM *rise* in volatility, while the Canadian dollar shows a significant *reduction* in volatility. The results reported in Table 7.2c for the real effective MERM rates (deflated by a basket of wholesale price indices, using the standardised MERM weights for the top ten currencies) are much more clear cut. These show a fairly marked reduction in real exchange-rate volatility for *all* the EMS countries, a slightly less marked increase in volatility of the real US dollar rate, with no significant shift for the other currencies.

Let us summarise the results so far. There is strong evidence of reduced intra-ERM exchange-rate volatility post-March 1979, and signs of increased volatility in dollar and (to a slightly lesser extent) sterling rates. These results hold, moreover, for both real and nominal exchange rates.

d.   Testing for a shift in the conditional variance

In a large number of modern macroeconomic models, unanticipated disturbances have a far greater effect than anticipated disturbances. It is thus of some interest to attempt to test for a shift in the *conditional variance* of exchange-rate changes post-March 1979. That is to say, one should test for a shift in the variance of *unanticipated* movements in the exchange rate.

Rogoff (1985) has tested for a shift in conditional variance by essentially estimating the variance of the forward rate prediction error. Although Rogoff claims that his results are robust to the presence of small, time-varying risk premia in the foreign-exchange market, this method really implicitly assumes uncovered interest-rate parity – and, more important, conditional homoscedasticity of exchange-rate changes. Recent work by (in particular) Cumby and Obstfeld (1984) and Domo- witz and Hakkio (1985) has strongly suggested the presence of con- ditional heteroscedasticity – or, more particularly, autoregressive con- ditional heteroscedasticity (ARCH – see Engle, 1982) effects – in

$$e_t = e_{t-1} + u_t$$

$$h_t = E(u_t^2 \mid I_{t-1}) = \alpha_0 + \alpha_1 u_{t-1}^2$$

(a) German Mark Nominal Rates

Exchange rate	Pre-ERM α_0	α_1	mean $h_t^{1/2}$	Post-ERM α_0	α_1	mean $h_t^{1/2}$	Likelihood ratio
DMK–DKR	0.27 E–8 (4.18)	0.33 (1.52)	1.07	0.32 E–4 (4.11)	0.86 (2.48)	0.97	7.00 (0.03)
DMK–BFR	0.42 E–4 (4.55)	0.38 (1.70)	0.85	0.24 E–4 (4.23)	0.97 (2.56)	1.16	5.33 (0.07)
DMK–FFR	0.36 E–3 (5.01)	0.23 E–1 (0.20)	1.92	0.76 E–4 (5.84)	0.13 (1.01)	0.94	30.09 (0.00)
DMK–ITL	0.39 E–3 (4.13)	0.56 (2.13)	2.93	0.91 E–4 (5.15)	0.28 (1.50)	1.11	28.12 (0.00)
DMK–NGL	0.38 E–4 (4.01)	0.70 (2.47)	1.04	0.13 E–4 (5.17)	0.21 (1.50)	0.41	18.71 (0.87 E–4)
DMK–US$	0.57 E–3 (4.44)	0.26 (1.38)	2.80	0.10 E–2 (5.64)	0.14 (1.96)	3.03	6.87 (0.03)
DMK–CN$	0.76 E–3 (4.38)	0.22 (1.22)	3.12	0.85 E–3 (5.64)	0.12 (1.63)	2.76	4.18 (0.12)
DMK–JPY	0.43 E–3 (4.12)	0.34 (1.62)	2.57	0.47 E–3 (4.13)	0.33 (1.69)	2.63	0.09 (0.96)
DMK–UK£	0.38 E–3 (4.26)	0.49 (1.95)	2.70	0.49 E–3 (4.83)	0.09 (0.63)	2.32	2.61 (0.27)

Table 7.3 Maximum Likelihood ARCH Estimates[1]

Note:
[1] Figures in parentheses below coefficient estimates are *t*-ratios; those below test statistics are marginal significance levels. The likelihood ratio statistic tests for a shift in the coefficients post-March 1979.

exchange-rate innovations. At an intuitive level, the exchange rate will clearly be easier to forecast in some periods than in others.

It is, however, a 'stylised fact' concerning the foreign-exchange market that the (logarithm of the) exchange rate appears to approximate very closely to a random walk (see, e.g., Mussa, 1984, Goodhart, 1987, Goodhart and Taylor, 1987). Moreover, there is also some evidence that the current spot rate outperforms the current forward rate as a spot rate predictor (Fama, 1984, Goodhart, 1987). Accordingly, a tractable way of estimating the conditional variance might be to model the evolution of the exchange rate as a random walk with an ARCH disturbance.[4]

(b) US Dollar Nominal Rates

| Exchange rate | Pre-ERM | | | Post-ERM | | | Likelihood |
	α_0	α_1	mean $h_t^{1/2}$	α_0	α_1	mean $h_t^{1/2}$	ratio
US$–DKR	0.37 E–3	0.34	2.39	0.10 E–2	0.15	2.99	13.53
	(4.15)	(1.67)		(5.77)	(2.55)		(0.11 E–2)
US$–BFR	0.42 E–3	0.31	2.48	0.11 E–2	0.13	3.11	10.82
	(4.27)	(1.63)		(5.63)	(1.74)		(0.45 E–2)
US$–FFR	0.33	0.52	2.54	0.98 E–3	0.11 E–1	3.11	8.42
	(4.03)	(2.13)		(5.31)	(0.17)		(0.01)
US$–ITL	0.19 E–3	0.73	2.40	0.88 E–3	0.12	2.80	19.14
	(4.10)	(2.48)		(5.58)	(1.63)		(0.70 E–4)
US$–NGL	0.41	0.36	2.55	0.10 E–2	0.12	3.00	9.60
	(4.02)	(1.73)		(5.52)	(1.48)		(0.81 E–2)
US$–CN$	0.75 E–4	0.35	1.05	0.89 E–4	0.15	1.02	0.47
	(4.17)	(1.58)		(4.84)	(0.97)		(0.79)
US$–JPY	0.32 E–3	0.42	2.34	0.89 E–3	0.34 E–1	3.03	12.07
	(4.43)	(1.95)		(5.46)	(0.31)		(0.24 E–2)
US$–UK£	0.28 E–3	0.39	2.13	0.94 E–3	0.82 E–1	2.95	13.54
	(3.87)	(1.81)		(6.30)	(5.78)		(0.11 E–2)

Using the Lagrange multiplier test procedure suggested by Engle (1982), we detected the presence of first-order ARCH effects in the random walk innovations for a majority of the nominal bilateral exchange rates investigated. Accordingly, we decided to estimate models of the form:

$$e_t = e_{t-1} + u_t \tag{7.7}$$

$$h_t = E(u_t^2 | I_{t-1}) = \alpha_0 + \alpha_1 u_t - l^2$$

where e_t is the exchange rate and I_{t-1} is the information set at time $t-1$.

The system (7.7) was estimated by maximum likelihood methods, using the scoring algorithm described in Engle (1982). In each case, nine scoring steps were carried out; this was in every case more than adequate to achieve convergence in terms of the gradient around the inverse Hessian (Belsley, 1979, Engle, 1982). For each nominal bilateral exchange rate, the ARCH parameterisation was estimated for the pre- and post-EMS periods separately and a likelihood ratio statistic for a shift in the coefficients was constructed. The results are reported in Table 7.3.

Consider first the results for the German mark nominal bilateral rates (Table 7.3a). With the single exception of the mark–Belgian franc rate, there is a significant shift in the ARCH coefficients for the EMS currencies post-March 1979, and in each case the mean conditional standard deviation of exchange rates ($h_i^{1/2}$) is lower for the second period (this effect is particularly marked for the mark–lira and mark–Dutch guilder exchange rates). There is, however, no significant shift in the ARCH coefficients for the non-ERM mark exchange rates.

The ARCH estimates for the US dollar nominal bilateral rates (Table 7.3b) indicate (with the single exception of the US dollar–Canadian dollar rate) a significant shift in the coefficients and a *rise* in the conditional forecast variance post-March 1979.

The results for sterling nominal rates (not reported) showed no sign of a shift in conditional volatility post-March 1979.

Overall, therefore, these results tend to confirm our earlier findings for shifts in (unconditional) volatility – there is a significant reduction in the conditional variance of exchange-rate innovations for the ERM currencies against the mark, and signs of a significant *rise* in the conditional variance of US dollar exchange-rate innovations.

4   Interest-rate volatility and the EMS

a.   *Volatility transfer*

One anti-ERM argument which is sometimes advanced rests on the notion that advanced macroeconomic systems naturally generate a 'lump of uncertainty' which can be pushed from one point in the economy but which will inevitably reappear elsewhere (see, e.g., Batchelor, 1983; 1985). For example, it might be argued that removing or reducing exchange-rate volatility will inevitably induce a rise in interest-rate volatility. Such a conclusion might follow from inverting a standard exchange-rate equation and noting that the interest rate is the only other major 'jump variable' in the system. Such a phenomenon might be termed 'volatility transfer'. Insofar as the burden of increased interest-rate volatility falls more widely on the general public than that of exchange-rate volatility (which presumably falls mainly on the company, or more particularly the tradeable goods sector), then the welfare argument must hinge on which sector would find it easier to hedge the induced risk. Given that there already exist well-developed forward foreign-exchange markets, it is probable that such an argument would come down against membership of the ERM. However, it is not at all clear that ERM membership is in fact equivalent to 'inverting the

Exchange rate	Normal	Logistic	Double exponential	Cauchy
French franc	1.05	0.81	0.75	0.51
	(0.29)	(0.42)	(0.46)	(0.61)
Italian lira	4.56	3.69	3.51	2.87
	(0.51 E–5)	(0.22 E–3)	(0.45 E–3)	(0.41 E–2)
Dutch guilder	2.91	2.37	2.25	1.85
	(0.36 E–2)	(0.02)	(0.02)	(0.06)
German mark	0.81	0.41	0.38	−0.84
	(0.42)	(0.68)	(0.71)	(0.40)
US dollar	−3.29	−2.60	−2.53	−2.01
	(0.10 E–2)	(0.92 E–2)	(0.01)	(0.04)
Canadian dollar	−2.77	−2.17	−2.11	−1.42
	(0.56 E–2)	(0.03)	(0.03)	(0.15)
Japanese yen	1.15	0.92	0.96	0.88
	(0.25)	(0.36)	(0.34)	(0.38)
UK sterling	6.10	5.10	5.10	5.49
	(0.11 E–8)	(0.34 E–6)	(0.35 E–6)	(0.41 E–7)

Table 7.4 Test Statistics for a Shift in Interest-rate Volatility After March 1979: Onshore Short Rates[1]

Note:
[1] See note to Table 7.2.

exchange-rate equation'. Insofar as membership enhances the credibility of policy, there may be a significant reduction in speculative attacks on the exchange rate and hence a *reduction* in the volatility of short-term interest rates (if the authorities use interest rates as at least a short-term measure for 'leaning into the wind'). Alternatively viewed, there may be a shift in the economic structure according to the Lucas (1976) critique.

In an attempt to shed some light on these arguments, we carried out the non-parametric volatility shift tests outlined above, for monthly changes in both onshore and offshore short-term interest rates; the results are reported in Table 7.4. From our discussion in the previous sub-section, the effective operation of French and Italian exchange controls for much of the post-ERM period would be expected to achieve a reduction in onshore interest rate volatility, and this is borne out (at least for the Italian case). There is also, however, strong evidence of a reduction in Dutch onshore interest-rate volatility whilst the converse is true for US and Canadian onshore rates. Interestingly, there is also evidence of a reduction in the volatility in UK onshore interest rates.

b.   Capital controls and the EMS

It has been argued that exchange controls over capital flows have been a particularly important feature of the functioning of the EMS. The two major member countries outside Germany – France and Italy – have deployed substantial measures of capital control. Belgium, with its two-tier market arrangements, has discriminated between commercial (or current account) and capital transactions.

The significance of these controls was first effectively highlighted by Rogoff (1985), who noted the substantial violations of (covered) interest parity exhibited by France and Italy. Subsequently, Giavazzi and Giovannini (1986) and Giavazzi and Pagano (1985) have analysed and documented further the impact of these controls. Despite anecdotal suggestions that the measures have been ineffective, a contrary impression of effectiveness is indicated by the wedge between 'offshore' (Euro) interest rates and 'onshore' (domestic) interest rates for the countries concerned. Accordingly, we employed the non-parametric tests outlined above to test for a shift in the volatility of the offshore–onshore (short-term) interest-rate differential post-March 1979, for most of the countries considered above. The results are reported in Table 7.5; they do indeed indicate a sharp rise in the offshore–onshore interest-rate differential for the franc and lira, while there is some evidence of a reduction in volatility of the differential for the mark and guilder. Given that the relaxation of UK and Japanese exchange control was almost contemporaneous with the formation of the EMS, it is hardly surprising that Table 7.5 reveals strong evidence of a reduction in the UK and Japanese offshore–onshore differentials.

In the absence of an exchange-rate agreement and capital controls, equilibrium for a system characterised by inflation differentials of the kind noted in the previous section could be expected to imply a steady depreciation of the high-inflation countries' nominal exchange rates *vis-à-vis* the low-inflation 'anchor' country (Germany) at a rate just equal to the difference in interest and inflation rates. With an agreement to restrain the movement of the exchange rate and only to adjust by way of periodic realignments, the interest differential has to oscillate in order to compensate for the switch from a situation in which a realignment is expected to a situation in which it has just occurred, although the degree of oscillation may be mitigated if central rates are realigned before parity limits are reached. Capital controls attenuate this compensatory interest-rate fluctuation and prevent the possibility of destabilising speculation. On the assumption that they do not contain the needed adjustment permanently, or for periods long enough to induce major distortion in

Exchange rate	Normal	Logistic	Double exponential	Cauchy
French franc	−2.70	−2.71	−1.98	−2.01
	(0.49)	(0.47)	(0.54)	(0.36)
Italian lira	−2.55	−2.46	−2.43	−2.20
	(0.12)	(0.14)	(0.14)	(0.03)
Dutch guilder	2.73	2.26	2.15	1.86
	(0.64×10^{-2})	(0.02)	(0.03)	(0.06)
German mark	2.41	1.89	1.84	−1.30
	(0.02)	(0.06)	(0.06)	(0.19)
US dollar	−1.56	−1.18	−1.13	−0.79
	(0.12)	(0.24)	(0.26)	(0.43)
Canadian dollar	−1.43	−1.10	−1.07	−0.59
	(0.15)	(0.27)	(0.29)	(0.56)
Japanese yen	3.67	3.27	3.38	4.71
	(0.24 E–3)	(0.10 E–2)	(0.72 E–3)	(0.25 E–5)
UK sterling	5.71	4.74	4.75	4.93
	(0.11 E–7)	(0.22 E–5)	(0.20 E–5)	(0.84 E–6)

Table 7.5 Test Statistics for a Shift in Interest-rate Volatility After March 1979: Onshore–Offshore Differential[1]

Note: [1] See note to Table 2.

the real rate of exchange, a case in favour of their use would be that they reduce the perceived welfare losses of fluctuating interest rates and remove the prospect of the 'peso problem' phenomenon (Krasker, 1980). In the context of the present functioning of the EMS, it has been argued that it is the inflation-constraining, underindexed crawling-peg realignment policy that speculation might otherwise have made impossible. Without the controls, the market might have forced the authorities' hand and liquidated the overvaluation of weak currencies which the authorities have used as a weapon in their campaign against inflation. This would be the strong case for controls, illustrating the welfare-enhancing effects of the action of 'throwing sand in the wheels' of finance, as advocated by Tobin (1982) some years ago and by Dornbusch (1986) more recently. If there is anything in this argument, the prospect for the future functioning of the EMS gains added interest in the context of the liberalisation of controls in France and Italy and the possible full participation by the UK, with its liberal payments regime, in the system.

5   Conclusion

The EMS has defied predictions of its imminent demise and thereby built
up a stock of credibility with the market – as also with governments. We thus found unequivocal evidence that the ERM has brought about a reduction in both the conditional and unconditional variance of exchange-rate changes – and, far from having purchased this reduction at the cost of increased interest-rate volatility, there is also some evidence of a reduction in the volatility of interest rates for ERM members. We attribute this to the enhanced credibility of the exchange-rate policies of these countries.

In detail, however, the operation of the EMS has clearly owed something (at times) to the controls over capital flows by France and Italy. The present phase of liberalisation in these countries has highlighted the need for changes. Indeed, it is now recognised by ERM member countries that there is a need for constant monitoring of the system and changes in its mode of operation from time to time. In addition, it has also become accepted that more explicit co-ordination of monetary – particularly interest-rate – policy may be necessary, especially in the event of British accession.

Let us conclude by pointing out a number of questions and issues which remain. To a large extent in this study we have been concerned with the extent to which the EMS has met its short- to medium-term objectives, and what have been the costs of attaining them. Although we found some evidence of the importance of the use of capital controls by some ERM members over the period, we have not addressed the question of *how* volatility has been reduced – whether through intervention at the margins, intra-marginal intervention or whatever. This remains a possible avenue for future research. In addition, given the findings of this study, it would seem appropriate to examine whether the longer-run objectives of the system have been met, and whether or not the long-run credibility of the ERM is open to question. As we have noted, the fundamental long-run issue concerns *real* exchange rates, and primarily the size or level of *misalignment* rather than *volatility*. A related issue concerns currency substitutability within the ERM.

Following Canzoneri (1982), we can say that the creation of an exchange-rate union converts external shocks affecting member countries asymmetrically into symmetric ones; if the permanence of the union is credible, one member's currency is as good as another's and an external shock inducing a flight of capital into (say) the mark, should affect the franc and lira in the same way, relieving pressure on the cross rates. Indeed, a diminution of the exposure of German competitiveness to sentiment against the dollar was apparently a major motivation of German interest in the founding of the EMS (Ludlow, 1982). It would therefore seem of some interest to examine for the substitutability of ERM member currencies during the period of operation of the EMS.

In Artis and Taylor (1988b) we address these twin issues of misalignment and currency substitutability and hence examine the longer-run credibility of the ERM.

APPENDIX: DENSITY AND ASYMPTOTIC SCORE FUNCTIONS FOR THE NON-PARAMETRIC TESTS[1]

Distribution	Density Function $f(x)$	Asymptotic Score Function $\psi(u)$
Normal	$(2\pi)^{-\frac{1}{2}}\exp(-\frac{1}{2}x^2)$	$\{\Phi^{-1}(u)\}^2 - 1$
Logistic	$e^{-x}(1 + e^{-x})^{-2}$	$(2u - 1)\ln\{u/(1 - u)\} - 1$
Double Exponential	$\frac{1}{2}\exp(-|x|)$	$-\ln(1 - |2u - 1|) - 1$
Cauchy	$\pi^{-1}(1 + x^2)^{-1}$	$2\tan^2\{\pi(u - \frac{1}{2})\}[1 + \tan^2\{\pi(u - \frac{1}{2})\}]^{-1} - 1$

Note: [1]The asymptotic score function is defined in relation (7.4) in the text. $\Phi(\cdot)$ denotes the standard normal distribution function, i.e.:

$$\Phi(u) = \int_{-\infty}^{u} (2\pi)^{-\frac{1}{2}} \exp(-\frac{1}{2}u^2)du$$

NOTES

* At the time of preparation of this study, Mark Taylor was at the Bank of England (now at the University of Dundee). We are grateful to John Flemming, Chris Taylor, Roger Clews, Tony Latter and other economists at the Bank of England for comments on a previous version of this study, as well as to conference delegates at the Money Study Group Conference (Oxford) September 1987 and at the CEPR – Banca d'Italia Conference on the EMS (Perugia, Italy) September 1987. The usual disclaimer applies. Any views expressed are those of the authors and in no way should be construed as representing the views or policies of the Bank of England past or present. Michael Artis acknowledges the administrative support of the CEPR and financial support from the Ford and Alfred P. Sloan Foundations under the CEPR programme 'Macroeconomic Interactions and Policy Design in Interdependent Economies'.

1 Ludlow (1982) gives a detailed and informative account of the negotiations leading to the institution of the EMS.

2 See Section 4 below, and Artis and Taylor (1988a).

3 Another relevant distribution would have been Student's t. However, the score function (7.4) for this distribution would have been very difficult to compute. A possibility not considered is that there was a change in distribution of ERM exchange-rate changes post-March 1979 (e.g., shifted from normal to

Cauchy). Tests for this kind of behaviour could conceivably be based on likelihood ratio tests, although one might suspect that the discriminatory power of such procedures would be low.

4 As noted above, heteroscedastic normal exchange-rate changes would account for the appearance of leptokurtosis and this is therefore an alternative interpretation to that offered above. A more general approach would be to estimate the conditional variance non-parametrically (see, for example, Pagan and Ullah, 1986). This possibility is currently under investigation by the present authors.

REFERENCES

Akhtar, M. A. and R. S. Hilton (1984). 'Exchange Rate Uncertainty and International Trade: Some Conceptual Issues and New Estimates for Germany and the United States', Federal Reserve Bank of New York Research Paper, No. 8403 (May).

Artis, M. J. and M. P. Taylor (1988a). 'Exchange Controls and the UK Experience', in A. S. Courakis and M. P. Taylor (eds), *Policy Issues for Interdependent Economies*, London, Macmillan (forthcoming).

(1988b). 'Some Issues Concerning the Long-Run Credibility of the European Monetary System', in R. MacDonald and M. P. Taylor (eds), *Exchange Rates and Open Economy Macroeconomics*, Oxford, Basil Blackwell.

Bank of England (1984). 'The Variability of Exchange Rates: Measurement and Effects', *Bank of England Quarterly Bulletin*, Vol. 24, pp. 346–9.

Batchelor, R. A. (1983). *Evidence* to House of Commons Select Committee (1983).

(1985). *Evidence* to House of Lords Select Committee (1985).

Belsley, D. (1979). 'On the Efficient Computation of the Non-Linear Full-Information Maximum Likelihood Estimator', paper presented to the European meeting of the Econometric Society (Athens).

Boothe, P. and A. Glassman (1987). 'The Statistical Distribution of Exchange Rates: Some Empirical Evidences', *Journal of International Economics*, Vol. 22, pp. 297–319.

Canzoneri, M. (1982). 'Exchange Intervention Policy in a Multiple Country World', *Journal of International Economics*, Vol. 13, No. 3/4.

Cumby, R. E. and M. Obstfeld (1984). 'International Interest Rate and Price Level Linkages under Flexible Exchange Rates: A Review of Recent Evidence', in J. F. O. Bilson and R. C. Marston (eds), *Exchange Rate Theory and Practice*, Chicago, University of Chicago Press.

Cushman, D. O. (1986). 'Has Exchange Risk Depressed International Trade? The Impact of Third Country Exchange Risk', *Journal of International Money and Finance*, Vol. 5, pp. 361–79.

Domowitz, I. and C. S. Hakkio (1985). 'Conditional Variance and the Risk Premium in the Foreign Exchange Market', *Journal of International Economics*, Vol. 18, pp. 47–66.

Dornbusch, R. (1986). 'Exchange Rate Economics, 1986', Royal Economic Society Conference (July).

Engle, R. F. (1982). 'Autoregressive Conditional Heteroskedasticity with Estimates of the Variance of UK Inflation', *Econometrica*, Vol. 50, pp. 987–1007.

European Commission (1982). 'Documents Relating to the European Monetary System', *European Economy* (July).

Fama, E. F. (1984). 'Forward and Spot Exchange Rates', *Journal of Monetary Economics*, Vol. 14, pp. 319–38.

Giavazzi, F. and A. Giovannini (1986). 'The EMS and the Dollar', *Economic Policy*, Vol. 2 (April), pp. 456–85.

Giavazzi, F. and M. Pagano (1985). 'Capital Controls and the European Monetary System', in F. Giavazzi (ed.), *Capital Controls and Foreign Exchange Legislation*, Euromobiliare Occasional Papers, No. 1 (June).

Goodhart, C. A. E. (1986). 'Should the UK join the EMS?', LSE (mimeo).
  (1987). 'The Foreign Exchange Market: A Random Walk with a Dragging Anchor', LSE Financial Markets Group Discussion Papers.

Goodhart, C. A. E. and M. P. Taylor (1987). 'Why Don't Individuals Speculate in the Forward Foreign Exchange Market?', LSE Financial Markets Group Discussion Paper, No. 17.

Hajèk, J. and Z. Sidak (1967). *Theory of Rank Tests*, New York and Prague, Academic Press.

House of Commons Select Committee (1985). 'The European Monetary System', 13th Report from the Treasury and Civil Service Committee, and Evidence, London, HMSO.

House of Lords Select Committee (1983). 'The European Monetary System', 5th Report from the Summit Conference on the European Community, and Evidence, London, HMSO.

International Monetary Fund (1983). 'Exchange Rate Volatility and World Trade', IMF Occasional Papers, No. 28 (July).

Krasker, W. S. (1980). 'The "Peso Problem" in Testing the Efficiency of Forward Exchange Markets', *Journal of Monetary Economics*, Vol. 6, pp. 269–76.

Lucas, R. E. (1976). 'Econometric Policy Evaluation: A Critique', in K. Brunner and A. H. Meltzer (eds), *The Phillips Curve and Labor Markets*, Carnegie–Rochester Conference Series on Public Policy, No. 1, pp. 19–46.

Ludlow, P. (1982). *The Making of the European Monetary System*, London, Butterworths.

Melitz, J. (1985). *Evidence* to the House of Commons Select Committee (1985).

Mussa, M. (1984). 'The Theory of Exchange Rate Determination', in J. F. O. Bilson and R. C. Marston (eds), *Exchange Rate Theory and Practice*, Chicago, University of Chicago Press.

Padoa-Schioppa, T. (1983). *Evidence* to the House of Lords Select Committee (1983).

Pagan, A. and A. Ullah (1986). *The Econometric Analysis of Models with Risk Terms*, CEPR Discussion Paper, No. 127.

Rogalski, R. J. and J. D. Vinso (1977). 'Price Level Variations as Predictors of Flexible Exchange Rates', *Journal of International Business Studies* (Spring–Summer), pp. 71–81.

Rogoff, K. (1985). 'Can Exchange Rate Predictability be Achieved Without Monetary Convergence? Evidence from the EMS', *European Economic Review*, Vol. 28, Nos. 1–2 (June–July), pp. 93–115.

Tobin, J. (1982). 'A Proposal for International Monetary Reform', *Eastern Economic Journal*, Vol. 4 (3–4) (July–October), pp. 153–9, reprinted in J. Tobin, *Essays in Economics: Theory and Practice*, Cambridge, Mass., MIT Press.

Ungerer, H., O. Evans and P. Nyberg (1983). 'The European Monetary System: the Experience 1979–82', IMF Occasional Papers, No. 19 (May).

Ungerer, H., O. Evans, T. Mayer and P. Young (1987). 'The European Monetary System: Recent Developments', IMF Occasional Papers, No. 48 (December).

Westerfield, J. M. (1977). 'Empirical Properties of Foreign Exchange Rates under Fixed and Floating Rate Regimes', *Journal of International Economics*, Vol. 7, pp. 181–200.

Williamson, J. (1985). *The Exchange Rate System* (revised edn), Policy Analyses in International Economics, No. 5, Institute for International Economics (June).

Discussion

EMIL-MARIA CLAASSEN AND ERIC PERÉE

The Artis and Taylor study contains a great deal of interesting material with which to assess the achievements (if any) of the EMS. The aim of the founders of the EMS was to create a zone of monetary stability in Europe in order to avoid the potentially disruptive effects of exchange-rate fluctuations. Has the EMS lived up to the expectations of its supporters? Artis and Taylor's answer is equivocal. They address two major issues: (1) Has the EMS reduced the short-term volatility of exchange rates? (2) Has the EMS helped in stabilising real exchange rates, and hence competitiveness of member countries? Even though the authors recognise that welfare costs of sustained exchange-rate misalignments are likely to be larger than that of short-run volatility (pp. 188–9), the bulk of the study is devoted to an analysis of the high-frequency component of the exchange-rate time series. We shall comment on these two issues in their order of appearance in the original study, now available as Artis and Taylor (1988).

1   Volatility of nominal rates

Statistical problems of parametric approaches to the measurement of exchange-rate volatility lead the authors to adopt an innovative non-parametric approach. Adoption of a new methodology does not alter the picture given by the data and results obtained in previous studies carry over in this one – since March 1979, exchange-rate volatility has been significantly reduced inside the EMS (what one would expect from a fixed but adjustable exchange-rate system), while at the same time the US dollar has exhibited much more variability. Furthermore, intra-EMS volatility has been sufficiently reduced to render EMS-effective exchange rates more stable (what one would not necessarily expect).

The authors concentrate their analysis on the monthly rate of change in exchange rates; however, results from other studies lead us to believe that this achievement of the EMS would be confirmed for other short-term periods as well. However, the choice of end-of-month data excludes in many cases the phenomenon of high volatility, in particular for interest rates around realignments – actual or potential. The EMS is characterised by periods of quiescence followed by periods of turbulence; volatility will be higher during the latter than during the former, and in all likelihood the difference will not be negligible.

Should the volatility issue really be considered as a 'success' of the EMS, and does it really matter? The enhanced predictability of EMS exchange rates may have simplified the conduct of industrial and financial business, but risks resulting from short-term exchange-rate variations can easily – albeit not costlessly – be hedged in financial markets. The existence of markets to diversify exchange risk away is therefore likely seriously to limit the welfare gains of reduction in volatility. The evidence presented by Artis and Taylor does not point to a transfer of volatility to another part of the economy (at least with respect to onshore interest rates) where such a volatility could be less easily hedged or fall on agents less able to cope with the risk.

Once the analysis is made with the interest-rate differential between onshore and offshore markets, the evidence suggests an increase in volatility for France and Italy, countries using capital controls. The question then becomes: how really harmful is this volatility? This is open to debate, but the definition of EMS parities in nominal terms calls for adjustments of parities when inflation rates diverge among member countries and when these countries are not symmetrically affected by shocks arising in the rest of the world. The cooperative nature of negotiations leading to realignments in addition to non-economic factors (e.g., political considerations) are bound to put some strain on interest rate differentials unless the authorities always act before such market developments occur.

One of the major problems of the present EMS is the existence of one-sided expectations for exchange-rate adjustments, and therefore potential low-risk speculative gains. Capital controls in weak-currency countries are often viewed as a necessary means to limit speculative outflows and make maintained membership in the EMS feasible. The current trend in favour of foreign-exchange liberation and the proposed phasing-out of capital controls raise the question of whether the EMS can work without restrictions on capital flows.

Artis and Taylor document the imperfect substitutability among EMS currencies; the mere existence of capital controls is a sufficient condition to explain this phenomenon. As a matter of fact, the EMS is a regional exchange-rate zone where the Deutsche mark is the only currency having the status of world currency. This means that the EMS currencies are not symmetrically affected by developments in the world monetary scene, especially US dollar movements. There is no clear-cut way out of this dilemma; future strengthening of the EMS could perhaps rest on the developments of the ECU as a parallel currency having a larger role in the international monetary system.

No explanation for the reduced volatility in intra-EMS exchange rates is provided by the authors. The reason for less volatility may be found in the more frequent interventions by central banks. With respect to interventions, one has to distinguish between those at the margin and intramarginal ones; the former are compulsory when two currencies hit the limit of the bilateral fluctuation band and they have to be pursued by the two central banks concerned in using each other's currency. The reduced volatility may be explained by the second type of interventions, the intramarginal ones. In a recent study by Francesco Giavazzi and Alberto Giovannini (1987), one obtains the interesting information that Germany never intervenes intramarginally in EMS currencies, whereas there are important intermarginal interventions by other EMS countries. Furthermore, when Germany intervenes, it does so with respect to the US dollar, and most dollar interventions within the EMS are in fact coming from Germany. Consequently, the rules of the EMS with respect to the reduced volatility of bilateral exchange rates seem to reflect in many cases an assignment according to which the Bundesbank – the 'German Monetary Area' – is concerned with the dollar rate of the EMS and the other $(n-1)$ EMS countries manage the intra-EMS rates with intramarginal interventions in EMS currencies.

2   Volatility of real rates and the notion of misalignment

Let us now come to the question of the stabilisation of real exchange rates, a related subject with which the authors deal in the extended version of their study (Artis and Taylor, 1988). The authors address this question by testing for a unit root in real exchange rates. Their results lead to a rejection of the purchasing parity hypothesis (PPP) both before March 1979 and after that date. This is a usual result in the literature: only a few studies have been unable to reject the PPP hypothesis, in all cases in the very long run. The authors nevertheless abstain from drawing any strong conclusions and their cautious approach is unwarranted. Their argument is that the data period over which the EMS has been observed is too short to enable one to infer the very long-run properties of the system.

Beside the usual discussions about the appropriateness of the price indexes used, some additional comments are in order. At the beginning of the EMS it was common to claim that weak-currency countries had joined the system at an undervalued rate to avoid as much as possible any strain on the EMS in its early days. If this is true, it offers one good reason for the rejection of PPP. Furthermore, the exchange rate has proved a powerful weapon to fight inflation, and inflation-prone countries have probably accepted some (temporary) losses of competitiveness inside the EMS in order to reduce their inflation rates, especially in an environment where the dollar was appreciating, and minimising the export losses resulting from an appreciation inside the EMS. The above arguments are apparently leading in opposite directions. The point is that they appeared successively.[1] All this does not necessarily mean that real exchange rates are (and will be) stable inside the EMS but rather that the utmost caution is in order. The happy fact for the supporters of the EMS in the Artis–Taylor study is that the speed (in a probabilistic sense) at which misalignments have been building up has been significantly reduced. In view of the fact that welfare costs of exchange-rate misalignments are probably non-negligible, this finding tends to support the idea that the EMS has achieved some of its aims.

Our last remark concerns the notion of misalignment which has become very popular and which comes out of the distinction between volatility as a short-run phenomenon and misalignment as a long-run phenomenon. As a matter of fact, the major issue with real exchange rates is not their volatility – which represents some nuisance within the system – but their *level* of misalignment. The benchmark for assessing whether a currency is over- or undervalued is provided by PPP. This is the case in the Artis–Taylor study as it is the case in many others. It should be emphasised that the PPP doctrine simply represents the proposition of the neutrality of money for an open economy. It is a hypothesis according to which relative prices – and consequently the real exchange rate – remain unaffected (in the very long run) by monetary disturbances. It follows that only in those circumstances when monetary factors dominate exchange-rate developments, is one allowed to use PPP estimates as a benchmark for observing the over- and undervaluations of a currency. Those circumstances could be hyperinflations or a situation of very long-run comparisons during which *real shocks* are transitory and cancel each other out over time. However, the last decade has been dominated by a wave of real shocks: extreme alterations in the relative prices of oil and other commodities, large swings in fiscal stances, and enormous changes in real interest rates. In such a world – dominated by real disturbances – it must be fundamentally misleading – in theory and for policy prescriptions – for the EMS and for the IMS to use PPP as a yardstick for misalignments.

NOTE

1 Giavazzi and Pagano (1986) have claimed that inflation-prone countries have to pay for the credibility they gain by joining the EMS with a permanent appreciation of their real exchange rate. They showed that Italian competitiveness has deteriorated by about 30 per cent between 1979 and 1985. Their computation is, however, highly dependent on the index used, and overlooked the above considerations.

REFERENCES

Artis, M. J. and Taylor, M. P. (1988). 'Exchange Rates and the EMS: Assessing the Track Record', CEPR Discussion Paper, No. 250.
Giavazzi, F. and A. Giovannini (1987). 'Models of the EMS: Is Europe a Greater Deutschmark Area?', in R. Bryant and R. Portes (eds), *Global Macroeconomics: Policy Conflict and Cooperation*, London, Macmillan, pp. 237–760.
Giavazzi, F. and M. Pagano (1986). 'The Advantage of Tying One's Hands: EMS Discipline and Central Bank Credibility', CEPR Discussion Paper, No. 135; (1988) *European Economic Review* (June).

8 The Stability and Sustainability of the European Monetary System With Perfect Capital Markets

JOHN DRIFFILL

1   Introduction

This study looks at the question of whether, and under what circumstances, the European Monetary System (EMS) might be stable and sustainable without the support of capital controls. Most of the countries participating in it have maintained capital controls over the years since the start of the EMS (1979), and these controls are widely thought to have been essential to its successful operation, permitting intermittent and at least partly predictable discrete realignments to take place without large capital flows and large fluctuations in onshore interest rates in devaluing countries. Currently, exchange controls are being dismantled, and discussions are now under way to remove all remaining controls, following the meeting of European Commission finance ministers in Nyborg (Denmark) in September 1987. The question of how the EMS is expected to operate in the absence of controls is one which naturally arises.

A variety of views on the possibility of sustaining something like the EMS in its present form without capital controls have been expressed. Giavazzi and Pagano (1986), for example, have commented that the effects of greater capital mobility would be greater volatility of short-term interest rates but that the costs would be relatively small, because direct costs are offset by the greater credibility of low inflation policies in countries such as Italy with relatively high inflation.

Obstfeld (1985), talking more generally about managed exchange regimes, has remarked:

> Given the comparative disadvantage of fixed rates in the face of certain disturbances, the credibility problem is likely to arise under any arrangements limiting exchange rate flexibility. It is therefore an open

211

question whether such arrangements would be stable in the absence of pervasive capital controls.[1]

It is clear that there exist, under almost any circumstances, combinations of monetary and fiscal policies which are capable of sustaining a system of managed exchange rates – without capital controls, and without violent fluctuations in interest rates or speculative attacks on currencies. The question is whether or not countries would be willing to pursue the necessary policies. The answer is not clear either from recent evidence of their behaviour or from analysis of the operation of the EMS to date.

An appropriate way of analysing these questions formally would be to set out the situation as a game played by EMS member countries, and to look for equilibrium outcomes using appropriate solution concepts. This method has been followed fruitfully in recent work on the EMS by, for example, Giavazzi and Giovannini (1986, 1987, 1988), and Begg and Wyplosz (1987).

Begg and Wyplosz (1987) considered interactions among EMS countries – including the use of capital controls – as a non-cooperative game in which governments do not commit themselves at the outset; they find that capital controls will be used in equilibrium if the cost of setting them up is sufficiently small. Their analysis focusses on two countries with initially different inflation rates, and so is probably a more apt model of the early years of the EMS than of the years ahead. In their concluding remarks they commented that:

> we have seen [that] the incentives to form an EMS are sensitive to the initial conditions inherited by member countries. This raises the intriguing possibility that an EMS formed to fight inflation might disintegrate once unemployment not inflation was the main concern, especially if both the success on inflation and the extent of the unemployment problem were unanticipated at the date the bargain took place to hammer out the operating rules of the EMS.

The EMS may be currently changing its rules in response to unexpected circumstances, as conjectured by Begg and Wyplosz (though not in the way in which they envisaged), in that imminent collapse of the EMS does not appear likely. However the removal of capital controls now – when inflation differentials between EMS countries have narrowed substantially – is implicitly predicted by their analysis, reflecting the lower benefits of capital controls relative to the costs now that inflation differentials between participants have narrowed.

Giavazzi and Giovannini (1987) and Giavazzi and Pagano (1986) also carry out exercises in positive game-theoretic modelling of policy, and investigate the incentives for high-inflation countries to peg their exchange rates to a low-inflation country. They postulate objective functions for governments, and examine the gains associated with optimal policy in and out of the EMS.

In principle, the game-theoretic approach to modelling the effects of removing capital controls on the EMS is the right one to follow. The credibility of a managed exchange-rate regime and the monetary and fiscal policies of participants is crucial to how it works. Indeed, the use (or non-use) of capital controls in the system should be modelled as an endogenous choice of participants in it, as it is in the study by Begg and Wyplosz. The difficulty with this approach is that the problem has to be kept dramatically simple in order to produce a tractable model. In addition, it requires rather specific assumptions to be made about government objectives and the structure of the game.

In the case of the EMS, government objectives, and the motivation for the EMS, are not clear. Giavazzi and Giovannini have emphasised the idea that high-inflation members are disciplined to run tighter macroeconomic policies by participating in it. In this view, the EMS would offer no benefits to Germany, which would carry the burden of encouraging other members to reduce their inflation faster than they would have done in the absence of the EMS. Complementary to this is the view that the EMS allows countries (1) to cooperate in setting real exchange rates amongst themselves, which would offer benefits to Germany, and (2) to stabilise real exchange rates over time. (Rogoff, 1985 discusses this aspect of the EMS.) Proponents of this view argue that the European countries actually wanted to lower inflation rates in the 1980s, and would have done so with or without the EMS.

Given the difficulties of embracing all these aspects of the EMS, I have not attempted to construct a formal model. Instead, this study examines an issue which is a preliminary to the question of what policies would be *chosen* by EMS members – namely, the issue of what policies are available to them, in the absence of capital controls, consistent with the stability and sustainability of the EMS. The issue of whether any such policies would be credibly pursued by members of the EMS is addressed only informally.

The study is laid out as follows. Section 2 considers the way in which the EMS has operated over the last eight years with capital controls. Section 3 discusses the broad implications of perfect capital mobility for policies consistent with sustainability of the EMS, in the light of the literature on 'speculative attacks'. Section 4 then discusses various exchange-rate policies under perfect capital mobility, and their implications for interest rates, real exchange rates, and monetary policy. Section 5 contains some concluding remarks.

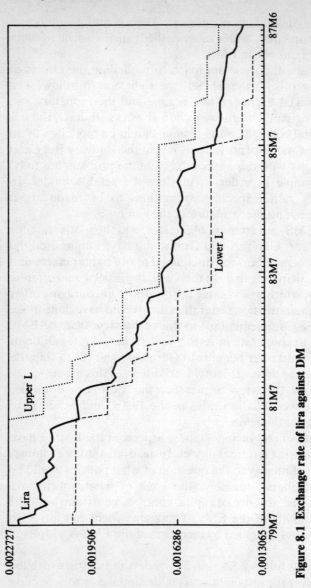

Figure 8.1 Exchange rate of lira against DM

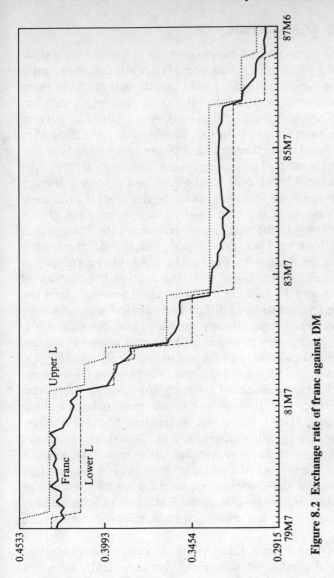

Figure 8.2 Exchange rate of franc against DM

2   The EMS with capital controls

France and Italy have maintained capital controls of various sorts since 1979, when the EMS was set up. Realignments of central exchange rates have taken place on eleven occasions since then, though not all of these are regarded as being 'major realignments'.[2] The franc–mark rate has been changed seven times, and the lira–mark rate eight. The path of these two exchange rates and the bands within which they are allowed to move – ± 2.25 per cent for the franc and ± 6.07 per cent for the lira – are shown in Figures 8.1 and 8.2. The changes in the franc central rates have typically exceeded the 4.5 per cent band-width, and involved discrete jumps in the exchange rate. The changes in the lira central rates have always been less than the 12 per cent band-width, but have not always avoided a discrete jump in the actual spot exchange rate, though that would theoretically have been possible. Notably in July 1985, there was a run on the lira and a devaluation by 8 per cent against other currencies in the exchange-rate mechanism. Since then, the lira has been devalued twice (6 April 1986 and 12 January 1987) by small amounts, and the lira–mark spot rate appears to have drifted fairly smoothly downwards.

The importance of capital controls in permitting these devaluations is evidenced by the divergences between onshore and offshore interest rates for the franc and lira in the months just before a realignment (see, for example, Giavazzi and Pagano, 1985, and Giavazzi and Giovannini, 1987), and the lack of a pronounced tendency for onshore short-term interest rates in France and Italy to rise in the months before these realignments. Rogoff (1985) finds that there has been less intra-European exchange-rate volatility during the EMS period, and attributes it to capital controls rather than more coordination of monetary policy as a result of the EMS. Melitz and Michel (1986) have argued the case that capital controls are not the complete explanation for the absence of large-scale speculative movements inside the EMS, and that uncertainty about realignment dates and the menace of further capital controls are also important.

The realignments which have taken place appear to have resulted substantially from the inflation differences between EMS countries (Figure 8.3), resulting from differences in monetary and fiscal policies, rather than any other source of shocks.[3] Figure 8.3 illustrates inflation rates for Germany, France, and Italy for the period July 1979–June 1987, and shows that differences in inflation rates have narrowed somewhat during the last few years.[4]

The periods in which nominal exchange rates have been fixed have been associated with rises in the real exchange rates of France and Italy, as

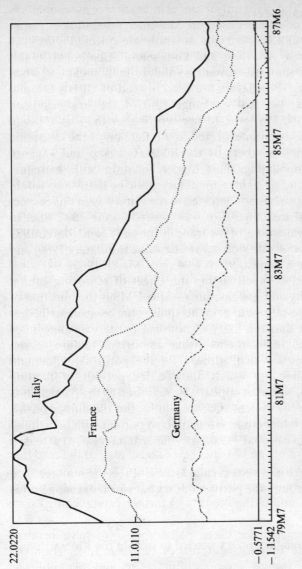

Figure 8.3 Inflation rates

Figure 8.4 indicates. (This gives only a coarse indication of movements in real exchange rates, since it is based on consumer price indices rather than relative normal unit labour costs or wholesale prices. Figures 4.6 and 4.7 in the study by Giavazzi and Giovannini, Chapter 4 in this volume, show that the same assessment is valid, broadly speaking, when unit labour costs or GDP deflators are used instead of CPIs.) Despite periodic devaluations, the real exchange rate of the lira has risen persistently and in June 1987 was 17 per cent higher than its value in January 1980. This has been interpreted as a reflection of the discipline imposed on inflationary members by the EMS (Giavazzi and Pagano, 1986) by not accommodating their higher inflation with matching devaluations, and inducing tighter monetary policies than they would otherwise pursue. France has not behaved in the same way in this respect as has Italy. The real exchange rate was lower in June 1987 than in January 1980. The devaluations of the franc in June 1982 and March 1983 brought the real exchange rate well below the value in January 1980, and it has remained within a range 0.95 to 1.04 since March 1983.

A question which arises in discussing the effect of removing capital controls on the stability and sustainability of the EMS is the question of what kinds of exchange-rate arrangements qualify for being described as 'the EMS'. It is clear that the fixity of nominal parity exchange rates (except for occasional realignments) is an important feature of the system. An arrangement which allowed for the parities to fluctuate constantly through time, or which allowed for periods of floating between realignments, would, it appears, be regarded by the participants as a radical change in the system. Consequently, the remainder of this study will focus upon stability in a system of fixed parities with occasional realignments, where 'occasional' is taken to mean at intervals of at least a year, on average.

The second key feature of a system called 'the EMS' is the maintenance of the narrow bands around the parity rates within which exchange rates can float.

3   Conditions on monetary policy needed to sustain the EMS without capital controls

Any form of managed floatation of exchange rates imposes some restrictions on monetary policy, though capital controls weaken their force. The recent literature on speculative attacks on fixed exchange-rate systems provides a framework within which to analyse the sustainability of a managed exchange-rate regime like the EMS, as for example in the study by Maurice Obstfeld (Chapter 9 in this volume). Most of the

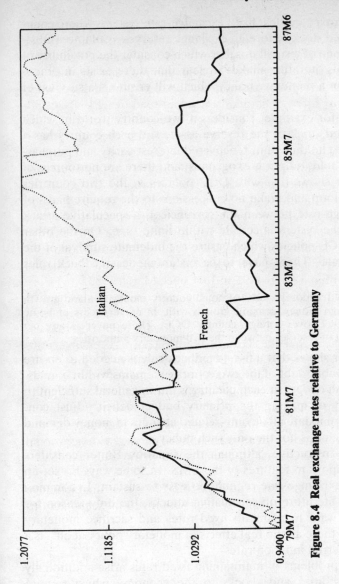

Figure 8.4 Real exchange rates relative to Germany

literature in this area considers fixed exchange-rate systems where countries have a limited stock of foreign exchange reserves available. (Obstfeld's analysis is one of a small number which consider the possibility of realignment.) This literature makes it clear that there exists in practically any situation a monetary policy which will ensure the survival of the system.

Buiter (1986b), for example, considers a two-country world in which there exists a fixed stock of the reserve asset, and each country has a minimum required holding of it. Uncovered interest parity and purchasing power parity hold, output is exogenous, and there are no sources of stickiness. Buiter shows that with DCE policies in the two countries (which are open-loop and make no concessions to the requirements of the fixed exchange rate between the currencies), a speculative attack and collapse of the system is certain within finite time. On the other hand there *are* DCE policies which ensure the indefinite survival of the fixed exchange rate. These have to be instantaneous feedback rules which

> match any [random] excess of home country money demand growth over foreign money demand growth with an equal excess of home country DCE over foreign country DCE. There never is any net movement of reserves between the two monetary authorities.[5]

In addition Buiter shows that a fiscal feedback rule is needed to ensure that the relative public debt of the two countries remains within bounds. A balanced overall budget in each country is not in general sufficient to do this. A policy of making the primary budget deficit adjust continuously to accommodate all income-related changes in money demand is sufficient, though it is not the only such policy.

This analysis is instructive, although the situation Buiter considers excludes some important features of the EMS. In some ways his set-up makes the fixed exchange-rate regime too easy to sustain. In common with most of the literature on speculative attacks, the only reason for countries not to want to maintain fixed rates and sacrifice monetary autonomy – since there are no real effects of monetary policy at all – is a difference in preferred inflation rates.

In practice, the problems of maintaining fixed rates arise additionally from nominal rigidities and shocks to the economy which require changes in the real exchange rate. These are costly to effect by means of price and wage changes and relatively cheaper to effect by nominal exchange-rate adjustment. Their existence does not alter the proposition that there almost always exists a monetary policy consistent with the maintenance of a managed or fixed exchange-rate system. It does, however, reduce its attractiveness. This consideration may make stated commitments to fixed exchange rates not credible, and lead to speculative attacks when such shocks do occur.

In other respects, Buiter's analysis imposes tighter conditions on monetary policies consistent with fixed rates than would be needed in the EMS. He assumes a fixed stock of the reserve asset – a condition which may be inappropriate to the EMS since members of the exchange-rate mechanism can, at least in principle, create unlimited reserves for defending exchange rates amongst participants by swaps. With unlimited reserves, any monetary policy is consistent with survival of the system. In practice, the availability of reserves to defend parities is limited by the reluctance of low-inflation countries to supply their currencies to other central banks in amounts large enough to weaken their control on the domestic money supply and inflation rate. The recent attempts to make the EMS operate more symmetrically may make more reserves available. In addition, the bands within which exchange rates can float (and the possibility of realignments) enlarge the range of monetary policies consistent with sustainability of the EMS.

Realignment of exchange-rate parities following a speculative attack did not form part of Buiter's analysis, but has been considered by Obstfeld (1984, and Chapter 9 in this volume). Obstfeld (1984) shows that when central bank policy is to follow a speculative attack by devaluation, the timing of the attack depends on the size of the anticipated devaluation – the larger the expected devaluation, the sooner the speculative attack occurs – and in a more complicated way on the length of time between the abandonment of the old parity and the establishment of the new. These conclusions are based on an assumption that the central bank in question is expanding domestic credit at a constant exogenous rate, unaffected by the devaluation. Obstfeld's analysis in Chapter 9 shows that if the devaluation fully (or more than fully) accommodates real depreciation in the exchange rate which has occurred since the last devaluation, then instability may result.

While no exchange-rate system as complex as the EMS – embodying both narrow bands around the central rates and the possibility of realignment – has been analysed from the point of view of its susceptibility to speculative attack, the existing literature suggests some broad conclusions. It suggests that changes in central rates and bands could be made under the EMS, provided that they were associated with credible plans for future growth of the money stock which implied no discontinuity in the path of the actual spot exchange rate.[6] The periodic adjustment of the central rates could allow nominal exchange rates to adjust gradually to accommodate (at least partially) the differences in inflation rates that persist among EMS members, and to allow changes in real exchange rates (in response to real shocks) to take place without relying totally on changes in wages and goods prices.

While removing capital controls need not prevent EMS central rates and the surrounding bands from being altered from time to time, it probably restricts the size of anticipated changes in bands which can be made without causing a speculative attack or violent fluctuations in short-term interest rates.

4   Three possible models of an EMS without capital controls

a.   'Soft' bands

The speculative attack literature suggests that modelling formally the operation of an exchange-rate regime that involved floating within narrow bands, subject to periodic adjustment, would be difficult, in general. A straightforward special case would be one in which the bands within which floating occurred were purely 'decorative' – soft bands – and as soon as any currency touched the edge (or earlier) the band would be shifted down so that the new central rate equalled the current spot rate.[7] In this case, the exchange rate would be floating, driven by whatever money-supply policy was in force, whether a highly-contingent feedback rule which would be consistent with a fixed exchange rate, an open-loop rule, or whatever. Realignment *per se* would have no implications for the evolution of the exchange rate or the interest differential, and would not be associated with particularly large interest differentials relative to times when realignments did not occur. Under such a regime, the volatility of interest rates would be closely related to the volatility of expected exchange-rate changes. A monetary policy which was designed to stabilise the exchange rate would also stabilise the interest differential.

The conclusion that removal of capital controls would lead to greater volatility of interest rates in the EMS rests on the assumption that realignments would always occur 'too late', and be associated with expected rapid depreciation of the actual exchange rate following the shift in the central rates. (It may also result from extrapolating from the behaviour of offshore interest rates under a regime supported by capital controls, to the behaviour of onshore rates under a regime without such controls.)

On one hand this was the experience under the Bretton Woods system, and it may be argued that the same behaviour would emerge in the EMS. To the extent that the EMS is a disciplinary device, as assumed by Giavazzi and Giovannini, this may be true. Those countries subject to its discipline and unwillingly (in the short term) constrained to tighten their macroeconomic policy may find themselves up against the edge of the bands for some time before being forced painfully and substantially to realign.

On the other hand, the EMS differs in having established a practice of making realignments frequently, almost regularly, and in having wider bands within which currencies float. In addition, there is at least a stated intention among EMS members to achieve a common inflation rate and otherwise make their monetary and fiscal policies consistent with each other. The evidence of volatility of offshore interest rates under a regime supported by capital controls should not be taken as an indication that the same volatility would characterise onshore rates in the absence of capital controls because the removal of controls would constrain (and alter) the choice of policy followed by participants in the EMS.

It may be argued that a system of bands which change so readily is hardly worthy of the name.[8] However, with appropriately-designed monetary and fiscal policies it would involve realignments as infrequently as desired, on average, and from that point of view be indistinguishable from a system of 'hard bands'. Current annual inflation rates in Germany, Italy, and France are roughly 0, 3, and 4.5 per cent and forecasts for the next few years are of the same order of magnitude. Realignments at roughly yearly intervals of the central rates for the lira and franc against the mark by those amounts would fall well inside the existing bands, and allow the currencies to fall smoothly over time, although random fluctuations of exchange rates around the constant real exchange-rate values may induce more frequent realignments. Roughly annual realignments would follow the pattern established over the first eight years of operation of the EMS.

b.   Slow realignments

An alternative to a policy of allowing exchange rates to drift downwards gradually within (nominally-fixed) bands which themselves made occasional discrete downward shifts, would be to effect desired changes in central parities rapidly, though in a continuous way, and then to maintain a period of roughly constant nominal exchange rates within a fixed band. What may be envisaged are thus occasional periods when the central rates move rapidly, though not instantly, to new values, which are then maintained for a relatively long period of time. This would imply a path of short-term interest rates in France, for example, which were roughly equal to German ones during periods when the central exchange rate was constant, and higher during periods when the central rate of the franc was being gradually devalued relative to the mark. Such a policy would imply the real exchange rate in France rising during periods of constant nominal rates, interspersed with periods when the real exchange rate would fall back during periods when readjustments were being made. It is not clear why such a policy would be preferred to one of continuous devaluation, which involved a roughly constant real exchange rate. Unless imposing the costs of variations in real exchange rates is one of the ways the EMS seeks to discipline its more inflationary members.

c.   *Random realignments*

A third possible policy which might be considered as a means of achieving exchange-rate realignments under the EMS with no capital controls might be to make a realignment a random event. Melitz and Michel (1986) suggest this mechanism as one way in which the EMS in the past has allowed realignments without very large capital flows and interest-rate movements. Their model assumes a limited amount of possible speculation which reflects the presence of capital controls. They propose a policy under which a realignment occurs certainly between two extreme dates, but is a random event within the interval, uniformly distributed over it. This policy rule is consistent with asset market equilibrium given their assumption of limited amounts of speculative funds, but would not be consistent with perfect capital markets and unlimited speculative funds, since the hazard rate – the probability of devaluation occurring in the coming interval of time given that it has not occurred already – approaches one as the latest possible date of devaluation approaches. Since the exchange rate then is devalued by a finite amount, this would imply an indefinitely large interest differential on short-term franc assets.

A similar policy which might be considered with perfect capital markets is to have devaluation in the next time interval with a constant probability, and by an amount which would restore the exchange rate to some fundamental value (such as a constant real exchange rate, or a partial adjustment towards it), like the 'speculative bubbles' in Blanchard and Watson (1982). This would entail the French short-term interest rate being higher than the German rate by an amount equal to the probability of devaluation times the size of the devaluation, should one occur over the time interval. Short-term rates in France would thus rise with the time since the last devaluation, as would the real exchange rate. This policy would make large short-term interest rates in France less likely (but large deviations from the fundamental exchange rate more likely) than the policy discussed by Melitz and Michel.

It is not clear why such a policy would be advantageous relative to one which maintained the real exchange rate and the nominal interest differential roughly constant over time. It seems perverse to introduce something like a speculative bubble into the path of real exchange rates and interest rates. It may be argued that a policy of randomly-timed devaluations is not consistent with cooperation among EMS members in the determination of real exchange rates. They would be hard to keep as a surprise if meetings of EMS finance ministers were needed to fix new central rates. A contingency plan worked out in advance might be necessary.

5   Conclusions

A number of writers have expressed surprise at the survival of the EMS over the past eight years, even though it has been supported by capital controls. The stability of the system without them in the future is an important question. The literature on managed exchange rates and speculative attacks suggests that while removing capital controls restricts further the combination of monetary and fiscal policies consistent with the stability of the system, there exist such policies. Avoidance of speculative attacks on currencies and of large fluctuations in interest rates requires that central rates in the EMS are changed frequently enough, and by sufficiently small amounts, so that actual exchange rates are effectively floating and large expected rates of change of exchange rates are avoided. This requires monetary and fiscal policies that generate the necessary exchange-rate stability.

In this study, three (out of the many) possible methods of accommodating the EMS to the removal of exchange controls were considered, these being (1) 'soft bands', (2) slow realignments, and (3) random realignments. 'Soft bands' involves modelling the system as one in which currencies are realigned immediately and by a small amount when the edges of existing bands are reached. The burden of keeping currencies within an existing band, so as to control the frequency of realignment, is then placed upon monetary and fiscal policy, rather than exchange-market intervention. Slow realignments involves limiting the pace at which currencies' central rates are changed, when changes are necessary. The third scenario needs no elaboration. Of these, for reasons discussed in Section 4, the first appears to be the most satisfactory approach, and need not entail more interest-rate volatility in the EMS. Indeed, it may well entail less.

The implications of an EMS without capital controls for members' macro policy do not seem to be particularly severe. Current and projected inflation differences could be accommodated by shifts in central rates at roughly annual intervals by amounts which leave actual spot rates floating freely within the ± 2.25 per cent (± 6.0 per cent for Italy) bands. Feedback rules for interest rates seem to be able to maintain floating exchange rates within fairly narrow bounds (as in the recent experience of the UK, which has been able to maintain the pound sterling within a very narrow range relative to the Deutsche mark for most of 1987). The lira seems to have been floating well inside its band for the last two years, during which time the central rate has been changed twice by amounts which are small relative to the band-width.

Of course, maintaining exchange rates within narrow ranges in the absence of capital controls may require close coordination of interest rates: an interest-rate change in Germany may have to be followed in the UK if the pound is to remain stable relative to the mark. However, this degree of coordination of interest-rate policy appears to have been achievable.

Without specifying an objective function and comparing the costs of optimal policies under various regimes, conclusions about the credibility and stability of a system of managed floating without capital controls are tentative. Nevertheless, the recent experience of the EMS and the implications of free capital movements do not suggest that such a regime is bound to be unstable.

APPENDIX: DATA FOR FIGURES 8.1–8.4

Data on price levels and exchange rates in Figures 8.1–8.4 are monthly figures taken from *International Financial Statistics* (data to the end of 1985) and the European Commission publication *Eurostatistics* (for data for 1986 and 1987).

Price Level – Consumer prices, general index. Inflation rates are $100 \cdot ($CPI
Data $(t) - CPI(t - 12))/CPI(t - 12)$.

Exchange – Exchange rate expressed as the price of 1 ECU. *IFS* data is for end
Rate   of month; *Eurostatistics* gives monthly average figures.
Data

Central – data from various issues of the *Bulletin* of the European Communi-
Rates and   ties' Commission.
Parity
Grid

NOTES

1 Obstfeld (1985), p. 442.
2 Melitz and Michel (1986) describe only those of October 1981, June 1982, and March 1983 as major. Since they wrote, substantial realignments have taken place, in July 1985 and April 1986.
3 Other shocks do affect the relative strengths of currencies in the EMS

exchange-rate mechanism, but these do not appear to have been a major cause of realignments. For example, it is widely acknowledged that when the dollar is weak, the Deutsche mark tends to rise within the EMS. See for example Melitz (1988). The tensions within the EMS thereby caused by dollar fluctuations seem mostly to have been absorbed.

4 The year-on-year growth rate of the CPI for June 1987 was 4.42 per cent for Italy, 3.27 per cent for France, and 0.16 per cent for Germany. The National Institute's forecasts for inflation are:

	1987	1988	1989	1990	1991
Germany	−0.1	0.3	0.0	0.2	0.0
France	3.0	2.3	2.3	3.0	3.3
Italy	4.9	6.2			

Source: National Institute Economic Review (August 1987).

5 Buiter (1986b), p. 35.

6 A policy rule which appears infeasible in the absence of capital controls and with perfect capital markets is one of anticipated devaluations at regular intervals. Giavazzi and Pagano (1986) compute the optimal inflation rate in a country which belongs to the EMS, assuming devaluations at fixed intervals, and assuming that the policymaker cares about the interest rate on assets of a given maturity at issue. The optimal policy involves discrete devaluations. This is inconsistent with the conventional assumption made in the literature on efficient financial markets that foreseeable discontinuities in asset prices cannot occur.

7 Nigel Lawson appeared to be proposing something similar for a wider system of target zones at the annual meeting of the IMF. The *Financial Times* (1 October 1987) reported 'if the time came to adjust one currency's value, the movement in its central rate would be confined within the existing band. This would prevent markets from being given a one-way bet and allow central banks to retain tactical flexibility'.

8 For example, Obstfeld (1985) remarks 'if the notion of a target zone is to have any content, there will be some occasions when the central bank takes a stand against exchange movements it views as unwarranted. Disagreement between the markets and the authorities in these circumstances would entail massive reserve movements harmful to financial stability'.

REFERENCES

Begg, D. and C. Wyplosz (1987). 'Exchange Rates, Capital Controls, and the EMS', in Richard Portes and Ralph Bryant (eds), *Global Macroeconomics: Policy Conflict and Cooperation*, London, Macmillan.

Blanchard, O. J. and M. W. Watson (1982). 'Bubbles, Rational Expectations, and Financial Markets', in Paul Wachtel (ed.), *Crisis in the Economic and Financial System*, Lexington, Mass., Lexington Books.

Buiter, W. H. (1986a). 'Fiscal Prerequisites for a Viable Managed Exchange Rate Regime: A Non-technical Eclectic Introduction', CEPR Discussion Paper, No. 129.

(1986b). 'A Gold Standard Isn't Viable Unless Supported by Sufficiently Flexible Monetary and Fiscal Policy', CEPR Discussion Paper, No. 125.

Giavazzi, Francesco, and Alberto Giovannini (1986). 'The EMS and the Dollar', *Economic Policy*, Vol. 2 (April), pp. 456–74.

(1987). 'Models of the EMS: Is Europe a Greater Deutschmark Area?', in Richard Portes and Ralph Bryant (eds), *Global Macroeconomics: Policy Conflict and Cooperation*, London, Macmillan, pp. 237–76.

(1988). 'The Role of the Exchange-rate Regime in a Disinflation: Empirical Evidence on the European Monetary System', Chapter 4 in this volume.

Giavazzi, F. and M. Pagano (1985). 'Capital Controls and the European Monetary System', in F. Giavazzi (ed.), *Capital Controls and Foreign Exchange Legislation*, Euromobiliare Occasional Papers, No. 1 (June).

(1986). 'The Advantage of Tying One's Hands: EMS Discipline and Central Bank Credibility' (May) (mimeo); (1986) CEPR Discussion Paper, No. 135; (1988) *European Economic Review* (June).

Melitz, J. (1985). 'The Welfare Case for the European Monetary System', *Journal of International Money and Finance*, Vol. 4, pp. 485–506.

(1988). 'The Prospect of a Depreciating Dollar and Possible Tensions Inside the EMS', CEPR Discussion Paper, No. 97. Also (1988) in *Schweizerische Zeitschrift für Volkswirtschaft und Statistik*, No. 1.

Melitz, J. and P. Michel (1986). 'The Dynamic Stability of the European Monetary System', CEPR Discussion Paper, No. 96.

Micossi, S. (1985). 'The Intervention and Financing Mechanisms of the EMS and the Role of the ECU', Banca Nazionale del Lavoro *Quarterly Review* (December), pp. 405–24.

Obstfeld, M. (1984). 'Balance of Payments Crises and Devaluation', *Journal of Money Credit and Banking*, Vol. XVI, No. 2 (May), pp. 208–17.

(1985). 'Floating Exchange Rates: Experience and Prospects', Brookings Papers on Economic Activity, No. 2, pp. 369–450.

Oudiz, G. (1985). 'European Policy Coordination: An Evaluation', CEPR Discussion Paper, No. 81.

Padoa-Schioppa, T. (1985). 'Policy Coordination and the EMS Experience', in W. H. Buiter and R. H. Marston (eds), *International Economic Policy Coordination*, New York, Cambridge University Press.

(1987). 'Efficiency, Stability, and Equity', Report of a Study Group appointed by the European Commission (April).

Rogoff, K. (1985). 'Can Exchange Rate Predictability be Achieved Without Monetary Convergence? Evidence from the EMS', *European Economic Review*, No. 28, Nos. 1–2 (June–July), pp. 93–115.

Thygesen, N. (1984). 'Exchange-Rate Policies and Monetary Targets in the EMS Countries', in Rainer Masera and Robert Triffin (eds), *Europe's Money. Problems in European Monetary Co-ordination and Integration*, Oxford, Oxford University Press.

Discussion

DANIEL GROS

The topic of this study, 'Can the EMS survive the planned abolition of capital controls?' might fill a conference volume, but the author limits himself to a discussion of some twenty pages. Why? I believe the reason is that the problem is at the same time both very simple and very complex. It is simple because if you start from first principles the answer is indeed quite obvious: once the nominal exchange rate is fixed (or precommitted), the domestic authorities can no longer control the money supply; all they have to do is to fix a path for domestic credit which does not imply a continuous loss of reserves. In this sense, I would agree with the author that there certainly exists a set of monetary and fiscal policies that makes the EMS sustainable even without capital controls and that does not seem to be too 'severe'. In this simple view, monetary shocks would be accommodated by reserve movements and a real shock would have to be accommodated by movements in prices and wages. The monetary authorities would not have to do anything, they would just have to accept the resulting fluctuations in reserves and interest rates.

But things do not seem to be quite so simple. If one takes the impossibility theorem by Padoa-Schioppa (Chapter 12 in this volume) it seems that there is a view that the EMS in its present shape could not survive the abolition of capital controls.

What determines this difference of view? The fact that the simple view does not take into account political realities. The simple view works well in the case of the Netherlands. The Dutch case is instructive because most observers would probably agree that it is clear why it works: the Dutch central bank follows almost every move of the Bundesbank. But most observers would also agree that it would be politically absurd to expect countries like France and Italy to behave this way. The real and interesting problems arise therefore when it is recognised that for some countries it is politically unacceptable to face a complete loss of monetary sovereignty.

But if EMS members like France and Italy try to conduct an independent monetary policy, realignments become inevitable sooner or later. At this point, it would still be possible to make the EMS viable with a simple rule: just do everything necessary to keep the (market) exchange rate from jumping. But the same political reasons that made it impossible to precommit monetary policy to the defence of the exchange rate will make it difficult to at least impose the constraint on monetary policy that the exchange rate cannot jump; especially since the rule 'keep the exchange rate on a continuous path' is much more vague and that makes it difficult to judge whether any specific action taken by the central bank makes it more or less likely that this target will be reached. Once the public realises that there is a possibility that the exchange rate jumps from time to time, the situation becomes complicated since it will change into a game between the public and the authorities. For this sort of game, one can think of many different rules and outcomes.

The framework proposed by Maurice Obstfeld (Chapter 9 in this volume) is a good example of this. In his study, the equilibrium is stable as long as the authorities follow a sensible policy – that is, as long as they do not accommodate 100 per cent all nominal shocks.

Given that the economic prerequisites for having a sustainable EMS without capital controls are quite simple, one might have asked why capital controls were introduced in the first place. This should give some indication of why the authorities were unwilling to subordinate their policies to the constraints imposed by free capital flows, and what difficulties can be expected if capital controls are lifted.

In France and Italy, the aim was presumably to keep domestic nominal and real interest rates low in the face of rapid inflation and a depreciating currency.[1] This rationale should no longer be operating in the present much more stable environment of lower inflation rates (as well as lower inflation rate differentials) and stable (intra-EMS) exchange rates. This implies that one should be relatively optimistic about the willingness of the French and Italian authorities to accept the external constraint imposed by the EMS without capital controls. But it has also been argued that in the case of Italy an additional aim of the capital controls was to keep interest rates on the public sector debt as low as possible. This rationale continues to exist since the debt–GNP ratio has risen even further during recent years and the deficit remains high as well. Rudiger Dornbusch emphasises (Chapter 2 in this volume) this public finance aspect when he argues that the optimal inflation rate in the fiscally weak countries is definitely not zero and might be around 6–10 per cent. This suggests that either the nature of the EMS has to change, or that the fiscally-weak countries will experience difficulties in trying to stay in the EMS without capital controls. If the countries with high deficits and public debt–GNP ratios adopt such a policy without the protection of capital controls, they would also have to adopt a crawling-peg policy inside the EMS since inflation differentials of this size cannot be accommodated by only occasional realignments. This is hardly compatible with the aim of creating a zone of monetary stability in Europe.

In conclusion, I would therefore say that the author is certainly correct in saying that the economic prerequisites for a stable EMS are not too severe, but what might be lacking is the political will to make this simple view come true.

NOTE
1 As an aside, I would like to note that Belgium gets off rather lightly in discussions about capital controls, simply because its controls are labelled differently – namely, a dual exchange-rate system.

9 Competitiveness, Realignment, and Speculation: The Role of Financial Markets*

MAURICE OBSTFELD

1 Introduction

Since its inauguration in March 1979, the Exchange-Rate Mechanism (ERM) of the European Monetary System (EMS) has functioned with the aid of frequent currency realignments – to date, more than one per year on average. In the eyes of many observers, the strategy of frequent realignment has allowed the system to survive in spite of the rather divergent macroeconomic policies pursued by the 'Big Three' of the EMS, France, Germany, and Italy.[1] An apparently critical element in minimising the financial disruption caused by realignments has been the control over cross-border financial flows maintained by France and Italy. The large onshore–offshore interest differentials that have emerged during currency crises suggest that capital controls have played an important role in insulating the French and Italian financial systems from the full force of speculative capital movements.

Current and planned measures liberalising the external capital accounts of France and Italy call into question the continued viability of a widely-understood EMS policy of periodic realignment. Yet the speculative response of capital flows to expected parity change is an area that has received little attention in the academic literature.[2] The relative neglect of the role parity changes play in balance of payments crises is puzzling: empirically, devaluation fears are a leading – perhaps *the* leading – factor behind currency flight, just as speculative inflows are often inspired by hopes of revaluation. A further shortcoming of the existing literature is that, for the most part, it stops short of analysing the possible *real* macroeconomic effects of exchange-rate crises.

This study is intended as a first step in evaluating the real and monetary effects of EMS-type realignment policies in a setting of free cross-border

232

financial flows. A simple model that serves as the study's analytical framework is sketched in Section 2. The precise question then asked is: what kinds of equilibria can arise when markets expect a loss of home competitiveness against foreign goods to lead to realignment? Although much work remains to be done, the results of a preliminary investigation are quite suggestive.

The first set of results, described in Section 3, concerns a situation in which there are no *fundamental* factors (such as fiscal expansion) behind domestic inflation. Instead, Section 3 analyses the economy's behaviour under exchange-rate rules that allow cumulative inflation automatically to trigger realignment. The key finding is that such rules can induce multiple equilibria. Specifically, if realignment is expected to maintain or enhance external competitiveness, the economy has two equilibria. One of these involves an inflationary spiral in which speculators force a collapse of the fixed exchange rate and a depreciation of the currency to its new peg. When realignment is expected to aim at a real appreciation of the domestic currency, however, there is only one equilibrium: the inflation–depreciation spiral cannot occur.

These results suggest that under conditions of capital mobility, a systematic realignment policy may have disruptive effects – in financial markets, in the output and labour markets, and on domestic inflation. Although the results are model-specific and therefore should not be taken too literally, they also provide a rationale for the recent EMS practice of *only partially* offsetting differential inflation through currency realignment.[3]

A second set of results, explained in Section 4, studies expected realignment in a setting where domestic price inflation is already being driven by fundamentals (here, fiscal expansion). The possible equilibria of the economy depend on how fully the authorities attempt to offset past inflation through currency depreciation. If devaluation is large relative to past inflation, an exchange-rate collapse occurs as soon as an expansionary fiscal policy is enacted, but before any real appreciation has occurred. In the face of smaller devaluations, the fixed exchange rate can coexist with domestic inflation for some time before the inevitable collapse occurs.

2   The model

A simple model with sticky output prices is the setting for the discussion; in line with the likely evolution of financial arrangements within the EMS, perfect capital mobility is assumed. Three basic hypotheses are (1) that the exchange rate is pegged entirely through the intervention of the home central bank, (2) that the home central bank has only a limited capacity to defend the exchange rate (in a sense to be made precise below), and (3) that the fixed exchange rate must be abandoned (at least temporarily) once this capacity has been exhausted. These hypotheses do not square perfectly with the facts of the EMS, but they lead to a useful benchmark model on which more realistic analyses can be built.

The analytical framework is the overshooting model of Dornbusch (1976) and Mussa (1977), as set out in the survey by Obstfeld and Stockman (1985). In the following description, variables other than interest rates are natural logarithms, and a variable such as $Dz(t)$ is the (right-hand) time derivative of z at time t. Perfect foresight is assumed, so no distinction is made between actual and expected rates of change.

With free capital mobility and perfect substitution between domestic- and foreign-currency bonds, the onshore domestic interest rate, $i(t)$, is related by interest parity to the (fixed) foreign rate, i^*, and the expected rate of domestic currency depreciation, $De(t)$:

$$i(t) = i^* + De(t) \tag{9.1}$$

The exchange rate $e(t)$ is the price of foreign currency in terms of domestic.

If $m(t)$ is the home money supply, y the (fixed) level of domestic output, and $p(t)$ the money price of output, equilibrium in the money market occurs when:

$$m(t) - p(t) = \gamma y - \lambda i(t) \tag{9.2}$$

Let p^* be the (fixed) foreign-currency price of foreign output, which is distinct from domestic output. Aggregate demand for domestic output is:

$$d(t) = \phi[p^* + e(t) - p(t)] - \sigma[i(t) - Dp(t)] \tag{9.3}$$

Because the price of home output is sticky, aggregate demand and supply can differ in the short run.

Imbalances in the output market contribute to price adjustment, however, and the model's final element is an equation to describe price dynamics. Let $\bar{p}(t)$ denote the output price that would currently clear the goods market; as in Mussa (1977), this price is defined as the solution to:

$$y = \phi[p^* + e(t) - \bar{p}(t)] - \sigma[i(t) - Dp(t)] \tag{9.4}$$

Then the inflation rate is given by:

$$Dp(t) = \theta[d(t) - y] + D\bar{p}(t) \tag{9.5}$$

where θ measures the sensitivity of inflation to excess output demand. The second term in equation (9.5) is central to the discussion below, as it captures the pure effects of inflationary expectations on the price level.

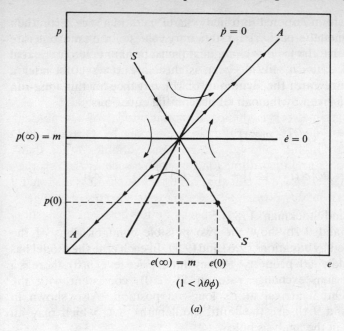

$$(1 < \lambda\theta\phi)$$

(a)

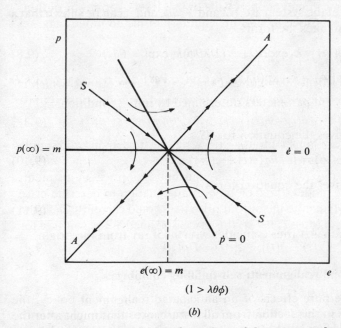

$$(1 > \lambda\theta\phi)$$

(b)

Figure 9.1 The two possible configurations of the system under a floating exchange rate

Assume now (for notational simplicity) that i^*, y, and p^* are zero. Then for a constant money stock, m, the stationary values of the exchange rate and price level are $e(\infty) = p(\infty) = m$, and the stationary value of the real exchange rate, $x(t) = p^* + e(t) - p(t)$, is therefore $x(\infty) = 0$. Under a floating exchange rate, the dynamics of convergence to this long-run equilibrium are given by the pair of differential equations

$$De(t) = \frac{1}{\lambda} [p(t) - p(\infty)] \tag{9.6}$$

$$Dp(t) = \theta\phi[e(t) - e(\infty)] + \left(\frac{1}{\lambda} - \theta\phi\right) [p(t) - p(\infty)] \tag{9.7}$$

(see Obstfeld and Stockman, 1985).[4]

Figures 9.1a and 9.1b show the two possible configurations of the system described by equations (9.6) and (9.7). In each case the model has the familiar saddlepath property: for any initial price level $p(0)$, there is a unique equilibrium exchange rate on SS, $e(0)$, consistent with the economy's eventual arrival at its long-run position. Also shown in Figures 9.1a and 9.1b are the 'anti' saddlepaths AA, which play an important role in the analysis below.

The two roots of the system are $1/\lambda$ and $-\theta\phi$, and it can be shown that a general solution takes the form:

$$e(t) - e(\infty) = k_1 \exp(t/\lambda) - (1/\lambda\theta\phi)k_2 \exp(-\theta\phi t) \tag{9.8}$$

$$p(t) - p(\infty) = k_1 \exp(t/\lambda) + k_2 \exp(-\theta\phi t) \tag{9.9}$$

where k_1 and k_2 are parameters determined by initial conditions.

Setting $k_1 = 0$ gives the equation for SS:

$$p(t) - p(\infty) = -\lambda\theta\phi[e(t) - e(\infty)]. \tag{9.10}$$

Setting $k_2 = 0$ gives the equation for AA:

$$p(t) = e(t). \tag{9.11}$$

The unstable path AA thus coincides with a 45° ray from the origin.

3   Inflation and realignment: self-fulfilling equilibria

To focus on the pure effects of an anticipated realignment policy, the model abstracts in this section from all disturbances that might alter the long-run equilibrium level of external competitiveness. The model thus concentrates on monetary factors alone, and asks if, even under these relatively uncomplicated conditions, expected realignments can have disruptive effects on the macroeconomy. In particular, can expected realignments lead to equilibria that look like inflation–devaluation spirals?

The answer depends on the mechanism in place to fix the exchange rate. Here I assume that the policy authority allows the exchange rate to float once private capital outflows have reduced the domestic money stock to a *positive* lower bound of m_0. Such a situation would arise, for example, if the central bank's external credit lines provided insufficient foreign exchange to purchase outstanding domestic credit and if other tools for reducing the domestic component of the monetary base were unavailable.

The realignment rule followed by the policy authority must now be specified. Imagine that the exchange rate is initially fixed at the level $\bar{e}$ and that the corresponding long-run price level is $\bar{p}$. (To these prices there corresponds an endogenously-determined money stock $\bar{m} = \bar{p} + \gamma y - \lambda i^* = \bar{p}$.) The policy authority's rule is to devalue the currency to an exchange rate of $\bar{e}' > \bar{e}$ if the price level reaches the trigger value of $\tilde{p} > \bar{p}$.

Suppose first that $\bar{e}' \geq \tilde{p}$. The interpretation of this condition is that when p reaches the trigger point, the authorities devalue the currency to a level that (at a minimum) restores current external competitiveness to its long-run value. Clearly, one equilibrium of the model is the one in which nothing happens and the economy remains at the initial equilibrium, $e = \bar{e}$, $p = \bar{p}$. With no shocks disturbing markets, there is no reason for p ever to reach its trigger level and bring the realignment policy into play.

There is, however, a second equilibrium, illustrated in Figure 9.2. (The analysis henceforth assumes, without loss of generality, that the configuration of Figure 9.1a is the relevant one.) In this equilibrium, speculators mount an attack on the currency as soon as the realignment rule becomes known. Private capital outflows reduce the money supply to m_0 and force the central bank to withdraw from the foreign-exchange market: the economy is now on an unstable path of the *floating-rate* system associated with a money supply equal to the minimum level m_0. The collapse results in a sharp currency depreciation (to $e(0)$), after which e and p rise together in an inflation–depreciation spiral. When p reaches $\tilde{p}$, $e = \bar{e}'$ and the central bank can peg the exchange rate at this new level if no further realignment is expected.[5] Subsequently, rising domestic prices erode any short-term gain in competitiveness as p rises to its new long-run level $\bar{p}' = \bar{e}'$.

This second equilibrium is driven entirely by self-fulfilling expectations that there will be a crisis followed by inflation and a realignment.[6] Since a

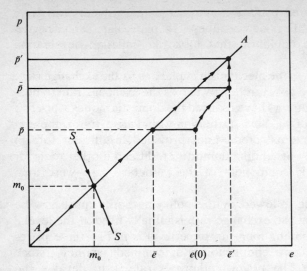

Figure 9.2 Equilibrium when speculators mount an attack on the currency

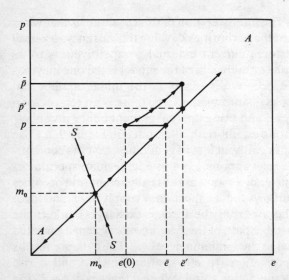

Figure 9.3 Non-equilibrium in which the currency initially appreciates

speculative attack causes a depreciation of the domestic currency, each
speculator has an incentive to join in if he believes an attack is about to
occur. The immediate real currency depreciation helps pull domestic
prices up until the trigger price level is reached. In this alternative

equilibrium, the exchange rate reaches its new peg just as the trigger price level is reached, so there is no need for a discrete antipicated jump in the exchange rate, which would be inconsistent with asset-market equilibrium (Krugman, 1979). Although the exchange-rate collapse causes an immediate real depreciation, the currency subsequently appreciates in real terms during the transitional float that precedes the return to realigned fixed rates.

Perhaps surprisingly, there is only one equilibrium – the first of the two described above – when $\bar{e}' < \bar{p}$, so that the policy authority realigns without attempting fully to offset the price inflation that has occurred in the past. To see this, consider Figure 9.3. In the case shown there, the only exchange-rate paths avoiding a discrete jump at the moment of realignment call for an *appreciation* of the currency just after the attack that drives the central bank from the exchange market. This immediate appreciation means that the hypothesised speculative attack in fact never occurs: no individual speculator would find it profitable to participate. The economy thus remains at $e = \bar{e}$, $p = \bar{p}$ if it is believed that the realignment policy will not fully offset past inflation.

To understand the difference between the present case and the last one, observe that the post-attack change in the exchange rate is influenced by two factors, the initial drop in the money supply (from $\hat{m}$ to m_0) *and* the expectation that the exchange rate will be pegged at the level $\bar{e}'$ in the future. The first factor pushes the price of foreign currency downward after the attack, the second pushes it upward.[7] The second factor dominates when the realigned exchange rate is more competitive because it is only by depreciating initially that the real exchange rate can be higher also when the central bank re-enters the foreign-exchange market.

The case $\bar{e}' = \bar{p}$ is a borderline case in which both equilibria are possible. In this case, the authorities peg at a nominal exchange rate that maintains the original level of competitiveness, given that p is at the trigger point. The initial speculative attack leaves the floating exchange rate at its pre-attack level $\bar{e}$, after which e and p rise together along AA until p reaches $\bar{p}$. At this point, the currency is again pegged and the economy is at a new stationary position.[8]

4 Attacks that are justified by fundamentals

Section 3 establishes the existence of multiple equilibria under an accommodative realignment rule. Central to the discussion was the precise form of the authorities' exchange-rate rule: under alternative rules the multiplicity can disappear. If the policy rule is to realign only

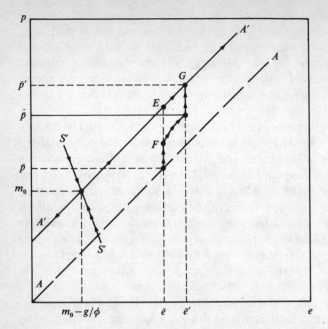

Figure 9.4 Reaction of the economy to fiscal stimulus followed by realignment

after the *real* exchange rate has appreciated by a given amount, for example, the inflationary paths of Section 3 are no longer supported by the policy rule, because the attack that sets off the inflation leads to a temporary gain in competitiveness, not a loss.

Section 4 demonstrates how speculative attacks can nonetheless occur when realignment is prompted by a current or prospective loss in external competitiveness due to *fundamental* factors. (In contrast, the inflations prompting the realignments described in the previous section were entirely the result of the prospect of accommodation.) Once again, the behaviour of the model turns on the degree to which the authorities attempt to offset inflation through devaluation.

Under the posited conditions of a fixed exchange rate and interest parity, continuing domestic-credit expansion by the authorities would lead to steady foreign reserve loss rather than to real currency appreciation. I therefore assume that the source of real appreciation is, instead, fiscal. With a fixed exchange rate and a sticky price level, fiscal expansion induces temporary excess output demand and thus a gradual price-level rise that appreciates the currency in real terms and eventually restores output-market equilibrium. The specific scenario analysed is one in which fiscal expansion sets off domestic inflation, but the market expects the policy authority to devalue some time before the full upward adjustment of the home price level is complete.

The model used in the previous sections can be extended to allow for aggregate-demand shocks such as fiscal-policy shifts. Write the aggregate-demand equation (9.3) as:

$$d(t) = \phi[p^* + e(t) - p(t)] - \sigma[i(t) - Dp(t)] + g$$

where g is a demand-shift factor.

The steady state of the floating-rate model becomes $p(\infty) = m$, $e(\infty) = m - g/\phi$, for any constant money supply m. The equation of the unstable linear path AA is now $p(t) = e(t) + g/p$: a rise in g causes a parallel leftward shift of AA in Figures 9.1a and 9.1b.

Figure 9.4 shows one example of how the economy can react to a fiscal stimulus followed by realignment. Initially $g = 0$ and the long-run values of the price level and exchange rate are shown as $\bar{p}$ and $\bar{e}$; a rise in g sets prices moving upward. (The nominal money supply also must rise over time, as a result of official intervention, to maintain equilibrium in the money market.) So long as the exchange rate remains fixed at $\bar{e}$, the economy moves vertically toward point E, the new long-run position that would eventually be reached in the absence of an exchange-rate change. Point E lies on $A'A'$, the 'anti' saddlepath associated with a level g of the demand shift parameter.

Assume now that the market expects the authorities to realign the exchange rate at $\bar{e}'$ once the price level reaches $\bar{p}$. In this case, an attack occurs at point F, so that the economy is placed on a path of the floating-rate system associated with the minimal money supply m_0 (and the saddlepath $S'S'$). The equilibrium path is the unique one with the property that e reaches $\bar{e}'$ just as p reaches $\bar{p}$. No discrete jump in e takes place at the moment of repegging (though there is a sharp capital inflow that raises m), and the economy converges afterward to point G as inflation falls to zero. Clearly the devaluation has no long-run effect on the real exchange rate, but it does cause a higher long-run price level.

Two features of the path just described deserve emphasis. First, even though the eventual attack is perfectly foreseen, there is an initial period following the fiscal impulse during which prices rise, the capital account is in surplus, and the exchange rate remains fixed. The pattern of capital inflows and real currency appreciation followed by external crisis is reminiscent of events that accompanied the stabilisation plans undertaken in Latin America's Southern Cone in the late 1970s. Second, competitiveness continues to deteriorate during the transitional period of floating (since p is rising faster than e below $A'A'$, which itself has a 45°

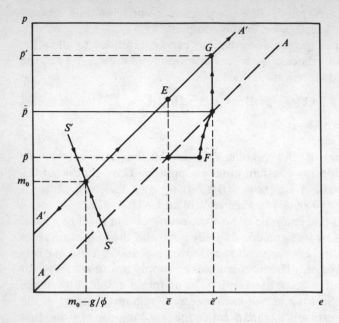

Figure 9.5 Another adjustment path

slope). Realignment thus occurs after *steady* deterioration in competitiveness, in contrast to the example of the last section. There, the real exchange rate first depreciated (as a result of collapse), then appreciated as realignment approached.

As Figure 9.5 shows, however, other adjustment paths are possible. In Figure 9.5, the authorities' realignment policy calls for a devaluation so large that competitiveness is (temporarily) restored to its original (pre-fiscal expansion) level. In this case, the fiscal expansion sparks an *immediate* collapse, and a nominal currency depreciation to point F. The associated real currency depreciation is completely reversed during the transitional float that brings the economy to $e = \bar{e}'$, $p = \bar{p}$. After repegging, there is a further loss in competitiveness as inflation brings the economy to point G. Once again, there is no ultimate gain in competitiveness as a result of the exchange-rate change.

The lesson of this example is that the expectation of an overenergetic attempt to restore competitiveness despite a structural shift in the real exchange rate can set off an immediate run on the currency. Such runs occur even before any real appreciation emerges, and thus may appear to be without foundation in market fundamentals. Nonetheless, they are the result of rational anticipations of future exchange-rate policy.

The fiscal-policy shock analysed here is not the only one calling for a change in the long-run real exchange rate. A very plausible situation involves expected devaluation after an adverse shift in the demand for domestic exports. (Such a devaluation could have the advantage, in principle, of shortening the period of recession that results from the shock.) A puzzling result is easy to verify using the techniques employed above: in many cases an equilibrium does not exist.

Obviously, much of the analysis above rests heavily on the assumption of continuous-time trading. A discrete-time model would allow devaluations that were not preceded by transitional floats, although paths similar to those analysed above would still be possible. Arguably, the continuous-time trading assumption is reasonably close to reality.

5   Implications and extensions

The model examined above is simple, but its implications are stark. A policy of attempting to accommodate domestic inflation through *real* devaluation can lead to multiple rational-expectations equilibria. One of these involves an exchange crisis and a subsequent spiral of inflation and depreciation that ultimately leave the economy with a permanently higher price level and exchange rate. In contrast, a policy of partial accommodation – if credible – precludes the inflationary equilibrium. As noted in the introduction, this reasoning may provide one rationale for the failure of EMS realignments fully to accommodate differential inflation in recent years.[9]

Exchange-rate crises can also arise in response to realignments that attempt to offset inflation due to expansionary fiscal policy. Inflation and real appreciation may continue for some time before a collapse occurs, even though an eventual collapse is anticipated by the market. A sufficiently large anticipated devaluation may, however, cause an immediate attack that itself postpones the inevitable real appreciation.

The model used above clearly leaves many unanswered questions. For example, is a single-country analysis applicable to situations in which several EMS members may be intervening to defend a parity?[10] A related question concerns the equilibria that arise when the authorities' ability to defend a rate is *not* limited in the manner assumed above, so that the authorities *can* – and do – purchase the entire money supply to defend the exchange rate. This possibility would appear to rule out the multiple equilibria of Section 3, but not obviously to preclude the attacks of Section 4, since the public could reduce its money holdings to zero just before devaluation.

At a deeper level, one must ask whether there are plausible policymaker preferences that might generate the types of realignment rules examined in this study. All of these questions raise difficult problems for economic analysis, but they are central to understanding the present and prospective functioning of the EMS.

APPENDIX: ALGEBRAIC ANALYSIS OF SELF-FULFILLING EQUILIBRIA

An algebraic analysis of the inflationary equilibrium discussed in Section 3 clarifies some aspects of self-fulfilling paths. Such an analysis can be based on equations (9.8) and (9.9), the general solutions for the dynamic system describing the floating-rate model.

To construct an inflationary equilibrium, one must find a transition time T and constants k_1 and k_2 such that $e(T) = e'$ and $p(T) = \bar{p}$ when $e(t)$ and $p(t)$ follow the equations:

$$e(t) - m_0 = k_1 \exp(t/\lambda) - (1/\lambda\theta\phi)k_2\exp(-\theta\phi t) \tag{A9.1}$$

$$p(t) - m_0 = k_1 \exp(t/\lambda) + k_2\exp(-\theta\phi t) \tag{A9.2}$$

that is, when the post-attack floating rate is determined in a system with money supply m_0. One initial condition is given by the stickiness of prices: $p(0) = \bar{p}$. So there are three conditions – one initial, two terminal – to determine the unknown parameters T, k_1, and k_2.

The solution for T is given implicitly by the non-linear equation:

$$A(T) = B(T) \tag{A9.3}$$

where

$$\begin{aligned} A(T) &= [\bar{\bar{p}} - m_0 - (\bar{p} - m_0)\exp(-\theta\phi T)]/ \\ &\quad [\bar{e}' - m_0 + (1/\lambda\theta\phi)(\bar{p} - m_0)\exp(-\theta\phi T)] \\ B(T) &= [\exp(T/\lambda) - \exp(-\theta\phi T)]/[\exp(T/\lambda) + (1/\lambda\theta\phi)\exp(-\theta\phi T)]. \end{aligned} \tag{A9.4}$$

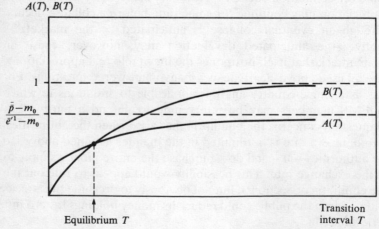

Figure A9.1 How T is determined by the equation $A(T) = B(T)$

Figure A9.1 illustrates how T is determined by (A9.3). Note that as $T \to \infty$, $A(T) \to (\bar{p} - m_0)/(\bar{e}' - m_0)$ while $B(T) \to 1$. Thus, for realignment rules such that $\bar{e}' \geq \bar{p}$, at least one intersection of $A(T)$ and $B(T)$ is guaranteed. Intersections are also possible for some non-accommodative realignment rules, of course, but these do not define equilibria because the currency would have to *appreciate* immediately after the speculative attack that sets off the inflation.

One case that is easy to analyse explicitly is the borderline case referred to above, in which $\bar{e}' = \bar{p}$. In this case the solution to (A9.3) is:

$$T = \lambda \log[(\bar{p} - m_0)/(p_0 - m_0)] \tag{A9.5}$$

Direct calculation shows that the appropriate initial conditions are

$$k_1 = \bar{p} - m_0 \quad \text{and} \quad k_2 = 0,$$

which imply that the equilibrium floating exchange rate immediately after the attack is:

$$e(0) = \bar{e}$$

the original peg. After the attack, the exchange rate therefore moves toward its new peg along the path AA in Figure 9.2. The adjustment process is in this case a pure inflation that does not affect relative output prices.

NOTES
* I am grateful for helpful conversations with Guillermo Calvo and Stephen O'Connell and for critical comments from participants in the Conference on the EMS, especially Marcus Miller. I also had the benefit of presenting these results in a seminar at the Research Department of the International Monetary Fund. All errors are, however, my own. Financial support from the National Science Foundation and the Alfred P. Sloan Foundation is acknowledged with thanks.
1 Among recent reviews of the EMS experience are Collins (1987), Giavazzi and Giovannini (1986), Rogoff (1985), and Ungerer *et al.* (1986).
2 Exceptions include Blanco and Garber (1986), Feenstra (1985), Gros (1987), and Obstfeld (1984). As will become apparent below, some of Feenstra's conclusions, although reached in a financial setting more descriptive of some developing economies than of Europe, are quite relevant for analysing prospective developments in the EMS.
3 See, for example, Giavazzi and Pagano (1988).
4 Equations (9.6) and (9.7) follow from (9.1), (9.2), and the fact that under price-adjustment rule (9.5), the real exchange rate is driven to its long-run value of zero according to the equation $Dx(t) = -\theta\phi x(t)$.
5 A similar response to anticipated devaluation is analysed by Feenstra (1985) in a flexible-price model of currency substitution based on utility maximisation. Notice that, in contrast to the case discussed in Obstfeld (1984), the length of the transitional period of floating is *endogenous* here. This is also true of the transitional float analysed in Section 4.
6 The alternative equilibrium provides another example of the type of self-

fulfilling crisis described in my 1986 study. The role of self-fulfilling accommodative policies is studied in a different context by Corden (1986).

7 See, for example, Flood and Garber (1983) or Obstfeld and Stockman (1985).

8 An algebraic analysis is given in the Appendix.

9 A natural question is whether capital controls preclude multiple equilibria by preventing – or at least minimising – speculative reserve outflows. Models of anticipatory wage and price setting, such as Calvo (1983), suggest a tentative negative answer. The question, however, deserves a thorough analysis.

10 For a clear account of EMS intervention arrangements, see the study by Mastropasqua, Micossi, and Rinaldi (Chapter 10 in this volume).

REFERENCES

Blanco, H. and P. M. Garber (1986). 'Recurrent Devaluation and Speculative Attacks on the Mexican Peso', *Journal of Political Economy*, Vol. 94 (February), pp. 148–66.

Calvo, G. A. (1983). 'Staggered Contracts and Exchange Rate Policy', in Jacob A. Frenkel (ed.), *Exchange Rates and International Macroeconomics*, Chicago, University of Chicago Press for the National Bureau of Economic Research.

Collins, S. M. (1987). 'PPP and the Peso Problem: Exchange Rates in the EMS', Harvard University (manuscript).

Corden, W. M. (1986). 'Exchange Rate Depreciation, the Current Account and Wages', *Economic Record*, Special Issue, pp. 14–21.

Dornbusch, R. (1976). 'Expectations and Exchange Rate Dynamics', *Journal of Political Economy*, Vol. 84 (December), pp. 1161–76.

Feenstra, R. C. (1985). 'Anticipated Devaluations, Currency Flight, and Direct Trade Controls in a Monetary Economy', *American Economic Review*, Vol. 75 (June), pp. 386–401.

Flood, R. P. and P. M. Garber (1983). 'A Model of Stochastic Process Switching', *Econometrica*, Vol. 51 (May), pp. 537–51.

Giavazzi, F. and A. Giovannini (1986). 'The EMS and the Dollar', *Economic Policy*, Vol. 2 (April), pp. 456–85.

Giavazzi, F. and M. Pagano (1988). 'The Advantage of Tying One's Hands: EMS Discipline and Central Bank Credibility', *European Economic Review* (June).

Gros, D. (1987). 'Tranquil and Turbulent Periods in the EMS and the Possibility of Self-fulfilling Crises', CEPS (manuscript).

Krugman, P. (1979). 'A Theory of Balance-of-Payments Crises', *Journal of Money, Credit and Banking*, Vol. 11 (August), pp. 311–25.

Mussa, M. (1977). 'A Dynamic Theory of Foreign Exchange', in Michael J. Artis and A. Robert Nobay (eds), *Studies in Modern Economic Analysis*, Oxford, Basil Blackwell.

Obstfeld, M. (1984). 'Balance-of-Payments Crises and Devaluation', *Journal of Money, Credit and Banking*, Vol. 16 (May), pp. 208–17.

   (1986). 'Rational and Self-fulfilling Balance-of-Payments Crises', *American Economic Review*, Vol. 76 (March), pp. 72–81.

Obstfeld, M. and A. C. Stockman (1985). 'Exchange-Rate Dynamics', in Ronald W. Jones and Peter B. Kenen (eds), *Handbook of International Economics*, Vol. 2, Amsterdam, North-Holland.

Rogoff, K. (1985). 'Can Exchange Rate Predictability be Achieved Without Monetary Convergence? Evidence from the EMS', *European Economic Review*, Vol. 28, Nos. 1–2 (June–July), pp. 93–115.

Ungerer, H., O. Evans, T. Mayer and P. Young (1986). 'The European Monetary System: Recent Developments', IMF Occasional Papers, No. 48 (December).

Discussion*

MARCUS MILLER

To help understand the economic implications of abolishing capital controls within Europe, Maurice Obstfeld provides a fascinating 'first step in evaluating the . . . effects of EMS-type realignment policies in a setting of free cross-border financial flows'. In this discussion we first outline the approach he adopts (and the conclusions he derives) and then briefly compare this with an alternative approach suggested by Paul Krugman (1987).

Obstfeld adopts a sticky-price, deterministic macroeconomic model with perfect capital mobility – which exhibits 'overshooting' of the exchange rate in response to monetary changes if the exchange rate is allowed to float (see Dornbusch, 1976, Appendix). Assuming, however, that the exchange rate is initially fixed, he asks what effects announcing a policy of realignment might have in such a setting. The specific policy is that of repegging the rate at a lower level if the domestic price level reaches a 'trigger point'.

As there are no shocks disturbing the model, there is no reason for the price level ever to rise to the trigger level: so one equilibrium is where the announcement has no effect. Indeed this seems to be *the* rational-expectations solution!

But Obstfeld goes on to consider what might happen if the announcement were to cause a 'run' on the currency, followed by a contraction of the money stock and an exhaustion of reserves, so the rate has to float. The answer provided is obtained by finding what trajectory for the now-floating rate will take the price level from its current level to the trigger level (allowing for a discontinuity in the rate at the time of the announcement but not at the time of refixing). Note that the trajectory which satisfies this boundary condition necessarily involves the unstable root of the model. Indeed, where the policy of realignment is precisely to accommodate past inflation, it is, in fact, the unstable eigenvector.

The principal conclusion of that part of the study dealing with purely monetary disturbances is that a policy of more-than-accommodating inflation may induce a fall in the currency and a rise in the price level to the trigger point. So the policy announcement causes a devaluation–inflation spiral. (It is argued, however, that a policy of less-than-full accommodation does not cause any effect on the economy.)

One could criticise this ingenious argument for using a rational-expectations theory of floating rates for analysing what appears to be an 'irrational' run on the currency. But, even in its own terms, some questions remain unanswered. One of these is what would occur if the policy announcement *also* included the symmetrical possibility of revaluing if the price level were to fall. If both revaluation and devaluation were overaccommodating to the same extent would the exchange rate remain stable? Or would it move? And if so, which way?

Currencies in the EMS are not (as in Obstfeld's study) pegged, allowed to float, and repegged: rather they are allowed to move within 'bands', and it is these bands which are shifted at times of realignment. This raises the question of how the analysis might be adapted to fit more closely that reality of these EMS arrangements.

It happens that Y. Choe (1987) has recently used a very similar model to study the behaviour of a rate floating within an exchange-rate band. He concludes that the commitment to stabilise the rate at the edge of the band makes feasible paths which involve the unstable root of the system. Indeed Choe argues that a multiplicity of paths are possible, and concludes that the exchange rate is in fact *indeterminate*.

Both Obstfeld and Choe work with the same sort of model and get results which suggest multiple equilibria. An alternative approach which makes no use of these unstable trajectories has been developed by Krugman (1987) (and has been applied to a Dornbusch style of model by the author of this note in joint work with Paul Weller (1988)).

In order to analyse the behaviour of a floating rate inside an exchange-rate band, Krugman's approach essentially restricts the system to the stable manifold of the system. Because the system is assumed to be stochastic, the relevant manifold is no longer given by the stable eigenvectors of the system.

If the defence of the band is believed to be fully credible the solution for the rate is found to lie on a non-linear manifold which is biased away from the usual stable manifold, towards the centre of the band. This stands in stark contrast to Choe's conclusions. If the defence of the band is less than 100 per cent credible, one gets less of a bias in the band, as agents allow for the possibility of either a realignment or a float (if the country effectively leaves the EMS). This provides an alternative answer to some of the issues raised by Obstfeld.

It appears therefore that there are two rather sharply contrasting approaches now being developed to analyse the effects of deregulating capital movements in Europe – both, in different ways, making use of rational-expectations assumptions. Personally, I find the 'stable but stochastic' approach more attractive; but it is probably too early to come to a considered judgement as to which is better.

NOTE
* Thanks are due to Paul Weller for helpful discussions on the subject of this comment.

REFERENCES
Choe, Y. (1987). 'The Indeterminacy of Short-run Exchange Rates in a Managed Float Regime', Woodrow Wilson School Discussion Papers in Economics, No. 128, Princeton University (May).
Dornbusch, R. (1976). 'Expectations and Exchange Rate Dynamics', *Journal of Political Economy*, Vol. 84 (December), pp. 1161–76.
Krugman, P. R. (1987). 'The Bias in the Band: Exchange Rate Expectations under a Broad-Band Regime', paper presented to NBER Conference on the EMS, NBER, Cambridge, Mass. (December) (mimeo).
Miller, M. H. and P. Weller (1988). 'Currency Options, Target Zones and the Dollar', Department of Economics, University of Warwick (April) (mimeo).

Discussion

HERAKLES POLEMARCHAKIS

Maurice Obstfeld's study is succinct and to the point. Its stated purpose is to study the equilibria of economies in which financial capital flows freely across countries and intervention by monetary authorities takes the form of realignment of exchange rates. Its stated finding is the possible multiplicity to equilibria. More specifically: (i) Independently of fundamental factors, exchange-rate rules can induce multiple equilibria, in particular two, one of which 'involves an inflationary spiral in which speculators force a collapse of the fixed exchange rate and a depreciation of the currency to its new peg'. (ii) When inflation is 'being driven by fundamentals (here, fiscal expansion), the possible equilibria of the economy depend on how fully the authorities attempt to offset past inflation through currency depreciation. If devaluation is large relative to past inflation, an exchange-rate collapse occurs as soon as an expansionary fiscal policy is enacted, but before any real appreciation has occurred. In the face of smaller devaluations, the fixed exchange rate can coexist with domestic inflation for some time before the inevitable collapse occurs'.

Such considerations are very interesting, even important, for the theory as much as for the practice of economic policy. However, possible objections can be raised about the model employed by Obstfeld, and its interpretation.

First, the model. It is traditional, an aggregative model, but in a tradition economists have come to find increasingly embarrassing: markets do not clear and prices respond to excess demand; the optimisation of individuals is ignored as are expectations other than instantaneous changes. Variables are selectively ignored.

That utility maximisation is left in the background is not important. After all, we know that little if anything is preserved by aggregation. Budget constraints, however, do aggregate, and it is budget constraints which macroeconomic models in the tradition Obstfeld has chosen to follow ignore. That markets fail to clear is a fine modelling assumption as long as individual demand behaviour is correctly specified: the trades realised by individuals in one affect their choices in other markets – at least when budget constraints are satisfied. Admittedly, such modelling shortcomings are displayed even by recent and influential studies in open-economy macroeconomics.

Second, the results and their interpretation. The model reduces to two differential equations in the price level and the exchange rate, both endogenous variables. The equations of the dynamic system are first derived for the regime of flexible exchange rates. The regime of pegged exchange rates is much simpler, and is superimposed on the former. The system as the monetary authority shifts from one regime to the other is heuristically specified, leaving one with an uneasy feeling, but I do not think the flaw is a major one. What I simply do not understand is the reference to multiple equilibria. The laws of motion of the price level and the exchange rate are derived from the discrepancy between supply and demand away from equilibrium. Along any path, the price level and the exchange rate may or may not converge to equilibrium, but it is erroneous to confuse convergence to equilibrium with equilibrium behaviour along the path. In models with genuine multiplicity of equilibria, markets clear every period, and the distinction arises between degenerate equilibrium paths along which variables do not change over time (steady states), and equilibrium paths along which variables do change over time. In Obstfeld's framework, away from the rest point, markets are not guaranteed to clear.

The story Obstfeld wants to tell makes economic sense. It should be possible to formalise it in an equilibrium framework.

10 Interventions, Sterilisation and Monetary Policy in European Monetary System Countries, 1979–87*

CRISTINA MASTROPASQUA, STEFANO MICOSSI and ROBERTO RINALDI

1 Introduction

This study examines the functioning of the Exchange-Rate Mechanism (ERM) of the European Monetary System (EMS) over its eight-year history (March 1979–June 1987). It concentrates on the role of intervention in foreign-exchange markets and domestic monetary instruments in maintaining ERM cohesion; the analysis of individual countries' behaviour is complemented by that of their interactions, with a view to describing the rules and patterns of monetary coordination implicit in the system's exchange-rate constraint.

In order to highlight the 'rules of the game', and the different positions and policy approaches of the system's members, we have focused on four countries: Germany, as the monetary 'leader'; Belgium, as a small country basically behaving as an exchange-rate pegger; and France and Italy, two large countries with heterogeneous economic structures and economic performances that have diverged (albeit decreasingly so) from that of the leading country through most of the EMS's life.

The study is organised as follows. Section 2 examines the intervention rules and intervention patterns within the ERM; Section 3 presents evidence on the behaviour of the four sample countries, notably as regards the different ways they have combined intervention, exchange-rate and interest-rate flexibility in their policy approach; Section 4 offers more detailed discussion of various institutional aspects of monetary management and monetary coordination within the system and presents preliminary evidence on the sterilisation techniques used to 'decouple' interventions from domestic monetary conditions; and finally, Section 5 presents the results of econometric estimates of individual countries' sterilisation policies, as well as of certain aspects of monetary policy interaction within the ERM. The main findings and open issues are summed up in the concluding Section 6.

252

2   Intervention rules and intervention patterns

The Agreement of 13 March 1979 between the central banks of the EEC 'laying down the operating mechanisms and procedures of the EMS' (henceforth the Central Banks' Agreement) contains very few explicit rules concerning interventions in foreign-exchange markets.

Interventions are compulsory and should be carried out in Community currencies on an automatic basis and without limits of amount when a currency reaches the lower or upper margin *vis-à-vis* any one of the other currencies in the ERM. The foreign exchange required for these interventions can be obtained through the very short-term financing facility (VSTF), a network of mutual credit lines by means of which each central bank makes its own currency available to the others, again on an automatic basis and without limits of amounts. The resulting debtor balances may be settled not only in convertible currencies but also in ECUs, which in practice mobilises part of central banks' gold holdings.[1]

On the other hand, intramarginal interventions – i.e., those undertaken within the EMS band – are basically unregulated,[2] except insofar as it is stipulated that (1) interventions in Community currencies are subject to prior authorisation (through concertation) by the central bank issuing the intervention currency and should be discontinued if they produce undesirable effects on that currency; (2) interventions in dollars are subject to a milder requirement of 'concertation', the main purpose of this provision being to avoid interventions that could weaken EMS cohesion or accentuate dollar trends in foreign-exchange markets.

Unlike those at the margin, intramarginal interventions do not enjoy automatic access to the VSTF, and in practice until recently such financing was unavailable.[3] The build-up of reserves in Community currencies was also discouraged, and the ECU was set up more like a credit instrument than a reserve asset.

These provisions reflected the expectation – stemming from the experience of the 'snake' – that most interventions would take place at the margin. Since the obligation to intervene applies to the central bank of both the strong and the weak currency, there was at least a formal implication of symmetry in the sharing of intervention burdens; symmetry was meant to be reinforced, in the original system's design, by the identification of the country responsible for domestic policy adjustment through the indicator of divergence. The willingness of prospective creditor central banks to accept intervention obligations was predicated on the assumption that a country whose currency had fallen to the lower margin would not long be able to put off a decision either to devalue or to take policy action to move its currency back to a less uncomfortable

Table 10.1 Basic Macroeconomic Data for Selected ERM Countries (Yearly Averages)

	GDP/GNP[1]	CPI[1]	ULC[2]	$ exchange rate[1]	DM exchange rate[1]	DM exchange rate[1]	Intra-ERM exchange rate[1]	Intra-ERM exchange rate[1]	Current b.o.p.[3]	Trade balance vis-à-vis ERM (billion dollars)[4]
Belgium										
1973–8	2.9	8.8	7.7	5.7	-2.1[5]	-1.4[6]	1.1[5]	-1.0[6]	0.6	0.12
1979–82	1.3	6.8	3.7	-8.8	-4.4	-4.4	-2.4	-5.2	-3.5	0.12
1983–5	1.0	6.3	2.8	-8.3	-2.4	-1.4	-0.6	-1.7	0.1	-0.36
1986–7*	1.8	1.4	0.7	25.0	-1.3	-1.2	0.4	0.6	3.3	0.0
France										
1973–8	3.5	10.1	10.7	1.9	-5.6	-2.0	-2.0	-1.0	0.1	-14.4
1979–82	1.7	12.4	11.0	-8.8	-4.5	2.0	-2.0	2.2	-0.7	-25.2
1983–5	1.2	7.6	4.1	-9.8	-4.6	1.1	-2.0	1.2	-0.4	-19.2
1986–7*	1.6	2.9	1.5	21.0	-4.3	-1.4	-3.0	-0.1	0.4	-15.9
Germany										
1973–8	2.5	5.1	5.4	8.0	–	–	6.2	1.0	1.3	15.6
1979–82	1.1	5.3	4.3	-4.6	–	–	4.4	-0.4	-0.7	21.6
1983–5	2.4	2.6	-0.6	-6.0	–	–	3.2	-0.2	1.5	13.8
1986–7*	1.9	0.3	3.1	27.6	–	–	2.9	2.6	3.6	23.2
Italy										
1973–8	2.9	15.4	17.2	-6.0	-13.0	-2.7	-10.9	-2.0	-0.8	-9.5
1979–82	1.2	17.5	14.1	-10.9	-6.6	3.1	-4.7	2.8	-1.1	-17.8
1983–5	2.2	11.0	9.1	-10.8	-5.0	1.6	-3.4	1.5	-0.3	-13.8
1986–7*	2.9	5.3	4.1	20.8	-4.6	-1.5	-3.0	-0.5	0.5	-11.2

Notes:

*Data for 1987 are based on forecasts except for exchange rates and for trade balances, which were calculated on the basis of data to June 1987.

[1]Percentage change over the period; a minus sign indicates depreciation.

[2]Unit labour costs (in manufactures).

[3]Percentage ratios to GNP/GDP, period average.

[4]Cumulated balances within periods.

[5]Nominal.

[6]Real: deflated with (relative) producer prices of manufactures.

Source: Bank of Italy, IMF, OECD.

	1979	1983	1985	1987[2]
Convertible currencies	39.0	59.9	67.0	78.9
– dollars	35.3	46.5	42.4	59.0
– EMS currencies	3.2	10.2	19.7	14.4
– others	0.5	3.2	4.9	5.5
ECUs	26.6	49.9	43.5	42.0
Net position on the IMF[3]	7.3	14.2	· 14.1	12.9
Others[4]	−4.4	−16.7	−16.2	−16.7
Total	68.5	107.3	108.4	117.1
Memorandum item:				
Euromarket deposits[5]	–	28.7	37.1	45.4

Table 10.2 Official Net Reserves of Countries in the EMS Exchange-rate Arrangements[1]

Notes:
[1]Outstanding amounts in billions of US dollars at the end of the period (excluding gold holdings).
[2]End of June.
[3]Including SDRs.
[4]Other assets minus official short-term liabilities.
[5]Monetary authorities' net liabilities reported to the BIS (not available for Ireland).

Source: BIS, Monthly Statistical Series.

position in the band. The refusal to grant access to the VSTF for intramarginal interventions reflected fears that in this case there would be a stronger temptation for debtor countries to seek a way out of their troubles by swelling creditors' monetary base through VSTF-financed interventions.

Actual developments differed from expectations in a number of ways. Practically on the morrow of the inception of the EMS the second oil shock reopened large imbalances in member countries' foreign payments and pushed inflation up, with relatively stronger adverse effects on weaker economies (Table 10.1). As it turned out, this was instrumental in strengthening the consensus for effective adjustment policies in the early years of the EMS, with the exchange-rate constraint performing an important disciplinary function in promoting downward convergence of inflation.[4] The claims for symmetry, which had seemed so important in the negotiations leading up to the establishment of the EMS, were superseded by common acceptance of the principle of convergence towards the best performer. One important consequence was that EMS

		1979–82[1]		1983–5		1986–7[2]	
US dollars	P	31.4[8]	17.2[9]	22.2[8]	15.1[9]	30.8[8]	20.9[9]
	S	99.3	54.3	56.8	38.6	8.0	5.4
EMS currencies[3]							
– at the margin[4]		20.5	11.2	15.4	10.5	22.4	15.2
– intramarginal	P	10.6	5.8	28.9	19.7	32.8	22.2
	S	18.6	10.2	19.6	13.3	50.6	34.3
Others[5]	P	0.1	0.1	3.2	2.2	1.3	0.9
	S	2.2	1.2	0.9	0.6	1.7	1.1
Total							
– gross		182.7	100.0	147.0	100.0	147.6	100.0
– net[6]		−78.0	−42.7	−24.4	−16.6	7.0	4.7
Memorandum items:							
– recourse to VSTF[7]		17.1	9.4	7.2	4.9	17.9	12.1
– ECU spot settlements of intervention		6.4	3.5	1.3	0.9	0.7	0.5

Table 10.3 Foreign-exchange Intervention by Countries in the EMS Exchange-rate Arrangements

Notes:
[1]For 1979, March to December.
[2]For 1987, first six months.
[3]Currencies of countries participating in the exchange arrangements.
[4]Purchases or sales.
[5]From 1985 onwards, the figures include interventions in the private ECU market.
[6]A minus sign indicates net sales.
[7]Very short-term financing facility (VSTF).
[8]Cumulative amount (billions of US dollars).
[9]Percentage shares of the total. P = purchases; S = sales.

Source: EMCF, BIS.

countries generally maintained domestic monetary conditions consistent with the need to finance their current external deficits on international markets, so that they did not experience serious strains in their official reserve positions (Table 10.2), nor did they have to rely systematically on EMS credit mechanisms. This helped build mutual confidence and cooperation between the central banks of the system.

Interventions in foreign-exchange markets were substantial in these early years, with a large excess of sales over purchases (see the 1979–82 figures in Table 10.3). They were, however, mostly in dollars (over 70 per cent of the gross total), and fairly evenly distributed among the member countries. It was natural to use the dollar, since it still constituted a large

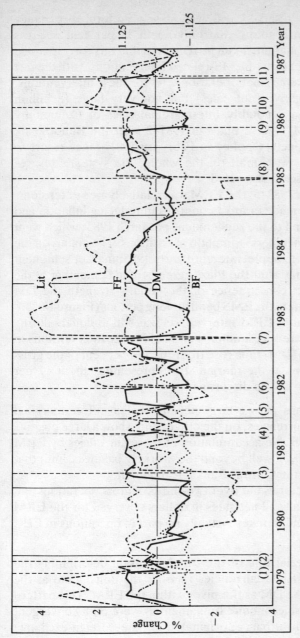

Figure 10.1 Intra-EMS exchange rates, percentage changes *vis-à-vis* central rates

Source: Bank of Italy.

Realignments: (1) 24 Sept. 1979: DM +2, KD −3; (2) 30 Nov. 1979: KD −4.8; (3) 23 Mar. 1981: LIT −6, (LST +22.7); (4) 5 Oct. 1981: DM +5.5, FF −3, LTT −3, FOL +5.5, (LST −9.9); (5) 22 Feb. 1982: KD −3, BF −8.5, (LST +8.3); (6) 14 Jun. 1982: DM +4.25, FF −5.75, LIT −2.75, FOL +4.25; (7) 22 Mar. 1983: DM +5.5, FF −2.5, LIT −2.5, KD +2.5, BF +1.5, FOL +3.5, IRL −3.5, (LST −13.9); (8) 22 Jul. 1985: DM +2, FF +2, LIT −6, KD +2, BF +2, FOL +2, IRL +2, (LST +5.4), (DRA −13.3); (9) 7 Apr. 1986: DM +3, FF −3, KD +1, BF +1, FOL +3, (LST −15.3). (DRA −36.9); (10) 4 Aug. 1986: IRL −8; (11) 12 Jan. 1987: DM +3, BF +2, FOL +3, (LST −18.3), (DRA −12.1).

proportion of official reserves and was strong in foreign-exchange markets. It is also worth noting that only about 11 per cent of gross intervention was at the margin; it can be reckoned that this corresponded to between 20 and 25 per cent of EMS-related interventions, with the rest taking the form of intramarginal operations. As for these interventions, their balance was negative (net sales) but not very large (8 billion dollars); most of them – notably intramarginal sales of Community currencies (mostly DM) – took place in 1981–2 after the Bundesbank shifted to a tighter monetary policy in February 1981. Since resort to Community currencies was small on the whole, the system's reserve mechanisms were not seriously tested.

In the ensuing period, 1983–5, the ERM was relatively free of tensions, thanks to the progress made in most countries in reducing inflation and external imbalances, and to the realignment of March 1983, which went some way in restoring members' competitive positions. The dollar, on the other hand, continued to appreciate until early 1985; market sentiment really turned bearish only after the Plaza agreement in September of the same year. As a direct consequence of the dollar's strength the DM remained relatively weak in the EMS band for long periods (Figure 10.1).[5]

More than 50 per cent of ERM intervention was still in dollars during this period, but the share was smaller than in 1979–82. Interventions in Community currencies (DM) thus rose from 26 to 44 per cent of the gross total, with interventions at the margin still representing about 11 per cent. A distinct pattern can be discerned:

(a) Dollar interventions show a large negative balance; intramarginal interventions in EEC currencies, on the other hand, show a large positive balance, leading to a sizable accumulation of these currencies by ERM central banks (Table 10.2), well beyond the 'working balances' limit that had been envisaged in the Central Banks' Agreement.

(b) The Bundesbank carries out over two-thirds of gross operations and is responsible for virtually all net sales in dollars observed for the ERM group; on the other hand, it takes virtually no part in operations in EEC currencies.

This highlights the special role of the Bundesbank in determining the exchange rates of the ERM currencies vis-à-vis the dollar, and at the same time the role of the DM as the pivot within the ERM. This pattern becomes visible because economic fundamentals were on a convergent path and the main disturbance originated in the foreign-exchange markets – the appreciation of the dollar.

The considerable increase in intramarginal interventions in DM and the accumulation of DM balances by ERM central banks were again tolerated since they did not involve creation of the reserve currency or place demands on the system's financing mechanisms. To a large extent official DM balances were held in the Euromarkets, either directly or through the BIS (Table 10.2).

In 1986–7 the system returned to an international environment and a pattern of relative economic positions within the EMS that more closely resemble those envisaged when the system was designed. During 1986 and the first half of 1987 the dollar went down fairly rapidly; after a point further declines were resisted increasingly by European central banks through a combination of (sometimes very substantial) interventions in foreign-exchange markets and interest-rate adjustments. In Europe, inflation differentials have fallen to their lowest values since the late 1960s; however, the strength of the DM has been augmented by Germany's large external surplus and the weakening external positions of most other European countries, as well as by the remaining divergences in fiscal positions. In addition, low growth of demand in Germany and widening bilateral trade deficits with Germany in most of the other ERM countries have raised doubts as to the authorities' willingness to continue to assign top priority in national policies to exchange-rate stability within the ERM.

Rapid progress in lifting foreign-exchange restrictions – notably in France and Italy – has also increased the potential scale of intervention required to preserve EMS stability, and may aggravate the conflict between domestic monetary objectives and ERM cohesion. This is all the more likely in that inflation differentials have become quite small (three, four percentage points at the most), while gyrations in the forward premiums or discounts on ERM currencies tend to be rather large at times of unsettled foreign-exchange markets. Appropriate interest-rate differentials supportive of ERM cohesion may thus prove to be more costly in terms of domestic policy objectives.

The new environment is well reflected in the recent pattern of interventions. Substantial net purchases have been made in US dollars, net sales in Community currencies. Gross operations in dollars fell to about a quarter of the total and those in Community currencies rose to 72 per cent; 15 per cent consists of interventions at the margin, and 34 per cent of intramarginal sales; all in a context of interventions running at annual rates almost double those observed in the two preceding periods.[6]

The dramatic increase in the share of interventions in EEC currencies obviously reflects the fact that dollar interventions no longer offered an appropriate means for supporting weak currencies within the EMS in view of the dollar's persistent weakness and the goal of avoiding its further depreciation. While all the ERM countries shared in large dollar purchases, the Bundesbank was again not involved in intramarginal interventions in EEC currencies; it did, however, make substantial interventions at the margin, notably on the occasion of the January 1987 realignment. On this and other occasions rigid defence of exchange rates and insufficient coordination of interest-rate policies (see Section 3) led to very large interventions in relatively short periods, with resulting strains in the the system's mechanisms.

Eventually, the authorities modified the rules of the system. The possibility of obtaining intervention currencies was considerably expanded in 1985 with the introduction of an ECU mobilisation mechanism that – subject to a requirement of 'need' – allows participating central banks to obtain dollars or EEC currencies in exchange for a fraction (up to approximately 60 per cent) of their official ECU holdings, for a limited period of time but without restrictions on the type of intervention involved. Even more significant changes were approved by the Committee of Governors in September 1987: although no automatic access to the VSTF for intramarginal interventions is allowed, there is now a presumption that such financing will be available, up to a maximum limit and under certain conditions,[7] for intramarginal interventions that have been agreed upon by the central bank issuing the intervention currency. *De facto*, the 50 per cent limit on the obligation to accept ECUs in settlement of debts under the VSTF has also been lifted (with the proviso that this should not lead to an unbalanced reserve composition for creditor countries or an excessive accumulation of net debtor–creditor ECU positions with the EMCF). Since VSTF will also be available for intramarginal interventions, the improvement in the usability of the ECU is substantial.

The system's mechanisms have thus been adapted to meet the greater need for EEC currencies for interventions, arising notably from increased financial integration and capital mobility. It has also been agreed, however, that this should go hand in hand with more flexible interest-rate policies, as well as a willingness to make fuller use of the EMS fluctuation band to increase the perception of risk among operators. There is, in other words, a clear implication that every effort should be made to limit resort to intervention by adjusting interest rates more rapidly and by not providing speculators with rigid reference points for position taking in foreign-exchange markets.[8]

3 Interventions, interest rates and exchange-rate flexibility in the management of the ERM

In principle, a central bank that is confronted with (upward or down-ward) pressure on its currency can intervene in foreign-exchange markets, adjust money-market interest rates, 'absorb' part of the pressure on the exchange rate itself (as long as there is room within the band), or give in and ask for a central rate realignment.

All these actions to resist pressure have advantages and drawbacks, depending on the circumstances. Interventions can be effective in countering minor tensions and smoothing very short-term oscillations in currency demand and supply; they can be counterproductive if the markets consider current rates of intervention to be unsustainable. Interest-rate changes can also be of help provided they are prompt and large enough; once expectations of exchange-rate changes take hold of the markets, however, the interest-rate changes required may become unrealistically large. Half-hearted action in the early phase of exchange-rate pressures may sometimes excite rather than calm agents' expectations. Finally, exchange-rate flexibility within the band may help increase the perception of two-way risk in open position taking; but it may also be perceived by the markets as the first sign of surrender, notably when currencies fall to the margin. Evidence of cooperation between the central banks whose currencies come under opposite pressure can make intervention and interest-rate action more effective.

Member countries' recourse to these alternative measures has differed, and has evolved over time in response to changes in the environment and the lessons of experience.[9] Table 10.4 presents data on net interventions by ERM countries in the three periods previously identified, and (within each period) in sub-periods identified on the basis of the band position of the DM; Table 10.5 shows various measures of exchange-rate and interest-rate variability; Table 10.6 provides some evidence on ERM central banks' behaviour in periods of exchange-rate tension.

The Bundesbank intervened only intramarginally in EEC currencies in the early years of the EMS at times of DM weakness, but was involved in substantial interventions at the margin[10] in EEC currencies, notably in 1986–7. The bulk of its interventions, however, were in the dollar market and were mostly not ERM-related and concentrated in periods when the DM was tension-free. As for the other central banks as Table 10.4 shows, recourse to interventions was particularly ample in periods when the DM was strong; the dollar was widely used to meet ERM-specific tensions (see the left section of Table 10.4) in the early years of the system but much less so subsequently; intramarginal interventions in EEC

	Strong DM DM ≥ 1[1]			Weak DM DM < −1.5[1]			Rest of period 1 > DM ≥ −1.5[1]		
	1979–82[2]	1983–5	1986–7[3]	1979–82[2]	1983–5	1986–7[3]	1979–82[2]	1983–5	1986–7[3]
Belgium[4]									
Dollars	–	–	–	–	–	–	–	–	–
EMS currencies	–	–	–	–	–	–	–	–	–
– at the margin	–	–	–	–	–	–	–	–	–
France									
Dollars	−11.6	−4.4	0.5	−0.5	−2.3	0.9	−3.1	−1.3	7.6
EMS currencies	−3.9	0.7	−14.9	5.6	3.4	8.4	2.3	5.0	−2.8
– at the margin	−4.2	1.5	0.0	2.7	2.3	8.5	0.3	0.3	−2.0
Germany									
Dollars	−5.6	−4.8	1.2	−5.5	−3.4	0.1	−8.5	−10.4	2.1
EMS currencies	1.9	−0.3	0.1	−2.4	−0.6	−0.5	−0.6	0.6	3.7
– at the margin	1.5	−0.3	0.1	−0.7	−0.6	−0.5	−0.5	0.1	3.7
Italy									
Dollars	−4.3	−2.3	0.7	−2.5	3.7	1.3	−11.0	−4.7	2.8
EMS currencies	0.8	−1.1	−1.4	−0.1	1.2	3.1	0.0	0.5	−1.4
– at the margin	0.0	0.0	0.0	0.0	0.0	0.0	0.0	0.0	0.0
Total ERM									
Dollars	−30.0	−14.5	1.7	−8.5	−2.4	2.6	−29.4	−17.5	18.4
EMS currencies	−11.9	−4.9	−25.6	0.7	6.2	12.3	−2.6	7.0	−1.7
– at the margin	−6.6	−3.2	−1.7	1.1	2.1	6.4	−0.6	−0.1	−1.8

Table 10.4 Net Interventions in Foreign-exchange Markets by Selected ERM Central Banks (Billions of US Dollars)

Notes:
[1]Intervention data are selected on the basis of the DM position in the EMS narrow band in terms of percentage divergences from central rates vis-à-vis the currency in opposition (monthly figures of band position are obtained as median of daily figures).
[2]For 1979, March to December.
[3]For 1987, first six months.
[4]Not available.

Source: BIS.

currencies were resorted to increasingly over time. Italy, with its wider oscillation band, never went to the margin; compared with the other ERM countries, it also shows a higher share of dollar interventions throughout the life of the EMS.

It can be seen that in 1986–7 sizable interventions in EEC currencies were concentrated in periods when the DM was hovering in the central region of the band. To a greater extent than in the past, participating central banks – other than the Bundesbank – were 'taking a view' on the desirable position of their currency within the band, and maintained their currencies in relatively appreciated positions even at the cost of substantial interventions. Consequently, what had seemed a well-established relation between the position of the DM in the band and the pattern of interventions has become blurred.

In general, interventions patterns are to be examined in the context of countries' stances regarding both the position of their currency in the band and the flexibility of interest rates on domestic markets.

The first two columns of Table 10.5 provide measures of band utilisation and the third one of actual exchange-rate variability, while the last column gives alternative measures of short-term interest-rate variability (based on daily data on domestic call money rates).

The special regime (wide band) of the lira within the ERM is reflected in a clear tendency to make less than full use of the band and at the same time to offer a flexible exchange-rate response to pressures (see also Figure 10.1); it appears that, together with increased flexibility in day-to-day exchange-rate management (see the standard deviation figures of the first and third columns of Table 10.5), over time there has been a decreasing utilisation of the band. It is also apparent that interest-rate changes provided little support in meeting exchange-rate tensions in the early years of the EMS (1979–82), but were increasingly important in the ensuing periods, reflecting growing financial markets' interdependence as well as a changed policy attitude.

Turning to the countries in the narrow band, the position of the DM can be seen as primarily the result of the other central banks' exchange- and interest-rate policies (relative to the Bundesbank's medium-term monetary course). German interest rates show low variability, with a marked reduction over time. Nevertheless, at times of strong pressures on the dollar, large capital inflows have made it difficult for the German authorities to achieve full sterilisation (German monetary aggregates overshoot the targets throughout 1986–7); this is also reflected in increased interest-rate variability in the last period.

As for France, the franc was kept preferably in the upper part of the band, often close to or at the upper margin. Over time, its median

	Max bilateral spread[2]		Average spread[3]		Nominal exchange-rate variability		Interest-rate variability	
	Median	St. Dev.	Median	St. Dev.	Intra-ERM[4]	Vis-à-vis DM		
Belgian franc								
Mar. 1979–May 1987	−1.88	0.63	−0.95	0.57	0.21	0.23	0.30[5]	1.56[6]
Mar. 1979–Mar. 1983	−1.99	0.77	−1.04	0.60	0.28	0.30	0.25	1.37
Apr. 1983–Dec. 1985	−1.87	0.41	−0.87	0.54	0.13	0.16	0.24	1.83
Jan. 1986–May 1987	−1.78	0.47	−0.97	0.54	0.08	0.08	0.25	1.51
French franc								
Mar. 1979–May 1987	1.48	1.23	0.38	0.59	0.26	0.27	0.26	0.24*
Mar. 1979–Mar. 1983	1.50	1.40	0.38	0.67	0.33	0.34	0.16	0.23*
Apr. 1983–Dec. 1985	1.54	1.07	0.38	0.46	0.14	0.17	0.10	0.27
Jan. 1986–May 1987	1.48	0.96	0.32	0.62	0.22	0.21	0.09	0.20
Deutsche mark								
Mar. 1979–May 1987	0.80	1.71	−0.04	0.45	0.16	–	0.35	0.45
Mar. 1979–Mar. 1983	−0.71	1.79	−0.07	0.54	0.20	–	0.25	0.61
Apr. 1983–Dec. 1985	0.82	1.61	−0.02	0.33	0.13	–	0.08	0.16
Jan. 1986–May 1987	1.31	1.77	0.06	0.39	0.09	–	0.08	0.23
Italian lira								
Mar. 1979–May 1987	1.87	2.60	0.72	1.62	0.28	0.31	0.28	2.33*
Mar. 1979–Mar. 1983	1.45	2.64	0.25	1.55	0.26	0.31	0.04	0.72*
Apr. 1983–Dec. 1985	2.67	2.58	1.40	1.73	0.23	0.24	0.26	2.99
Jan. 1986–May 1987	2.04	1.20	1.17	0.59	0.40	0.40	0.28	2.33

Table 10.5 Measures of EMS Band Cohesion and of Exchange-rate and Interest-rate Variability[1]

Notes:

*Data are available from 13 May 1981.

[1] All measures are calculated on daily data.

[2] Percentage divergences from central rates *vis-à-vis* the currency in opposition; these equal +2.25 when the bilateral rate *vis-à-vis* the currencies of the narrow band reaches the intervention margin (±6 for the lira).

[3] Weighted average (with ECU weights) of bilateral divergences from central rates *vis-à-vis* the currencies of the narrow band; it equals ±2.25 when all the bilateral rates reach the intervention margin (±6 for the lira).

[4] Standard deviation of absolute percentage changes in the weighted average (with ECU weights) of bilateral exchange rates *vis-à-vis* the currencies in the narrow band.

[5] Domestic call money rates: coefficient of variation.

[6] Domestic call money rates: standard deviation of the residuals of 'best' ARMA interpolations.

Source: Bank of Italy and (for interest rates) national sources.

	Interest rates[1]				Deutsche mark exchange rates		Band width		Interventions	
	Domestic		Eurorates							
Belgium[10]										
Oct. 1981	−1.2[2]	−1.0[3]	0.0[2]	0.5[3]	0.1[4]	0.1[5]	2.1[6]	1.2[7]	−[8]	−[9]
Jun. 1982	−2.6	−1.7	0.0	1.0	−0.1	−0.1	2.1	1.5	−	−
Mar. 1983	3.7	4.0	2.7	2.7	0.0	−0.3	2.2	1.3	−	−
Mar. 1984*	4.3	3.8	1.4	1.4	0.0	−0.3	2.2	1.7	−	−
Jan. 1987	0.7	0.6	0.2	0.1	−0.3	−0.3	1.2	1.1	−	−
France										
Oct. 1981	1.1	1.0	9.7	9.0	0.1	−0.5	1.7	0.8	63	122
Jun. 1982	−0.1	−0.6	4.8	10.1	0.0	−0.2	1.7	1.0	61	155
Mar. 1983	0.1	0.1	37.4	37.5	−1.0	−1.1	2.0	0.5	43	311
Mar. 1984*	0.1	0.2	0.1	0.2	−0.1	−0.8	1.9	0.1	38	195
Jan. 1987	1.2	1.7	0.9	1.4	−1.1	−1.2	1.4	0.9	27	182
Germany										
Oct. 1981	0.0	0.0	0.0	0.2	−	−	2.1	0.7	4	21
Jun. 1982	−0.3	−0.5	0.2	−0.4	−	−	2.1	0.7	1	15
Mar. 1983	0.1	−1.2	−0.4	−0.4	−	−	2.1	0.5	10	198
Mar. 1984*	0.0	0.0	−0.1	−0.1	−	−	2.2	0.5	12	86
Jan. 1987	−0.1	0.2	−0.2	0.1	−	−	2.0	0.8	24	261
Italy										
Oct. 1981	1.2	0.5	5.5	4.5	−1.3	−2.0	1.4	1.3	9	78
Jun. 1982	0.0	0.0	0.0	−0.5	0.0	−0.7	2.8	1.5	6	23
Mar. 1983	0.1	0.1	6.5	6.5	−3.1	−3.1	2.4	2.1	18	202
Mar. 1984*	−0.7	−1.5	0.2	0.9	−0.6	−2.4	3.7	0.9	20	136
Jan. 1987	1.2	2.4	0.7	1.1	−0.5	−0.7	2.9	1.1	22	192

Table 10.6 Interest Rates, Exchange Rates and Interventions in Selected Periods of Pressure Within the ERM

Notes:

*Pressure not leading to realignment.
1 Domestic call money rates; 2 days Eurorates.
2 Percentage point difference between the median values in the period of pressure (15 days) and in the month preceding it.
3 Percentage point difference between the median values in the period of pressure and in the last but one month preceding it.
4 Percentage change of the median value in the period of pressure over the median value in the month preceding it.
5 Percentage change of the median value in the period of pressure over the median value in the last but one month preceding it.
6 Percentage divergence from central rates *vis-à-vis* the currency in opposition: median of absolute values in the period of pressure.
7 Weighted average of bilateral divergences from central rates *vis-à-vis* the currencies of the restricted band: median of absolute values in the period of pressure.
8 Expressed as a percentage quota of the total (gross) intervention undertaken by EMS central banks during the pressure period).
9 Expressed as a percentage of the yearly average of gross intervention undertaken by the country.
10 Not available.

Source: BIS.

position has come down towards the centre of the band, while the variability measures seem to point to an increased rigidity in day-to-day management. The flexibility of interest rates seems modest, of a similar order of magnitude to that observed for Germany. Variability was greater in 1983–5 than in 1986–7, in spite of the removal of foreign-exchange restrictions.

By contrast, the Belgian franc tended to remain low in the band and repeatedly went to the lower margin *vis-à-vis* one or another of the ERM currencies. Over time, the median position of this currency tended to move away from the lower margin, and flexibility in day-to-day management seems to have declined somewhat. Interventions were often very large; on a net basis, however, they have recently declined considerably in line with the strengthening of the external position. The flexibility of interest rates was high until 1983, in spite of the fact that a two-tier exchange-rate system (still in operation) helped to absorb pressures on the exchange rate.

Further insights into countries' approaches come from closer scrutiny of their behaviour in selected periods of tension. Table 10.6 presents evidence on the use of the different instruments: changes in interest and exchange rates and related interventions (e.g., the share of total gross EMS interventions carried out by each central bank in each period and, for each central bank, the ratios of monthly rates of intervention in periods of pressure to average rates of intervention during the year). The DM was always strong and downward pressure involved the other three currencies.

Table 10.6 confirms the pattern of responses that has been described above. Comparison of the first and second columns highlights the role of foreign-exchange controls in Italy and France in isolating (at least in the short term) domestic interest rates from international markets in the early EMS years (Giavazzi and Pagano, 1985; Micossi and Rossi, 1986; Gros, 1987). What is striking is the generally modest role that interest rates played in the three larger countries in most episodes. More pronounced interest-rate changes are observed in the weak-currency countries, in the period 1984–5, following the relaxation of exchange and credit controls in Italy and France. In early 1984 pressures were successfully resisted by Belgium and France, with determined joint use of the three instruments. In January 1987, before the realignment, there was also an interest-rate response in France, but the exchange rate was initially defended rather rigidly (leading to large-scale interventions) until just before the realignment, when the Banque de France let its currency drop to the margin. The exchange-rate column in Table 10.6 confirms that exchange-rate flexibility was always fairly important to

Italy's responses; greater exchange-rate flexibility was instrumental in reducing the need for intervention.

Insufficient coordination of interest-rate responses and rigid defence of exchange rates in narrow ranges sometimes gave rise to an unstable pattern of reserve flows, mirrored in very large interventions (Belgium and France in 1983, Belgium in 1984, and France, Italy and eventually Germany, after its currency rose to the margin, in January 1987).

On the other hand, it is confirmed that the Bundesbank interventions become relevant only after the DM has reached the upper margin *vis-à-vis* some other currency in the ERM, as in the March 1983 and January 1987 episodes; interest-rate responses seem in most cases to have played a negligible role.

4 Interventions in foreign-exchange markets and domestic monetary conditions: some basic facts

The ERM countries have a great variety of institutional settings and approaches to monetary policy,[17] although during the 1970s almost all of them adopted quantitative approaches involving control of monetary or credit aggregates. Targets in terms of monetary aggregates were adopted by Germany (central bank money), and France (M2 and M3); the Netherlands and Ireland set target ranges for credit aggregates (respectively, monetary institutions' credit to the private and public sectors, and monetary institutions' credit to the private sector). In Italy, monetary policy is geared to both a money and a credit variable (respectively, M2 and credit to the private sector). Denmark and Belgium publish 'normative forecasts' of the expansion of respectively a monetary and a credit aggregate, while in practice attributing great importance to exchange-rate developments *vis-à-vis* the DM. With the possible exception of the latter countries, there is no formal arrangement for the *ex ante* coordination of monetary policy targets for purposes of ERM cohesion.

The setting of independent monetary objectives by more than one country within the ERM can only by chance be consistent with the exchange-rate constraint.[12] In practice, consistency has been ensured by a combination of flexible management of monetary targets and occasional central rate realignments. These have been necessary because convergence towards the best performer (notably in terms of inflation) has been gradual. The existence of foreign-exchange controls in some ERM countries has provided additional leeway for divergent monetary courses, especially in the early years of the EMS.[13]

Another important factor in ERM cohesion is that irrespective of the chosen intermediate target, all the participating central banks share operating procedures that involve smooth management of interest rates and accommodation of short-term disturbances in money markets. This implies routine sterilisation of short-term gyrations in the foreign component of the monetary base. While such an approach can often moderate exchange-rate variability – at least in the sense that there is less incentive to move from one currency to another in the expectation of interest-rate changes – it is liable to generate short-term policy conflicts and accentuate the risk of instability in the presence of exogenous shocks in the foreign-exchange markets. Indeed, it is an established result that routine sterilisation of interventions by all countries within a pegged exchange-rate area can lead to explosive reserve behaviour.[14]

A further aspect of interdependence within the ERM is the system's increasing use of the participants' currencies (the DM in particular) for reserve holding and interventions. It is important to distinguish between interventions that affect the monetary base of the country issuing the intervention currency and those that do not.[15] The first case obtains when (say) the Bank of Italy supports the lira by selling DM made available through the VSTF (or otherwise directly by the Bundesbank). Barring offsetting operations in the foreign-exchange or capital markets, there will be an equal effect of opposite sign in the money markets of the two countries (e.g., expansionary in Germany and contractionary in Italy). This can make interventions more effective by inducing supportive changes in interest-rate differentials.

The situation is different, however, if the Bank of Italy intervenes using DM balances held on the Euromarkets: in this case there is still a (potentially) contractionary impulse on Italy's monetary base, but no effect on Germany's since the Bundesbank observes no change in its overall liabilities (except insofar as the shift of DM deposits may entail changes in the aggregate demand for the DM monetary base by commercial banks). In this case, the (potentially) supportive monetary effects of interventions are asymmetrical; the burden of monetary adjustment falls on the intervening country.

This second case has actually been prevalent within the EMS, since most interventions in EEC currencies have been made with balances held in the Euromarkets; indeed this has been a main reason why the considerable increase in the scale of operations in DM has not provoked stronger resistance by the Bundesbank.[16] By contrast, large expansionary effects on the German monetary base have sometimes been produced in connection with interventions at the margin preceding

| | Interventions[1] | Official reserves[1,2] | Current balance of payments[1] | Monetary base growth[3] | Contributions[4] | |
					Foreign component[2]	Interventions
Belgium[5]						
1979: 2/1982: 4	–	–3.1	–14.6	7.7	2.4	–
1983: 1/1985: 4	–	0.3	0.1	4.1	3.7	–
1986: 1/1987: 2	–	0.1*	3.6*	0.9	5.8	–
France						
1979: 2/1982: 4	–3.8	–0.7	–17.1	27.8	17.0	–4.6
1983: 1/1985: 4	2.7	9.6	–5.1	0.9	3.6	1.1
1986: 1/1987: 2	–0.9	–0.9	2.6	7.3	4.2	–0.8
Germany						
1979: 2/1982: 4	–17.2	–9.5	–24.9	4.6	–1.1	–7.1
1983: 1/1985: 4	–19.3	1.6	28.1	4.9	–0.5	–10.8
1986: 1/1987: 2	5.9	15.4	57.5	2.9	5.9	5.3
Italy						
1979: 2/1982: 4	–14.6	–6.7	–21.8	21.2	9.9	–5.4
1983: 1/1985: 4	–3.1	0.8	–4.4	13.7	3.5	–1.1
1986: 1/1987: 2	5.1	4.7	1.3	3.5**	0.7**	5.3**

Table 10.7 Interventions, Official Reserves and Monetary Base in Selected EMS Countries

Notes:

*1986: 1/1986: 4.

**1986: 1/1987: 1.

[1] Billions of US dollars, cumulated flows in reference periods.

[2] There are substantial unexplained differences between the data on official reserves (net of valuation adjustments), taken from BIS sources, and the monetary base data, which are from IMF sources.

[3] In per cent.

[4] The contributions to monetary base growth are obtained from the ratio of total flows of the relevant variable to beginning-of-period monetary base stocks.

[5] Not available.

Source: BIS, IMF.

realignments, particularly when these have been delayed and widely anticipated by the markets.

Finally, some observations regarding sterilisation techniques are in order. Inspection of intervention and official reserve flow data (Table 10.7) shows that they have been rather loosely related, especially when net interventions were strongly negative. In part this discrepancy is explained by offsetting recourse to official borrowing (by the central bank or the Treasury); the proceeds of such loans are not usually sold on the market and thus do not lead to liquidity creation. Movements in official reserves are also offset through swaps with commercial banks: in this case, both the domestic liquidity and the foreign-exchange effects of interventions cancel out. This technique has been widely used by Germany (to sterilise its own and other countries' interventions) and France, and to a lesser extent also by other ERM members.

Other offsetting techniques in foreign-exchange markets are available,[17] though they have played a less important role: interventions of opposite sign within the VSTF period, settlement of debtor balances in the creditor currency – and, as already noted, use of currency balances held in the Euromarkets and the redepositing of weak currencies acquired through interventions in these markets.

The right-hand side of Table 10.7 makes it clear that countries have largely 'decoupled' the evolution of the external component of the monetary base from interventions; whatever adjustment has been undertaken in domestic monetary policies in response to external developments, it seems that it has not usually been achieved by (semi-) automatic 'rules of the game' involving less than full sterilisation of intervention.

This does not necessarily mean that the effects of interventions on the foreign component of the monetary base – and thereby on domestic monetary conditions – have always been nil or have never played a stabilising role at times of pressure. Indeed, in all countries there have been occasions when developments in the foreign-exchange markets have influenced domestic monetary conditions.

Some rough evidence of this is presented in Table 10.8 – i.e., the correlation coefficients (calculated on monthly data) between interventions, foreign base and total monetary base changes for the three different periods examined above. The only general result – as could be expected – is the great variety of behaviour in the different periods, with direct sterilisation in foreign-exchange markets and sterilisation in domestic money markets being used in complementary fashion to obtain the desired result for total base growth. Germany appears to stand out for its systematically weaker correlations both of interventions and of the

	Mar. 1979–Dec. 1982		Jan. 1983–Dec. 1985		Jan. 1986–Jun. 1987	
	Inter-ventions[1]	$\Delta^2 fa$[3]	Inter-ventions	Δfa	Inter-ventions	Δfa
Belgium						
Δfa	0.66*	–	0.16	–	0.63*	–
Δm[4]	0.47*	0.76*	0.11	0.99*	0.36	0.27
France						
Δfa	0.24	–	0.59*	–	0.74*	–
Δm	– 0.09	0.82*	– 0.03	– 0.16	– 0.47*	– 0.12
Germany						
Δfa	0.45*	–	0.61*	–	0.90*	–
Δm	0.08	0.13	0.10	0.20	– 0.55*	– 0.54*
Italy[5]						
Δfa	0.17	–	0.76*	–	0.85*	–
Δm	– 0.03	0.77*	0.24	0.46*	– 0.31	– 0.14

Table 10.8 Correlation Coefficients Between Interventions, Changes in the Foreign Component of the Monetary Base and the Total Monetary Base

Notes:
*Statistically different from zero on the basis of the approximate confidence bounds $\pm 2/\sqrt{N}$, where n is the number of observations within each period.
[1]Interventions: foreign-exchange interventions, monthly flows in US dollars.
[2]Δ: first difference operator
[3]fa: change in the monetary base foreign component, monthly flow (converted in US dollars on the basis of monthly-average exchange rate).
[4]m: change in the monetary base, monthly flow (converted in US dollars on the basis of monthly-average exchange rate).
[5]For Italy, the third period ends with March 1987.

Source: BIS, IMF.

foreign component with changes in the total base. Note that in 1986–7, when interventions were largely reflected in the foreign component, the correlation of both variables with total base flows turns large and negative, indicating 'aggressive' sterilisation operations in the money market.

For the other three countries, there are periods when interventions seem to play an immediate role in determining domestic monetary conditions. Belgium stands out as the most respectful of the rules of the game, notably in 1979–82 and 1983–5 (correlation coefficients always positive and relatively high). France, on the other hand, seems to have acted more systematically to offset the potential monetary consequences of interventions in the two earlier periods and to have been more willing to accept them in 1986–7. Italy stands in between, with a tendency to accommodate (and accept) expansionary impulses stemming from interventions and to sterilise contractionary ones.

All in all, the very variety of behaviour makes it apparent that there is hardly any automatic feedback rule ensuring supportive adjustment of monetary conditions when exchange rates come under pressure; rather, when such an adjustment takes place it is largely the product of discretionary policy decision.

5   Sterilisation and monetary policy interactions

Even though intervention in foreign-exchange markets has mostly been sterilised by offsetting operations in foreign exchange and capital markets (Section 4), there have been substantial variations in official reserves and the foreign component of monetary base in all the ERM countries (Tables 10.2 and 10.7).

The pattern of monetary coordination in the ERM is thus further revealed by the estimation of central banks' reaction functions relating monetary base creation through domestic channels to changes in the foreign component of the monetary base and to variables representing the domestic objectives of monetary policy (inflation and growth), as in Herring and Marston (1977a, 1977b) and Obstfeld (1983).

The estimated equation is as follows:[18]

$$\frac{\Delta da}{m_{-1}} = a + b\pi + cg + d\,\frac{\Delta fa}{m_{-1}} + u \tag{10.1}$$

To the extent that monetary base growth is determined in the light of domestic objectives, changes in the foreign component must be offset by equal and opposite changes in the domestic component; the coefficient d must therefore approach a value of -1. Smaller absolute values of d can be taken to indicate that monetary policy objectives are modified in response to developments in the balance of payments and official reserves.

Estimation of equation (10.1) is complicated by the fact that the foreign component of the monetary base cannot safely be considered an exogenous variable. Indeed, changes in the domestic component are liable to affect interest rates in domestic markets and, through this channel, international capital flows and the foreign component. Hence, the fa variable is correlated with the error term, implying inconsistency of OLS estimates and the need to resort to simultaneous equation methods of estimation. Rather than attempt to estimate a full structural model of money markets, we specified an equation for the variable *fa* that included the other exogenous variables of (10.1) and, in addition, the current external balance and lagged values of the domestic and foreign component of monetary base creation; we then proceeded to estimate the two-equation system with two-stage least squares (2SLS). We also tried to improve the efficiency of OLS parameter estimates by using Zellner's seemingly unrelated regression technique (SUR) to take full account of the correlations between the residuals of the estimated reaction functions that may arise under fixed exchange rates.

Equation (10.1) has been estimated, with quarterly data covering 1979:1/1986:4, for Belgium, France, Germany, and Italy. The results obtained with OLS, SUR and 2SLS are given in Table 10.9.[20] Though they may not be the best obtainable for each individual country, the uniformity and simplicity of the model allow some useful comparisons.

Indeed, a clear difference emerges in sterilisation behaviour. Germany shows a coefficient for the variable *fa* of around − 0.8 (and indeed not statistically different from − 1) with OLS and − 0.6 with 2SLS (statistically, though only marginally, different from − 1), while for the other three countries the value of the coefficient is around − 0.3 (Italy and Belgium) or − 0.4 (France).

The domestic objective variables do not perform very well in Italy's equation (the positive sign for inflation implies at least partial accommodation); the inflation variable is significant in the Belgian, French and German equations, with small negative coefficients indicating non-accommodation; the output variable has a significant (albeit small) effect only in the French equation.

A major difficulty in estimating these equations is, of course, the fact that the relationship between monetary base and the other main macroeconomic variables was affected, to a varying degree, by financial innovation and the accompanying adaptations of regulatory structures. These changes were particularly significant for Italy, where the reserve requirement on bank deposits was repeatedly modified during the 1980s. On the other hand, no simple way of taking these complex phenomena into account seemed to yield significant improvements in the estimated equations while permitting the meaningful cross-border comparison.

Evidence on the interrelationships that arise in monetary policy management within the ERM has been sought through the estimation of vector autoregression (VAR) models relating Germany's monetary base to that of each of the other three countries and the corresponding bilateral exchange rate. Such models can be thought of as reduced forms

Dependent variable $\frac{\Delta da^1}{m-1}$		Independent variables									
		$\frac{\Delta fa^2}{m-1}$	Inflation	Output	Time[3]	Constant	s1[3]	s2[3]	s3[3]	R2 (corr.)	DW
Belgium[8]	OLS[4]	−0.31 (4.60)	−0.014 (2.04)	n.s.[7]	−0.002 (3.13)	0.068 (3.54)	–	–	–	0.42	2.0
	SUR[5]	−0.29 (4.62)	−0.018 (2.67)	n.s.	−0.002 (3.50)	0.075 (4.13)	–	–	–	–	2.0
	2SLS[6]	−0.35 (3.71)	−0.017 (2.16)	n.s.	−0.003 (3.19)	0.087 (3.39)	–	–	–	0.33	1.6
France[9]	OLS	−0.39 (4.72)	−0.011 (1.68)	0.018 (1.95)	−0.002 (3.67)	0.080 (3.32)	–	–	–	0.48	2.2
	SUR	−0.40 (5.10)	−0.013 (2.15)	0.021 (2.44)	−0.002 (4.06)	0.080 (3.86)	–	–	–	–	2.2
	2SLS	−0.38 (2.36)	−0.012 (1.73)	0.016 (1.64)	−0.002 (3.07)	0.090 (2.95)	–	–	–	0.26	2.2
Germany[10]	OLS	−0.82 (5.70)	−0.008 (1.50)	n.s.	–	0.033 (4.25)	−0.036 (3.35)	−0.030 (2.98)	−0.006 (0.54)	0.65	2.4
	2SLS	−0.64 (3.28)	−0.010 (1.86)	n.s.	–	0.036 (4.76)	−0.037 (3.58)	−0.036 (3.67)	−0.008 (0.85)	0.59	2.3
Italy[11]	OLS	−0.28 (1.87)	0.006 (1.49)	n.s.	–	0.014 (0.81)	0.017 (1.35)	−0.033 (2.58)	−0.016 (1.25)	0.41	2.1

Table 10.9 Policy Reaction Functions of Monetary Authorities of Selected EMS Countries (Estimation Period: 1979: 1–1986: 4)

Notes:

[1]Δda: change in the domestic component of the monetary base.

[2]Δfa: change in net foreign assets (the data are not adjusted for valuation changes, since time series for the latter were not available).

[3]time: a (linear) time trend; s1, s2 and s3: seasonal dummies.

[4]OLS: ordinary least squares.

[5]SUR: Zellner's seemingly unrelated regressions.

[6]2SLS: two-stage least squares; instruments for fa in the 2SLS estimation are a time trend, seasonal dummies, lagged foreign and domestic components of the monetary base, the current account balance and the other exogenous variables.

[7]n.s.: the coefficient is not statistically different from zero.

[8]Belgium: inflation is measured on consumer prices, the output variable by the deviations from trend of industrial output.

[9]France: inflation is measured by the percentage change in the GDP deflator, the output variable by the deviations from trend of GDP.

[10]Germany: inflation is measured on consumer prices, the output variable by the deviations from trend of industrial output.

[11]Italy: inflation is measured by the percentage change in the GDP deflator, the output variable by the deviations from trend of GDP.

Source: BIS, IMF.

of very simple two-country structural models of money markets and their interactions in a pegged exchange-rates area, as follows:[20]

$$m_s = m_d(i, i^*, \mathring{e}, k, z) \tag{10.2}$$

$$m_s^* = m_d^*(i, i^*, \mathring{e}, k, z^*) \tag{10.3}$$

$$i^* = i + \mathring{e} + k \tag{10.4}$$

$$m_s^* = \bar{m}_s^* \tag{10.5}$$

$$\mathring{e} = \epsilon - \bar{e} \tag{10.6}$$

Equations (10.2) and (10.3) are standard base (money) market equilibrium conditions, equation (10.4) is the interest-parity condition, equation (10.5) the leading country's money supply rule, equation (10.6) the definition of $\mathring{e}$, the expected rate of change of the exchange rate. It is assumed that exchange-rate expectations are formed (in the short term) on the basis of static or regressive expectations, so that $\mathring{e}$ is defined by the difference between a constant and the current exchange rate. The leading country sets its independent money supply rule; the other country fixes the exchange rate at level $\bar{e}$ and intervenes in the foreign-exchange market to keep it there. Equation (10.3) thus determines the German interest rate i^*; equation (10.4), for a given value of $\bar{e}$, the other country's interest rate i; equation (10.2), this latter country's money supply. The reduced form of this model expresses the second country's money supply and the two interest rates as functions of Germany's money supply, the second country's exchange-rate objective and the other exogenous variables. Assuming constancy of all exogenous variables we can thus write, differentiating with respect to time:

$$\mathring{m} = \phi(\mathring{m}^*, \mathring{e}) \tag{10.7}$$

Estimation of equation (10.7) with VAR techniques can thus be seen as a test of the model's ability to describe the relation of each country's monetary policy to that of Germany.

Empirically, we treated (10.7) as one equation in a broader vector autoregressive model where the variables $(\mathring{m}, \mathring{m}^*, \mathring{e})$ are potentially endogenous. To obtain wide-sense stationarity, the two variables $\mathring{m}$ and $\mathring{m}^*$ have been calculated as first differences of the log of base money; they have been further filtered by a time trend and when necessary (on the basis of the corresponding autocorrelation function) by seasonal dummies; $\mathring{e}$ is the first difference of the log of the exchange rate and no filter has been applied to it. The optimal lags of each independent variable in each equation of the model have been selected by resort to Akaike's final-prediction-error (FPE) criterion; search of the optimal lag structure has been limited to a maximum of six lags. The significance of the added variables in each equation has then been tested with likelihood ratio statistics.

The estimation results are reported in Table 10.10. Overall they confirm the validity of equation (10.7) in describing the monetary interactions between the selected countries; in particular, the growth rate of the monetary base of Belgium, France and Italy is significantly influenced by German base money and by the exchange rate *vis-à-vis* the DM. For Italy, the exchange-rate effect is stronger, pointing to the larger role played by this variable in reconciling divergent monetary behaviour.[23]

The results obtained for the equations in which Germany's monetary base is the dependent variable are not in full accordance with our stylised money market model. In all cases m_G is correlated with the other country's m, implying that m_G cannot be safely thought of as a constant or univariate autoregressive process. The same result (i.e., interdependence between the base money markets) was largely confirmed by estimation of the same VAR models subject to a more stringent information criterion, as well as by canonical correlation analysis of the three-variable vector defined for each pair of countries. In all two-country models – and even in the general model including all the countries (and variables) – the German base appears correlated with the lagged values of other countries' monetary base.

This would imply that equation (10.5) of our stylised model does not fully describe monetary interactions among the selected countries. One obvious reason is that on a number of occasions interventions were carried out by the exchange-rate peggers using the leading country's currency: this evidence points to the need to take account explicitly in the model of the effect of third-country interventions (in DM) on Germany's money supply.

We have therefore modified our model as follows:

$$m_s^* = \bar{m}_s^* + \sum_{j=0}^{T} \tilde{d}_j fa_{-j} \qquad (10.5')$$

In line with our findings pointing to a sterilisation coefficient for Germany close to -1 with quarterly data, we tested the hypothesis that the short-run (monthly) effects of the foreign component are transitory, and thus introduced the restriction $\sum_{j=0}^{3} \tilde{d}_j = 0$ on the coefficients of (10.5').

By reformulating equation (10.5') and the restriction on the $\tilde{d}$ parameters in the policy reaction function specified earlier, we obtained:[22]

Germany and Belgium

Dependent variable[1]	Independent variables[2]		$\chi^2(m_G)$	$\chi^2(m_B)$	χ^2 (BF/DM)
m_G	m_G (2)	m_B (2)	—	5.1 (7.8)	—
m_B	m_G (6)	m_B (1)	17.0 (1.0)	—	9.1 (0.3)
BF/DM	m_G (0)	m_B (0)	—	—	—

Germany and France

Dependent variable[1]	Independent variables[2]		$\chi^2(m_G)$	$\chi^2(m_F)$	χ^2 (FF/DM)
m_G	m_G (2)	m_F (2)	—	7.7 (2.2)	—
m_F	m_G (5)	m_F (6)	13.3 (2.0)	—	17.5 (0.7)
FF/DM	m_G (0)	m_F (0)	—	—	—

Germany and Italy

Dependent variable[1]	Independent variables[2]		$\chi^2(m_G)$	$\chi^2(m_I)$	χ^2 (Lir/DM)
m_G	m_G (2)	m_I (5)	—	22.1 (0.0)	—
m_I	m_G (5)	m_I (3)	12.3 (3.2)	—	15.0 (1.0)
Lir/DM	m_G (0)	m_I (0)	—	—	—

Table 10.10 Vector Autoregression Models of Monetary Base in Germany and Third Countries and the Exchange Rate for Selected EMS Countries (Estimation Period: 1979: 3/1986: 12)

Notes:

[1]Variables for each model are percentage changes of the monetary base (m) and of the bilateral exchange rate against the DM (BF/DM = Belgian franc, FF/DM = French franc, Lir/DM = Italian lira).

[2]In parentheses the number of lagged values included for each variable. The autoregression models have been identified with Akaike's final prediction error: FPE $= (N + K + 1)/(N − K − 1)$. RSS, where N is the number of observations, K the number of lagged variables and RSS the sum of squared residuals. $\chi^2(Z) = − N \ln(\text{RSS}_{\text{UN}}/\text{RSS}_{\text{RS}})$ is the likelihood ratio statistic where RSS_{UN} is the sum of the squared residuals of the unrestricted model and RSS_{RS} is the sum of the squared residuals of the restricted model by the null hypothesis that lagged values of the independent variable Z do not affect the dependent variable. The statistic is asymptotically distributed as a χ^2 with degrees of freedom equal to the number of lags of the independent variable. Marginal significance levels are reported in parentheses.

Source: BIS, IMF.

$$\frac{\Delta da^*}{m_{-1}} = a + b\pi + cg + \sum_{j=0}^{3} d_j \left(\frac{\Delta fa^*}{m_{-1}}\right)_{-j} + u,$$

$$\sum_{j=0}^{3} d_j = -1 \qquad\qquad\qquad (10.5'')$$

We estimated equation (10.5″) and tested the restriction on the basis of monthly data assuming that the parameters d_j lie on an Almon polynomial of degree 2. The hypothesis of full sterilisation within the three-month period is not rejected: the F associated with restriction $\sum_{j=0}^{3} d_j = -1$ is well below the critical value for a confidence level of 95 per cent. However, the pattern of lagged responses does not fully conform to expectations (in particular, we fail to find an impact coefficient d statistically smaller than -1). The hypothesis that German monetary policy is characterised in the short run by flexibility in correcting for ERM-related external disturbances is thus not fully confirmed. Further work will be needed here, perhaps with a different methodology.

6   Conclusions

A few main conclusions seem worth stressing. There can be little doubt that the track record of the ERM is on the whole a good one, especially in view of the troubled international environment during most of its life.

However, actual developments differed from expectations in many respects. The system's robustness has been enhanced more by the policies autonomously pursued by member countries (which fostered adjustment and convergent performances) than by constraints of automatic rules of the game built into its mechanisms. Technically, these mechanisms proved flexible and were adapted to changing circumstances and developments thanks to close cooperation among the participating central banks. There were two crucial ingredients in this cocktail: on the one hand, the flexibility of the 'leading' central bank in accommodating (most of the time) the system's need for its currency and in managing its monetary targets; on the other, proper use of the system's reserve and credit mechanisms by weak-currency countries, notably in the sense that resort to these mechanisms was not sought in the main to finance balance of payments deficits or sustain 'divergent' monetary courses.

As to the model of monetary coordination that prevailed within the ERM, ample evidence has been presented to show that Germany has played the nth country's role of supplying the system with a monetary standard – the 'nominal anchor' – and, increasingly, with the intervention and reserve currency. The other countries have 'followed', using the

ERM exchange constraint as their compass and disciplinary policy standard, while gaining leeway through realignments and – in the case of more pronounced divergences in performance – exchange controls.

This model of coordination is obviously asymmetric; it has placed most of the burden of adjustment on the weak-currency countries. It should be recognised in fairness that it carries some merit for the results of the system and that no obvious alternative was (or is) available.

At the same time, we cannot conclude that the ERM is problem-free. There is first, in the background, a 'real', fundamental problem in that the 'leading' country seems able to provide the system with a stable nominal anchor, but not with an engine for growth. Unlike the United States under the Bretton Woods system, Germany has enjoyed the benefit of a generally somewhat undervalued currency in real terms – as a reflection of the exchange-rate discipline accepted by higher-inflation countries – and has 'subtracted' real growth from her partners through rising bilateral trade surpluses; on average, Germany's growth rate of domestic demand has been lower than that of its partners. There is a genuine risk that the EMS 'real' straitjacket may not be acceptable to all the participant countries forever, especially in view of their different unemployment situations and demographic trends.

Secondly, there is a monetary management problem. The evidence that has been presented shows that, in general, countries have adhered to the asymmetric-model rules of the game, thus ensuring ERM cohesion. Short-term management, however, has not been faultless. There has been somewhat excessive reliance on sterilised interventions, on occasion with the aim of rigidly defending a particular exchange-rate level, and insufficiently supportive use of domestic monetary instruments (interest rates). And, at times of great strain stemming from external shocks (the dollar), there has been insufficient coordination of responses, and sometimes even contradictory actions by participating central banks.

The need for closer monetary coordination is enhanced by the increased mobility of capital – and, somewhat paradoxically, by the fact that inflation differentials are now smaller than the band-width. As a result, the relative weight of 'pure' financial factors in the determination of interest-rate differentials is greatly increased, and so are the potentially destabilising effects of uncoordinated interest-rate policies when the system comes under strain. The (potential) conflict between external and domestic objectives of monetary policy is made more acute. There is a real danger that exchange-rate stability may give way, with the system evolving towards a crawling peg.

The recent changes in the system's mechanisms seem to go some way towards overcoming these difficulties. They make the reserve mechanisms of the system more flexible and enlarge the means available to meet pressures. Without a parallel improvement in management techniques, however, these enhanced mechanisms will not ensure greater exchange-rate stability. More flexible interest-rate policies are needed, as well as greater automaticity of adjustment in domestic monetary conditions in response to interventions in foreign-exchange markets. Fuller and more flexible use of the oscillation band can also help; but its benefits should not be overestimated unless greater consistency in domestic monetary conditions can be brought about.

It is also essential that the signals given by the central banks whose currencies are coming under opposing pressures be made more consistent. Within the ERM, this will require the leading country to accept a greater degree of symmetry in short-term monetary adjustment. In principle, this is not inconsistent with preserving its medium-term monetary course and the system's stable nominal anchor. In practice, it will require a degree of consensus on medium-term policy objectives that simply does not exist today.

NOTES

* The authors are indebted to W. Rieke, the Foreign Department of the National Bank of Belgium, F. Giavazzi and L. Spaventa for useful comments, and to R. Giannini, M. A. Antonicelli and B. Bucci for excellent research assistance.
1 For fuller description of ERM intervention, reserve and credit mechanisms see Micossi (1985).
2 Article 3.5 of the European Council Resolution of 5 December 1978 'on the establishment of the EMS and related matters' (Brussels Resolution) also states that 'an ECU basket formula will be used as an indicator to detect divergences between Community currencies', and Article 3.6 stipulates that 'when a currency crosses its threshold of divergence, this results in a presumption that the authorities concerned will correct this situation by adequate measures', including 'diversified interventions'. This provision could be seen as entailing an explicit role for intramarginal intervention; in practice, however, it has played virtually no role in the management of the system.
3 A number of changes in EMS mechanisms, decided upon by the Committee of Governors in September 1987, are discussed at the end of this section.
4 This is reflected in higher inflation countries' currencies appreciating in real terms *vis-à-vis* the DM, as a direct consequence of the policy decision to avoid full exchange-rate accommodation of inflation differentials.
5 The relationship between dollar weakness *vis-à-vis* the DM, and DM strength in the EMS band has been assessed, in particular, by Micossi and Padoa-Schioppa (1985) and Giavazzi and Giovannini (1985).
6 This increase is only in part EMS-related, since dollar-support interventions increased considerably during this period.

7 The maximum limit is equal to double the debtor quota in the short-term monetary support; it has also been agreed that the intervening central bank will make parallel use of its balances of the intervention currency 'in amounts to be agreed', and that the issuing central bank may ask that settlement of resulting debtor balances in the VSTF be made in its own currency.

8 Indeed, this new approach has been successfully applied in October 1987 when the ERM came under strain owing to the breakdown of the Louvre Agreement and the ensuing sharp fall in the dollar.

9 See Report No. 59 of the Dalgaard Group.

10 Interventions at the limit carried out before realignments were in most cases subsequently reversed quite rapidly, often within the same month; this lowers the reported figures for interventions at the limit.

11 See Caranza (1985).

12 The problem does not arise for countries targeting domestic credit, since the total supply of money and other financial assets can then be determined by the balance of payments according to the 'rules of the game'.

13 Some evidence is presented in Giavazzi and Pagano (1985) and, for Italy alone, in Micossi and Rossi (1986).

14 See De Grauwe (1977). The sufficient conditions for stability of reserve flow equations in an interdependent system were derived formally by Aoki (1977).

15 This aspect was first systematically analysed by the Committee of Governors' Experts Group chaired by M. Raymond (1985); see also Masera (1986).

16 This point is made by Michielsen and Rey (1986).

17 See Caesar (1986).

18 m is monetary base, da and fa are respectively the domestic and foreign components of monetary base, π is inflation and g the (percentage) deviation of output (GNP or industrial production) from trend, u a stochastic term, Δ the first difference operator. Current time subscripts are omitted.

19 We have omitted SUR and 2SLS results when they did not lead to an improvement on OLS. The current account balance, lagged by one quarter, was also used as an instrumental variable in 2SLS: the results were not significantly different from those shown in Table 10.9. Giavazzi (1987, pp. 24–6) has raised an additional problem regarding the estimation of a policy reaction function of the kind we have used. He claims that if equation (10.1) is derived as a reduced form of a structural model, with exogenous shocks affecting both variables fa and da, there may be correlation between the foreign component of the monetary base and the disturbance term as the result of errors in the monetary base variables. In our view, however, this problem does not arise since the policy reaction function (10.1) is a structural equation.

20 m = monetary base; i = money market interest rate; $\mathring{e}$ = exchange rate (foreign currency per DM, with dot over variable indicating rate of change); k = risk premium; z = vector of other relevant exogenous variables. The asterisk identifies the leading country's (Germany's) variables; a bar over variables identifies policy objectives.

21 VAR models with different dynamic specifications from those reported in Table 10.10 have been selected through the Akaike information criterion:

$$AIC = N[\ln(|\Sigma_p|)] + 2^{2pk^2}$$

where N is the number of observations, $|\Sigma_p|$ is the generalised variance of estimated variance–covariance matrix of the disturbance terms of an order-p model and k is the number of variables.

The models identified by minimising AIC with respect to p (which always show a lower lag order than those reported in Table 10.10), show that Germany's monetary base is significantly correlated with each of the other countries' corresponding variable. Canonical correlation analysis (Theil, 1971), applied to current and future values of the vector time series $(\dot{m}, \dot{m}^*, \dot{e})$ as dependent variables, and to current and past values of the same vector time series as explanatory variables, basically confirms this result.

22 Equation (10.5″) can be easily obtained from equation (10.5′) by putting $m_s^* = da^* + fa^*$:

$$da^* = \dot{m}_s^* + \sum_{j=0}^{T} \tilde{d}_j fa^*_{-j} - fa^* = \dot{m}_s^* - (1 - \tilde{d}_0)fa^* + \sum_{j=1}^{T} \tilde{d}_j fa^*_{-j}$$

By use of the difference operator and dividing all terms by m^*_{-1}:

$$\frac{da^*}{m_{-1}} = \sum_{j=0}^{T} d_j \left(\frac{fa^*}{m_{-1}}\right)_{-j}$$

where $d_0 = (\tilde{d}_0 - 1)$; $d_j = \tilde{d}_j, j = 1, 2, \ldots T$.
The restriction

$$\sum_{j=0}^{T} \tilde{d}_j = 0$$

on the coefficients of (10.5′) can then be reformulated as:

$$\sum_{j=0}^{T} d_j = -1$$

Introducing the policy goals of the reaction function (π and g), we obtain equation (10.5″) of the text.

REFERENCES

Akaike, H. (1970). 'Statistical Predictor Identification', *Annals of the Institute for Statistical Mathematics*, No. 2.

Aoki, M. (1977). 'A note on the stability of the interaction of monetary policies', *Journal of International Economics*, Vol. 6 (February).

Bini Smaghi, L. and R. S. Masera (1987). *L'evoluzione degli accordi di cambio dello SME: marzo 1979 – marzo 1987*, in *L'unificazione monetaria e lo SME*, Bologna, Il Mulino.

Black, S. (1983). 'The use of monetary policy for internal and external balance in ten industrial countries', in J. Frenkel (ed.), *Exchange Rates and International Macroeconomics*, Chicago, University of Chicago Press.

Caesar, R. (1986). 'German Monetary Policy and the EMS', paper presented at the SUERF Colloquium on *International Monetary and Financial Integration – The European Dimension*, Luxembourg (9–11 October).

Caranza, C. (1985). '*La politica monetaria nella CEE: problemi ed esperienze a confronto*', *Quaderni della Cassa di Risparmio di Torino* (December).

De Grauwe, P. (1977). 'Monetary interdependence among major European countries', in R. Z. Aliber (ed.), *The Political Economy of Monetary Reform*, Chicago, University of Chicago Press.

Giavazzi, F. (1987). 'Exchange Controls and Sterilization: the German Experience and Lessons for Korea' (mimeo).

Giavazzi, F. and A. Giovannini (1986). 'The EMS and the Dollar', *Economic Policy*, Vol. 2 (April), pp. 456–85.

(1987). 'Models of the EMS: is Europe a Greater Deutschmark Area?', in R. Portes and R. Bryant (eds), *Global Macroeconomics: Policy Conflict and Cooperation*, London, Macmillan, pp. 237–76.

Giavazzi, F. and M. Pagano (1985). 'Capital Controls and the European Monetary System', in F. Giavazzi (ed.), *Capital Controls and Foreign Exchange Legislation*, Euromobiliare Occasional Papers, No. 1 (June).

Gros, D. (1987). 'The effectiveness of capital controls and their implications for monetary autonomy in the presence of incomplete market separation', IMF Staff Papers (December).

Group of Experts of the Committee of Governors chaired by M. Raymond (1985). *Report No. 27 on Current Monetary Policies in EEC Member Countries* (December).

Group of Experts of the Committee of Governors chaired by M. Dalgaard (1987). *Report No. 59 on the Working of the European Monetary System* (May).

Herring, R. J. and R. C. Marston (1977a). *National Monetary Policies and International Financial Markets*, Amsterdam, North-Holland.

(1977b). 'Sterilization Policy: the Trade-off Between Monetary Autonomy and Control Over Foreign Exchange Reserves', *European Economic Review* (December).

Masera, R. S. (1986). 'An increasing role for the ECU', *Temi di Discussione*, Banca d'Italia (June).

Masera, R. S. (1987). *L'unificazione monetaria e lo SME*, Bologna, Il Mulino.

Michielsen, J. and J.-J. Rey (1986). 'European Monetary Arrangements: Their Functioning and Future', paper presented at the SUERF Colloquium on *International Monetary and Financial Integration – The European Dimension*, Luxembourg (9–11 October).

Micossi, S. (1985). 'The intervention and financing mechanisms of the EMS', Banca Nazionale del Lavoro *Quarterly Review* (December).

Micossi, S. and T. Padoa-Schioppa (1985). 'Can Europeans control their interest rates?', Brussels, CEPS Paper, No. 17 (February).

Micossi, S. and S. Rossi (1986). 'Restrictions on international capital flows: the case of Italy', prepared for the Symposium on *European Factor Mobility: Trends and Consequences*, University of Kent at Canterbury (30 June–2 July).

Obstfeld, M. (1982). 'Can we sterilize: Theory and evidence', *American Economic Review*, Vol. 72, No. 2 (May).

(1983). 'Exchange Rates, Inflation and the Sterilization Problem', *European Economic Review* (March–April)

Russo, M. and G. Tullio (1987). 'Monetary Policy Coordination Within the European Monetary System: Is There a Rule'?' (Chapter 11 in this volume).

Theil, H. (1971). *Principles of Econometrics*, New York, John Wiley.

Discussion

WOLFGANG RIEKE

This study deals with issues which are right at the centre of discussions that led to the recent agreement between EMS central banks on changes in the system. It is instructive reading even for those who have been close to the operation of the system since its beginnings.

The study describes correctly the intervention policies of participating central banks and their monetary policy reactions, against the background of a growing consensus for effective domestic adjustment covering a broader range of policies outside the responsibility of central banks.

The description of intervention rules and policies of central banks given in Section 2 does not call for much commentary. The preference for a 'parity grid' type intervention system was indeed based on the view that the intervention obligations should be symmetrical.

It should be recalled that the alternative proposal was that the ECU market value of each participating country's currency should be held within a narrow margin around its ECU central rate, thus concentrating intervention on the central bank whose currency deviated from the average by a certain margin. Apart from the technical problems of such a mechanism there were clearly fundamental objections against that concept. The divergence indicator with its presumption of action on the part of the deviating partner – its central bank or government – was a left-over of that debate, and has never played a major role.

The assumption that a country whose currency had fallen to the lower limit would not long be able to put off action to deal with the situation in one way or another was, of course, part of the argument for the parity grid. Over the years exchange-rate adjustment was, however, not only initiated by weak-currency countries but on occasion as a concerted action by countries with weak and strong currencies.

Intramarginal intervention was not originally expected to play the role it came to play over the years, and there was originally little or no discussion of its financing through the very short-term financing mechanism. As intramarginal intervention became popular with certain countries, demands for their inclusion in very short-term financing (VSTF) were raised. They were resisted for some years for the reasons mentioned on p. 255. I shall come back to this point.

It is probably quite correct that the second oil shock and its inflationary impact were instrumental in strengthening the consensus for effective adjustment policies. Some would claim that this is the secret of success of the EMS, rather than the mechanism itself. According to that view, the discipline implicit in the system was at best additional to the overwhelming need to bring inflation under control, EMS or not. The EMS discipline helped certain partner countries in the task, but it was not the prime force causing them to pursue anti-inflationary adjustment.

This conclusion is supported by the fact that some countries outside the EMS were no less successful than EMS countries in controlling inflation and reducing their external imbalances. But it is probably true that the EMS through its consultation procedures and peer pressures facilitated common acceptance of convergence towards the 'best performer' as a guiding principle. EMS countries on the whole have maintained domestic monetary conditions consistent with the needs of the system, though some of them also had large-scale recourse to foreign currency credit to help finance their current account deficits through intervention or otherwise.

Some attention is paid in the study to the role of dollar appreciation and later depreciation as a source of tension (or its absence) within the EMS. The thesis was developed at an early stage that dollar weakness or strength would affect the Deutsche mark more than other non-reserve EMS currencies and could thus cause tension even though the fundamentals within the system were on track. In fact, this has not consistently happened for a variety of reasons: for one thing, other EMS partners allowed their interest rates to react more flexibly than in the past, as is rightly explained elsewhere in the study; for another, dollar rates at times moved, without great sums of money being transacted in the markets, especially as the dollar retreated from its peaks.

Still, intervention was substantial at times within the EMS, and at times of Deutsche mark weakness large Deutsche mark balances were built up with the consent of the Bundesbank, to be used later to support partner currencies. How effective the intervention was is a question for debate. In February 1981, the Bundesbank raised its interest rates by three percentage points to support the Deutsche mark, which suggests that large-scale Deutsche mark purchases by EMS partners were not enough to hold rates stable. At other times Deutsche mark intervention by Germany's partners seems to have been more effective even over longer periods and may indeed have reduced the overall cost of stabilising exchange rates in the system, as is often claimed.

This takes me straight to section 4 (as I have little to say on Section 3, which deals with the statistical evidence on intervention, interest rates and exchange rates). Here the distinction between interventions that affect the monetary base of the country issuing the intervention currency and those that do not is discussed at some length. As far as intramarginal intervention is concerned, I have always seen some considerable logic in the notion that the country undertaking such intervention should be held responsible for its effectiveness, through supporting monetary policy action as necessary. After all, there is no obligation to intervene intramarginally, only the desire by one partner to hold the exchange rate *vis-à-vis* one or more partner currencies at a certain position within the band, based on his conviction that he should and can do so. If there is no obligation to intervene intramarginally – and given that views on its advisability might differ among participants – why should there be an obligation at the other end to ensure its effectiveness? In fact, clear responsibility of the intervening central bank to see that its own intervention is effective may explain why indeed it had an impact as intended. Undue reliance on the partner central bank's willingness to tolerate the monetary effects might encourage even greater recourse to intramarginal intervention by individual central banks as a means to stabilise the exchange rate, with doubtful results as intervention volumes accumulate. The issue of burden-sharing might have to be judged differently if intramarginal intervention is undertaken as part of a concerted action.

New rules have now been adopted by EMS central banks, allowing very short-term financing of intramarginal intervention up to certain limits under a presumption that agreement by the issuing central bank to the use of its currency for intramarginal intervention will also extend to its financing through mutual central bank credit. This should not be interpreted as meaning that the partner central bank will from now on be fully involved in the financing of such intervention on a permanent basis. As the authors correctly state, the availability of very short-term financing for intramarginal intervention should be seen to 'go hand in hand with more flexible interest-rate policies as well as a willingness to make fuller use of the EMS oscillation band to increase the perception of risk among operators'. In any case, access to very short-term financing is limited in amount and subject to conditions. Any evidence of unduly large and permanent use of the facility for that purpose is likely to cause more critical scrutiny of a partner's intentions when he wishes to intervene inside the band. Intramarginal intervention after all remains subject to agreement by the issuing central bank.

As we have often emphasised, the question of sterilisation versus non-sterilisation of exchange-market intervention is largely a 'non-issue' in the German monetary policy context. The critical parameter for monetary policy is the level of short-term money market interest rates under the control of the central bank.

The effect of intervention and other transactions involving foreign-exchange inflows and outflows to and from the Bundesbank are taken into account in the estimation of the banks' needs of central bank money to meet their requirements for cash and for meeting the minimum reserve requirements set by the Bundesbank. There is thus quasi-automatic sterilisation so defined, within a margin of error or miscalculation of the demand for central bank money in the system.

In these circumstances non-sterilisation has to be essentially equated with discretionary action taken to influence the liquidity needs of the banks via interest rate changes. Unless the discount and Lombard rates are moved, this occurs in small steps via the flexible application of security repurchase agreements with the banks. But action in this area has various motives; it should not be related too closely to the behaviour of the exchange rate and to intervention in the exchange market. The Deutsche mark counterpart of intervention and other foreign-exchange transactions of the Bundesbank is merely one component of the overall determination of the central bank money needs of the system at a certain level of interest rates under the control of the central bank.

This does not mean that there is no monetary effect of intervention, or that the Bundesbank takes no account of the interests of other countries and that it carries none of the burden of defending exchange rates in the EMS. For one thing, intervention in response to pressures on the exchange rate normally will have its counterpart in the effects on the money supply of an inflow from abroad via the non-bank sector; the central bank will not be able to offset this through its sterilising action on bank liquidity. There will thus remain a residuum of non-sterilisation which the central bank could correct only through action on interest rates that would affect the money supply.

Moreover, the Bundesbank does take account of its partners' interests both implicitly and explicitly. It does so implicitly to the extent that less inflation in partner countries implies less inflation in Germany and thus leaves room for an easier monetary policy than would otherwise be the case. And it has often done so explicitly in situations when its own action might have added to potential tensions or even triggered them – by refraining from raising interest rates as required, in principle, on domestic grounds. Needless to say, external considerations are not allowed to dictate monetary policy over any length of time, as this might conflict with the primary objective of domestic price stability.

11 Monetary Policy Coordination Within the European Monetary System: Is There a Rule?*

MASSIMO RUSSO and GIUSEPPE TULLIO

1   Introduction

By drawing on the analysis of the role of monetary policy in balance of payments adjustment under different monetary systems and exchange-rate arrangements, this study aims at focussing on the crucial issues involved when attempting to set rules for monetary policy coordination in a system of fixed but adjustable exchange rates such as the European Monetary System (EMS). A proper functioning of the balance of payments adjustment mechanism is crucial for the stability of an exchange-rate system. In turn, the proper working of the adjustment mechanism can be sought either through 'rules' which make the adjustment automatic or through prompt 'discretionary' changes in monetary policy, which requires a close degree of cooperation among the central banks of the member currencies (and the political willingness to subordinate, when necessary, internal objectives to the external constraint).

After recalling the main lessons from the gold standard and the Bretton Woods system, the analysis will focus on the EMS as it works at present. These are all systems of fixed but, in different degrees, adjustable exchange rates.[1] In Section 2 the two main lessons from the earlier international monetary regimes are summarised, that is: first, that in a system of fixed exchange rates the money supply of at least $n-1$ participants must remain endogenous, if the adjustment mechanism is to work smoothly. To put it differently, a fixed monetary rule for the total stock of money (but not for the domestic component of the monetary base) is incompatible with a system of fixed exchange rates, unless such a rule is reserved (implicitly or explicitly) to a recognised leader of the system. Second, a stable system needs a rule governing 'world' inflation, or (however measured) the inflation target of the group of countries participating in it, as well as a rule governing the reaction of countries' economic policies to deviation of actual inflation from the desired path.

292

Section 3 of the study is devoted to an analysis of the degree of monetary policy coordination and convergence of inflation and interest rates reached by EMS countries. In particular, we investigate the role of Germany in the fight against inflation and the balance of payments adjustment mechanism within the EMS. No explicit rule concerning inflation exists at present in the EMS. However, there has been an accepted unwritten rule since 1982–3, that is: Germany decides its domestic inflation rate and all other members adopt policies gradually to adjust their own to it – i.e., the German inflation rate has become the target inflation rate of the system.

Section 4 deals with the question of how the working of the EMS could be improved by making the balance of payments adjustment mechanism more symmetrical than has been the case so far. It is found that this will also require a rule guaranteeing low and stable inflation in all member countries. Four possible co-ordination rules for monetary policy are examined: first, the adoption, *ex ante*, of an aggregate money supply rule for the member countries, an application to the EMS of the proposal McKinnon (1984) made for Japan, the United States and Germany in the context of the reform of the international monetary system. Second, a rule derived from the first involving the expansion of the domestic component of the monetary base (i.e., money of domestic origin) in each member country coupled with the non-sterilisation of international reserve flows. Third, a nominal income rule adopted by each member country that should, however, be consistent with both their (independently-determined) growth and inflation objectives and the aim of convergence within the system. Fourth, a rule consisting of the adoption of a common inflation target pursued by each country individually and, for each member, a suitable monetary policy, designed to achieve it.

2   Lessons from the gold standard and Bretton Woods

a.   The gold standard

1876 can be considered as the beginning of the classical gold standard in continental Europe. By that year, Germany had completed the transformation of its monetary system from a predominantly silver standard to a gold standard. From 1876 and until 1913, all major industrial powers of the world, including the United States, were operating under the rules of the gold standard with London being the financial centre of the system. During this period, the central exchange rates between the currencies of the major countries were never changed. It follows that expectations that exchange rates would remain fixed were very firmly held. Member countries gave up entirely their monetary policy independence in favour of free trade in most industrial goods, free capital mobility and fixed exchange rates.[2] Private capital flows are believed to have been relatively large and proved to be generally of an equilibrating nature because expectations that there would be no change in exchange rates were so firmly held. The need for actual gold flows to finance current account disequilibria was therefore relatively limited (Bloomfield, 1959; 1963). Nevertheless, financial crises occurred in 1884, 1890, 1893, and 1907. Fiscal policies were not a source of disturbance, as budget deficits were modest in size, as were government revenues and expenditures relative to GDP.

The gold standard was a unique system characterised by an automatic rule governing the balance of payments adjustment and another governing the determination of the world price level. Thus the latter was outside the control of governments (including Britain, which was then issuing the key currency of the system). However, this proved not enough to guarantee perfect world price stability, as insufficient gold production and German purchases of gold led to world deflation until 1896, while large gold discoveries and new processes to extract gold led to world inflation from about 1896 to 1913. A weighted average index of consumer prices in the United Kingdom, France and the United States fell by about 26 per cent from 1876 to 1896 and increased by about 19 per cent from 1896 to 1913 (an annual rate of 1 per cent per year, no mean feat by today's standards). The gold standard in fact possessed an *automatic stabilising mechanism which tended to bring the world price level back to long-run equilibrium.*[3] However, the equilibrium world price level was not impervious to all types of shocks. In particular, a shift in the flow demand for industrial gold or a shift in the flow supply of gold could lead to a permanent change in world prices. Moreover, the stabilisation process appears to have been extremely slow, as shown by the long periods of deflation and inflation.

The independence of the equilibrium world price level from the fiscal and monetary policy of the key currency country and the automatic adjustment of world inflation (for at least some types of shocks) were unique features of the gold standard. Neither the Bretton Woods system nor the EMS have these properties.

The balance of payments adjustment mechanism under the gold standard worked as follows: assume an inflow of capital into Germany. The private discount rate in Berlin (the key market interest rate) fell and the differential between this rate and the official discount rate of the Reichsbank widened, making it less advantageous for commercial banks to discount bills at the Reichsbank. This led to a fall of earning assets and liabilities of the Reichsbank. The reduction in the Reichsbank's liabilities in turn led to an increase in its liquidity ratio – i.e., the gold or metal cover of notes and other short-term liabilities outstanding (mainly deposits held by banks). Since the liquidity ratio was the main factor influencing the Reichsbank's decisions to change the discount rate, the Reichsbank was promptly led to reduce the discount rate.[4]

From 1896 to 1913 – the period during which the adjustment mechanism worked most smoothly – there were in Germany 98 changes of the discount rate (or 5.4 changes per year on average). The variability within the year of the level of notes outstanding was also extremely high: the difference between the highest and the lowest level of Reichsbank notes outstanding as a fraction of their average yearly total reached a maximum of 74.6 per cent in 1912 and a minimum of 23.8 per cent in 1877. A similarly high variability of the discount rate and of the amount of notes issued is found for the Bank of England.[5] The role of central bank notes outstanding can be compared with that of the monetary base or the money stock in today's industrial countries. As a result of the subordination of the discount rate policy to external objectives and of the possibility of central banks borrowing from each other in times of crises, balance of payments disequilibria and international gold flows were limited.

The conclusion that we wish to draw from this analysis is that the balance of payments adjustment mechanism between the main industrial countries worked well during the gold standard. In the case of Germany and the United Kingdom, both the Reichsbank and the Bank of England were ready to accept a sufficient variability of the discount rate and an even greater one of the relevant monetary aggregate, thus making the adjustment relatively symmetrical. This experience shows that : *monetary targeting is incompatible with a smoothly working and symmetric balance of payments adjustment mechanism under fixed exchange rates.* The system would have broken down if two major countries had attempted to target money.

The gold standard was far from a perfect system. The world price level was too dependent on gold discoveries and its automatic adjustment mechanism very slow to operate. Moreover, there were government interferences with trade and capital flows between the major countries, although on a moderate scale by subsequent standards. In addition, the balance of payments adjustment between the core countries of the system and the developing countries of the periphery was asymmetrical, with a disproportionate share of the burden falling on the latter. Nevertheless, in terms of variability of output and inflation, the gold standard compares well with the post-Second World War Bretton Woods system, at least for the major countries (Eichengreen, 1984; Sommariva and Tullio, 1987a, Chapter 1).

What worked well was the balance of payments adjustment mechanism between the major countries. The policies of their central banks, which aimed predominantly at stabilising their respective liquidity ratios and maintaining internal convertibility, made this result possible. There was no conflict between the internal (convertibility) objective and the external objective of balance of payments equilibrium. There were some interferences into the free movement of gold on the part of the main central banks, which resulted in changes in transport costs. For instance, the Reichsbank changed at times the location of its gold window from Hamburg to Berlin. Nevertheless, the effects on gold flows of these forms of capital controls must have been minimal, as suggested by the fact that over 95 per cent of the variance of annual German international gold flows from 1878 to 1912 can be explained without the need of dummy variables for 'capital controls' (Sommariva and Tullio, 1987b).

The gold standard collapsed in 1914 when the internal convertibility of notes into gold was abolished. The war effort of individual countries led to high budget deficits, inflation and a collapse in world trade. The gold standard which emerged after the First World War can hardly be called a system. Internal convertibility of notes into gold was not reintroduced in most countries. The war had caused large gold flows towards the United States and the United Kingdom or towards countries which had not participated in the war, at the expense of the other continental European countries. As a result, the world distribution of monetary gold became very uneven, with the United States and France possessing a very large fraction of it.[6] In addition, the balance of payments adjustment mechanism did not work smoothly, as domestic objectives were not subordinated to the external one (Hawtrey, 1947) and free trade and free capital mobility became the exception rather than the rule. There was virtually no attempt at coordinating policies, nor was the United States ready to provide the necessary leadership (Kindleberger, 1976). Budget deficits and external indebtedness grew rapidly, especially in Germany in the second half of the 1920s. As a result of the reconstruction, the introduction of flexible exchange rates especially in the early 1920s,[7] and the lack of coordination of economic policies, business cycles were less synchronised in this period than before the First World War. Table 11.1 shows that the United Kingdom, France and Germany were in the same phase of the business cycle in 83.1 per cent of the months from September 1878 to August 1914, while they were in the same phase in only 45.5 per cent of the months between June 1919 and July 1932.

Countries	Sept. 1879– Aug. 1914	Jun. 1919– Jul. 1932
United Kingdom, France, Germany	83.1	45.2
United Kingdom, France, Germany, United States	53.5	35.6

Table 11.1 Percentage of Months During Which Countries Were in the Same Phase of the Business Cycle

Source: Morgenstern (1959).

b.   The Bretton Woods system and the special role of the US

Relative to the gold standard, the Bretton Woods system was characterised by (a) a greater degree of exchange-rate flexibility (which
entailed a greater variability of expectations of exchange-rate changes
and consequently at times large destabilising capital flows), (b) a greater
asymmetry in the balance of payments adjustment mechanism, due to
the role of the dollar as a reserve currency and the insufficient response of
American interest-rate policy to the United States' balance of payments
fluctuations, and (c) a very weak mechanism tending to stabilise the
world price level, especially after about 1960 when the United States
decided not to make its monetary policy responsive to the continuous fall
in the ratio of its gold holdings to its dollar liabilities.[8]

Although at times the asymmetry in the balance of payments adjustment mechanism caused tensions in relation to the proper division of the
burden of adjustment, the system worked well as long as the reserve
currency country followed policies consistent with maintaining world
inflation at a low and stable level and did not cause a shortage of reserves
or create an excess supply of international liquidity. The strains became
severe when the United States embarked upon a fiscal and monetary
expansion which was incompatible with world price stability. This led
ultimately to the breakdown of the system as other major countries –
particularly Germany and Japan – were not prepared to renounce their
low-inflation objective. This experience underscores the need in a
Bretton Woods-type system to maintain the price stability of the key
currency.

Scholars of international monetary systems are divided as to the degree
of responsibility to be attributed to the United States for the 1971
collapse of the Bretton Woods system. Some tend to attribute greater

	End of 1969	End of 1972	End of 1977
Foreign dollar claims	78	146	363
On United States government and banks	49	85	210
On foreign branches of United States banks	29	61	153
International monetary reserves	79	159	319
Foreign exchange	33	104	244
Dollars and Eurodollars	20	81	197

Table 11.2 The Inflationary Explosion of International Liquidity (Dollar Figures in Billions)

Source: Triffin (1978).

responsibility to policies followed by the United States since 1964–5, while others emphasise the inherent defects of the system, such as the insufficient world gold production and the ensuing need on the part of the reserve currency country to supply the international reserves needed to finance increased world trade and world economic growth, leading to the well-known 'Triffin dilemma'. By 1975, Harry Johnson concluded: 'The fact that the root cause of the disturbance that shocked and finally wrecked the International Monetary System's adjustable peg was a world inflation, originating in President Johnson's failure to accompany the escalation of the war in Vietnam in 1965 with an appropriately large increase in taxes, is by now generally accepted' (Johnson, 1975).

Table 11.2 shows the huge increase in dollar holdings from 1969 to 1972. Triffin (1978) does not take a clear position as to the United States' responsibilities, but he considers the increase in dollar holdings resulting from large-scale intervention to sustain the exchange rate of the dollar as the cause of the acceleration of world inflation in the 1970s.

Triffin had in 1957 already foreseen the collapse of the Bretton Woods system; he was wrong, however, in forecasting its timing. He explained later that the system had survived longer than he had expected because of United States' political pressure on Germany and Japan, bureaucratic routine on the part of central bankers in investing their surpluses in the largest financial market of the world, fears of 'rocking the boat' and above all reluctance on the part of other countries to see their currencies appreciate *vis-à-vis* the US dollar (Triffin, 1978). Robert Heller attributes the large increase in official dollar holdings in those years to a shift in the private demand from US dollars to other currencies. The US liquid

	United States	10 Other industrial countries[1]	Difference 10 − US	Average difference
1961	2.9	12.7	9.8	
1962	2.1	11.0	8.9	9.2
1963	2.8	11.7	8.9	
1964	4.1	8.6	4.5	
1965	4.3	9.3	5.0	
1966	4.6	8.3	3.7	
1967	3.9	7.4	3.5	3.7
1968	7.0	8.1	2.1	
1969	5.9	8.3	2.4	
1970	3.8	8.2	4.4	
1971	6.8	16.7	9.9	
1972	7.1	16.1	9.0	8.5
1973	7.3	13.9	6.6	

Table 11.3 Monetary Growth in Domestic Currencies, 11 Industrial Countries (Percentage Changes in Annual Averages)

Note:
[1]The countries are: Belgium, Canada, France, Germany, Italy, Japan, Netherlands, Sweden, Switzerland, United Kingdom.

Source: McKinnon (1986).

liabilities to private non-residents fell from US$28.23 billion at the end of 1969 to US$21.77 billion at the end of 1970 and US$15.09 billion at the end of 1971. During the same period US liabilities to foreign governments increased from US$16 billion at the end of 1969 to US$50.65 billion at the end of 1971 as central banks made large interventions in support of the US dollar (Heller, 1976).[9] Heller also shows that the growth of the US money supply was lower than in other countries and concludes that monetary policy in the United States was not excessively expansionary in those years and hence could not have triggered the shift in private portfolios.

Table 11.3 reports the rate of growth of M1 for the US and for the average of ten industrial countries (excluding the US) from 1961 to 1973. In virtually every year the rest of the world's money supply grew faster than that of the US. The excess of monetary growth in the rest of the industrialised world with respect to that in the US is particularly marked in the period 1961–3 and 1970–3. A somewhat higher rate of growth of money abroad can be justified for the average of the period by the higher rate of economic growth that the countries of the 'periphery' experienced during the period. The difference in real economic growth between Europe and the US was particularly high in the early 1960s as a result of the creation of the Common Market and the ensuing productivity gains from increased trade within the community, the still relatively large technological gap, and the scope for shifts in employment from low to high productivity sectors. The differences in money growth in the period 1970–3 appear for the most part to be caused by other factors.

Individual countries' money stocks are not good indicators of the degree of ease or restrictiveness of monetary policy under a fixed exchange-rate regime with perfect capital mobility, since they are endogenously determined. As Swoboda and Genberg (1977) have shown, the only truly exogenous monetary variables under Bretton Woods were the domestic component of the US monetary base (the Federal Reserve's claims on the government and commercial banks), what they call 'the outside portion' of international reserves – i.e., international reserves not created via balance of payments deficits of the reserve currency country (or countries) – and to some extent the domestic components of the monetary base of the central banks of the rest of the world. The latter in fact becomes partly endogenous if these central banks try to sterilise international reserve flows. It follows that if one wants to say something about the degree of restrictiveness of US monetary policy at the end of the Bretton Woods system, one has to look at the domestic components of the monetary base. This is done in Table 11.4, which also shows the US balance of payments deficit and the rates of inflation in the US and abroad.

The large US balance of payments deficits of the early 1970s were clearly related to the excessive growth of the domestic component of the US monetary base (reflecting in turn the fiscal imbalance), while the expansionary 'European' monetary policy in the period 1968–9 retarded the collapse of the Bretton Woods system. The excess of the growth of the domestic component of the US monetary base over the foreign growth rate was − 17.4 per cent in 1968, − 9.7 in 1969 and swelled to 13.5 in 1970 and 34.6 in 1971. In the second half of the 1960s the favourable relative inflation performance of the US had also ended, which could have by itself caused a downward shift in the private demand for US dollars, as pointed out by Heller (1976).

The US balance of payments deficits reached unprecedented levels in 1970–2, swelling the stock of dollars held by foreigners and the world money stock. This inflow of international reserves could be sterilised only in part by surplus countries by reducing the domestic component of the monetary base in 1970 to 1971, which thus became itself partially

	Domestic components of base money (% changes)		US balance of payments (in billions of US dollars)	Excess of US inflation over the rest of OECD[2]
	US	Rest of OECD[1]		
1960	5.7	10.1	−3.12	0.28
1961	6.0	6.6	−1.35	−1.64
1962	9.3	18.1	−2.41	−3.22
1963	6.2	8.8	−1.99	−3.38
1964	8.5	10.1	−1.27	−2.18
1965	8.5	9.6	−1.17	−2.44
1966	9.9	10.6	−0.10	−2.11
1967	9.7	11.5	−3.34	0.64
1968	6.8	24.2	1.73	0.14
1969	3.4	13.1	2.59	0.73
1970	10.0	−3.5	−10.25	0.82
1971	14.5	−20.1	−28.17	−1.77
1972	0.6	36.0	−10.91	−2.58
1973	10.3	28.5	−4.03	1.63

Table 11.4 Changes in Domestic Component of Monetary Base and US Balance of Payments

Notes:
[1]The countries are: the ten in Table 11.3 plus Denmark and Australia.
[2]Inflation is measured by the consumer price index. The countries are the ten in Table 11.3 plus Denmark and Australia.

Source: Tullio (1979).

endogenous. In 1972 and 1973 the surplus countries gave up the attempt to sterilise reserve inflows, as indicated by the large rate of increase of the domestic component of their monetary base, thus speeding up the acceleration of world inflation. Swoboda and Genberg (1977) have shown that because of the special role of the dollar as an international reserve asset in the Bretton Woods system and the rest of the world's practice of holding dollar reserves in the form of US Treasury bills and US or Eurodollar bank deposits (rather than in the form of deposits at the Federal Reserve System), an increase in the domestic component of the monetary base of the US had a comparatively larger effect on the world money stock than an equal dollar increase in the domestic component of the monetary base of the rest of the world. The habit of keeping dollar reserves in this form implied an automatic sterilisation of the US balance of payments deficits.[10]

The magnified effect of US domestic credit policies on the world money stock – and therefore on world inflation – also implied that the balance of payments adjustment mechanism worked asymmetrically, with the largest share of the burden of adjustment falling on the countries of the periphery. Also in this respect the Bretton Woods system differed from the classical gold standard. As to the countries of the periphery, the balance of payments adjustment mechanism worked as follows: if (say) expectations of a sterling crisis developed, capital would flow out of the UK, putting upward pressure on British interest rates and downward pressure on the British money supply, as the Bank of England was obliged, under the rules, to intervene in the foreign-exchange market to support the pound. The smooth operation of this 'automatic' mechanism implied that the Bank of England did not (and could not) fully sterilise the effect of the losses in reserves on the domestic monetary base – i.e., the Bank of England had to let the British money supply fall.[11] To the extent that capital was flowing to other countries of the periphery, the adjustment mechanism would work symmetrically, as other countries experienced (in the absence of sterilisation) a multiple increase in the money stock and a fall in interest rates. To the extent that capital flowed to the US, the burden of adjustment would fall mostly on the UK, since the US money stock and interest rates were largely unaffected because of automatic sterilisation, as US banks' liquidity was not altered as a result of the change in the holder of their liabilities (from the UK monetary authorities to other monetary authorities, or to the private sector).

The preceding analysis of the Bretton Woods system suggests the following conclusions: domestic monetary stocks were not the proper indicators of monetary policy, while domestic components of the monetary base were, both in the case of the leading country and for countries of the periphery that did not sterilise reserve flows; a major defect of the system – that impeded the smooth and symmetric working of the balance of payments adjustment mechanism – was that the money stock of the leading country was not allowed to reflect balance of payments deficits and surpluses; finally, a monetary system without a rule guaranteeing stability of the world price level or without a central reserve currency country pursuing a stable inflation target is bound to collapse sooner or later. Michael Parkin (1977) has shown that two rules would be required for the long-term sustainability of a fixed exchange-rate system: a rule determining the growth rate of the domestic component of the monetary base in each country and a rule determining the growth of the world money supply. As will be seen later, the above analysis has some important implications for the significance of the money supply in Germany as an intermediate target and as an indicator of monetary policy during the EMS period.

3   The working of the EMS, 1979–87

This section is divided into three parts. The first analyses the degree of convergence of exchange rates, inflation rates and interest rates achieved so far by EMS members participating in the exchange-rate agreement, and discusses whether the establishment of the EMS has contributed to the reduction of inflation in member countries. Existing studies on the degree of convergence will be surveyed and new updated results based on the 'principal component analysis' will be presented. In light of these considerations, we then discuss the leading role of Germany within the EMS and analyse the contribution that German monetary policy has made to the reduction of inflation in the system. Finally, the working of the balance of payments adjustment mechanism within the EMS will be described, and the problems arising from monetary targeting and from sterilisation of international reserve flows dealt with.

a.   The degree of convergence of exchange rates, inflation and interest rates and the degree of coordination of monetary policy within the EMS

Average inflation in the EMS – as measured by the private consumption deflator – has fallen steadily from a peak of 11.6 per cent in 1980 to 2.3 per cent in 1986 (Table 11.5). The dispersion of inflation both in relation to the mean and to the lowest level has also declined considerably from its peak in 1980. Measures of dispersion of real GDP growth rates show instead that a downward trend is discernible only after 1982. Measures of dispersion of monetary growth also indicate that the EMS period has to be divided into two sub-periods: one of high average monetary growth rates and insufficient convergence of monetary policy lasting until the general realignment of March 1983, and the succeeding years of falling average monetary growth rates and reduced dispersion. The key factor behind the greater convergence of real growth rates and of monetary policy in the second sub-period was the change in France's economic policy. Also the shift in economic policy in Italy since 1981 played an important role, as the authorities accepted their exchange rate appreciating in real terms to reduce inflation. In Ireland, a major shift in economic policy also occurred in 1981 resulting in a real appreciation of the Irish punt. As in Italy, progress in improving the budget deficit was slow, but the current external imbalance and inflation were reduced markedly. In Denmark the policy shift occurred in 1982–3.

	1961–70	1971–8	1979	1980	1981	1982	1983	1984	1985	1986
A. Private consumption deflator										
Average increase	3.7	8.8	8.7	11.6	11.4	9.9	8.1	6.2	5.0	2.3
Deviation from mean	0.6	3.0	4.0	5.0	4.6	4.3	4.1	3.0	2.4	2.4
Deviation from lowest	1.2	3.5	4.8	5.8	5.4	5.2	5.3	3.7	3.0	2.2
B. Real GDP										
Average increase	5.1	3.2	3.8	1.9	0.1	0.2	0.6	2.1	2.1	2.6
Deviation from mean	1.1	0.9	0.7	1.1	0.3	1.2	0.6	0.6	0.5	0.4
Deviation from highest	1.9	2.9	1.1	2.0	2.5	2.8	1.4	2.3	1.7	0.5
C. Money supply										
Average increase	11.5	14.6	12.9	9.7	8.7	9.5	10.2	8.4	7.7	6.9
Deviation from mean	2.1	3.7	4.0	3.4	2.5	2.3	3.5	3.1	3.2	1.5
Deviation from lowest	4.6	6.0	8.1	4.4	4.4	3.0	4.8	4.4	2.8	1.6

Table 11.5 Convergence in the EMS[1]

Note:

[1] The UK and Greece are excluded, because they are not part of the exchange-rate agreement.

Source: Commission of the European Communities.

The fact that inflation has been reduced and inflation, real GDP growth and the growth of money have tended to converge, at least after 1983, does not necessarily imply that they have done so because of the existence of the EMS. De Grauwe (1986) argues, for instance, that in non-EMS European countries inflation fell more sharply during the EMS period and at a lower cost in terms of foregone growth and investment than in EMS countries. An empirical study by the IMF (Ungerer *et al.*, 1986) finds instead that there is support for the hypothesis that 'the EMS has not laid the ground for a looser monetary policy but rather provided a framework in which anti-inflationary policies could be pursued more effectively'.[11] In a more recent study (Chapter 5 in this volume), S. M. Collins rejects the hypothesis that the EMS has contributed to reducing inflation in the area. Both studies regress inflation on money growth, output growth, and dummy variables for a set of EMS and non-EMS countries. However, the main effect of the EMS would be on the path of the money stock of countries which felt the constraint; hence regressions of this type cannot be conclusive. In addition, several countries outside the EMS behaved 'as if' they belonged to it throughout most of the period, while (at least in the early years of the EMS period) some members did not behave as 'full' members, as suggested by the principal component analysis presented below and in Appendix 1.

Be that as it may, the conclusion of the IMF study appears more in line with the belief on the part of European monetary officials that the EMS has indeed represented a binding constraint for high-inflation countries, which has been reinforced at times by the real appreciation of weak currencies in relation to the Deutsche mark. In this respect it can probably be said that the EMS has exerted a deflationary bias, given the objective of monetary stability pursued by Germany. This has occurred, however, with the consent of other members and is not in contradiction with the original objectives of the system. As Giavazzi and Giovannini (1987a), and Roubini (1987a) have shown, by joining a fixed exchange-rate regime under German leadership, more inflation-prone countries have gained 'credibility' in the disinflation process, provided realignments are not frequent and entail political as well as economic costs. More credibility would also imply a reduction of the output costs of a given amount of disinflation.[12]

The 1986 IMF study also compares indices of variability of exchange rates, and of their rates of change, of the rate of inflation, the rate of growth of money and domestic credit, and of interest rates in each year before and during the EMS period for the EMS countries and for a group of non-EMS countries. The study concludes that the EMS has brought

Variables[1]	Periods		
	1973:3–1979:2	1979:3–1983:2	1983:5–1986:3
Exchange rate[2]	0.56	0.70	0.83
Consumer price inflation	0.18	0.19	0.24
Nominal short-term interest rate	0.34	0.70	0.59
Nominal long-term interest rate	0.28	0.44	0.31
M1[3]	0.12	0.11	0.20

Table 11.6 Principal Component Analysis: Fraction of Cumulative Variance Explained by the First Principal Component, 17 Industrial Countries

Notes:
[1]All variables are expressed in percentage change except the interest rates.
[2]Bilateral exchange rates with the US dollars.
[3]Seasonally adjusted.

about a significant increase in convergence and greater exchange-rate stability among its members and that 'it does not seem that events exogenous to the EMS have led to the decline in exchange rate variability among participating currencies, since no such trend is evident elsewhere'. Other studies, including the most recent ones by Artis and Taylor (Chapter 7 in this volume), arrive at the same conclusion (Padoa-Schioppa, 1985, Russo, 1986). As to other variables, however, these studies do not reach similarly strong conclusions.

In order to gain more insights into the degree of convergence achieved by EMS countries a 'principal component analysis' has been carried out and the results shown in Appendix 1. The technique allows the isolation of common elements in a number of time series. It has been applied before to inflation rates in industrial countries under the Bretton Woods system to isolate a common 'world inflation' (Genberg, 1975; 1977) and to interest rates to analyse to what extent they can be explained by a world interest rate (Fase, 1976). It can be thought of as a correlation analysis generalised to a large number of time series.

Table 11.6 summarises the fractions of the cumulative variance explained by the first principal component for each of the variables considered. The fraction is standardised for the number of countries in the group for the reason explained in the footnote.[13]

	Periods		
	---	---	---
Variables[1]	1973:3– 1979:2	1979:3– 1983:2	1983:5– 1986:3
Exchange rate[2]	0.73	0.95	0.99
Consumer prices	0.34	0.26	0.48
Nominal short-term interest rate	0.40	0.76	0.79
Nominal long-term interest rate	0.49	0.49	0.36
M1[3]	0.20	0.16	0.24

Table 11.7 Principal Component Analysis: Fraction of Cumulative Variance Explained by the First Principal Component – EMS Countries Participating in Exchange-rate Mechanism

Notes:
[1]All variables are expressed in percentage change except the interest rates.
[2]Bilateral exchange rates with the US dollars.
[3]Seasonally adjusted.

Table 11.7 provides the same information, but the sample is now limited to the countries participating in the exchange-rate mechanism.

Several indications emerge from Table 11.7. First, the fraction of the variance explained by the first principal component is higher for exchange rates than for any other variable. This is in line with the requirements of the EMS which have exerted a stronger effect with time, but was also the case before the EMS was created. Second, the fraction is higher for all variables in the third period with respect to the first, except for nominal long-term interest rates.[14] Third, every number in Table 11.7 is higher than the corresponding one in Table 11.6, implying that EMS countries experienced both before and after the EMS greater convergence than the larger group of industrial countries. Furthermore, the increase in convergence of inflation rates in the third period seems to have been more pronounced for the EMS than for the larger group of countries, thus confirming the finding reported above by Ungerer *et al.*

b. The special role of Germany in the EMS, monetary targeting and the inflation objective

There is no explicit rule governing inflation in the EMS. An implicit rule has, however, been followed so far since 1982–3. Under this rule Germany's role in the EMS is similar to the role of the US under Bretton Woods: Germany decides its desired rate of inflation and other member

Exports

	United States			Germany		
	In world exports	In industrial count. exports	In EMS (incl. UK)	In EMS (excl. UK)	In world exports	In industrial count. exports
1950	17.6	28.3	12.1	19.5	3.4	5.4
1955	17.9	26.6	21.7	31.0	7.0	10.4
1960	17.4	24.6	27.0	36.0	9.6	13.6
1965	16.1	21.9	27.6	35.1	10.5	14.2
1970	15.1	19.7	30.4	36.7	11.9	15.6
1975	13.3	19.0	30.3	35.5	10.2	15.6
1980	11.7	17.8	29.2	35.0	10.2	15.6
1984	12.3	17.9	29.6	35.3	9.7	14.1
1985	11.9	16.9	29.9	35.8	10.3	14.6

Imports

	United States			Germany		
	In world imports	In industrial count. imports	In EMS (incl. UK)	In EMS (excl. UK)	In world imports	In industrial count. imports
1950	16.0	24.2	13.6	21.6	4.5	6.8
1955	13.6	20.2	18.2	27.6	6.3	9.4
1960	13.2	19.2	22.5	31.7	8.2	11.9
1965	12.9	17.7	25.4	33.1	9.8	13.4
1970	14.2	18.8	25.7	31.6	10.0	13.2
1975	12.8	18.0	24.9	30.2	9.1	12.7
1980	13.3	18.8	26.2	31.2	9.7	13.7
1984	18.4	26.1	25.9	31.5	8.3	11.7
1985	19.2	26.6	25.7	31.3	8.4	11.6

Table 11.8 Share of US and German Exports and Imports of Goods (Per cent)

Source: IMF, *International Financial Statistics*, various issues.

	United States		Germany	
	In industrial count. GDP	In EMS (incl. UK)	In EMS (excl. UK)	In industrial count. GDP
1954	45.88	10.19	15.33	6.80
1955	45.79	10.74	15.93	7.14
1960	44.74	13.28	19.11	9.05
1965	43.69	13.83	19.24	9.11
1970	42.04	15.54	20.12	9.82
1975	37.02	18.64	22.48	11.54
1980	35.41	22.74	26.71	14.11
1983	42.82	24.74	29.18	13.55
1984	45.36	25.17	29.63	13.12
1985	46.09	25.27	29.83	13.10

Table 11.9 Share of US GNP in Industrial Countries' GDP and of German GNP in EMS GDP

Source: IMF, *International Financial Statistics*, various issues.

countries converge to it. As a corollary, the asymmetry noted above in the working of the Bretton Woods system is also present in the EMS as it has operated so far – i.e., Germany is also in a position to set its monetary growth target geared to ensure its own desired inflation rate, while the other members adjust their monetary policy (i.e., their interest rates) to it. Bretton Woods survived and the EMS will survive as long as there is agreement on a low and stable inflation target and member countries are willing to subordinate their monetary policy to this objective. This crucial condition has been emphasised also by Matthes (1987) and is implicit in the stance of German economic policymakers. There are, however, several differences between the role that Germany can play in the EMS and that played by the US under Bretton Woods. The most important difference is in the economic size of the two countries in relation to the other members of the system (*'raumwirtschaftliches Potential'*, as Matthes calls it). The US was by far the largest country under Bretton Woods, whilst the economic size of France, Italy, and the United Kingdom is relatively closer to that of Germany. Table 11.8 shows the share of US exports of goods in world and industrial countries' exports and the share of German exports in EMS exports in selected years. The shares of imports are also reported. US exports were 28.3 per cent of industrial countries' exports in 1950, but by 1985 the ratio had fallen to 16.9 per cent. The share of German exports in EMS exports (excluding the UK) was 19.5 per cent in 1950 and 35.8 per cent in 1985. Looking only at the share of exports, Germany is therefore more important during the EMS period in relation to EMS members than the US was in relation to industrial countries under Bretton Woods. A similar conclusion is reached by looking at the share of imports. However, Germany is a much more open economy than the US. When GDP-weights are used, the US share in industrial countries was and still is larger than that of Germany in the EMS (Table 11.9). This makes the German economy much more vulnerable to foreign shocks than the US economy.

Another important factor is the size and sophistication of US financial markets in relation to those of Germany. The Deutsche mark will face strong competition from the French franc, if capital liberalisation in France is maintained and Paris becomes a major international financial centre – and, more importantly, if the pound sterling joins the ERM. Thus also prospectively the Deutsche mark cannot play the same role as the US dollar under Bretton Woods.

The third difference is the great importance German monetary authorities attach to price stability. Matthes argues that Germany's leading role in the EMS originates not so much from its economic size but rather from the importance it attributes to price stability, while the US and the dollar played (and still play) a leading role in the international monetary system, independently of whether the US pursues a stable inflation objective. He concludes, therefore, that Germany cannot depart from this low and stable inflation objective without endangering the EMS and her leading role in it.

The fourth difference is that while the US had no explicit money-supply target during the Bretton Woods period, Germany has one under the EMS. Tables 11.10 and 11.11 show Germany's monetary targets and their implementation, as reported by the Bundesbank, as well as EMS interventions in Deutsche mark. Except for 1978 and 1986–7 (years of rapid appreciation of the Deutsche mark *vis-à-vis* the US dollar and large interventions to stem the speed and extent of this appreciation), the Bundesbank was able to achieve the targets initially set. When compared with total interventions (within and outside the EMS), the liquidity impact of Deutsche mark interventions within the EMS was relatively small and temporary (except for 1979 and 1981), as most of the interventions were intramarginal and/or were later reversed (except for 1987, when purchases of Deutsche mark after the realignment of 12 January 1987 were considerably smaller than the large sales effected in the months leading to the realignment, see section B of Table 11.11). When read in conjunction with Table 11.12 (as well as with the findings of the principal component analysis mentioned earlier), the data show that

	Target: growth of the central bank money stock			Actual growth (rounded figures)	
	In the course of the year[1]	On an annual average	Qualification of target in the course of the year	In the course of the year[1]	On an annual average
1975	8	–	–	10	–
1976	–	8	–	–	9
1977	–	8	–	–	9
1978	–	8	–	–	11
1979	6–9	–	Lower limit	6	–
1980	5–8	–	Lower limit	5	–
1981	4–7	–	Lower half	4	–
1982	4–7	–	Upper half	6	–
1983	4–7	–	Upper half	7	–
1984	4–6	–	–	5	–
1985	3–5	–	–	5	–
1986	$3\frac{1}{2}$–$5\frac{1}{2}$	–	–	8	–
1987	3–6	–	–	–[2]	–

Table 11.10 Germany: Monetary Targets and Their Implementation (Per cent)

Notes:
[1]Fourth quarter to fourth quarter.
[2]Annualised growth rate through August *vis-à-vis* the base period for the target was 7.4 per cent.

Source: Bundesbank, *Annual Report*, 1983, and *Monthly Report*, various issues.

domestic credit expansion (defined as the growth of the domestic component of the central bank monetary liabilities) was endogenous in Germany, in the sense that it attempted to sterilise the effects of the change in net foreign assets on the growth of the money stock. This was not the case for the other EMS members, most of which did not even have money supply targets.

Throughout the period, inflation in Germany declined sharply in line with the deceleration of money supply growth. The exogeneity, or otherwise, of the national money stock in Germany under a system like the EMS has important implications for the determination of inflation in Germany and for the determination of the Deutsche mark–US dollar exchange rate. In order to make the point clearer, let us start by considering a system of perfectly floating exchange rates (no intervention of the central bank in the foreign-exchange market). Under

A. By calendar years

	Obligatory	Intramarginal	Total	Memo item affecting liquidity in Germany[2]
1979[3] Purchases	–	–2.7[4]	–2.7	–2.4
Sales	+3.6	+8.1	+11.7	+11.7
Balance	+3.6	+5.4	+9.0	+9.2
1980 Purchases	–5.9	–5.9	–11.8	–11.1
Sales	–	+1.0	+1.0	+0.6
Balance	–5.9	–4.9	–10.8	–10.5
1981 Purchases	–2.3	–8.1	–10.4	–10.3
Sales	+17.3	+12.8	+30.1	+25.3
Balance	+15.0	+4.7	+19.7	+15.0
1982 Purchases	–	–9.4	–9.4	–2.5
Sales	+3.0	+12.8	+15.8	+6.1
Balance	+3.0	+3.4	+6.4	+3.7
1983 Purchases	–16.7	–19.1	–35.8	–20.4
Sales	+8.3	+12.9	+21.2	+12.6
Balance	–8.4	–6.2	–14.5	–7.8
1984 Purchases	–	–30.2	–30.2	–0.8
Sales	+4.7	+7.6	+12.3	+4.4
Balance	+4.7	–22.7	–17.9	+3.6
1985 Purchases	–	–29.6	–29.6	–0.2
Sales	+0.4	+30.8	+31.1	–
Balance	+0.4	+1.2	+1.5	–0.2
1986 Purchases	–19.0	–33.6	–52.6	–12.1
Sales	+4.1	+76.0	+80.1	+3.8
Balance	–14.8	+42.4	+27.6	–8.4

B. By selected periods, net

21 March 1983 to 8 July 1985 From the first trading day after the realignment of 21 March 1983 to the end of major Deutsche mark purchases by partner countries	−11.8	−49.8	−61.6	−16.9
11 July 1985 to 4 April 1986 From the end of major Deutsche mark purchases by partner countries to the last trading day before the realignment of 6 April 1986	+0.7	+33.3	+34.0	+0.0
7 April 1986 to 7 July 1986 From the first trading day after the realignment of 6 April 1986 to the end of major Deutsche mark purchases by partner countries	−19.0	−10.9	−29.9	−10.3
8 July 1986 to 9 January 1987 From the end of major Deutsche mark purchases by partner countries to the last trading day before the realignment of 12 January 1987	+18.9	+44.1	+63.0	+17.4
12 January 1987 to 20 February 1987 From the first trading day after the realignment of 12 January 1987 to the last trading day before the Paris accord of 22 February 1987	–	−7.3	−7.3	−0.9
23 February 1987 to 31 March 1987 From the first trading day after the Paris accord of 22 February 1987 to the end of the quarter	–	−16.1	−16.1	−5.7

Table 11.11 Deutsche Mark Interventions in the EMS[1] (in Billions of Deutsche mark)

Table 11.11 (cont.)

Notes:
[1] Deutsche mark intervention by other central banks participating in the EMS exchange-rate mechanism and EMS interventions by the Bundesbank.
[2] Indicates the extent to which Deutsche mark interventions in the EMS and the settlement of creditor and debtor positions in the EMCF affected the net external position of the Bundesbank and thus the banks' provision with central bank money; excluding transactions connected with the winding-up of the 'snake', which was succeeded by the EMS.
[3] As from the beginning of the EMS on 13 March 1979. Discrepancies in the totals are due to rounding.
+ equals Deutsche mark sales or expansionary impact on liquidity in Germany.
− equals Deutsche mark purchases or contractionary impact on liquidity in Germany.

Source: Bundesbank Annual Report, 1986.

	Money supply[1]	Net domestic assets[2]	Prices[3]
1978	10.1	22.1	2.7
1979	8.2	23.6	4.1
1980	3.5	47.4	5.4
1981	4.7	16.2	6.3
1982	6.1	5.8	5.3
1983	6.7	13.2	3.3
1984	4.8	8.2	2.4
1985	5.6	5.7	2.2
1986	8.8	−3.6	−0.2

Table 11.12 Germany: Growth of the Money Stocks, the Bundesbank Net Domestic Assets, and Prices

Notes:
[1]Average money stock is defined as the annual averages of monthly narrow and quasi-money (*IFS*, lines 34 and 35, respectively).
[2]Domestic component of the monetary base is broadly defined as the domestic credit of the central banks, the sum of the following *IFS* lines: claims on central government, official entities and deposit money banks (*IFS*, 12a, 12b, and 12e).
[3]Inflation rates are based on the consumer price index (*IFS*, line 64).

Source: IMF, *International Financial Statistics.*

such a system the money stock is exogenous. Assuming a stable demand function for money, the rate of inflation in Germany will be determined by the following equation:

$$\dot{P}_{gt} = \sum_{i=0}^{n} w_i (\dot{M}_g - \dot{m}_g)_{t-i} \tag{11.1}$$

$$\ln m_g = a + b \ln y_g + c i_g + d \ln S'_g \tag{11.1a}$$

where a dot indicates a percentage change, ln the natural logarithm, P_g the price level, M_g the nominal money stock (= supply of money) and m_g the real demand for money.

Equation (11.1) says that inflation adjusts gradually towards its long-run equilibrium level due to the existence of transaction and information costs. Equation (11.1a) defines the real demand for money as a function of the nominal rate of interest (i_g), the uncovered interest rate differential between Germany and abroad (S'_g), reflecting the degree of currency substitution, and real output (y_g). In the long run, the price level is determined, according to equation (11.2) and (11.1a), by the quantity theory of money.

Under perfectly fixed exchange rates the Bundesbank is obliged to intervene in the foreign-exchange market and the German nominal money stock is no longer exogenous. Assuming that the whole world is on fixed exchange rates, German inflation is determined by world inflation and world inflation by world monetary growth and the world demand for real money.

$$\dot{p}_g = \dot{p}_w \tag{11.2}$$

$$\dot{p}_w = \sum_{i=0}^{n} v_i (\dot{M}_w - \dot{m}_w)_{t-i} \tag{11.3}$$

$$\ln m_w = a_w + b_w \ln y_w + c_w i_w \tag{11.3a}$$

where i_w is the world interest rate and y_w the world real output.

The EMS is a regional system, and in addition exchange rates between members have been adjusted. Therefore neither equations (11.1) and (11.1a), nor equations (11.2), (11.3) and (11.3a), correctly describe how inflation is determined in Germany. While so far inflation in Germany may have been still determined as in equations (11.1) and (11.1a), it is likely to be progressively determined according to equations (11.4) and (11.5) below, as realignments become less frequent and capital mobility increases:

$$\dot{P}_g = \dot{P}_{cms} + \dot{S}_{g/cms} \tag{11.4}$$

$$\dot{p}_{cms} = \sum_{i=0}^{n} z_i (\dot{M}_{cms} - \dot{m}_{cms})_{t-i} \tag{11.5}$$

$$\ln m_{cms} = a_{cms} + b_{cms} \ln y_{cms} + c_{cms} i_{cms} + d_{cms} \ln S'_{cms/\$} \tag{11.5a}$$

where $\dot{S}_{g/cms}$ indicates the rate of change of the effective exchange of the Deutsche mark *vis-à-vis* the other EMS members and $S'_{cms/\$}$ reflects currency substitution between the EMS block excluding sterling, and the dollar block.

Demand functions for money specified as in (11.5a) have been estimated by Bekx and Tullio (1987) for the aggregate of the countries participating in the exchange-rate mechanism and for the US from the third quarter of 1978 to the last quarter of 1986. The coefficient of the currency substitution term turns out to be significantly different from zero, indicating that in periods of dollar weakness the demand for US money tends to fall and the demand for EMS money tends to rise. Bekx and Tullio also show that the Deutsche mark–dollar exchange rate and the ECU–dollar exchange rate were explained during the EMS period reasonably well by the disequilibria in the money markets in the EMS (excluding the UK) and in the US, as suggested by the monetary approach to exchange-rate determination. The equations performed better when the currency substitution term was included in the demand functions for money in the respective currency blocks.

The disequilibrium in the German money market instead does not contribute significantly to the explanation of the Deutsche mark–dollar exchange rate, independently of whether one takes into account currency substitution or not. These results suggest that despite the exchange-rate realignments within the system, the monetary policy of France, Italy and other countries participating in the exchange-rate agreements had an impact on the Deutsche mark–dollar exchange rate. Although intuitive, the finding has strong implications for the working of the system. First, German monetary policy does not have the same effectiveness as under the flexible exchange-rate system of the pre-EMS period in influencing the exchange rate of the Deutsche mark (at least in the short run – i.e., between realignments). Second, to the extent that the monetary policy of France and Italy influences the Deutsche mark–dollar exchange rate it also influences the German inflation rate (at least between realignments). Mastropasqua, Micossi, and Rinaldi argue, in their recent study (Chapter 10 in this volume), that the German monetary base appears correlated with the lagged values of other EMS members' monetary bases. The partial compensation by Germany of contractionary or expansionary monetary impulses originating in other EMS countries seems consistent with a reduced role of German monetary variables in explaining domestic inflation and the Deutsche mark–dollar exchange rate. The finding by Giavazzi and Giovannini (Chapter 4 in this volume) that German inflation is underpredicted during the EMS period by a largely domestic model of the inflationary process may further strengthen this argument.

As controls on capital movements are reduced in Europe and currencies of member countries become better substitutes, the effectiveness of German monetary policy in influencing the German exchange rate and inflation may be reduced even more. Coordination of monetary policy between member countries around agreed inflation targets then becomes more important than at present, not only for other member countries but also for Germany.

c.   The balance of payments adjustment mechanism under the EMS

If under the EMS the 'automatic' balance of payments adjustment mechanism is to work smoothly, it should not differ much from that between non-reserve currency countries under the Bretton Woods system. If expectations of a devaluation develop, for instance, capital will tend to flow out of the member country concerned and this will put its currency under pressure. By intervening in the foreign-exchange market to prevent the exchange rate from falling outside the margin, the monetary authorities will lose international reserves; this will reduce the money supply and put upward pressures on domestic short-term interest rates. The opposite should occur in the country where capital will flow.

In comparison with the adjustment mechanism under Bretton Woods, the task of the monetary authorities is made, on the one hand, easier by the more frequent possibility of realigning and therefore by the fact of not having to defend unrealistic parities for too long. On the other hand, central banks have to deal more frequently with destabilising speculation, because markets discount the possibility and frequency of these realignments, and because capital is more mobile internationally.

Be that as it may, the smooth operation of this 'automatic' mechanism implies that, for instance, the Banque de France and the Bundesbank do not sterilise – or at least do not fully sterilise – the effects of changes in their international reserves on the money supply. Full sterilisation effectively leads to a breakdown of the automatic adjustment mechanism, if carried out by both the strong and weak currency members. Interventions performed by using reserves accumulated with the banking system of partner countries lead to changes in international reserves of the intervening country, but do not change the liquidity of the banking system of the country whose currency is used; this type of intervention is therefore asymmetric and shifts the burden of adjustment on the intervening country, as was the case under Bretton Woods.

The EMS statutes contain a clause that forbids the accumulation of reserves in members' currencies except for working balances. However, this rule is not enforced as (especially) Italy and France have accumulated large reserves in Deutsche mark, the main intervention currency. Interventions in US dollars lead to changes in international reserves in the intervening member country without influencing those of other member countries and are therefore also asymmetric in their effects. However, interventions performed by directly borrowing currencies from other member central banks increase the liquidity of the country that lends while reducing the liquidity of commercial banks of the intervening country, in the same way as interventions performed using working balances of partner currencies held at the issuing central banks and not with the banking systems. These types of intervention would automatically reduce the liquidity of the banking system of the weak currency and increase that of the strong currency, in a symmetric way.

This symmetry, however, is lost if one member country (or both) adheres to a monetary target. If only one has such a policy, the burden of adjustment is shifted on the countries which do not adhere strictly to a monetary rule. Giavazzi and Giovannini (1987a) present evidence of two types of asymmetries within the EMS. They show first that Germany and the Netherlands intervened very little at the margin in EMS currencies and that they hardly intervened within the margins, while France and Belgium did most of the intervention in EMS currencies. They also show that the EMS period is associated with a reduction in the volatility of interest rates in Germany, and an increase in France, especially of offshore rates.[15] The fundamental asymmetry lies in the practice of sterilising interventions, since this is not possible in a durable manner for countries facing downward pressure on the exchange rate, no matter how the financing of interventions is shared. Mastropasqua, Micossi, and Rinaldi, in Chapter 10 estimate that Germany sterilised foreign reserve flows to a significantly greater extent than other EMS members. The sterilisation coefficient that they obtained is not significantly different from -1.0 for Germany, while for France, Italy, and Belgium it falls between -0.30 and -0.40. Roubini (1987b) shows that symmetric intervention rules are a necessary but not sufficient condition for an exchange-rate system to be symmetric; central banks must also refrain from sterilising foreign reserve flows. Asymmetry, however, was – and is – appropriate when inflation still needs to be reduced in the countries that do not have a money supply target, but becomes less appropriate as low inflation levels are reached and commitment to anti-inflation policies is credibly undertaken. It is also appropriate if demand shocks are originating in one country only, but not if all countries are faced with the same external shock.

Why does Germany then insist on adhering to a monetary target? Her reasons are not unfounded and should be clear from the discussion in the previous sections: since the present world monetary system has no built-in mechanism to guarantee the stability of the world price level (as the gold standard did), and since the EMS also has neither an explicit low-inflation objective nor a built-in mechanism to guarantee the return to an acceptable rate of inflation, if an exogenous shock should occur, Germany has made a hybrid compromise between monetary targeting, which should guarantee a stable and low German inflation in the long run, and a fixed but adjustable exchange-rate system such as the EMS.

If more symmetry is desired, the European monetary system needs an agreement on the target inflation rate and on a rule subordinating monetary (and fiscal) policies of member countries to the agreed inflation objective.

4　The balance of payments adjustment mechanism and the inflation objective within the EMS

This section will investigate the implications for the EMS of the adoption of 'rules' for the co-ordination of monetary policies to facilitate balance of payments adjustment and to contribute to the objective of reducing inflation and/or keeping it at a low level. By drawing on the existing literature, four possible rules will be examined: an EMS-wide money supply target, a target expressed in terms of expansion of the domestic component of the monetary base in each country with the agreement not to sterilise international reserve flows among members, nominal income targets for each member country and an appropriate inflation target for the area as a whole.

Before going into the details of the analysis, it is useful to state which EMS institutional setting we have assumed for the foreseeable future. It is *not* assumed that powers are transferred to the FECOM or other central institutions as envisaged in the 'second stage' of the EMS.[16] We assume, however, an increased degree of capital mobility between the member countries, in line with the declared objective of reducing and eliminating existing capital controls. Greater capital mobility has obvious implications for the degree of monetary cooperation which is consistent with the present exchange-rate system: interest-rate policy will have to be better coordinated and more subordinated to external objectives than has been the case in the past. The analysis developed below would also not change substantially if Italy narrowed its exchange-rate band or if the UK joined the exchange-rate agreement. On the other hand, it is assumed that no individual currency is by design recognised as the reserve currency of the system because this would be politically unacceptable and is contrary to the stated objective of placing the ECU at the centre of the EMS.[17]

a.　First rule: an EMS-wide ex ante money supply target

McKinnon has drawn the economic policymakers' attention to the implications of currency substitution between the major currency blocks for domestic monetary targeting and exchange-rate developments.[18] He suggested that domestic monetary targets be abandoned in favour of a worldwide (US plus Japan plus Germany) monetary target.

His proposal is based on the assumption that each country's inflation depends on the world money supply rather than on its own money supply. By regressing US price inflation on US money growth, world money growth and the effective exchange rate of the dollar from 1973 to 1984 he purports to show that world money growth and changes in the effective exchange rate explain US inflation better than domestic money growth (McKinnon, 1984). However, Spinelli (1983) performed tests on McKinnon's hypothesis for ten industrial countries from 1973 to 1980 and concluded that (except for France) domestic money performs better than world money to explain domestic inflation. The addition of world money among the explanatory variables only improves somewhat the explanatory power of the regressions.

Despite the inconclusive outcome of empirical tests of McKinnon's hypothesis for the major countries, the discussion of the previous section and in particular the results of Bekx and Tullio on the determination of the Deutsche mark–dollar exchange rate during the EMS period, suggest that the hypothesis may become with time plausible at the EMS level, if capital controls within the area are reduced further, realignments become less frequent, and the single market for goods and factors of production is achieved. Bekx and Tullio have already shown that the Deutsche mark–dollar exchange rate – and *a fortiori* the ECU–dollar exchange rate – are better explained by the EMS aggregate; changes in the ECU–dollar exchange rate significantly influence inflation in Europe. Imports of finished goods from the dollar area are important for most EMS member countries, and (under unchanged intra-EMS parities) inflation in each member country is influenced by inflation in other members via import price effects. Finally, as the stability of intra-EMS exchange rates tends to increase and the ERM tends to become more credible, wage demands by labour unions may also tend to converge and adapt to a common inflation objective.[19]

If capital controls among member countries are further reduced, as planned, expectations of realignments will lead to shifts of funds from countries which are likely to depreciate to strong-currency countries and currency substitution both on the demand side and on the supply side (via central bank interventions) will render domestic monetary stocks more volatile and less important as determinants of domestic inflation. It may therefore be worthwhile to analyse the implications of an aggregate money supply rule for the EMS.

The first step in the process of fixing a common money supply target ($\dot{M}_{ems}$) would have to be to agree on a common inflation target in the EMS (P_{ems}).[20] The second step would be to agree on the potential output growth for the EMS area ($\dot{Y}_{ems}$). Here the average will be arrived at by aggregating individual countries' potential growth rates, not a very easy process since some countries may show the tendency to overestimate their potential output growth to achieve a more relaxed monetary policy while others may have a tendency to do the opposite.[21] If these problems can be solved (and this is a big 'if'), then the target rate of growth of EMS-wide money can be obtained as follows:

$$\dot{M}_{ems} = \dot{P}_{ems} + \dot{Y}_{ems} \tag{11.6}$$

where changes in the velocity of the EMS-wide demand for money are assumed to be zero or to be accommodated by providing a range for the money supply growth target as is done in Germany.[22]

The adoption of an aggregate money supply rule for the EMS would, however, present several problems. First, keeping in mind that the ultimate objective of fixing an aggregate monetary target for the EMS would be to stabilise the inflation rate within the EMS, it is crucial to know whether the EMS-wide demand for money would be stable enough to generate the success of this rule. The study by Bekx and Tullio mentioned in the previous section seems to suggest that the EMS-wide demand for money may be better behaved than the German demand for money.[23] Even with the inclusion of a term reflecting currency substitution, the degree of autocorrelation of the residuals is significantly lower for the EMS-wide demand function than for the German one, during the EMS period. Formal stability tests of the parameters of the equations have, however, not been performed, nor have demand functions for money for other EMS member countries been estimated. More work is clearly required in this area. In addition, the stability of the demand for EMS-wide money may be reduced by the ongoing rapid pace of financial innovation in many member countries. Financial innovation may even accelerate in the next few years owing to the increased competition injected into national financial systems by the elimination of controls on capital flows and of barriers to the provision of financial services by European firms in any member country. Finally, while the instability due to currency substitution may be smaller for the EMS-wide demand for money than for the demand for money from each member country taken individually, it can still be substantial because the EMS currencies are freely floating as a block against the dollar, the yen and the pound.

Assuming that the EMS-wide demand for money can be estimated and predicted with sufficient accuracy, would it be feasible for European central banks to set *ex ante* targets and to achieve the desired EMS-wide monetary growth in the absence of an institutional change which creates a European central bank? There do not seem to exist at present the political conditions for the creation of such a central bank. Therefore, following McKinnon, an attempt is made in the next section to suggest operating procedures and rules to share the burden of adjustment among the members, under the present institutional framework.

b.   *Second rule: an individual domestic credit target for each member country with no sterilisation of reserve flows*

It will be shown in this section that if member countries fix individually the rate of growth for the domestic component of the monetary base according to a certain formula, and refrain from sterilising international reserve flows within the system, the balance of payments adjustment mechanism could work smoothly and symmetrically and the desired inflation target be achieved. The rule prescribed in this section is optimal in the sense that it satisfies the two requirements that a system with decentralised central banks and different monies needs. Assuming, for simplicity, that the monetary base multipliers are equal to one, we start by decomposing equation (11.6) into the monetary base growth of individual member countries, in the absence of interventions *vis-à-vis* third currencies, using first differences rather than percentage changes and expressing all monetary variables in a common currency:

$$\Delta M_{ems} = \Delta \sum_{i=1}^{7} M_i,$$

$$= \Delta \sum_{i=1}^{7} (DA_i + IR_i) = \sum_{i=1}^{7} (\Delta DA_i + \Delta IR_i) \qquad (11.7)$$

where DA is the domestic component of the monetary base and IR stands for international reserves.

Because interventions in member currencies cancel out, in the absence of interventions in third currencies:

$$\sum_{i=1}^{7} \Delta IR_i = 0 \qquad (11.8)$$

equation (11.7) becomes:

$$\Delta M_{ems} = \sum_{i=1}^{7} \Delta DA_i \qquad (11.9)$$

or in percentage terms:

$$\dot{M}_{\text{ems}} = \sum_{i=1}^{7} d_i \dot{D}A_i \tag{11.9'}$$

where

$$d_i = \frac{DA_i}{M_{\text{ems}}}$$

is the share of domestic assets of the central bank of country i in the total monetary base of the EMS.

Assuming that in each member country DA_i grows at the rate given by equation (11.6') (i.e., the proposed rule):

$$\dot{D}A_i = \frac{1}{a_i} (\dot{p}_i + \dot{y}_i) \tag{11.6'}$$

where $a_i = \dfrac{DA_i}{M_i}$

Substituting (11.6') into (11.9') yields the following equation:

$$\dot{M}_{\text{ems}} = \sum_{i=1}^{7} \frac{d_i}{a_i} \dot{p}_i + \sum_{i=1}^{7} \frac{d_i}{a_i} \dot{y}_i \tag{11.10}$$

which can be rewritten as:

$$\dot{M}_{\text{ems}} = \dot{p}_{\text{ems}} + \dot{y}_{\text{ems}} \tag{11.10'}$$

which is equivalent to the EMS-wide monetary base rule. The substitution of (11.6') into (11.9') shows first that if each country follows rule (11.6'), this is equivalent to the EMS-wide monetary base rule given by equation (11.6'). However, while there is a mathematical equivalence between equations (11.10') and (11.6'), their interpretations are quite different. If member countries follow the rule of equation (11.6'), equation (11.10') would hold *ex post*. If member countries jointly decide instead to follow rule (11.6), they would do so *ex ante*. Second, it shows what weights should be used to compute the aggregate EMS-wide inflation rate and GDP growth rate from individual country targets. The weights should be the share of each country's monetary base (money supply) in the EMS-wide monetary base (money supply), since:

$$\frac{d_i}{a_i} = \frac{M_i}{M_{\text{ems}}}$$

In Appendix 2 it is shown in a simplified two-country model that, if each country follows a rule like (11.6′), the exchange-rate system is stable. Vice-versa, if each country sterilises reserve flows – i.e., it fixes the total monetary base – the exchange-rate system is unstable or indeterminate. If only one country fixes the total monetary base, the system is stable. In this case it can be shown, however, that the speed of convergence is slower than in the case in which both countries do not sterilise reserve flows.

Some important assumptions under which rule (11.6′) has been derived, do not hold strictly at present. They are the assumption that exchange rates are perfectly fixed, the assumption that the productivity growth rates in the traded and non-traded goods sectors in each member country do not differ, and the assumption that member countries do not cheat about the sum of $\dot{y}_i$ and $\dot{p}_i$ in setting their target for $\dot{D}A_i$.

The possibility of realignments raises two problems. The first is technical: if in the ratio M_i/M_{ems}, M_i is expressed in a common currency using central rates, every time a weak currency i is realigned with respect to the common currency, the weight M_i/M_{ems} is reduced discontinuously. Conversely, if exchange rates for the conversion are kept constant the weight of high-inflation countries will increase through time. This problem can be overcome, however, by using fixed exchange rates for the conversion and by changing the weights every five years or so, for instance when the weight of member currencies in the ECU is changed.

The second problem has to do with currency substitution on the demand side: expectations of realignments can influence the demand for money in each country and lead to a higher or lower growth in the nominal demand for money than predicted on the basis of y_i or p_i. This can change the degree of restrictiveness or ease of monetary policy in each country, an occurrence which may lead to unwanted output and unemployment outcomes to the extent that domestic monetary growth will still matter (in addition to the global monetary growth) in the transition toward full monetary union. Capital controls will contribute to keeping the weight of domestic monetary policy higher than it would otherwise be.

Differential productivity growth in the traded and non-traded goods sectors leads to a further technical problem in the long run. If in one member country productivity in the traded goods sector grows faster than in the non-traded goods sector and because of institutional factors and market rigidities nominal wages are equalised across sectors, prices of non-traded goods will have to increase in relation to prices of traded goods. Inflation measured by the consumer price index will thus be higher in the high-productivity countries. It will then become necessary to distinguish between the common inflation rate measured by the prices of traded goods and the different inflation rates measured by the consumer prices or the GDP/GNP deflators. If $\dot{p}_i$ indicates the inflation rate measured by the price index of traded goods, equation (11.6') will have to be amended by adding a term reflecting differential productivity growth in the two sectors. This is mathematically tractable, as shown by Michael Parkin (1977).

A final problem could arise if some countries by design or error forecast wrongly the potential growth of output or the extent of the productivity bias, and hence consumer price inflation. Let us assume that a country desires a more relaxed monetary policy and intentionally overestimates the sum of $\dot{y}_i$ or $\dot{p}_i$. It will eventually incur a balance of payments problem. Unless the country reverses its policy, it will have to realign its exchange rate. Countries that underestimate the sum of $\dot{y}_i$ and $\dot{p}_i$ will be subjected to large international reserve inflows or pressure to revalue the currency. Thus eventually the market will force countries that make errors to fall back in line.

While a common monetary policy based on equation (11.6) seems unfeasible as long as there is no common European central bank, a rule such as (11.6') has some appeal. First it allows the money stock in each country to vary in order to accommodate balance of payments fluctuations, thus helping to smooth and make more rapid the balance of payments adjustment process. Second each central bank is attributed a precise responsibility consistent with its inflation objective and its potential output growth. A co-operative approach could be adopted in fixing the inflation objective for each member country, consistently with the desired degree of convergence. The Committee of Central Bank Governors and/or the Monetary Committee could become the forum for these discussions. Once exchange rates become permanently fixed, there will be the same inflation objective for each member. If countries feel that more convergence is needed before this rule can be applied, they can in the meantime retain the principle of non-sterilisation of international reserve flows among members of the system, which is an important ingredient of the rule implicit in equation (11.6').

There is no need for a stable relationship between DA_i and output, for the proposed rule to work. All that is needed is a stable relationship between the total monetary base and output and shocks involving symmetric shifts in the demand for money deriving from autonomous portfolio adjustments. Only for this type of shock will the control of DA_i allow stabilisation of both nominal output and the balance of payments.

The essential appeal of a rule *à la* McKinnon within the context of the EMS lies in the symmetry of the balance of payments adjustment and the specificity of the required common inflation target. It is an optimal rule in response to symmetric shifts in the demand for money deriving from autonomous portfolio adjustments; it is not, however, an optimal rule in the case of asymmetric demand or supply shocks, whether originating within or outside the EMS. It is also not optimal in the case of an asymmetric monetary shock (a velocity change) deriving from an autonomous change in money demand (or money supply shock) in one member country only or in the currency area as a whole. In these cases, the appropriate response would have to be a realignment (in case of asymmetric external demand or supply shocks) and/or corrective action in the member country originating the shock, be it monetary or demand related. This in turn will require the resolution of difficult conflicts in identifying the nature of the shock and in deciding on the appropriate asymmetric response (burden sharing).

  Countries that have very large and growing public debts may show more reluctance to adopt a rule like (11.6'). The implications of the rule for real domestic interest rates and the derived constraints for fiscal policy of both the quasi-fixity of exchange rates and the resulting high real interest rates would have to be accepted by the parliament and the government. These constraints may be seen as contributing to the effort to reduce the public debts and deficits in those countries and may therefore be quite useful. The large public debts and deficits in some member countries and the danger (however remote) of monetisation of these debts suggest that a monetary policy rule like the one proposed in this section may not be enough to guarantee the long-run stability of the EMS. A rule involving fiscal policy may have to supplement the monetary policy rule.

c.   Third rule: nominal income targeting by each member country

James Meade (1984) suggested that the whole panoply of demand management policies for the control of money expenditure should be used to keep total money expenditures on the products of labour (i.e., money GDP or money national income) on a steady and moderate growth path. In an open economy, according to Meade, monetary policy has a comparative advantage on the level of the exchange rate, so that most of the burden to keep money GDP on a stable moderate growth path would have to fall on fiscal policy. The level of real wages and changes in wage differentials should instead be used to guarantee full employment. He calls this policy strategy 'New Keynesianism', as opposed to 'Orthodox Keynesianism' which is aimed at manipulating money expenditure to control the level of employment. The orthodox Keynesianism led to excessive inflation due to the lack or unfeasibility of an appropriate incomes policy and the existence of labour market rigidities.

Meade's proposal has some appeal for the EMS because it would allow the endogeneity of the money supply necessary for the smooth working of the balance of payments adjustment process within the system. It would thus be consistent with the adoption of the rule described in the previous section. Money GDP targets could be set for each country individually but in a coordinated fashion consistently with a declining inflation rate in the higher-inflation countries and a low and stable inflation rate in the low-inflation countries. Fiscal policy would be the primary instrument to stabilise nominal GDP, while monetary policy could follow the rule outlined in the previous section (or at least follow the rule of non-sterilisation of international reserve flows).

Nominal GDP targeting could also be used as a non-contingent rule: as a velocity-adjusted money growth target. This would be particularly appropriate if asymmetric velocity changes are expected (because of financial innovation, liberalisation of capital movements, etc.). Money growth could then follow the path implied by the announced target for nominal GDP without necessarily implying a feedback to fiscal policy, since this would depend on whether the authorities concerned were prepared to fine tune or not.

Williamson and Miller (1987) have recently suggested the following rules for monetary and fiscal policy to manage a system of real effective exchange rates with target zones involving the major currencies of the world. They propose nominal domestic demand and the real effective exchange rate as targets of economic policy. The three rules are:

(a) That national fiscal policies should be designed with a view to achieving national target rates of growth of domestic demand.
(b) That differences in short-term interest rates among countries should be revised to prevent the deviation of currencies from their target ranges.
(c) That the average level of world interest rates should be revised up (or down) if the growth of aggregate nominal demand for the participating countries as a group exceeds (falls short of) the target growth.

These rules could equally well be applied to the management of the ERM. Rule (b) bears close similarities with the domestic component of the monetary base rule outlined in the previous section. The two rules imply the same 'reaction' of interest rates in the case of shocks involving the balance of payments. In fact, assume for instance, an asymmetric positive productivity shock in the domestic country which leads to a strengthening of competitiveness and of the exchange rate. In the case of an interest-rate rule, the interest rate will have to fall to slow down the appreciation of the exchange rate; in the case of a rule related to the domestic component of the monetary base, the unsterilised inflow of foreign currency will also lead to a reduction in the interest rate and slow down the appreciation.

Rule (c) allows to solve the so-called '$n - 1$ problem'. Since in an n-country world there are only $n - 1$ exchange rates, $n - 1$ interest-rate differentials are enough to stabilise them. The nth interest rate (and the average interest rate) can be used to stabilise the whole system's aggregate demand. Thus Williamson and Miller's 'blueprint' is a reformulation of the rule of the previous section with an aggregate nominal demand rule added, to solve the problem of velocity shifts for the area as a whole. It is a truly symmetric rule.

One problem with nominal income targets (or nominal demand) is caused by the fact that the lags of economic policy are variable, and often long. If an unexpected fall in money expenditure occurs, it takes time before fiscal measures influence money expenditures. Furthermore there are lags between the recognition that a fiscal stimulus (or contraction) is needed and the time the policies change can be implemented, as fiscal policy cannot normally be changed during a given fiscal year. Keeping money expenditure precisely on a desired path may be easier said than done. However, the setting of annual or biannual targets rather than quarterly ones could make the task easier.

Generally, the view behind the nominal income rule is one of more 'activism' of fiscal policy. According to the 'activist' view, fiscal policy should be actively used to support weak business cycles and dampen excessive aggregate demand growth. This view contrasts with the view behind the monetary rule described by equation (11.6') in the previous section which is based on 'non-activism'. While in principle the two rules could coexist, it is important to understand this difference.

The extent to which fiscal policy can be used 'actively' to even out the business cycle depends in part on the level of the public debt and budget deficit in the country. If disequilibria accumulated from the past are large, the 'room for manoeuvre' is limited. A nominal income rule for each of the member countries would thus imply severe asymmetries between members, as countries like Italy and Belgium should not lose sight of the long-term objective of reducing public debts and budget deficits. For them, an announced rule to reduce the ratio of the government deficit to GDP by one or more percentage points per year may be more compatible with the monetary rule implicit in equation (11.6') than using fiscal policy actively to achieve a given nominal income or demand target.

d.   *Fourth rule: a common inflation target and a monetary rule for each country individually*

The above sections have tried to show: (1) that the symmetric working of any pegged exchange-rate system is incompatible with a rigid money supply rule. This is true for the gold standard, for Bretton Woods, as well as for the EMS; (2) that it is important for the system to have some anchor for inflationary expectations and a mechanism tending to stabilise inflation, such as under the gold standard; (3) that there is no precise 'rule' which could be optimal in all circumstances. McKinnon (1977) has therefore proposed that member countries should agree upon the final (rather than intermediate) target – i.e., a common inflation target, measured by the prices of traded goods, which under fixed exchange rates will be the same for all members. The rate of inflation of traded goods prices on which an agreement is easiest would probably be zero. Wholesale prices are the existing index which best approximates an ideal index of traded goods prices. Consumer price inflation will be different among members if productivity in the traded and non-traded goods sectors grows at differential rates, given existing labour market rigidities. The proposed rule is the following: if the targeted EMS inflation rate accelerates above the intended path, monetary policy should be restricted in a coordinated fashion with countries where it accelerates more, adopting a relatively more restrictive stance. The Monetary Committee may become the inflation forum where the performance of EMS inflation is evaluated and changes in monetary policy suggested to the central banks of member countries.

Fiscal policy could also be restricted in order to assist monetary policy in reducing inflation when it accelerates, and expanded when inflation falls below zero. Because the lags with which monetary and fiscal policy affect inflation may be long, targets may have to be set for periods longer than one year. It would seem preferable to set the inflation targets in terms of 'underlying' inflation rates and not actual inflation rates: i.e., exogenous price shocks should be removed from actual inflation (oil shocks, maybe also indirect taxes).

McKinnon's proposal to target a common (and low) rate of inflation based on a common index seems appealing if the difference between productivity growth in the traded and non-traded goods sectors is significant. A case could also be made to target consumer prices because the latter are more stable and less influenced by exchange-rate developments and also because they represent the politically more sensitive inflation rate. As convergence of real economic performance among member countries proceeds with the creation of the internal market and the ensuing further integration of the real economies, the economic significance of the productivity bias is likely to become smaller, thus strengthening the case for targeting consumer prices rather than wholesale prices.

This proposal presents technical problems which are not easy to solve: the adjustment of consumer prices for the effects of exogenous shocks to arrive at the 'underlying inflation rate', and above all the agreement on the relative importance of the various factors affecting inflation: money, wages, fiscal policy, import prices. There are still large theoretical differences among European central banks as to the relative importance of each factor for inflation. In addition there is the problem of the long and variable lags between policy changes and inflation. An analysis of what existing econometric models of the various countries could tell in this respect would take us beyond the scope of this study. However, if EMS member countries find this rule appealing, then a comparative study of these models should certainly be commissioned.

5 Conclusions

This study has analysed the working of the gold standard, the Bretton Woods system, and of the EMS so far. The lessons drawn from this analysis are first that in a fixed exchange-rate system the money supply cannot be exogenously determined by the monetary authorities of individual countries without interfering with the balance of payments adjustment process. This is the more true the greater the degree of capital mobility in a system. However, in each system and to different degrees, a leader has emerged providing the 'anchor' to the system and having a greater degree of monetary autonomy than the other members. The second lesson is that a properly-functioning fixed or adjustable exchange-rate system needs a rule governing inflation. The gold standard had such a rule, albeit an imperfect one, Bretton Woods did not and the EMS does not. To the extent that in the latter two systems the nth country (the 'leader') has also provided an acceptable inflation anchor, the system has operated satisfactorily but in an asymmetric manner.

Having established that a properly-functioning exchange-rate system needs rules governing inflation and rules guaranteeing smooth balance of payments adjustment, in Section 4 four rules were discussed that could lead, under a broadly unchanged institutional setting, to an improvement in the functioning of the EMS system. While these rules were proposed in the wider context of the international monetary system, they could be extended to the EMS proper. They are not intended to be proposals for reform but only working hypotheses to stimulate the discussion. The rules discussed were: a common EMS-wide money supply target *à la* McKinnon fixed *ex ante*, a rule which consists in setting the growth rate of the domestic component of the monetary base in each country on the basis of the inflation target and of potential output growth (coupled with no sterilisation of interventions), a nominal demand/income target rule *à la* Williamson–Miller and the rule to target monetary policy (and fiscal policy?) at a commonly agreed measure of inflation. It was found that no rule could provide an 'optimal' response to all shocks, particularly when based on intermediate targets. In particular, while symmetry was a desirable feature, it would not provide, *per se*, a desirable outcome in all circumstances. Therefore, the need for concentrating on a final target (i.e., inflation) and adapting the policy response to the nature and origin of the shock must prevail in the present institutional context.

The EMS has been since its inception and still is in a transition stage. Initially there was no agreement (not even implicit) on inflation and the system had to undergo several realignments. After 1983 an implicit agreement on inflation emerged, namely to converge towards the German inflation rate and to let Germany determine the 'anchor' inflation rate of the system. Discretionary coordination of monetary policy and to a lesser extent of fiscal policies emerged, but given the initial inflation differentials and the different disequilibria accumulated from the past, realignments were still necessary. At present we have substantially greater convergence of inflation, and inflation differentials are smaller than the permitted fluctuation of exchange rates within the band. Roughly since 1986 a new challenge to the system is emerging, the increased degree of capital mobility. Independence of monetary policy, fixed exchange rates and totally free capital mobility are not consistent with each other. In the future, the independence of monetary policy will have to be constrained by more rigid rules, since the major achievements of the EMS, a relative stability of real exchange rates among members, should not be abandoned, and free capital mobility, albeit with safeguard clauses, is a necessary building block of a truly common European market for goods, services and factors of production.

The rule implied by equation (11.6'), that members expand the domestic component of the monetary base according to the targeted inflation rate and the potential output growth, seems to be the most promising of all those discussed if symmetry is desired and appropriate. Its main implication is the non-sterilisation of intra-EMS international reserve flows, but this would be appropriate only in response to symmetric shifts in the demand for money in member countries. Therefore, a degree of asymmetry will remain necessary in response to other shocks, involving the use of fiscal policy in a coordinated fashion as well. The recent agreement for the financing of intramarginal interventions by the monetary authorities in an *ad hoc* manner goes in this direction. It is to be part of and supplemented by stricter surveillance with a view to identifying the appropriate response to incoming shocks. At the same time central banks could consider putting their credibility more on achieving final economic policy targets (inflation) rather than domestic monetary growth, as suggested by the fourth rule.

Coordination of monetary policies will remain difficult if realignments are large and provide incentives for one-way bets, and therefore destabilising speculative capital movements. Given the achieved convergence of inflation rates, this problem would be lessened if realignments were infrequent, but nevertheless remained small so that any new agreed band would overlap with the previous one. To maintain the 'disciplinary' character of the system, they should also not completely offset inflation differentials, however measured, unless flanked by credible stabilisation policies. While such a realignment rule – cum monetary policy coordination – would be sufficient in the face of disturbances generated within the system, it may prove too rigid in cases of external shocks, such as the recent sharp depreciation of the US dollar. In this case, a temporary widening of the margins of the currency which has so far played the central role may prove the less costly option, waiting for the time when all currencies of the system become better substitutes for each other.

APPENDIX 1: PRINCIPAL COMPONENT ANALYSIS OF SELECTED VARIABLES, 17 INDUSTRIAL COUNTRIES

Consider first the monthly rate of change of the bilateral exchange rate with the US dollar. The principal component analysis has been made for the bilateral exchange rates of 16 industrial countries: the seven countries participating in the EMS Exchange Rate Mechanism (Germany, France, Italy, the Netherlands, Belgium, Denmark, Ireland) plus the United Kingdom, Spain, Norway, Sweden, Austria, Switzerland, Canada, Australia and Japan. The analysis has been carried out separately for three time periods: March 1973 to February 1979, March 1979 to February 1983, May 1983 to March 1986.

The first period goes from the beginning of floating to the starting of the EMS. The second period goes from the beginning of the EMS up to the general realignment of March 1983. The third period starts in May 1983 (after the disturbances caused by the March realignment had settled down) and ends with the month preceding the general realignment of April 1986. Thereafter there have been two more realignments in August 1986 and January 1987. It was not possible to update the analysis for lack of data.

The principal component analysis gives some insights into how closely the various currencies in the group fluctuated *vis-à-vis* the US dollar in the three

A. Cumulative variance and Eigenvalues

	Variance	Eigenvalues
Princ 1	0.585	9.360
Princ 2	0.685	1.600
Princ 3	0.757	1.159
Princ 4	0.821	1.018
Princ 5	0.872	0.809
Princ 6	0.906	0.549
Princ 7	0.933	0.438
Princ 8	0.954	0.337

B. Coefficients of correlation with principal components

	Princ 1	Princ 2	Princ 3
Ireland	0.687	−0.491	0.118
United Kingdom	0.687	−0.491	0.119
France	0.853	−0.006	0.015
Italy	0.606	−0.437	0.059
Belgium	0.962	0.156	−0.079
Germany	0.941	0.235	−0.056
Denmark	0.952	0.192	−0.104
Netherlands	0.938	0.164	−0.053
Austria	0.942	0.223	−0.074
Norway	0.908	0.227	−0.041
Sweden	0.864	0.218	−0.162
Switzerland	0.843	0.039	0.052
Australia	0.177	0.074	0.885
Canada	−0.165	0.637	0.447
Spain	0.377	−0.381	0.038
Japan	0.597	−0.276	0.289
Variance	0.585	0.685	0.757
Eigenvalues	9.360	1.600	1.159

Table A11.1 Rate of Change of Bilateral Exchange Rates with US Dollar, 16 Currencies, Period 1973: 3 to 1979: 2

A. Cumulative variance and Eigenvalues

	Variance	Eigenvalues
Princ 1	0.722	11.554
Princ 2	0.803	1.297
Princ 3	0.860	0.909
Princ 4	0.905	0.725
Princ 5	0.931	0.405
Princ 6	0.952	0.341

B. Coefficients of correlation with principal components

	Princ 1	Princ 2	Princ 3
Ireland	0.977	−0.127	0.067
United Kingdom	0.682	−0.057	−0.533
France	0.962	−0.034	0.109
Italy	0.965	−0.025	0.032
Belgium	0.953	−0.024	0.094
Germany	0.965	−0.070	0.021
Denmark	0.956	−0.014	0.175
Netherlands	0.964	−0.103	0.174
Austria	0.960	−0.074	0.220
Norway	0.884	0.162	−0.080
Sweden	0.649	0.231	−0.468
Switzerland	0.900	0.022	0.211
Australia	0.706	0.568	−0.115
Canada	0.518	−0.495	−0.292
Spain	0.692	−0.503	−0.266
Japan	0.646	0.595	−0.103
Variance	0.722	0.803	0.860
Eigenvalues	11.554	1.297	0.909

Table A11.2 Rate of Change of Bilateral Exchange Rates with US Dollar, 16 Currencies, Period 1979: 3 to 1983: 2

A. Cumulative variance and Eigenvalues

	Variance	Eigenvalues
Princ 1	0.839	13.424
Princ 2	0.910	1.129
Princ 3	0.951	0.660

B. Coefficients of correlation with principal components

	Princ 1	Princ 2	Princ 3
Ireland	0.992	−0.061	0.021
United Kingdom	0.838	0.020	0.413
France	0.992	−0.091	−0.022
Italy	0.970	−0.077	−0.093
Belgium	0.991	−0.079	−0.030
Germany	0.992	−0.074	−0.050
Denmark	0.990	−0.075	−0.021
Netherlands	0.994	−0.066	−0.036
Austria	0.992	−0.073	−0.057
Norway	0.981	−0.017	0.076
Sweden	0.984	−0.032	−0.006
Switzerland	0.975	0.054	0.063
Australia	0.437	0.723	−0.493
Canada	0.462	0.742	0.426
Spain	0.962	−0.072	−0.017
Japan	0.826	−0.029	−0.192
Variance	0.839	0.910	0.951
Eigenvalues	13.424	1.129	0.660

Table A11.3 Rate of Change of Bilateral Exchange Rates with US Dollar, 16 Currencies, Period 1983 to 1986: 3

A. Cumulative variance and Eigenvalues

	Variance	Eigenvalues
Princ 1	0.227	3.852
Princ 2	0.370	2.433
Princ 3	0.484	1.947
Princ 4	0.571	1.474
Princ 5	0.644	1.239
Princ 6	0.702	0.997
Princ 7	0.757	0.933

B. Coefficients of correlation with principal components

	Princ 1	Princ 2	Princ 3
Ireland	0.452	−0.514	0.299
United Kingdom	0.577	−0.338	−0.106
France	0.719	0.008	−0.069
Italy	0.084	−0.033	−0.745
Belgium	0.385	0.362	−0.193
Germany	0.581	0.114	0.222
Denmark	0.314	−0.458	−0.091
Netherlands	0.541	−0.324	−0.347
Austria	0.673	0.416	0.333
Norway	0.610	0.354	0.122
Sweden	0.505	0.409	−0.419
Switzerland	0.144	−0.242	0.567
Australia	−0.237	−0.458	−0.336
Canada	0.288	−0.511	0.374
Spain	0.503	0.531	−0.028
Japan	0.342	−0.386	−0.440
United States	0.551	−0.410	0.015
Variance	0.227	0.370	0.484
Eigenvalues	3.852	2.433	1.947

Table A11.4 Consumer Prices, Rates of Change, 17 Countries, Period 1979: 3 to 1983: 2

A. Cumulative variance and Eigenvalues

	Variance	Eigenvalues
Princ 1	0.236	4.005
Princ 2	0.346	1.883
Princ 3	0.450	1.769
Princ 4	0.529	1.330
Princ 5	0.594	1.119
Princ 6	0.656	1.053
Princ 7	0.714	0.978
Princ 8	0.764	0.858

B. Coefficients of correlation with principal components

	Princ 1	Princ 2	Princ 3
Ireland	0.643	−0.161	0.339
United Kingdom	0.588	0.123	0.434
France	0.643	−0.213	−0.298
Italy	0.579	−0.242	−0.196
Belgium	0.699	−0.083	−0.193
Germany	0.602	0.508	0.266
Denmark	0.240	−0.271	−0.186
Netherlands	0.595	−0.278	0.024
Austria	0.452	0.667	0.121
Norway	0.292	0.352	0.235
Sweden	0.227	0.492	−0.060
Switzerland	0.348	0.271	−0.249
Australia	0.535	−0.480	−0.060
Canada	0.049	0.269	−0.703
Spain	−0.010	−0.191	0.081
Japan	0.669	−0.189	0.039
United States	0.194	0.252	−0.744
Variance	0.236	0.346	0.450
Eigenvalues	4.005	1.883	1.769

Table A11.5 Consumer Prices, Rates of Change, 17 Countries, Period 1973: 3 to 1979: 2

A. Cumulative variance and Eigenvalues

	Variance	Eigenvalues
Princ 1	0.282	4.800
Princ 2	0.424	2.410
Princ 3	0.523	1.687
Princ 4	0.612	1.505
Princ 5	0.677	1.109
Princ 6	0.739	1.048
Princ 7	0.787	0.823

B. Coefficients of correlation with principal components

	Princ 1	Princ 2	Princ 3
Ireland	0.454	−0.346	0.435
United Kingdom	0.361	0.294	0.441
France	0.782	0.145	0.233
Italy	0.725	0.198	−0.211
Belgium	0.765	−0.205	0.332
Germany	0.783	−0.179	−0.097
Denmark	0.572	0.542	0.014
Netherlands	0.666	0.458	0.005
Austria	0.461	−0.665	−0.088
Norway	0.332	−0.159	−0.638
Sweden	0.389	−0.197	−0.368
Switzerland	0.495	−0.161	0.088
Australia	−0.224	0.221	−0.020
Canada	0.100	−0.599	0.236
Spain	0.194	−0.594	−0.402
Japan	0.301	0.515	−0.544
United States	0.672	0.092	0.116
Variance	0.282	0.424	0.523
Eigenvalues	4.800	2.410	1.687

Table A11.6 Consumer Prices, Rates of Change, 17 Countries, Period 1983: 5 to 1986: 3

A. Cumulative variance and Eigenvalues

	Variance	Eigenvalues
Princ 1	0.378	6.046
Princ 2	0.730	5.627
Princ 3	0.856	2.021
Princ 4	0.904	0.769
Princ 5	0.931	0.427
Princ 6	0.954	0.367

B. Coefficients of correlation with principal components

	Princ 1	Princ 2	Princ 3
Ireland	0.752	−0.472	0.241
United Kingdom	0.734	−0.538	0.049
France	0.712	−0.354	0.001
Italy	−0.262	−0.858	0.337
Belgium	0.368	−0.833	0.224
Germany	0.767	0.562	−0.219
Denmark	0.046	−0.592	−0.597
Netherlands	0.866	−0.112	−0.221
Austria	0.839	−0.101	−0.112
Norway	−0.363	−0.798	−0.339
Sweden	−0.529	−0.821	0.114
Switzerland	0.877	0.405	−0.152
Australia	0.281	−0.808	0.379
Canada	0.085	−0.832	−0.400
Japan	0.949	0.054	0.149
United States	−0.134	−0.217	−0.924
Variance	0.378	0.730	0.856
Eigenvalues	6.046	5.627	2.021

Table A11.7 Nominal Long-term Interest Rates, 16 Countries, Period 1973: 3 to 1979: 2

A. Cumulative variance and Eigenvalues

	Variance	Eigenvalues
Princ 1	0.718	11.481
Princ 2	0.859	2.266
Princ 3	0.918	0.945
Princ 4	0.944	0.416
Princ 5	0.960	0.258

B. Coefficients of correlation with principal components

	Princ 1	Princ 2	Princ 3
Ireland	0.750	−0.197	0.554
United Kingdom	0.576	−0.690	0.312
France	0.951	0.214	−0.128
Italy	0.889	0.426	0.049
Belgium	0.952	0.177	−0.159
Germany	0.890	−0.323	0.007
Denmark	0.796	0.341	0.022
Netherlands	0.847	−0.463	−0.042
Austria	0.960	−0.103	−0.009
Norway	0.856	0.437	−0.102
Sweden	0.878	0.282	−0.265
Switzerland	0.937	−0.243	−0.102
Australia	0.865	0.434	0.097
Canada	0.965	−0.060	0.056
Japan	0.245	−0.672	−0.617
United States	0.895	−0.273	0.093
Variance	0.718	0.859	0.918
Eigenvalues	11.481	2.266	0.945

Table A11.8 Nominal Long-term Interest Rates, 16 Countries, Period 1979: 3 to 1983: 2

A. Cumulative variance and Eigenvalues

	Variance	Eigenvalues
Princ 1	0.606	9.696
Princ 2	0.762	2.500
Princ 3	0.850	1.398
Princ 4	0.896	0.747
Princ 5	0.935	0.620
Princ 6	0.955	0.325

B. Coefficients of correlation with principal components

	Princ 1	Princ 2	Princ 3
Ireland	0.898	−0.238	0.104
United Kingdom	0.580	−0.355	−0.291
France	0.895	0.362	−0.077
Italy	0.669	0.641	−0.016
Belgium	0.941	−0.115	0.083
Germany	0.934	0.258	0.021
Denmark	0.860	−0.164	0.008
Netherlands	0.924	0.346	−0.036
Austria	0.834	0.057	0.105
Norway	−0.768	0.348	−0.398
Sweden	0.085	−0.735	−0.509
Switzerland	0.525	−0.727	−0.342
Australia	0.121	0.507	−0.748
Canada	0.875	−0.103	0.173
Japan	0.876	0.239	−0.352
United States	0.916	−0.176	0.174
Variance	0.606	0.762	0.850
Eigenvalues	9.696	2.500	1.398

Table A11.9 Nominal Long-term Interest Rates, 16 Countries, Period 1983: 5 to 1986: 3

sub-periods. It is also interesting to see whether the data are able to isolate an EMS block of currencies within the larger group and whether some countries which are not formally part of the exchange-rate agreements *de facto* behaved as if they were. Such candidates could be Switzerland, Austria, Norway and (at times) Sweden, as their currencies followed the Deutsche mark quite closely. On the other hand, the analysis could indicate that countries which are formally members of the EMS have *de facto* not behaved as good members due to the use of larger margins of fluctuations, frequent realignments or divergent economic policies. (Italy and France could have been two countries belonging to this sub-group.)

Table A11.1 summarises the results of the principal component analysis of bilateral exchange-rate changes with the US dollar for the first period (1973: 3–1979: 2). Tables A11.2 and A11.3 contain the results for the two EMS sub-periods. Section A of each table shows the cumulative variance explained by the first principal components and Section B contains the correlation coefficients of each country's variable with the first three principal components. In Table A11.1 the first principal component is highly correlated with the currencies of the DM area. The bilateral US dollar exchange rates of the following countries have a correlation coefficient higher than 0.90: Belgium, Germany, the Netherlands, Austria and Norway. France, Sweden and Switzerland have a correlation coefficient between 0.80 and 0.90. Ireland, the United Kingdom and Italy between 0.60 and 0.70. The exchange rates of the non-European countries have a much lower correlation coefficient. Thus the first principal component can be identified with the Deutsche mark area.

As to the second sub-period, Section B of Table A11.2 indicates that the first principal component still represents the Deutsche mark area with France, Italy, Ireland and also Switzerland now moving closer to it (correlation coefficient greater than or equal to 0.90 for all these countries). Spain also moves closer, while during this period Norway and Sweden had a more independent exchange-rate policy than before. During the second EMS sub-period Section B of Table A11.3 indicates that the EMS group showed an even greater cohesion, with Austria, Norway, Sweden, Switzerland and Spain now *de facto* behaving as if they belonged to the group.

What emerges from the analysis of Section B of Tables A11.1–A11.3 is that the original Deutsche mark area of the period of free floating developed into a more cohesive exchange-rate system comprising not only the countries which formally joined the exchange-rate agreement, but also Austria, Switzerland, Spain, Norway and Sweden. The fraction of the cumulative variance of bilateral exchange-rate changes explained by the first principal component increases from 59 per cent during the floating rate period to 72 per cent in the first EMS sub-period and 84 per cent in the second.

The same statistical analysis is presented in Tables A11.4–A11.6 for consumer prices, the US having been added to the group of countries. Even though the fraction of the variance explained by the first principal component is much smaller than for bilateral exchange rates, a European block of countries can be identified in each sub-period. This block widens in time to comprise additional countries and becomes more cohesive in the second EMS sub-period. During this period France, Italy, Germany, Belgium and (to a lesser extent) Denmark and the Netherlands seem to form a block with high (and growing) cohesion. US inflation also has in this period a much higher correlation with the first principal component than in the previous ones, reflecting the common external shock of the increase in oil prices and the priority given in all industrial countries to the fight against inflation. These findings do not say anything about whether the EMS has led to a faster reduction of inflation in the member countries.

The results of the principal component analysis for the 17 nominal long-term interest rates are presented in Tables A11.7–A11.9. During the first EMS sub-period (i.e., 1979–83), a remarkable degree of convergence of nominal long-term rates seems to emerge between Europe and the North American continent with only British and Japanese interest rates showing greater independent behaviour (Table A11.7). The very high interest-rate policy in the US probably helped to bring about this increased convergence, as European countries tried to contain the depreciation of their currencies with respect to the US dollar. This occurred at times of growing financial integration. As to the second EMS sub-period there is also no evidence of an independent EMS block, with Germany and the US being among the countries possessing the highest correlation with the first principal component. Tables A11.7–A11.9 seem to suggest that no common independent European capital market has emerged yet, not even in the second EMS sub-period. They suggest instead a strong domination of the US capital market on the other countries in the 1980s and a remarkably high and increasing worldwide integration of capital markets. This confirms Micossi and Padoa-Schioppa's findings (1984).

As to the principal component analysis of nominal short-term interest rates (not shown here), there is also no evidence of a greater convergence in the EMS group of countries. This is not surprising, however, as a smoothly working balance of payments adjustment mechanism within a fixed exchange-rate system requires that movements in the short-term interest rate be subordinated to the achievement of exchange-rate stability.

The principal component analysis of the rates of change of the money stocks (also not presented here) shows that the first three principal components explain a very low fraction of the variance of the money stocks. In addition, there is no evidence of a cohesive EMS block. Again this is hardly surprising: the data used are monthly; under a system of pegged exchange rates the money stock has to be subordinated to the achievement of exchange-rate stability and to balance of payments adjustment. This implies short-run changes of the money stocks of member countries which at times go in opposite directions. Thus, as with short-term interest rates, the inability to find evidence within the EMS of a common growth rate of the money stock on a monthly basis may indicate more rather than less monetary policy coordination. Furthermore a greater monthly variability of the money stocks and less monthly convergence is perfectly compatible with greater convergence of annual monetary growth, as shown in Table 11.5.

APPENDIX 2: STABILITY ANALYSIS OF A TWO-COUNTRY MODEL UNDER ALTERNATIVE MONETARY RULES AND EXCHANGE-RATE REGIMES

1   Introduction

This Appendix is intended to study the stability of an EMS-like agreement under alternative monetary rules. In particular the rule developed in Section 4b of the study will be investigated. The contribution of non-sterilisation of international reserve flows to the stability of the EMS will be demonstrated.

Any movement toward less frequent changes of parities and the removal of barriers to capital mobility will fundamentally change the operating conditions of the EMS and require new rules for coordinating monetary policy. Fixed exchange rates and unrestricted capital flows will necessarily be accompanied by a very high degree of currency substitution among the currencies of countries participating in the exchange-rate mechanism (ERM), a situation which is already observable to some extent in the present less than perfect state of monetary integration.

The monetary rules considered are two: (1) a rule consisting of controlling the total monetary base, with its implied sterilisation of foreign-exchange reserve variations; and (2) a rule consisting of controlling the domestic component of the monetary base.

The implications for stability of the adoption of these two rules will be evaluated both under the assumption of partially variable managed exchange rates and under the assumption of perfectly fixed exchange rates.

2   Stability analysis of a managed exchange-rate regime

For analytical purposes, the actual exchange-rate agreement of the EMS will be modelled as a managed exchange-rate regime. The regime is potentially a floating one, but exchange-rate movements are damped down through foreign-exchange market intervention. We shall examine which monetary rules return the exchange rate to its equilibrium level and the relative speed of convergence.

We shall consider two countries that are sufficiently large relative to each other so as to exert significant reciprocal influences and shall refer to them as Germany and Italy. The analysis will rely on the monetary mechanism of the balance of payments adjustment and exchange-rate determination.

In each economy, wealth is held in the form of money and goods, so that any excess demand for money must spill over into an excess supply of goods, just as an excess supply of money means that there is an excess demand for goods. The demand for money is characterised by a stable relationship which depends on real income. It also depends on the interest rate, but we shall ignore this complication as we shall not consider interest-rate adjustments. We shall also neglect the role of currency substitution.

In a closed economy, when there is an excess supply of money, the accompanying excess demand for goods will lead to a rise in prices unless increased supplies are forthcoming. In this way real cash balances adapt and equilibrium is reestablished in the goods and money markets. This mechanism is not immediately operative in an open economy. An excess supply of money will lead to an excess demand for goods in general, and in so far as this can be expended on imports, there will be no tendency for prices to rise. Instead a trade deficit will be incurred. If the exchange rate is free to vary, this will result in a depreciation of the domestic currency. In a similar manner, an excess supply of the foreign currency will lead to a trade surplus at home and a consequent appreciation of the exchange rate. The above reasoning is incorporated in the following equation:

$$\dot{S} = \alpha(M - PY) - \beta(M^* - P^*Y^*) \quad \alpha, \beta > 0 \tag{A11.1}$$

where S is the exchange rate (the price in Italian lire of a Deutsche mark), M is the Italian monetary base, P the price level in Italy and Y the level of output. Asterisks indicate the corresponding variables for Germany.

Under freely-floating exchange rates and instantaneous adjustment of portfolios, equation (A11.1) would determine the level of the exchange rate, and not its evolution. However, in our context changes in the exchange rate are tempered (or exacerbated) by intervention of the central banks of the two countries in the foreign-exchange market. This formulation ignores the existence of a band around the central parities. For the analysis of the stability of the system which concerns us here this neglect is not of very great importance, especially if the banks are sufficiently large (as in the case of Italy). Intervention can either lean against the wind, or with it. In the simplest case, Italian intervention in the foreign exchanges can be modelled as:

$$\dot{R} = -\gamma(S - S_0) \tag{A11.2'}$$

where $\dot{R}$ is the change in the level of international reserves held by the central bank, and S_0 is the central parity of the Italian lira with the Deutsche mark, the target exchange rate. γ is a policy parameter: it expresses the attitude of the Italian bank. When γ is positive, the bank is considered as leaning against the wind; when negative, it reinforces the pressures of the foreign-exchange market on the rate of exchange. The larger γ is in absolute value, the stronger the reaction of the central bank.

In equation (A11.2') above, changes in reserves are rigidly guided by the foreign-exchange market intervention rule. Remaining balance of payments disequilibria were absorbed by changes in the exchange rate. Consistently with the narrow bands of variation in exchange rates around the central parities in the exchange-rate mechanism, we allow, however, disequilibria resulting from excess or deficient private holdings of real cash balances to influence both exchange rates and reserves. Consider Italy once again. Suppose for a moment that the central bank intervenes to keep exchange rates firmly pegged. Then the entire disequilibrium in private holdings of cash balances will spill over into changes of international reserve holdings of the central bank:

$$B = -\delta_1(M - PY) + \delta_2(M^* - P^*Y^*) \quad \delta_1, \delta_2 > 0 \tag{A11.2}$$

where B is the change in reserves held by the Italian central bank as a consequence of private transactions.

Now let the central bank relax its rigid stance. If B is negative, the Italian monetary authorities will partially let the lira depreciate, partially absorb the excess supply of Italian lire by selling Deutsche mark. Therefore:

$$\dot{R} = B + \gamma(S - S_0)$$

where $\dot{R}$ represents actual changes in international reserves held by the Italian central bank.

In the above illustration, $\gamma < 0$ with the bank reinforcing private market pressures by accepting a larger fall in international reserves. When γ is positive, the Italian central bank buys marks when the Italian lira tends to depreciate. The latter is clearly not the behaviour that central banks normally adopt. The two basic equations now are:

$$\dot{S} = \alpha(M - PY) - \beta(M^* - P^*Y^*) \tag{A11.1}$$

$$\dot{R} = \gamma(S - S_0) - \delta_1(M - PY) + \delta_2(M^* - P^*Y^*) \tag{A11.2}$$

The above model is closed by introducing the following identities:

$$M = D + R \tag{A11.3}$$

$$M^* = D^* + R^* \tag{A11.4}$$

where D refers to the domestic credit component of the monetary base.

The two equations define the monetary base for Italy and Germany as the sum of domestic credit available from the central bank and its holdings of international reserves.

The final identity links the holdings of international reserves by the two countries with each other. Let R be the total availability of (outside) international reserves measured in marks. Then:

$$SR + R^* = \bar{R} \tag{A11.5}$$

We shall evaluate reserves at the central parity exchange-rate level. Moreover, without loss of generality, we shall normalise this level to unity. We thus obtain:

$$S_0 R + R^* = R + R^* = \bar{R}$$

Given equation (A11.2), equation (A11.5) determines the change in German holdings of international reserves.

(i) We shall first suppose that neither Italy nor Germany sterilises the effects of international reserve flows on their monetary bases. The domestic credit component is held constant since output is held fixed as well as prices. The resulting differential system is the following:

$$\begin{pmatrix} \dot{S} \\ \dot{R} \end{pmatrix} = \begin{bmatrix} 0 & \alpha + \beta \\ \gamma - (\delta_1 + \delta_2) \end{bmatrix} \begin{pmatrix} S \\ R \end{pmatrix}$$
$$+ \begin{pmatrix} \alpha(D - PY) - \beta(D^* + \bar{R} - P^* Y^*) \\ -\gamma - \delta_1(D - PY) + \delta_2(D^* + \bar{R} - P^* Y^*) \end{pmatrix}$$

where S_0 has been normalised to unity.

The characteristic equation of the above system is:

$$\lambda^2 + (\delta_1 + \delta_2)\lambda - (\alpha + \beta)\gamma$$

the roots of the equation are:

$$-\frac{(\delta_1 + \delta_2)}{2} \pm \frac{((\delta_1 + \delta_2)^2 + 4(\alpha + \beta)\gamma)^{1/2}}{2}$$

Intervention rule (i): $\gamma > 0$
With γ positive, the system has a saddlepoint behaviour. This requires an initial discretionary intervention in order to attain the unique convergent path.
Intervention rule (ii): $\gamma < 0$
With γ negative, the Italian central bank reinforces the movement of reserves initiated by adjustment of private cash balances to desired levels. In this case, the system is asymptotically stable. Any initial point leads to equilibrium either monotonically or with fluctuations depending on the sign of

$$[(\delta_1 + \delta_2)^2 + 4(\alpha + \beta)\gamma]$$

Central bank behaviour in relation to interventions in the foreign-exchange market is generally characterised by a negative γ. Actual behaviour leads therefore to a stable system.

(ii) Now suppose that Italy intervenes on the foreign exchanges and does not sterilise the effects of reserve flows; whereas Germany does sterilise the effects of reserve changes on its money stock. This form of asymmetric non-sterilised intervention has characterised the EMS so far.

In this case, the following equation must be added to the five listed above:

$$\dot{D}^* = -\dot{R}^*, \quad \text{or equivalently,} \quad M^* = \bar{M}^* \tag{A11.6}$$

The differential system now becomes:

$$\begin{pmatrix} \dot{S} \\ \dot{R} \end{pmatrix} = \begin{bmatrix} 0 & \alpha \\ \gamma - \delta_1 \end{bmatrix} \begin{pmatrix} S \\ R \end{pmatrix} + \begin{pmatrix} \alpha(D - PY) - \beta(\bar{M}^* - P^*Y^*) \\ -\gamma - \delta_1(D - PY) + \delta_2(\bar{M}^* - P^*Y^*) \end{pmatrix}$$

The characteristic equation now is:

$$\lambda^2 + \delta_1\lambda - \alpha\gamma$$

with roots:

$$\lambda = -\frac{\delta_1}{2} \pm \frac{(\delta^{1/2} + 4\alpha\gamma)^{1/2}}{2}$$

Once again, if $\gamma > 0$, the system is characterised by saddlepoint behaviour, whereas if $\gamma < 0$, the system is asymptotically stable.

The sterilisation of international reserve flows by Germany affects the relative speed of convergence to equilibrium of the exchange rate and of reserves. When Italy intervenes as it normally does ($\gamma < 0$), then sterilisation by Germany slows down the convergence of the system as can be seen by comparing the larger of the two roots in the two cases described above (case (i) – symmetric non-sterilisation by both countries, and case (ii) – non-sterilisation by Italy and sterilisation by Germany).

If, moreover, Italy behaves such that $\gamma > 0$ and is on the convergent path, then the speed of convergence is further hampered.

(iii) If now Italy intervenes on the foreign exchanges and sterilises the effects of reserve changes, whereas Germany allows reserve changes to affect its monetary base, conclusions about the stability of the system are like those in case (ii).

(iv) The system breaks down if both countries refuse to allow their monetary base to be influenced by the international reserve flows. It provokes the continuous accumulation of reserves by one country and a continuous loss by the other.

3   Stability analysis of a fixed exchange-rate regime

With the transition to credibly-fixed exchange rates between the member countries of the EMS and the removal of barriers to capital mobility, the degree of currency substitution between the member states will become very high indeed.

Under a regime of fixed exchange rates, the entire brunt of disequilibria in private money holdings, that is, the adjustment of actual money holdings to the desired level, is borne by changes in international reserves at the central bank:

$$\dot{R} = -\delta_1(M - PY) + \delta_2(M^* - P^*Y^*) \tag{A11.7}$$

Moreover, in the absence of restrictions to capital flows, national currencies become perfect substitutes and only the total aggregates money stock will reveal stable behaviour. Furthermore, prices in the different countries will have to align themselves to each other:

$$P = P^* \tag{A11.8}$$

In such a world, excess supplies of money will be absorbed not only by an international transfer of reserves but also by an adjustment of prices in both countries. Consider a rise of output levels in Italy and the consequent shortage of real cash balances. The resulting movement of reserves toward Italy will provoke a shortage in Germany. Hence, the output shock will ultimately be absorbed by price changes:

$$\dot{P} = \dot{P}^* = (M + M^* - P(Y + Y^*)) \tag{A11.9}$$

International reserve changes in both countries are directed toward the maintenance of fixed exchange rates. It remains to determine the behaviour of domestic credit. Assume the domestic component of the monetary base is targeted to a permanent zero rate of inflation. Two other alternatives will be considered, namely, the targeting of domestic credit to temporary changes in prices; and the targeting of the total monetary base to the same end.

(a) Consider first the case in which the domestic component of the monetary base is kept constant. In Section 4b of this study the rule proposed was that the domestic component of the monetary base should grow at the same rate as the sum of desired inflation and potential output (equation (A11.6′)). Since here derived inflation is assumed to be zero and potential output is assumed to be constant, the case considered here is the dynamic version of rule 4b. The system reduces to two equations:

$$\begin{pmatrix} \dot{R} \\ \dot{P} \end{pmatrix} = \begin{bmatrix} -(\delta_1 + \delta_2) & \delta_1 Y - \delta_2 Y^* \\ 0 & -\eta(Y + Y^*) \end{bmatrix} \begin{pmatrix} R \\ P \end{pmatrix}$$

$$+ \begin{pmatrix} -\delta_1 D + \delta_2 D^* + \delta_2 \tilde{R} \\ \eta D + \eta D^* + \eta \tilde{R} \end{pmatrix}$$

with characteristic equation:

$$[(\delta_1 + \delta_2) + \lambda][(Y + Y^*)\eta + \lambda]$$

and roots:

$$\lambda = -(\delta_1 + \delta_2) \quad \text{and} \quad -\eta(Y + Y^*)$$

Since both roots are negative, the system is asymptotically stable.

(b) Now suppose that both countries adapt the domestic component of the monetary base to counteract temporary price movements:

$$\dot{D} = -\alpha \dot{P}; \quad \dot{D}^* = -\beta \dot{P}^*$$

An unexpected rise in output in Italy will lead to an increase in Italian reserves and a fall in prices. If α and β are positive, the necessary adaptation of the Italian monetary base will be hastened, whereas the undesired reduction of the German monetary base will be neutralised. The complete system of differential equations is:

$$
\begin{bmatrix}
1 & 0 & 0 & 0 \\
0 & 1 & 0 & 0 \\
0 & \alpha & 1 & 0 \\
0 & \beta & 0 & 1
\end{bmatrix}
\begin{pmatrix}
\dot{R} \\
\dot{P} \\
\dot{D} \\
\dot{D}^*
\end{pmatrix}
$$

$$
=
\begin{bmatrix}
-(\delta_1 + \delta_2) & \delta_1 Y - \delta_2 Y^* & -\delta_1 & \delta_2 \\
0 & -\eta(Y + Y^*) & \eta & \eta \\
0 & 0 & 0 & 0 \\
0 & 0 & 0 & 0
\end{bmatrix}
\begin{pmatrix}
R \\
P \\
D \\
D^*
\end{pmatrix}
+
\begin{pmatrix}
\delta_2 \bar{R} \\
\eta R \\
0 \\
0
\end{pmatrix}
$$

with the roots of its characteristic equation equal to:

$$
\begin{aligned}
\lambda &= 0 \quad \text{(twice)} \\
&= -(\delta_1 + \delta_2) \\
&= -[(\alpha + \beta) + (Y + Y^*)]\eta
\end{aligned}
$$

The two zero roots correspond to the collinearity between the dynamics of the price level and domestic credit in the two countries. The other two roots are both negative if α and β are positive. The system is always stable in this case. If, however, α and β are negative, with large values, implying that the central banks accommodate a rise in inflation, then the system will exhibit saddlepoint behaviour.

(c) Both countries are now supposed to target their total monetary base to inflation:

$$
\dot{M} = -\alpha\dot{P}; \quad M^* = \delta\dot{P}
$$

In this case, three roots of the corresponding characteristic equation are zero, whereas the fourth is equal to:

$$
-(\alpha + \beta + Y + Y^*)\eta
$$

It is, consequently, negative for α and β positive. Under monetary base control, the system is characterised by hysteresis – that is, when subjected to shocks it will not return to its original equilibrium but to another one.

4   Conclusion

The examination of various monetary rules in the context of the monetary approach to the balance of payments, both under managed and fixed exchange rates, has led to a presumption in favour of rules based on control of the domestic component of the monetary base. This evaluation has been based on the criteria of stability, speeds of convergence and determinateness. The analysis of this Appendix confirms therefore that a rule like the one proposed in Section 4b of this study implies a stable system.

NOTES

* A first draft of this study was written when the authors were, respectively, Director General and Economic Adviser, Directorate General for Economic and Financial Affairs, Commission of the European Communities, Brussels. Mr Russo is now Director of the European Department at the International Monetary Fund, Washington, DC, and Mr Tullio is a member of the Research

Department of the Bank of Italy, Rome. Appendix 2 was written by Eric de Souza of the University of Louvain-la-Neuve in collaboration with Giuseppe Tullio. The authors are indebted for comments to their colleagues in the Commission, the Banca d'Italia, and the International Monetary Fund, in particular to Manuel Guitián, and Stefano Micossi, as well as to the other participants in this conference and the discussant Lucas Papademos; but the conclusions are their own and do not necessarily reflect the views of their previous or current employers. Mr Nouriel Roubini of Harvard University provided extensive and very useful comments, which significantly affected the conclusions.

1 However (only under the gold standard) central exchange rates were perfectly fixed between major currencies.
2 The system, however, may have been more asymmetric than claimed here, with the UK playing a central and more dominant role and the Bank of England 'conducting the International Orchestra' (Eichengreen, 1987).
3 This equilibrating property resulted from the fact that, with a fixed nominal gold price, profits in gold production and thus world gold output were raised by a fall in the world price level and reduced by an increase.
4 See Sommariva and Tullio (1987a–b) for a theoretical model explaining the determinants of the German discount rate under the classical gold standard and for empirical tests showing that changes in the liquidity ratios explain changes in the discount rate.
5 See *Vergleichende Notenbankstatistik* (1925) and Charles Goodhart (1972, 1984).
6 An even more dramatic concentration of gold in US hands occurred during the Second World War. Valued at 35 dollars an ounce the US gold stock amounted to US$8,500 million in 1931 and US$26,000 million at the end of the Second World War.
7 Germany had flexible exchange rates until the monetary reform of 1923. All major industrial countries had returned to fixed exchange rates by 1928. The period of fixed exchange rates was very short and lasted until about 1931, when sterling was devalued.
8 It must be pointed out, however, that the fall in this ratio was also due to the sharp increase in the demand for dollar reserves which resulted from world economic growth, the growth in world trade and the insufficient world gold production. This indicates that the proviso of adequate international reserves is also an important condition for the smooth functioning of a fixed exchange-rate system.
9 This situation recurred in 1987, after the decision to stabilise the dollar exchange rate *vis-à-vis* other key currencies (the 'Louvre' agreement).
10 A practice which is being repeated with respect to the Deutsche mark in the EMS, with similar consequences.
11 The 'follower' country indeed cannot 'sterilise' its losses of foreign reserves because any such credit expansion could bring another round of reserve losses equal to the domestic credit expansion (a point noted by Mr N. Roubini).
12 It should be noted that the size and duration of a member currency's real appreciation could be considered as a measure of the extent to which the monetary authorities concerned have not been able to 'borrow credibility' from the Bundesbank. Furthermore, as suggested by Melitz (Chapter 3 in this

volume), to the extent that credibility is bought at the expense of competitiveness, the gains of credibility have to be weighted against the output loss resulting from the real appreciation of the exchange rate. Thus, for countries like France and Italy, EMS participation may reduce welfare.

13 The reason for this standardisation is that we wish to compare the fraction of the cumulative variance of each variable explained by the first principal component in the analysis relating to the group of 17 industrial countries with that relating to the EMS countries only. This is done in Tables 11.6 and 11.7 below. For instance the first number in Table 11.6 is obtained from Table A11.1 in Appendix 1 as follows (for $n = 16$):

$$
0.56 = \frac{f - \dfrac{1}{n}}{1 - \dfrac{1}{n}} = \frac{0.59 - 0.0625}{1 - 0.0625}
$$

where f is the fraction of the variance explained by the first principal component reported in Table A11.1.

14 The fact that long-term nominal interest rates show less cohesion in the third period may be due to inflation differentials, which were still significant, and risk premia related to larger differences in budget deficits in relation to domestic savings.

15 It could be argued, however, that offshore rates of currencies which are subject to capital controls are inherently more volatile because, as the internal and external markets are separated, the external ones bear the brunt of shocks. As they are generally small markets, their volatility is inherently high.

16 The conclusions of the European Council meeting at Bremen on 6–7 July 1978 state that 'not later than two years after the start of the scheme, the existing arrangements and institutions will be consolidated in a European Monetary Fund'. The second stage is also mentioned in point 1.4 of the Resolution of the European Council of Brussels on 5 December 1978.

17 Italy and France have, however, accumulated Deutsche mark balances which they use for interventions, against the original rules of the system. See also Section 3c where the issue of interventions under the EMS is discussed.

18 Under perfectly fixed exchange rates, which are expected to prevail forever, all currencies become perfect substitutes in investors' portfolios (on the demand side). Substitutions on the supply side (via central bank interventions) will then become an important factor in changing the stock of money.

19 This has been an argument frequently used by the supporters of the entry of sterling into the ERM – especially in 1986, when wages were growing very rapidly in the UK.

20 This common inflation target should not be an average, but the lowest possible inflation rate acceptable to every member.

21 Note that when comparing measures of capacity utilisation for Germany, those by the Bundesbank are believed to be on the low side, and its estimates of potential output growth have been higher than those of other German forecasters. The *Sachverständigenrat* revised its estimate of the ratio of actual to potential output for 1986 from 98.5 per cent to 96.1 per cent, presumably to adapt its estimate to the one of the Bundesbank.

22 Switzerland instead announces its target as a point estimate equal to the growth of potential output and assuming zero inflation. Deviations from the target are, however, accepted if other data show no inflationary pressure and the deviation is not too large.
23 Other estimates, however, show a relatively stable demand for money in Germany.

REFERENCES

Aliber, R. (1978). 'The Integration of National Financial Markets: A Review of Theory and Findings', *Weltwirtschaftliches Archiv*, Vol. 114, pp. 448–80.
Artis, M. and M. Taylor (1987). 'Exchange Rates and the EMS: Assessing the Track Record', paper presented at the Conference on the EMS, Perugia (16–17 October).
Balassa, B. (1964). 'The Purchasing Power Parity Doctrine: A Reappraisal', *Journal of Political Economy*, Vol. 72 (December), pp. 584–96.
Bekx, P. and G. Tullio (1987). 'The European Monetary System and the Determination of the DM–US Dollar Exchange Rate', Brussels, Commission of the European Communities (May) (unpublished paper).
Bloomfield, A. (1959). *Monetary Policy Under the International Gold Standard, 1880–1914*, New York, Federal Reserve Bank.
   (1963). 'Short-Term Capital Movements Under the Pre-1914 Gold Standard', Princeton Studies in International Finance, No. 11.
Bordo, M. and A. Schwartz (eds) (1984). *A Retrospective of the Classical Gold Standard, 1821–1931*, Chicago, University of Chicago Press for the National Bureau of Economic Research.
Cassel, G. (1923). *La Monnaie et Les Changes Après 1914*, Paris, La Chapelle.
Collins, S. (1987). 'Inflation and the EMS', paper presented at the Conference on the EMS, Perugia, (16–17 October).
De Grauwe, P. (1986). 'Fiscal Policies in the EMS: A Strategic Analysis', International Economics Research Paper, No. 53, Catholic University of Louvain (October).
Deutsche Bundesbank (1976). *Deutsches Geld und Bankwesen in Zahlen*.
Dupriez, L. (1966). *Des Mouvements Economiques Généraux*, Tome II, Louvain, Editions Nauwelaerts.
Eichengreen, B. (1984). 'The Gold Standard in Theory and History', Harvard Institute of Economic Research, Discussion Paper, No. 1084 (September).
   (1987). 'Hegemonic Stability Theories of the International Monetary System', NBER Working Paper, No. 2193 (March).
Einaudi, L. (1944). *Problemi Economici della Federazione Europea*, Lugano, Nuove Edizioni di Capolago.
Fase, M. M. G. (1976). 'The Interdependence of Short-Term Interest Rates in the Major Financial Centres of the World: Some Evidence for 1961–1972', *Kyklos*, Vol. 29, Fasc. 1, pp. 63–96.

Genberg, H. (1975). *World Inflation and the Small Open Economy*, Stockholm, Swedish Industrial Publications.

(1977). 'The Concept and Measurement of the World Price Level and Rate of Inflation', *Journal of Monetary Economics*, Vol. 3 (April), pp. 231–52.

Giavazzi, F. and A. Giovannini (1987a). 'Models of the EMS: Is Europe a Greater Deutschmark Area?', in R. Bryant and R. Portes (eds), *Global Macroeconomics: Policy Conflict and Cooperation*, London, Macmillan, pp. 237–76.

(1987b). 'Interpreting European Disinflation: The Role of the Exchange Rate Regime', paper presented at the Conference on the EMS, Perugia (16–17 October).

Goodhart, C. (1972). *The Business of Banking*, London, Weidenfeld & Nicolson.

(1984). 'Comment to John Pippinger', in Michael Bordo and Anna Schwartz (eds), *A Retrospective on the Classical Gold Standard 1821–1931*, Chicago, University of Chicago Press, for the National Bureau of Economic Research.

Gros, D. (1987). 'The EMS and the Determinants of the European Price Level', Brussels, CEPS (unpublished paper).

Hawtrey, R. (1947). *The Gold Standard in Theory and Practice*, 5th edn, London, Longman.

Heller, R. (1976). 'International Reserves and World-Wide Inflation', IMF Staff Papers (March).

Johnson, H. G. (1975). 'World Inflation and the International Monetary System', Miami University Inflation Conference (15–16 May) (unpublished paper).

Kindleberger, C. (1976). 'Germany's Persistent Balance of Payments Disequilibrium Revisited', Banca Nazionale del Lavoro *Quarterly Review* (June), pp. 135–64.

Kouri, P. (1986). 'Stable Money and World Monetary Reform: Review and Prospect', *Report of the Shadow G-7 Group*, Citicorps Investment Bank, New York (June).

Masera, R. (1980). *L'unificazione monetaria e lo SME*, Bologna, Il Mulino.

Mastropasqua, C., S. Micossi and R. Rinaldi (1987). 'Interventions, Sterilization, and Monetary Policy in EMS Countries (1979–1987)', paper presented at the Conference on the EMS, Perugia (16–17 October).

Matthes, H. (1987). *Europäische Wirtschafts- und Währungsintegration, Erreichtes und Erstrebtes, Vortrag vor dem Institut für Kapitalmarktforschung an der Johann Wolfgang Goethe-Universität*, Frankfurt/Main (29 January).

McKinnon, R. (1977). 'Beyond Fixed Parities: The Analytics of International Monetary Agreements', in Robert Aliber (ed.), *The Political Economics of Monetary Reform*, London, Macmillan, pp. 43–55.

(1984). *An International Standard for Monetary Stabilization*, Washington, DC, The Institute for International Economics; Cambridge, Mass: MIT Press.

(1985a). 'The Dollar Exchange Rate and International Monetary Cooperation', Stanford University (January) (unpublished paper).

(1985b). 'What to Do About the Overvalued Dollar', Stanford University (March) (unpublished paper).

(1986). 'Monetary and Exchange Rate Policies for International Financial Stability: a Proposal', Economic Papers, No. 53, Brussels, Commission of the European Communities (November).

Meade, J. (1984). 'International Cooperation in Macro-Economic Policies', Economic Papers, No. 28, Brussels, Commission of the European Communities (February).

Melitz, J. (1987). 'Germany, Discipline and Co-operation in the European Monetary System', paper presented at the Conference on the EMS, Perugia (16–17 October).

Micossi, S. and T. Padoa-Schioppa (1984). 'Short-Term Interest Rate Linkages between the United States and Europe', *Rivista di Politica Economica*, No. 18.

Mitchell, B. (1975). *European Historical Statistics, 1750–1970*, London, Macmillan.

Morgenstern, O. (1959). *International Financial Transactions and the Business Cycle*, Princeton, Princeton University for the National Bureau of Economic Research.

Mundell, R. (1968). *International Economics*, New York, Macmillan, Chapter 20.

Padoa-Schioppa, T. (1985). 'Policy Cooperation and the EMS Experience', in W. H. Buiter and R. C. Marston (eds), *International Economic Policy Coordination*, Cambridge, NBER/Cambridge University Press.

Parkin, M. (1977). 'World Inflation, International Relative Prices and Monetary Equilibrium under Fixed Exchange Rates', in R. Z. Aliber (ed.), *The Political Economics of Monetary Reform*, London, Macmillan.

Roubini, N. (1987a). 'Leadership and Policy Co-operation in the EMS', Harvard University (August) (unpublished).

(1987b). 'Target Zones, EMS, and Policy Transmission Under Alternative Exchange Rate Regimes', Harvard University (August) (mimeo).

Russo, M. (1984). '*Cooperazione Monetaria Europea: Cinque Anni di Esperienza dello SME*', *Rivista Bancaria* (May–June).

(1986). 'Why the Time is Ripe', Lecture delivered to the Bow Group, House of Commons, London (19 May).

Sarcinelli, M. (1986). 'Monetary Integration, Exchange Rate Policies and Capital Markets in US–Europe Relations', *The International Spectator*, Vol. 21, No. 1.

Sommariva, A. and G. Tullio (1987a) *German Macroeconomic History 1880–1979 – A Study of the Effects of Economic Policy on Inflation, Currency Depreciation and Economic Growth*, London, Macmillan.

(1987b). 'The Determinants of the Official Discount Rate and of Liquidity Ratios During the Classical Gold Standard: An Econometric Analysis of the Objectives of Monetary Policy in Germany: 1876–1913', Economic Papers, No. 56, Brussels, Commission of the European Communities.

(1987c). 'International Gold Flows in Gold Standard Germany: a Test of the Monetary Approach to the Balance of Payments, 1880–1911', *Journal of Money, Credit and Banking*, Vol. 20, No. 1 (February), pp. 132–400.

(1987d). 'A Note on the Real Exchange Rate, Differential Productivity Growth and Protectionism in Gold Standard Germany, 1878–1913', *Weltwirtschaftliches Archiv* (June), pp. 354–62.

Spinelli, F. (1983). 'Currency Substitution, Flexible Exchange Rates and the Case for International Monetary Cooperation', IMF Staff Papers, No. 4 (December).

Swoboda, A. K. and H. Genberg (1977). 'Worldwide Inflation Under the Dollar

Standard', Discussion Paper, No. 12, Geneva, Graduate Institute of International Studies (January).

Tanzi, V. and T. Ter-Minassian (1985). 'The European Monetary System and Fiscal Policies', paper presented to the conference on tax coordination in the EEC, Rotterdam (22–24 August).

Triffin, R. (1978). 'Gold and the Dollar Crisis: Yesterday and Tomorrow', *Essays in International Finance*, No. 132, Princeton, Princeton University (December).

Tullio, G. (1979). 'Monetary Equilibrium and Balance of Payments Adjustment: An Empirical Test of the U.S. Balance of Payments (1951–73)', *Journal of Money, Credit and Banking*, Vol. 11 (February), pp. 68–79.

(1981). *The Monetary Approach to External Adjustment: A Case Study of Italy*, London, Macmillan; New York, St Martin's Press, Chapter 2.

(1987). 'Long-Run Implications of the Increase in Taxation and Public Debt for Employment and Economic Growth in Europe', Economic Papers, No. 49, Brussels, Commission of the European Communities (August); (1987) *European Economic Review*, Vol. 31 (April), pp. 741–80.

Ungerer, H., O. Evans, T. Mayer and P. Young (1986). 'The European Monetary System: Recent Developments', IMF Occasional Papers, No. 48 (December).

US Department of Commerce (1979). *Historical Statistics of the US*, Washington, DC, Department of Commerce.

Vergleichende Notenbankstatistik (1925). *Organisation und Geschäftsverkehr Europäischer Notenbanken, 1876–1913*, Berlin, Reichsdruckerei.

Williamson, J. and M. H. Miller (1987). 'Targets and Indicators: A Blueprint for the International Co-ordination of Economic Policy', Washington, DC, Institute for International Economics, Policy Analyses in International Economics, No. 22 (September).

Wyplosz, C. and D. Begg (1987). 'Why the EMS: Dynamic Games and the Equilibrium Policy Regime', Fontainebleau, INSEAD and London, Birkbeck College (May) (unpublished paper).

Discussion

LUCAS PAPADEMOS

Central banks participating in a system of fixed exchange rates, such as the European Monetary System (EMS), have to adopt explicit or implicit rules and operating procedures, which constrain both the choice of policy objectives and the use of policy instruments. As a result of the constraints imposed by the exchange-rate mechanism of the EMS, the policy objectives of any one member country must be compatible with the choices made by other members, while the efficiency of the instruments of monetary policy is affected by the response of the other participants in the system. There is general agreement that monetary policy coordination is necessary and desirable for the smooth functioning of the EMS. But there is less general agreement on the form or nature of this coordination and, in particular, on whether it should be based on explicit and fixed rules or on implicit and flexible cooperative arrangements.

Since its inception in 1979, the EMS has functioned remarkably well, considering the differences in 'initial conditions' among member states and the sizeable imbalances and disturbances that have affected international financial markets. The system has functioned well without the adoption of explicit rules other than those implied by the exchange-rate mechanism. The institutional setting has involved cooperation, but also decentralised decisionmaking on the choice of final objectives and on the conduct of intervention and interest-rate policies. Monetary policy in member states has enjoyed a certain degree of flexibility and independence, despite the constraint of the EMS, because exchange rates are not rigidly fixed but can fluctuate within certain limits, realignments may occur, and a number of member countries have imposed restrictions on some categories of capital movements. Nevertheless, monetary policy within the EMS is likely to face new challenges. As the European Communities advance towards full liberalisation of capital movements and complete freedom in the provision of financial services, the traditional instruments of policy cannot be employed effectively to achieve domestic objectives. Inevitably, the degree of autonomy in monetary policy will be further reduced. In addition, as the international monetary system after the Louvre Agreement has entered a new phase, in which stronger emphasis is laid on the stability of exchange rates, the need for increased coordination of monetary policy is becoming more important. In particular, the EMS needs an effective mechanism or rule which can help establish an 'anchor' to its price level or nominal income.

The study by Russo and Tullio provides a timely and stimulating analysis of many of the central issues faced in the formulation and conduct of monetary policy under a system of fixed but adjustable exchange rates, such as the EMS. The study is divided into four parts, the first being introductory. In the second, the authors review the experience from the gold standard and the Bretton Woods system in order to derive 'lessons' concerning the essential ingredients or necessary conditions for the stability of a system of fixed or 'quasi-fixed' exchange rates. The third part of the study focuses on the functioning of the EMS from 1979 until the present. Finally, the study examines how the functioning of the EMS could be improved by the adoption of a rule which would govern the setting of nominal targets in all member states. In particular, the authors evaluate the implications of four alternative coordination rules for monetary policy, which could improve the system by making the balance of payments adjustment mechanism more symmetric and by securing the objective of price stability. Their analysis, which is particularly timely for the reasons stressed above, leads them to propose one rule as the most promising alternative. According to Russo and Tullio, application of this rule does not call for fundamental changes in the institutional setting, but only for a higher degree of monetary coordination among member states.

The experience gained under the gold standard and the Bretton Woods system serves as a useful frame of reference for an analysis of the EMS. A first 'lesson' offered by history on the conduct of monetary policy in such a system is that monetary targeting by individual countries is, in general, incompatible with the smooth functioning of the balance of payments adjustment mechanism. A country may set a money target only if it plays a 'dominant' role in the system and acts as the accepted leader that provides a nominal anchor. Other countries may be able to pursue a money target only if it is consistent with that of the dominant member of the system. But this is not likely to be feasible in practice. The problems faced after the collapse of the gold standard were associated with the failure to coordinate economic policies and the lack of leadership observed after the abolition of the convertibility of banknotes into gold. The main factors which created tensions and eventually led to the collapse of the Bretton Woods system were the asymmetry in the balance of payments adjustment mechanism, and the absence of a central reserve currency pursuing the goal of price stability. The authors relate the US balance of payments deficits in the late 1960s and early 1970s to the evolution of the domestic components of the monetary base in the US and the other OECD countries, quantities which could be set exogenously under Bretton Woods. They argue that the special role of the dollar as an international reserve asset and the practice of most countries of holding dollar reserves in the form of US treasury bills and US and Eurodollar bank deposits, rather than in the form of deposits with the Federal Reserve, magnified the effects of US monetary policy on the world money growth and inflation and implied an 'automatic sterilisation' of the US balance of payments deficits.

In evaluating the performance of the EMS so far, Russo and Tullio focus on three issues: the contribution of the system to the convergence of nominal and real magnitudes in member states, the role of German monetary policy in the disinflation process, and the problems arising within the EMS from the sterilisation of foreign reserve flows. The conclusions of empirical studies reviewed by Russo and Tullio on the contribution of the EMS towards increasing convergence and reducing inflation are mixed. This is rather surprising and contrary to the common view, shared by most European central bank officials, that the EMS has not only imposed greater discipline on the policies of inflation-prone countries, but that it has indeed facilitated the disinflation process by allowing these countries to use the system to influence expectations and enhance the credibility of domestic policies. The studies, which raise doubts about the role of the EMS in promoting convergence and disinflation, point out that inflation in non-EMS countries since 1980 has fallen more sharply and at a lower cost than in EMS countries; that over a number of years (1979–82) monetary growth and inflation remained high within the EMS group and convergence was limited; and the higher degree of convergence achieved since 1983 has been partly due to exogenous factors, such as the decline in oil prices, and to fundamental changes in French and Italian monetary policies, which can not be attributed solely to the constraints imposed by the EMS.

To assess the contribution of the EMS to greater convergence, Russo and Tullio present fresh empirical evidence employing a 'principal component analysis', which allows the isolation of common elements in a number of time series. They compare the fractions of the cumulative variance explained by the first principal component of five variables for a sample of seventeen industrial countries with the corresponding fractions obtained for a sample that contains only the countries participating in the exchange-rate mechanism of the EMS. The variables analysed are exchange rates, inflation, nominal short-term and long-term interest rates, and money stock (M1).

I will comment on the authors' findings by restating somewhat the main results. (1) The fraction of the variance explained by the first principal component is higher for the exchange rate than for any other variable. This is true both of the complete sample and of the EMS countries, as well as of the periods before and after the creation of the EMS. However, the fraction explained is higher for the EMS countries and increases substantially after 1979. The latter result is not, of course, surprising for countries participating in a system of 'quasi-fixed' exchange rates. (2) For EMS countries, the fraction is higher for *all* variables in the most recent period (1983: 3–1986: 3) compared with the previous two periods, and especially compared with the first period (1973: 3–1979: 2) before the creation of the EMS. However, the fractions for inflation and the money stock are lower in the four years following the inception of the EMS. Furthermore, a similar (although less pronounced) pattern follows from a comparison of the fractions in the recent period and in the pre-EMS period for the complete sample of all 17 countries. (3) All fractions for all variables in all periods are higher for the EMS countries than for the larger group of countries. This suggests that the EMS countries have been characterised by a higher degree of convergence than the larger group, both before and after the EMS.

These results provide suggestive but not very conclusive evidence in support of the proposition that the EMS strengthened the convergence of nominal magnitudes, especially inflation, in the most recent period. However, the decline in the fraction of the variance of EMS inflation and money growth which is explained by the first principal component over the period 1979: 3–1983: 2, is puzzling, although consistent with the results of other studies. The fact that convergence has increased since 1979 for most variables (not only in the EMS group but also in the larger group of 17 industrial countries), indicates that some other common factor has influenced developments. These findings are hard to interpret because the economic interpretation of the first principal component is not obvious. It would have been informative if the authors had split the sample into EMS and non-EMS groups, and if they had included in their analysis a real variable, such as GDP growth.

Although the EMS does not at present incorporate an explicit rule for the determination of the system's price level, an implicit rule has been established since 1982. Germany has been setting a monetary growth target to achieve its own inflation objective, and other members, having agreed to the objective of disinflation, have adjusted their monetary policies to converge on it. Russo and Tullio discuss at some length the role of Germany in providing the nominal anchor for the system's price level. This issue is particularly relevant today. As EMS inflation has reached a fairly low level but unemployment has stubbornly remained high, a consensus on an acceptable trade-off between inflation and output growth may prove harder to reach, thereby weakening the effectiveness of the implicit rule. Moreover, the ability of Germany to control its money stock effectively may be eroded as a result of the constraints imposed by international agreements on exchange rates.

Germany's capability to determine its own and EMS inflation depends upon its relative economic size and ability to control its money supply. Russo and Tullio show that, on the basis of shares of exports and imports, Germany is more important during the EMS period in relation to EMS members than the US was under the Bretton Woods system in relation to the industrial countries. On the other hand, the German economy is much more open than the US economy, and thus more susceptible to external disturbances. Moreover, the German financial market is relatively small compared with the EMS and US financial markets.

Two sets of evidence are examined to assess Germany's capacity to control its money supply and to pursue unilaterally the objective of price stability. The evidence clearly shows that since 1979, Germany has been able to attain its monetary targets, except during the years (1986–7) of rapid appreciation to the DM against the US dollar, when large interventions were required to limit the speed and extent of this appreciation. Russo and Tullio show that the liquidity impact of DM interventions within the EMS was relatively small and temporary, and that the growth of the domestic component of the Bundesbank's monetary liabilities was endogenously determined in order to sterilise the effects of the change in net foreign assets on money growth. They conclude that 'inflation in Germany declined sharply, in line with the deceleration of money supply growth'. It is interesting to note, however, that although inflation did decelerate sharply and steadily after 1980, the money growth figures reported in their Table 11.12 have not exhibited a particularly sharp or monotonic decline since 1979.

The implications of other evidence reported on the determinants of German inflation are rather different. It is suggested that inflation in Germany can be described by a simple monetarist model which implies that German inflation equals EMS inflation, adjusted for the rate of change in the effective exchange rate of the DM against other EMS currencies, and that EMS inflation gradually adjusts to disequilibria in the market for aggregate EMS money. Bekx and Tullio, in an unpublished study (1987), have estimated demand functions for the aggregate money stock of countries participating in the exchange-rate mechanism (ERM) of the EMS. Russo and Tullio report that the DM–dollar and the ECU–dollar exchange rates can be explained reasonably well during the EMS period by the disequilibria in the US and the aggregate EMS money markets, while the disequilibrium in the German money market does not contribute significantly to the explanation of the DM–dollar exchange rate. The inference is that monetary policies in other ERM countries have had an impact on the DM—dollar exchange rate, and through that on German inflation.

Although the results reported on the role of the EMS money market in explaining German exchange rates are interesting and suggestive, it is difficult to assess their quantitative significance and the relative contribution of different factors to German inflation. The underlying model of the inflation process is simple and incomplete. It does not relate nominal interest rates to inflation and it does not specify the mechanism determining the EMS-wide money supply and, in particular, the effects of German monetary policy on the EMS-wide money stock. A testing of alternative hypotheses on the determinants of EMS inflation and an empirical analysis of the causal links between German and EMS inflation on the one hand, and German and EMS money growth on the other, are necessary to reach firm conclusions on these issues.

The implications for the EMS of the adoption of alternative rules for the coordination of monetary policy are examined in the fourth part of the study. These rules aim, in particular, at achieving the objective of price stability for the system and at improving the balance of payments adjustment. They belong to two different categories. Of the four rules examined, two are indeed rules which relate directly to the conduct of monetary policy and, in particular, to the setting of intermediate monetary targets or the setting and use of policy instruments. The other two rules, concerning nominal income targeting for each member country and a common EMS inflation target, define frameworks for the formulation and conduct of policy rather than specific operational rules constraining the implementation of policy. Indeed, the last two 'rules' necessitate considerable activism of both monetary and fiscal policies.

The first rule involves the fixing of an aggregate money supply target for the EMS as a whole. It is based on McKinnon's thesis (1984) that when currency substitutability is high between countries, each country's inflation depends on the entire system's money supply rather than on the domestic money supply. The empirical results of Bekx and Tullio, discussed above, seem to support this proposition, and the planned complete liberalisation of capital movements by 1992 will clearly strengthen the validity of the underlying hypothesis of high currency substitutability. Russo and Tullio propose to set the target rate of growth of the EMS-wide money stock on the basis of an agreed common inflation target and an agreed potential EMS output growth, on the assumption that the income velocity of the EMS-wide money stock is constant and stable. Anticipated short-term changes in velocity may be accommodated by the adoption of a range of money growth rates.

The implementation of this monetary rule is likely to cause considerable difficulties. As acknowledged by Russo and Tullio, it will not be easy for all members of the EMS to reach agreement on a desirable common inflation target and on potential output growth. This difficulty, however, must also be overcome in the context of other policies discussed below. The effectiveness of this rule will depend on the stability of demand for the aggregate EMS money stock. Although the empirical results cited above are promising, stability may be affected by ongoing financial innovations in many countries. Further to the difficulties recognised by Russo and Tullio, the conduct of a monetary policy which targets the EMS-wide money stock is likely to face other problems. In the first place, stability of demand for aggregate EMS money is a necessary but not a sufficient condition for the efficiency of a policy based on this rule. Alternative monetary strategies may be more effective, depending upon the economy's structural characteristics and the nature of shocks affecting the economy. Secondly, the measure of the money stock to be targeted is not specified, although one may infer that the authors have in mind a broad measure of money. A potentially serious difficulty in this case is that an attempt by central banks to fix such an aggregate may induce market behaviour and financial innovations in order to by-pass monetary control. This would destabilise the income velocity of money and undermine the efficacy of the first rule. Thirdly, the operational procedures required to achieve effective control of such an aggregate are also not specified. It is likely that, even in the absence of endogenous financial innovations, monetary authorities would face difficulties in achieving the target collectively, when there is instability in foreign-exchange markets and when there are agreements to stabilise the exchange rates of EMS currencies against other major currencies.

The second rule specifies an operational procedure for each central bank. This procedure aims at satisfying the constraint imposed by the exchange-rate mechanism in a symmetric way, while allowing a degree of flexibility in attaining domestic nominal income targets. On the assumption that interventions in member currencies sum up to zero, the proposed rule specifies that each central bank should set the rate of growth of the domestic component of the monetary base equal to a multiple of the desired rate of growth of nominal income in the respective country. The proportionality factor or 'multiplier' is the reciprocal of the share of the domestic assets of the central bank in the monetary base. It can be readily shown that, if all member states followed such a rule, the aggregate money supply of the EMS would grow at a rate which is given by a weighted average of the rates of growth of the domestic component of each country's monetary base, with weights equal to the share of the domestic assets of the country's central bank in the total monetary base of the EMS. Furthermore, if all countries followed this rule, it would result in an aggregate EMS-wide inflation and growth rate given by the weighted average of the individual countries' inflation and output growth rates, where the weights are the shares of each country's money supply in the EMS-wide money supply.

The appealing features of this rule are that it does in fact constrain the conduct of policy and that it appears to be applicable to a system of decentralised decisionmaking, such as the EMS at its present stage. Moreover, Russo and Tullio argue that, if each country follows such a rule, the exchange-rate system is stable, whereas a policy of fixing the total monetary base leads to instability. Nevertheless, adoption of such a rule does not generally constitute an optimal strategy for monetary policy, and the feasibility of this approach is open to question in the absence of a coordinated choice of final policy targets.

Some of the problems that a central bank must face in implementing this rule are noted by Russo and Tullio and relate to certain simplifying assumptions, namely that exchange rates are perfectly fixed, that the rates of productivity growth in the traded and non-traded goods sectors are equal, and that countries employ unbiased forecasts of potential output growth. The first two problems can be overcome by an appropriate adjustment of the rule, while persistent forecast errors would yield results that would force countries to adjust their estimates.

Further problems relating to other hypotheses underlying the analysis must be tackled. First, the rule fixes a narrow measure of the money supply, which may not exhibit a stable relationship to nominal income. The assumption that the monetary base multiplier has a value of one does not limit the effectiveness of the rule. But the assumption that the money multiplier and the income velocity of the monetary base are stochastically stable and invariant to policy actions, which may include sizeable variations in interest rates, is not likely to hold. Second, the rule is derived on the assumption that there are no interventions in third currencies, which is not realistic under present circumstances. Third, adoption of this rule by each country implies the targeting *ex post* of measures of aggregate EMS inflation and real income whose economic significance is unclear. Finally, as mentioned before, the applicability of this rule in the absence of a coordinated choice of inflation targets by member countries is questionable. Although Russo and Tullio state that a cooperative approach could be adopted in fixing the inflation target for each member country, consistently with the desired degree of convergence, the presumption is that each country can pursue its own inflation objective. But if member states do not choose inflation targets that are mutually consistent in the long run, this could lead to instability, for the proposed rule can not be invariant over time: it depends on the share of the domestic component of the monetary base in the total monetary base, a share which varies when the central bank sets a non-zero target growth rate for the domestic component of the base.

The other two rules discussed by Russo and Tullio – i.e., nominal income targeting by each member country and a monetary rule for each country with an EMS-wide inflation target – have three features in common: monetary policy focuses directly on the final policy objectives rather than aiming at them indirectly via the control of an intermediate target; fiscal policy is brought into the picture and it is employed jointly with monetary policy in order to control nominal income more effectively; finally, both policies imply active use of policy instruments, such as short-term interest rates. Consequently, these policies do not describe monetary coordination rules, but general macroeconomic strategies aimed at nominal income control and exchange-rate stability.

The Williamson–Miller (1987) prescription for monetary and fiscal policy geared to the management of a system of real effective exchange rates is an example of nominal income targeting. This approach requires: an active fiscal policy at the national level aiming at a domestic nominal income target; the management by central banks of interest-rate differentials to maintain exchange-rate stability; and the adjustment of the system's average interest rate to stabilise EMS nominal demand. The last 'rule' involves coordinated short-term variations in member countries' money growth in response to deviations of EMS inflation from the desired path. Clearly, such a rule presumes a discretionary approach to monetary management, both at the national and at the EMS level. In theory, these macroeconomic strategies could be more effective than the two money supply rules. In practice, however, their effectiveness may be limited by imperfect information on the economy's structure, time lags in the effects of both monetary and fiscal policies on the economy, and a failure to act promptly and in a coordinated way when shocks affect the system asymmetrically.

The Russo and Tullio analysis of alternative policy rules within the EMS and of the performance of the system so far is a valuable contribution to the ongoing debate on macroeconomic policy coordination. A conclusion which emerges from both the authors' analysis and my own comments is that no single rule can be considered as optimal *ex ante*, independently of the origin of the shocks affecting the economy and of its structure. Moreover, implementation of either the monetary rules or the more general macroeconomic strategies implies considerable difficulties for the conduct of monetary policy. Nevertheless, it is clear that the EMS needs an effective rule which can provide an anchor for the system's price level.

A feature of all the policies examined by Russo and Tullio is that, explicitly or implicitly, member states are required to choose a common target for aggregate EMS nominal income. Although it will not be easy to reach a consensus on such an objective, it will be necessary if the system is to function smoothly in the new environment of perfect capital mobility, low inflation and slow GDP growth within the EMS. Agreement on a common EMS nominal income target and efficient implementation of any of the policies discussed above would necessitate further progress in two directions: introduction of institutional changes in the structure of EMS central banks, which would allow more centralised decisionmaking in the formulation and conduct of monetary policy; and attainment of a higher degree of convergence of fiscal policies, so as to minimise undesirable consequences for the economy from potential conflicts between national fiscal policies and a European monetary policy.

REFERENCES

Bekx, P. and G. Tullio (1987). 'The European Monetary System and the Determination of the DM–US Dollar Exchange Rate', Brussels, Commission of the European Communities (May) (unpublished).

McKinnon, R. (1984). *An International Standard for Monetary Stabilization*, Washington, DC, Institute for International Economics; Cambridge, Mass,: MIT Press.

Williamson, J. and M. H. Miller (1987). 'Targets and Indicators: A Blueprint for the International Co-ordination of Economic Policy', Washington, DC, Institute for International Economics, Policy Analyses in International Economics, No. 22 (September).

IV The Future of the European Monetary System

12 The European Monetary System: A Long-term View

TOMMASO PADOA-SCHIOPPA

1 Introduction

I have been invited to contribute to this conference with a consideration of the long-term prospects of the European Monetary System (EMS). My approach will differ from that of the other studies in this volume: it will take the system as a variable, while they take it as given; it will be non-technical, while they develop their arguments with the help of sophisticated techniques. The reasons why a contribution of this kind was felt necessary are that the system is now sufficiently well established to justify expectations of its having a long life, that the tests it has still to pass may be so demanding as to change its shape, and that the view of a policymaker may be a useful input to an academic debate.

Let me start by explaining the meaning I shall give to three concepts that are central to my argument: 'long term', 'performance', and 'evolution' of the system.

What do we mean by 'long term'? Rinaldo Ossola used to say that the time horizon of a central banker is about three months. Between this extreme and Keynes's definition in terms of a lifetime, a measure of several years can be taken as a fair compromise. However, a definition based exclusively on the time dimension is too restrictive. It is more helpful to base it on the well-known distinction that the German language makes between *Prozesspolitik* and *Ordnungspolitik*: the former operates *within* existing institutions, instruments and markets; the latter acts *on* the existing framework. The 'long term' is the time horizon of *Ordnungspolitik*, which is the amount of calendar time actually lapsing before a change in the existing order becomes necessary and is enacted. I shall argue that the problem of the long-term evolution of the EMS may well require our attention earlier than it is generally believed.

The 'performance' expected from the monetary organisation of a group of economically interdependent and institutionally linked countries, such as the member states of the Community, is to foster trade integration and promote domestic price stability. An arrangement that is optimal for one purpose may not be the best for another. Thus, by stabilising nominal exchange rates, a fixed-rate system would be optimal for the promotion of macroeconomic discipline, but might distort price competitiveness, possibly leading to trade disruptions and imbalances. On the other hand, a crawling peg would ensure the stabilisation of real exchange rates (and thereby preserve the relative competitive position of member countries), but might undermine macroeconomic discipline by producing full accommodation of inflation differentials.

A satisfactory balance between the above two objectives must form the basis of an appropriate monetary system. In this study, a 'satisfactory trade and macroeconomic discipline' will be taken as the desired performance of the EMS for today and tomorrow.[1] This implies that exchange rates are managed in such a way as to avoid over-accommodation of price differentials or unwarranted changes in real exchange rates. Since 1979 the system has been quite successful in promoting such balance compared with what has occurred outside the area.

Finally, the 'evolution' of the EMS I have in mind is one whereby the system will succeed in maintaining or improving its performance as circumstances change. Adaptation of the system should build on what has already been achieved, without giving ground on either the price stability or on other fronts.

I will argue that the programme set for the development of the Community in the areas of trade, financial services and capital mobility is such that it requires the EMS to evolve to a *de jure* or *de facto* monetary union. I am not advocating the creation of a monetary union as an objective *per se*, possibly as a way to strengthen European integration or to fulfil a political commitment that dates back to 1974. Rather, I will base my arguments on the less ambitious aim of maintaining a system that will be able to provide the performance defined above and support the programme of completing the internal market.

The long-term evolution of the EMS can be seen as comprising three phases: the first phase, of consolidation, can be considered concluded; we are now living through the second, in which the 'inconsistent quartet' emerges; and we start to foresee the third, that of monetary union. I will now discuss the main features of these three phases.

The reasoning here pays only limited attention to external factors and relations with the rest of the world. In part this is done for the sake of simplicity, but more it is due to the conviction that the determinants of the life, development, or failure, of the EMS lie within the system itself and the Community, not outside.

2   Phase One: consolidation

The first phase has been one of consolidation, with the objective of protecting the acquired degree of Community trade integration from disruptive fluctuations in real exchange rates and promoting convergence on a low rate of inflation in member countries.

The performance of the system has been quite satisfactory, notwithstanding the second oil shock – an event that would have perhaps discouraged the entire enterprise if it had occurred on the eve instead of the morrow of the Jenkins–Giscard–Schmidt initiative. Average inflation in the EMS countries has fallen from 11 per cent in 1980 to 2 per cent in 1986; the difference between the highest and the lowest inflation rates has narrowed from sixteen to six percentage points. Despite high and rising unemployment (from 6 per cent in 1980 to 10.5 per cent in 1986), trade relationships within the Community have not been infected by the protectionist pressures that have emerged worldwide.

The period of consolidation has also been fruitful in establishing important practices and interpretations, thereby filling in and completing the system's 'written constitution'. Three such features, which we now consider an integral part of the EMS, were not taken for granted from the start and should be mentioned.

The first is the successful blend of rules and discretion by means of which the system functions. The rules apply to the management of exchange rates, which have to be maintained within compulsory margins between realignments. They enhance cooperation in intervention, market confidence and the credibility of the system itself. Discretion governs the timing and the magnitude of realignments. It is necessary both because the events that lead to a realignment are themselves difficult to forecast and because predictable parity changes would generate such speculative pressures that the system would break down.

The second feature is that central rates are the result of a truly collective decision. In this respect, the management of exchange rates has been effectively taken away from national hands and is conducted at the Community level. This is a crucial advance (and one the Bretton Woods system had failed to make), as changes in parities were normally decided unilaterally by the country concerned and simply communicated, for a 'multilateral blessing', to the IMF.

A third important feature is the positive interaction between exchange-rate and other policies (both monetary and real) fostered by the system in the nine years since 1979. In a way, this has disposed of the debate that flourished between 'economists' and 'monetarists' at the time of the Werner plan.

Acceptance of the principles and objectives of the system has reinforced policy cooperation both *among* member countries and *within* countries, between such policy-making bodies as central banks, fiscal authorities, trade unions and employers' organisations. Italy (July–September 1980), Belgium (February 1982), and France (March 1983) are the most significant examples of the behaviour of one or more macroeconomic agents having conformed to the stability-oriented option embodied in participation in the system.

Undeniably, the system's successful performance in the phase of consolidation owed something to the help of special factors and circumstances. First, the strong dollar attenuated intra-EMS pressures by diverting financial flows away from DM-denominated assets. Further, the gain in competitiveness of European producers *vis-à-vis* important non-EMS competitors partly offset the contractionary effects of disinflationary policies in EMS countries. Overall, the external environment was propitious in the phase of consolidation, notwithstanding the inflationary effects of the rising dollar and their different impact on member countries' economies.

Second, capital controls reduced the exchange-rate pressures associated with the higher inflation rates of France and Italy, whose participation in the system is the main difference between the snake and the EMS.

Finally, recognition of the need to give priority to the reduction of inflation also resulted in relatively easy acceptance of the policy leadership of the Federal Republic of Germany, the member country that is both economically strongest and most attached to monetary stability. The sensitive issues of coordination, leadership, and symmetry were thus not a major problem for several years.

3   Phase Two: the inconsistent quartet

The end of Phase One coincides with the disappearance of the favourable factors mentioned above. The reversal in the trend of the dollar was largely exogenous to the EMS and the Community. Improved inflation convergence and the relaxation of exchange controls stemmed, by contrast, from the very success of the system, although they are now posing new problems for its existence. Consolidation has led to lower inflation, and hence has made consensus more difficult to achieve on monetary objectives since national priorities may tilt in favour of growth in some countries and away from it in others. It has also inevitably restored the implementation of Articles 67–73 of the Treaty of Rome, concerning the full freedom of capital movements, as a credible item of the Community agenda.

The second phase of the EMS is marked by the emergence of a fundamental challenge to the system as capital controls are lifted and all the remaining non-tariff barriers in the trade of goods and services are removed as a consequence of fulfilling the programme set by the Single European Act. Unless new items are added to the agenda, the Community will be seeking to achieve the impossible task of reconciling (1) free trade, (2) full capital mobility, (3) fixed (or at any rate managed) exchange rates and (4) national autonomy in the conduct of monetary policy. These four elements form what I call an 'inconsistent quartet': economic theory and historical experience have repeatedly shown that these four elements cannot coexist, and that at least one has to give way.[2]

In Phase Two, which can be seen as having started in 1986, the full effects of the inconsistency have not yet been felt, because capital mobility is still incomplete. Short-term capital is not yet wholly transferable and the national markets for financial services are not open. However, the main allocative decisions of business and households regarding production, consumption and investment can already range freely across frontiers and no serious obstacles hinder the execution of payments. The difference between Phase Two and Phase Three is the extent to which this inconsistency manifests itself.

The question is whether the EMS mechanisms are adequate to allow the system to survive and to 'perform', as defined above, as effectively as it did in Phase One. Perhaps the challenge in this new phase does not originate so much from the objective of maintaining price stability (since inflation has been substantially lowered), as from the active dismantling of barriers to the exchange of goods and services and the liberalisation of sectors so far heavily protected.

The importance of this question about the adequacy of the EMS mechanisms is enhanced by the recent stipulation (in Basle and Nyborg), of an accord that modifies and improves some of the EMS mechanisms, making it less likely that there will be another round of revision during the present phase. The system may thus have to rely solely on what is already available.

In my opinion, the existing arrangements and mechanisms of the EMS are sufficient to preserve its performance, provided a significant change in attitude takes place in the way the system is managed, and provided participants are constantly aware of the dangers of the system's fragility.

Of course, there will continue to be instances in which pressures on exchange rates are wholly justified by cost and price divergences. As in the past, a realignment paralleled by other policy measures will be the appropriate response. In contrast with Phase One, however, there will be many other instances in which tensions will be fuelled by capital mobility, with minor 'real' divergences being nothing more than a pretext. The required change in attitude consists in *not* considering pressures in the exchange markets as a sufficient condition for a realignment. The only effective instrument to counter financial disturbances is a defence of the exchange rate through enhanced cooperation among monetary authorities and the willingness to subordinate domestic goals to exchange-rate stability when circumstances so required.

Interventions will be the first line of defence, and they may have to be on an unprecedented scale. Coordinated movements in interest rates, as agreed in Nyborg and tested last November, would provide the second line of defence. The problem is that these two instruments may be insufficient, even if used jointly and aggressively. Firstly, the financial assets that economic agents may ask their central bank to convert into a foreign currency are a large multiple of official reserves, and secondly, the size of the interest-rate changes needed to offset the expected return from a realignment may far exceed the central bank's room for manoeuvre.

In these circumstances, the two lines of defence mentioned above would need to be supplemented by a third. This would consist in a 'recycling mechanism' through which the 'system' would be ready to counteract destabilising capital movements by providing temporary accommodation of the demand for currency diversification, for the time and in the amount necessary to change market expectations. If a substantial proportion of economic agents in the area want to convert financial assets (not necessarily *monetary* assets) from currency A to currency B, the system should accommodate the change in preferences by withdrawing A-assets and issuing B-assets. If central banks are successful, this operation will end with a profit for the authorities and a loss for private agents, because A-assets are likely to carry a higher nominal yield than B-assets.[3]

There is an analogy here with the textbook case of a central bank response to a run on banks: the demand to convert deposits into banknotes should be fully accommodated, without worrying about the monetary statistics, to restore full confidence in the 'parity' between banknotes and deposits. The EMS case differs in that runs and the lender-of-last-resort function take a transnational and intercurrency form.

The technicalities of this mechanism are not too hard to work out in detail. The difficulties are of another kind, and there are several. Firstly, it may be difficult both to decide what is the cause of the market pressures and to agree that their nature makes defence of the existing parities appropriate. Some lack of convergence in price and cost developments will always exist and increase the attractiveness of the 'easier' option of a realignment, with exchange rates taking the full burden of adjustment. In the circumstances described above, a realignment would not serve the interests of the Community as a whole, nor serve those of individual countries. It could severely damage the export industry of the appreciating country and the pursuit of price stability of the depreciating one.

Secondly, decisions and action have to be taken *jointly*, to a much greater extent than was necessary between realignments during the earlier phase of the system. While joint discretionary action in Phase One was essentially confined to procedures or realignments, it will now be needed during the week rather than at weekends. This will require intense consultation and cooperation among central banks, almost to the point of their acting as the departments of a single monetary authority.

My conclusion with regard to Phase Two is that its objective is the survival of the system, and that it should not last too long.

4   Phase Three: monetary union

Phase Three will be characterised by the full implementation of items 1 and 2 of the inconsistent quartet – i.e., free trade and capital mobility – to the point of eliminating all nationality distinctions within the Community between economic agents, services and products. Note that 'trade' is to be taken as comprising services, and 'capital' as including financial assets of all possible maturities, including cash. The time horizon for reaching this stage and completing the internal market is 1992, the date set by the Single European Act, which has been approved and ratified by member states as an amendment to the Treaty of Rome.

In the monetary and financial area, the implementation of the programme implies the elimination of all the remaining restrictions on the full mobility of capital and the complete freedom for households, firms and financial intermediaries in different member states to demand and supply financial services. The money and credit available to economic agents in the Community will be the overall money and credit supply of the Community as a whole, limited only by their ability to gather information and cover transaction costs.

If nothing is done about items 3 and 4 of the inconsistent quartet, the inconsistency will emerge in full and the process of restoring consistency could develop in an uncontrolled and destructive way. It could take several alternative routes, possibly leading to a breakdown of the common market as a result of failure to complete the internal market by 1992, a reintroduction of comprehensive capital and exchange controls, or a transition from fixed to floating exchange rates. These would be only the first step towards a '*rémise en question*' of the whole '*acquis communautaire*'. The existing degree of trade integration and the painful problem of unemployment in most European countries would, sooner or later, make the unravelling of the existing Community arrangements unavoidable. Breaches of Community law, failures to adopt the national legislation necessary to implement Community directives, congestion in the presentation and examination of cases before the Court of Justice, a weakening of the policing action of the Commission for infringements of the law, growing recourse to safeguard clauses and retaliatory measures against foreign producers, would all be part of this unravelling scenario. The latter would not necessarily be visibly dramatic; it could advance in a creeping way and take the form of an historical decline.

In the long term, the only solution to the inconsistency is to complement the internal market with a monetary union. It would be unrealistic to expect the Community to be able to square a circle that has never been squared – i.e., to let national monetary policies follow their own course and yet expect macroeconomic and trade discipline to survive for the area as a whole.

The monetary union issue has an institutional and a functional aspect. The former concerns the legal provisions, the procedures of approval, etc.; the latter concerns the definition of the monetary regime. The debate on this subject, particularly in official circles, gives the impression that the functional aspects are sufficiently well identified – as regards both the definition and the solution of the problems – while the institutional aspects are the difficult ones. Since in most countries central banks occupy a rather delicate and special position, it is understandable that they should be particularly sensitive to the institutional problem. Moreover, it is in the institutional and legal field that the crucial questions of sovereignty and responsibility emerge in full. It is possible, however, that the alleged difficulties of the legal and institutional aspects of the problem actually conceal problems of political will or a natural reluctance to consider fundamental changes in the seemingly solid ground on which the existing institutions rest. If a satisfactory solution were found to the functional aspects of the problem, the solution of the institutional aspects might not be so difficult, apart from the problem of political will.

My aim here is obviously not to present a comprehensive analysis of the problems of creating a monetary union, nor even to identify all the aspects that would have to be considered. I will confine myself to some thoughts touching, in turn, on the functional and the institutional aspects.

5   Functional aspects of a monetary union

If the monetary union were set up, with one currency being declared *the* currency of the area and one central bank being created to issue and control it, the solution of the functional problems would be straight-forward and the process would repeat the historical experience of many nation-states. The difficulty in a top-down approach of this kind would be mainly political, the replacement of national currencies and national central banks being such a momentous move that most of the parties involved would not be willing to consider it except as part of a plan for full political union.

It is questionable, however, whether this move is really necessary. My own opinion is that it takes less than is usually thought to get the substance of a monetary union. In reality, it could be built on what already exists with little need for change in what is presently visible to economic agents. Let me briefly list some of the things that are dis-pensable.

It would not be necessary for the existing visible symbols of national monetary systems to disappear: currency denominations, banknotes and central banks could well continue to exist in a monetary union. This would not require much more 'tolerance' than was required to let Banco di Napoli and Banco di Sicilia continue to issue their banknotes for more than sixty years after the unification of Italy, or to let the Bank of Scotland issue pounds sterling today.

Fiscal policy does not have to be formally unified either. Let me explain why. In every political system, the overall budgetary function is shared by central and local governments; this is also true for the Community. The allocative considerations that guide the attribution of different tax and expenditure functions to different levels of government do not necessarily coincide with those presiding over the choice of an optimal currency area. Indeed, full coincidence of the geographical jurisdiction of the bulk of budgetary and monetary powers offers an opportunity, but also entails a danger. The opportunity is to conduct fiscal and monetary policy in a coordinated way. The danger is to use the printing press to finance the deficit. In a political union, the budget would almost by definition reach a size consistent with the scope of playing a macroecono-mic role since essential public goods such as defence, internal security and justice would be provided at the level of the union. The opportunity would be created, but also the danger.

The crucial question about fiscal policy, however, is whether there will be a serious risk of the monetary union being undermined by independent and possibly uncoordinated budgetary policies conducted by member countries. In other words: should item 4 of the inconsistent quartet include monetary policy only, or should it include fiscal policy as well?

In a monetary union with a fully integrated internal market but decentralised fiscal authorities, national governments would be subject to disciplinary factors that are now lacking in the Community. The first would be provided by the need to make recourse for their financing requirement to a large (and for them uncontrollable) capital market encompassing the whole area. In borrowing on that market, member countries would be seen solely with 'market-minded' eyes, not as the source of regulation and protection. They would be treated according to their creditworthiness, although the debt problem experienced in recent years shows how difficult the assessment is for sovereign borrowers. The second disciplinary factor would be the impossibility of monetising the debt, since the printing press would be at the level of the union.

Historically, the combination of these two factors has been considered, and proved, to be sufficient to promote fiscal discipline and coordination. With the exception of Australia, there is no constitutional system – not even among countries with a high degree of decentralisation and federalism – in which local government budgets are subject to the authority and control of the union.

In Europe, it can be argued that the size of member states relative to the size of the union – both in general economic terms and in terms of their respective budgets – makes it questionable whether a more binding process of fiscal policy coordination would be necessary to make the monetary union work. Of course, national fiscal policies will have to be consistent with participation in the union. They will have to react to real disturbances that cause a change in equilibrium exchange rates and avoid determining such changes. The elements of discipline outlined above should, in general, put sufficient pressure on member countries to bring about such consistency, although the presence of these elements does not rule out fiscal irresponsibility on the part of one member country with regard to the burden of taxation and the use of fiscal deficits for stabilisation purposes. Nor should it be forgotten how technically and politically difficult it would be to limit fiscal sovereignty for the purpose of stabilisation, since budgetary power is tied to the exercise of an allocative function and firmly placed in the hands of elected national parliaments. Formal coordination would certainly be desirable, but I do not think it should be regarded as a prerequisite for establishing the union.

Finally, turning to exchange rates, I wonder if their definitive and irrevocable fixity should be considered an indispensable aspect of the monetary union from the start. I would suggest that it should not, although I am aware that this runs counter to well-established convictions. Provided they remained under the firm control of the federal monetary authority and were decided only in special circumstances, parity changes could be the best policy instrument for coping with unusual developments in one country (the mind turns naturally to exceptional developments in the labour market or in the social field).

The notion of a currency area is economic, not geographical. The same portion of territory may (and usually does) simultaneously belong to more than one monetary area, depending on the different markets to which the various goods and residing agents belong. A vast territory such as the Community might well include sub-markets where local currencies could continue to be efficiently used.

What *is* then needed for a monetary union to exist? The simple answer is: *one* monetary policy and hence one monetary authority, entrusted with the necessary decisionmaking powers and operational instruments. This means that the supply of money for the whole Community – the one that will be available to every single economic agent in each country when capital markets are fully integrated – should be based upon the same monetary base – i.e., one base money aggregate should be the ultimate source of total money and credit in the whole Community. Again, this may not require the replacement of the national highpowered monies in the two layers of the system of money creation that exist in our countries and are described in textbooks. It may require adding a third layer, a Community monetary base that would play *vis-à-vis* national base monies the role that the latter play *vis-à-vis* bank deposits. This role is made up of customary and regulatory elements, such as the legal tender and lender-of-last-resort functions, wide acceptance of that money as a means of settlement, and the requirement that reserves proportional to the outstanding national base money be held in that instrument. The creation of such a third layer would not be a novelty. Indeed, it used to be occupied by gold; after which it was occupied by the dollar until the terms of the 'Triffin dilemma' came into full effect; contrary to the initial plan, the SDR has failed to occupy it.

It is natural to envisage the ECU as the base money of the Community. Each central bank would be allowed to expand its monetary base proportionally to the highpowered ECUs in its balance sheet, in much the same way as commercial banks can expand deposits only up to a maximum multiple to their holdings of highpowered money. ECU deposits with the European central bank would be the instrument for final payments among central banks, and perhaps among commercial banks as well.

In the meantime, the ECU we know, the so-called 'private ECU', would continue to function as a parallel currency, with all economic agents in the Community free to use it as they liked. Only a small share of the payments system in the Community economy would be occupied by the official ECU but that share would be a sufficient lever to organise a monetary union.

Of course, the main problem in this respect is that of defining the 'rule' and the techniques governing the creation of total highpowered ECUs. The latter should be central bank operations whereby base money is created against assets acquired by the European central bank. As to the former, rather than a mechanical rule, operational discretion should be allowed under the statutory mandate of promoting exchange-rate and price stability in the Community.

6   Institutional aspects of a monetary union

If the foregoing functional problems could be dealt with in a satisfactory way, what are now regarded as the most difficult aspects – namely the institutional ones – would probably prove less intractable than they seem today. I will discuss two: the relationships between political and monetary union, and the legal basis of the monetary union.

Without political union, it is argued, there can be no monetary union. While it would be paradoxical to think of a political union without a monetary union, economic analysis and historical experience support the view that the converse is possible. Neither the gold standard nor the Bretton Woods system, which in a way performed as a monetary union for some decades, were based on a political union. From an economic point of view, the relevant meaning of the term 'political union' is that the 'rule of law' should apply to the whole area, and that certain public goods should be provided at the highest level of government. As to the first proposition, the Treaty of Rome and the body of Community legislation that already exists (or is planned to exist by 1992) provides a unified rule of law for the whole Community in the field of economic activity. As to the second, I have argued above that a wider budgetary policy for the union is desirable but not actually indispensable, and also that it involves some danger for the independence of the monetary authority at the Community level.

I am not suggesting, of course, that the creation of a monetary union is simply a technical decision. It is a political decision of the greatest importance, since it touches fundamental questions of sovereignty and modifies the economic constitution of member countries. This is why technical institutions and authorities, such as central banks, have neither the right to impose it nor the right to impede it. The contribution they can (and should) be asked to make to the sound development of the monetary order of the Community is to explain and clarify what can (and cannot) be achieved with a given type of technical authority, to help design an appropriate new regime when the decision to implement one has been taken, and to operate the existing regime as well as possible. However, recognising these links between the technical and the political dimension of a monetary union does not mean that the latter is impossible without political union. It means that the new order needs to be created by an act of political will and provide for an appropriate relationship between the technical and political levels of responsibility. This would be very difficult to achieve by a loose group of countries without institutional links. It is possible for a structured constitutional system such as the Community.

The second aspect is the legal basis of monetary union. Without a new treaty, it is said, there can be no monetary union. This proposition is widely accepted and was at the origin of the insertion in the Single European Act of Article 102A which mentions in para. 2 that 'if the further development in the field of economic and monetary policy requires institutional modifications, the dispositions included in article 236 of the Treaty apply'. Again, neither the historian nor the economist would necessarily agree. The former would once again recall that the gold standard was never formally legislated, and could go back to the old eighteenth-century debate about the advantages and disadvantages of having a written constitution. The latter cannot ignore the very strong customary element embedded in every monetary system. Money was not invented by legislators, nor was it the consequence of creating a central bank. It was created by the needs of commerce, and only subsequently was it regulated by law and managed by central banks.

One can imagine a fully customary or a fully formal route to monetary union. The customary route would pass through growing *de facto* acceptance of the ECU as a convenient instrument gradually performing all the functions of money. In this process the ECU would develop an 'independent' exchange and interest rate as an increasing amount of goods and services were priced in it. There is room for ECU pricing both in the wholesale area of large contracts for primary goods and commodities and in the retail area for goods and consumers spread throughout the Community. As the need arose, essential stabilisation functions would be performed by member central banks, either individually or collectively. The EMCF and the BIS already provide a potential framework to be exploited to this end. They are the place where central bank governors meet at the same interval as the FOMC meetings at the Fed. The BIS is the institution that hosts the ECU clearing system and acts, with full operational capacity, as an agent for central banks. The monetary base function is now performed for the ECU system by member currencies and member central banks, but it could be exerted collectively and be based on the ECU if open-market operations in ECUs were developed further and official ECUs made available for such operations. An operational connection between the clearing and the official ECU would be the natural way to promote such a development.

I have argued elsewhere[4] that *if* the wind of habit blew with sufficient strength, developments along the customary route could go very far indeed without meeting unsurmountable legal or logical obstacles, perhaps to the point of eventually imposing the formalisation of a monetary union. The system would be one of monetary federalism, the ECU would be a widely and increasingly accepted parallel common currency for that layer of Community markets that spreads over the whole area. Consistency with the other currencies and monetary policies would be imposed together by irreversible full mobility of capital and growing cooperation among central banks.

A similar (but not identical) customary route seems to be envisaged by the Bundesbank when it outlines a situation in which many Community currencies would, after achieving the same degree of stability and 'openness', be fully interchangeable and provide equally attractive alternatives to the dollar.

The formal route, in turn, would involve a new treaty creating a European monetary authority and defining its status and functions, with a procedure similar to that establishing the Federal Reserve System and the International Monetary Fund. The new institution would replace or federate the existing central banks, and a common currency would replace or parallel the existing currencies. Decentralised solutions of monetary federalism, such as those outlined above, could be adopted as an alternative to the more traditional centralised ones, the functional and the institutional choices being to a large extent independent.

The two routes correspond to two extremes, both of which are possible but unlikely. I regard it to be both more realistic and more desirable to envisage a sequence of events in which the customary and the legal elements are dynamically intertwined. Of the two components of any modern monetary system, one, the currency, will be pushed primarily by the customary factor, while the second, the central bank, will require more legal and institutional initiatives to provide the necessary independence and operational capacity. Market forces and the political will would thus interact with each performing in its own field. Monetary authorities would remain as a technical entity placed in between, operating on markets for policy purposes.

7 Conclusions

The European Monetary System that we have known since 1979 is based on two obligations subscribed to by each participant: to maintain the market exchange rate within given margins around central rates, and to change the latter only in accord with the other participants. For nine years the two obligations have been fulfilled and the system has made a substantial contribution to lowering the average inflation rate in the Community and narrowing the earlier large inflation differentials, as well as preserving open trade in a period of rapidly rising unemployment in Europe and growing protectionism in the world at large.

Partly as a result of this success, the Community has set itself new and ambitious objectives to be achieved by the year 1992. These include the complete dismantlement of all physical and regulatory barriers to the free circulation of goods and services, and the complete liberalisation of capital movements, including short-term capital and monetary instruments. In implementing this programme, the problem will emerge of the contradiction between full trade integration, complete mobility of capital, fixity of exchange rates, and as yet unchallenged national autonomy in the conduct of monetary policy. This contradiction is demonstrated by economic analysis and confirmed by historical experience.

I have argued that the only solution to this contradiction that does not entail the undoing of the common market is to move towards a monetary union. Basically, this means adding a third obligation to the two mentioned above: the obligation to link the process of money and credit expansion in each country to that of a single monetary base for the whole Community. A monetary union requires a single policy, but not necessarily a single currency and even less a unique name. In turn, the oneness of policy requires operational instruments and regulatory powers, entrusted to an institution with full authority and operational independence.

The historical and political importance of creating a monetary union in Europe can hardly be underestimated. It would be a decisive step towards full political union, as the creation of a Community of defence in the early 1950s would have been. As such, it will have to reckon with traditions and attitudes that are deeply rooted in the habits, ideas and sometimes prejudices of economic agents, institutions, analysts and politicians. That such difficulties and obstacles can be surmounted is far from obvious, and perhaps is not even likely.

The considerations I have developed above are thus by no means meant to minimise the difficulty of moving to a monetary union; they are reflections developed on economic and technical grounds, not the programme of a politician. At this technical and economic level, it can be argued that a monetary union is a necessary complement of a fully integrated market, that there are no insurmountable technical difficulties in setting it up in a way that builds on existing realities, and that an institutionalised budgetary union is not a prerequisite. This in no way lessens the political difficulty, but it may help to have it called by its true name.

NOTES
1 For a broader definition of the concept of 'performance', see Padoa-Schioppa et al. (1987), Chapter 2.
2 See also Padoa-Schioppa (1985).
3 Attempts to defend the parity with funds raised in the market are likely to fail (except perhaps in the case of a small country) because they would leave unchanged the excess supply of the currency under attack in the Community market as a whole. What is needed is a means of offsetting the pressure of market participants by monetary authorities taking an equal and opposite exchange-rate position. With unchanged parities, this will not inflate the aggregate money supply of the EMS, nor will it stimulate demand in the country whose currency is more demanded. The overshooting of monetary targets set for that country is offset by a fall in velocity.
4 See Padoa-Schioppa (1988).

REFERENCES
Padoa-Schioppa, T. (1985). 'Squaring the Circle, or the Conundrum of International Monetary Reform', *Catalyst, a Journal of Policy Debate*, Vol. 1, No. 1 (Spring).
Padoa-Schioppa, T. (1988). The ECO's Coming of Age', in M. Nighoff (ed.), *The Quest for National and Global Economic Stability*, Dordrecht: Khuver Academic Publishers.
Padoa-Schioppa, T. *et al.* (1987). *Efficiency, Stability and Equity*, Oxford: Oxford University Press.

13 A New Phase in the European Monetary System – Exchange-rate Constraint, Capital Liberalisation and Policy Coordination: a Report of the Conference Panel Discussion

Introductory statement

Lamberto Dini

It will be a useful introduction to this policy panel if I briefly recall the changes in the EMS mechanisms recently decided upon by the Committee of Governors of the EEC, the considerations that led the Governors to adopt them, and the underlying analytical framework.

1 Changes in the environment and their impact on EMS mechanisms

The good performance of the EMS has been due above all to the policies of its members, notably their willingness to take account of the requirements of the exchange-rate constraint in setting domestic objectives.

The EMS has also benefited, however, from certain factors and circumstances whose influence may be less favourable in the future. In fact:

(a) As long as the dollar was strong and expected to remain strong, capital flows from Europe to the US tended to depress the DM relative to the other EMS currencies, and to strengthen EMS cohesion because of the DM's role as a dollar substitute in international portfolios. The opposite has occurred since the dollar started to decline: weakness in the dollar has caused strains and tended to amplify tensions generated within the EMS by divergences in economic performances and policies.

(b) The acceleration of financial integration and the removal of many of the exchange controls in France and Italy have increased capital mobility

385

in Europe. As a result, the external constraint on domestic policies has become more stringent and the potential repercussions on exchange rates of divergent monetary conditions in EMS countries have been enhanced.

(c) While inflation differentials have narrowed to their lowest values since the late 1960s, there remain significant differences between EMS countries in fiscal positions as well as in unemployment, demographic trends, and potential GDP growth.

(d) The priority assigned to reducing inflation and external deficits was an important cohesive factor in the early years of the EMS; there is a risk that the increased importance now attributed by member countries to 'real' macroeconomic performance may lead to less consensus on policy objectives.

These developments also have a bearing on the technical management of the EMS. The combination of reduced inflation differentials and increased mobility of capital means that financial factors must have recently played a major role in the determination of interest-rate differentials that are appropriate from the standpoint of exchange-rate stability. At the same time, the 'real' cost of adjusting interest rates in the light of external objectives is potentially higher. In other words, the potential conflict between the external and domestic objectives of monetary policy may have become more acute.

These developments have been accompanied by certain changes in the technical functioning of the EMS, some of the mechanisms of which seemed to require adaptation. Contrary to expectations, interventions have mostly been intramarginal. In addition, there has been a marked increase in the use of Community currencies for such interventions, notably since the dollar started to decline. The availability of these currencies was limited, however, since such interventions did not qualify for access to the very short-term financing (VSTF) facility.

2   Changes in EMS mechanisms and management techniques

The Governors have now agreed on a number of changes in EMS arrangements and mechanisms. One of their main purposes was to prevent the new conditions from loosening exchange-rate cohesion and causing the EMS to degenerate into a crawling peg. The changes are thus designed to strengthen the system and enhance its ability to forestall and cope with exchange-rate pressures.

(a) While agreeing that monetary policies will have to remain geared to price stability in the medium term, this objective will be pursued flexibly in the short term, leaving greater room for exchange-rate considerations in the determination of interest-rate policies.

It has been agreed that making fuller use of the EMS fluctuation band can help enhance operators' perception of the exchange-rate risk inherent in taking speculative positions.

More active use of interest rates and flexible management of exchange rates within the EMS band should help reduce the need for intervention in foreign-exchange markets.

Appropriate use of all the instruments available for maintaining exchange-rate stability will be assessed within a strengthened procedure for joint monitoring of member countries' economic performances and policies.

(b) At the same time, the Governors have agreed to increase the means available within the system for combating exchange-rate pressures. Specifically:

(i) There is now a presumption that when intramarginal interventions in EEC currencies are acceptable to the issuing central banks, they will also be eligible for VSTF within certain limits (i.e., twice the debtor quota of the debtor central bank in the short-term financing mechanism); the duration of financing under the VSTF has been extended by one month (to a maximum of three and a half months), and the amount that can be automatically renewed has been doubled (it will now be equal to twice the debtor quota in the short-term financing mechanism).

(ii) Moreover, it has been agreed that, without altering the formal rules that govern use of the official ECU, the settlement in ECUs of outstanding claims in the VSTF will be accepted beyond 50 per cent, and up to 100 per cent, provided that this does not result in an imbalanced composition of reserves or in excessive debtor and creditor positions building up within the EMCF. After two years of experience with this arrangement the formal rules relating to the official ECU will be reviewed.

3   The philosophy underlying the Governors' decisions

It is worth stressing that:

(a) The restrictions on the use of EEC currencies and the ECU for intramarginal interventions have now been greatly reduced. However, this is basically meant to increase the system's flexibility and to adapt it to changed circumstances; it is not meant to lead to systematically increased resort to EMS credit or to a build-up of net positions with the EMCF.

(b) The Governors have stressed the need for improved and more closely coordinated management of the EMS, as a way of preventing strains from developing and avoiding the need for intervention. They see the expanded scope for interventions primarily as a deterrent; there is a clear implication that greater use will have to be made of domestic monetary instruments to maintain exchange-rate stability.

(c) Increased availability of EEC currencies and strengthened coordination of interest-rate policies seem to imply greater symmetry in burden-sharing, at least in the short term. The reaffirmation of the commitment to monetary stability in setting medium-term objectives for monetary policy is the necessary counterweight, ensuring that the expanded facilities of the system do not endanger the stability-oriented policies of strong-currency countries.

A specific safeguard has been introduced, by allowing a creditor central bank whose currency has been provided through the VSTF for intramarginal intervention to ask for repayment in its own currency. In this way, any monetary effects of intervention on creditor countries will be entirely offset.

Of course, only continued adherence by all EMS members to the objectives of low inflation and exchange-rate stability can provide the ultimate safeguard.

Reflections on the EMS experience

Peter B. Kenen

The study by Tommaso Padoa-Schioppa (Chapter 12 in this volume) takes up several of the points I was planning to raise. I will not go over those points again, but will try to collect those that remain into a coherent presentation.

Two years ago, Emil Claassen asked me to give a paper at a conference in Florence. I promised to write one with the title 'The adjustable peg is alive and well and living in Europe'. I failed to keep that promise, and my failure may have spared me some embarrassment. If I were writing that paper now, I would have to turn the title into a question: '*Is* the adjustable peg alive and well and living in Europe?'

An answer to that question must weigh carefully the 'inconsistent quartet' issues that Padoa-Schioppa has examined. My own assessment leads me to believe that the EMS version of the adjustable peg may be in failing health. That assessment is influenced by some issues he did not raise, as well as those that figured in his analysis.

Let me focus narrowly on a single aspect of EMS experience. How have EMS members been able to agree on realignments with comparatively little market disruption or political commotion? Conversely, how have they been able to avoid realignments when the foreign-exchange market was signalling its view that a realignment was needed or impending?

Let us acknowledge at once that politics may be more helpful than economics in answering these questions, even as politics were more important than economics in explaining why the EMS came into being – a point that too many conference studies have overlooked when making cost–benefit calculations and measuring the value of the EMS as an engine of disinflation in the early 1980s. There *was* an economic case for creating the EMS, it is evoked by the well-known phrase about making Europe into a zone of monetary stability. But its founders were strongly influenced by the need to dramatise the long-term goal of European integration; let us not forget that when we appraise the performance of the EMS. We must set against its economic successes the lack of progress on the institutional side – the failure to create the European Monetary Fund – and must likewise appraise Padoa-Schioppa's proposals for further reform in the light of that long-term political goal, not get bogged down in technicalities.

The existence and cohesion of the European Community must surely take some credit for the successes of the EMS. No government has dropped out as France had left the earlier snake, rejoined it, and then left again, although influential voices were urging France to leave the EMS and allow the franc to float in the early days of the Socialist government. No government has blocked or walked away from negotiations concerning a realignment. And though it may be difficult to prove that the EMS has brought about convergence in its members' macroeconomic performance, there is encouraging evidence of close cooperation among the participating central banks to manage capital movements by managing interest-rate differences.

Turning from politics to economics, it is useful to look at the recent theoretical literature on collapsing exchange-rate regimes, to ask why the EMS has thus far escaped the fate predicted by that literature. There are three systemic reasons and one accidental one.

First, the frequency of realignments has allowed the EMS to make large cumulative changes in exchange rates, needed to offset changes in relative costs and prices, but to make them by small increments. Indeed, a significant number of realignments have been sufficiently small for the new and old bands to overlap. This means, of course, that the closing out of short positions after a realignment can cause the weak currency to appreciate rather than depreciate, and turn speculative profits into losses. In other words, speculators have not been offered the old one-way option that they exploited happily under the Bretton Woods system, when realignments were infrequent and had thus to be quite large. The convergence of inflation rates within the EMS – whether or not due to the EMS itself – should make it even easier to keep realignments small during the next several years, and this could improve the health of the adjustable peg. (It must be added, however, that other European countries may be increasingly reluctant to accept the German unemployment rate as the cost of accepting the German inflation rate and may therefore press for realignments large enough to alter real exchange rates.)

Second, expectations of a realignment have not been self-fulfilling, because of the unusual credit arrangements in the EMS. In the theoretical literature, the expectation of a realignment can bring a realignment about by producing speculative capital movements that devour the central bank's reserves and prevent it from continuing to peg the exchange rate. This happened under the Bretton Woods system. But EMS central banks have unusually deep pockets – access to the very short-term (credit) facility (VSTF). It is, of course, a *very* short-term facility, which means that central banks are not likely to abuse it by borrowing to finance long-lasting balance of payments deficits. But they can combat speculation effectively, especially when speculators can be convinced that they were wrong to gamble on a near-term realignment and thus induced to liquidate their short positions, giving central banks the resources they need to repay their drawings from the VSTF. (The recent changes in EMS credit arrangements described by Lamberto Dini give even greater importance to this point. Central banks combatting speculative pressures will be able to do so before their currencies reach their lower limits – the circumstance that often leads to large-scale speculation.)

I have deliberately emphasised the central banks' ability to engage in counter-speculation rather than the role of capital controls in limiting the volume of speculation. I do not deny the practical importance of French and Italian capital controls, which appear to be benign in normal circumstances but to bite hard at the margin, if only for short periods. But they must be dismantled by 1992, and it is important to realise that they have not been the only defence against speculative capital movements.

Third, the Deutsche mark is the only world-class currency in the EMS, and it has usually been the strong currency within the system. These circumstances have worked to limit the volume and duration of speculative flows. Suppose that the foreign-exchange market comes to expect a revaluation of the Deutsche mark *vis-à-vis* the French franc. Frenchmen will sell francs for Deutsche marks. But they are the only large holders of francs; anyone else wanting to speculate against the franc must borrow francs before selling them. This may limit the volume of speculation and turn it around rapidly (because Frenchmen need their francs for domestic transactions, and others will want to pay back their debts). Now let us imagine that Margaret Thatcher changes her mind, allowing Britain to become a full member of the EMS and bringing in another world-class currency. Suppose that the foreign-exchange market comes to expect a revaluation of the Deutsche mark *vis-à-vis* the pound. There are many more footloose holders of sterling than footloose holders of francs, and a much larger amount of money could flow from London to Frankfurt than currently flows from Paris to Frankfurt. Furthermore, this would not be borrowed money (though that would move too), which means that it might not return speedily to London. I find it easy enough to understand why Britain should want to participate fully in the EMS; I find it more difficult to explain other governments' enthusiasm for British membership, which could seriously impair the health of the adjustable peg.

The point I have just made about speculative flows was dependent in part on the strength of the Deutsche mark in the EMS. There would be large flows of footloose, non-resident money from Germany to other EMS countries if the foreign-exchange market came to expect a devaluation of the Deutsche mark. The historical accident I promised to invoke in explaining the success of the EMS is likewise dependent on the strength of the Deutsche mark. It has confronted the German authorities with a dilemma that is peculiarly acute for them and has made it easier for EMS members to agree on realignments. If the German authorities resisted a realignment, they would have to face another disagreeable prospect – a large and rapid increase of the domestic money supply consequent on borrowing by other central banks having to defend their currencies. If the Deutsche mark had not been the principal candidate for revaluation, or the German authorities had not been so strongly committed meeting their money-supply targets, disagreements about realignments would have been harder to resolve.

But two trends may be working to make realignments more difficult in the future, which could also thus impair the health of the adjustable peg. First, markets seem to be learning how to predict realignments, and the figures on reserve flows before and after realignments suggest that anticipatory capital flows have been getting larger. Second, and more worrisome, the movement to eliminate capital controls and the possible accession of the United Kingdom could bring into play a much larger volume of speculative funds.

These trends could impair the viability of the EMS if they lead the authorities to postpone realignments merely to disappoint the market's expectations. It would be better to go the other way by introducing an element of randomness into the timing of realignments, along lines discussed during the conference. I am not proposing that exchange rates be moved up and down merely to make noise and confuse the market. I *am* suggesting that it would sometimes make sense to realign exchange rates before it is perfectly clear that a realignment is required by a change in fundamentals, even at the risk of having to reverse it later.

The commitment to eliminate capital controls by 1992 will have broad consequences for the EMS and its member governments. The resulting increase in capital mobility will intensify the need for central banks to focus on exchange-rate stability, foregoing the use of monetary policy for any other purpose. In other words, there will be less scope for sterilised intervention. There will still be one degree of freedom in the system: aggregate (or German) monetary policy will still be available for the pursuit of macroeconomic stability. But that degree of freedom may be used up by the requirements of the global system – the need to stabilise the ECU (or Deutsche mark) *vis-à-vis* the US dollar. European governments must therefore be prepared to make more active use of fiscal policy, in a consistent but not strictly convergent fashion. And this will require a major change in political mythology: fiscal rectitude is fine, but not fiscal rigidity. And institutional changes may be needed to permit more frequent tax-rate changes; the demands of macroeconomic management cannot be made to wait until some long-planned tax reform has finally ripened.

Do not misunderstand me. I am not proposing a new attempt to fine-tune the European economy. I am merely calling for more flexibility in the use of the only policy instrument that will be available once monetary policy has to be assigned primarily to the maintenance of stable exchange rates. But I am also urging EMS members not to fall into the Bretton Woods trap – not to abandon exchange-rate adjustability until they are ready to move to 'Phase Three' in Padoa-Schioppa's proposal for progress toward full-fledged monetary union. Careful thought might also be given to John Driffill's suggestion (Chapter 8 in this volume) that there should perhaps be two sets of EMS members. Some might move quickly to truly fixed rates (or, at least, to very narrow margins); others should join Italy and maintain wide bands to give them scope for sizeable exchange-rate changes without also giving the market a one-way speculative option.

Finally, allow me to question the all-or-nothing character of the 1992 objective. It may not be impossible – and might be quite helpful – to modify rather than abolish French and Italian capital controls, leaving in place a system that bites even harder at the margin in times of intense speculative pressure, without inhibiting capital movements in more tranquil periods. This is perhaps a more satisfactory compromise than the system of dual exchange rates proposed by Rudiger Dornbusch. In an imperfect world with sticky prices, all policies and institutional arrangements are necessarily second best. The theory of optimal intervention tells us to remove the offending imperfection, the stickiness of prices in this instance, but that is not feasible. And the best of the available second-best policies may be to tamper with the markets that magnify the costs of the imperfection – financial markets in this instance. They are the ones that put pressure on nominal exchange rates, forcing realignments when rates are pegged and causing rates to overshoot when they are allowed to float. This is the appropriate framework in which to assess the maintenance of modified capital controls. I venture to predict, moreover, that capital controls will not be the only or most serious departure from the 1992 objective when that year arrives.

European currency: an Italian view*

Rainer S. Masera

1 Introduction

The political ideas and technical studies that were to lead up to the inception of the EMS on 13 March 1979 began to take on a recognisable shape ten years ago.

The revival of interest in the process of monetary unification in Europe is traditionally associated with the speech that Roy Jenkins (at the time President of the Commission of the European Communities) gave at the European University Institute in Florence on 27 October 1977. The idea of formulating a new framework for exchange rates in alternative to the snake gained ground between 1977 and 1978, when the German Chancellor (Helmut Schmidt) and the French President (Valéry Giscard d'Estaing) agreed on the desirability of giving new impetus to the process of monetary and exchange integration in Europe. The fall in the dollar during that period, coupled with exchange-rate fluctuations, was threatening the cohesion of the Community by tempting countries to undertake competitive devaluations. The view that the weakness of the US currency should be countered by an area of monetary stability in Europe gathered strength: a new Bretton Woods on the other side of the Atlantic.

The breadth of the political vision and the implications of the project resulted in stress being immediately placed on how exchange-rate stability and the creation of a European monetary symbol – the ECU – and a monetary fund involving the sharing of reserves were to be the cornerstone for promoting growth, gradually returning to full employ-ment, reducing regional disparities and completing the integration of the Community. In addition to the problems inherent in the convergence of currencies, there was also agreement on the need to focus on strengthen-ing the economies of the so-called less prosperous countries, which in the Community of nine included Italy.

The importance and comprehensiveness of the project enabled Italy to participate. The Prime Minister (Giulio Andreotti) was persuaded of the merits of the plan, which Schmidt and Giscard d'Estaing outlined for the first time at the European Summit held in Copenhagen in April 1978, in terms of the possibility it offered of promoting disinflation and growth in Italy by anchoring the country to Europe. The Governor of the Bank of Italy (Paolo Baffi) subsequently succeeded – in particular, by negotiating the 6 per cent fluctuation band directly with Chancellor Schmidt at the behest of Andreotti – in reconciling the strictness of the exchange-rate mechanism with the conditions of the Italian economy. The political choices that sealed Italy's participation proved to be complex and not without further consequences.

The ambitious and innovative political driving force behind the creation of the EMS was somewhat circumscribed in the meetings of the commit-tees of experts that worked out the operational details of the system during 1978. On the other hand, the actual working of the system in its more than eight years of existence can be considered a major success, if it is compared – as it should be – with the gradual disintegration of the international monetary system. However, the resilience of the exchange-rate mechanism and the downward convergence of inflation rates have not led to the institutional progress foreseen not only in the initial design but also in the documents establishing the EMS.

The actual operation of the system reveals just how important a contribution monetary and exchange-rate policies have made to narrow-ing inflation differentials and reducing the size of realignments. The procedures for arriving at agreement on changes in central rates – albeit difficult and sometimes tiring – have provided a basically satisfactory solution to the underlying problem of a fixed-but-adjustable exchange-rate system: given n currencies, only $n-1$ exchange rates can be determined independently.

The discipline imposed by the system – which has made itself felt in the determination of nominal incomes and the planning of budget balances – has encouraged the acceptance of changes in central rates that did not fully accommodate inflation differentials, thereby stimulating domestic and external monetary convergence. On the other hand, real exchange rates have never been allowed to get seriously out of line with the so-called economic fundamentals for any length of time, by contrast with developments among the major currencies with floating regimes.

The limited freedom of capital movements helped to curb speculative attacks against central rates, causing changes suggested by past or feared inflation to be delayed. For a long time, moreover, the appreciation of the dollar and the growing US deficit on current account mitigated tensions within the system, both by weakening competitive pressures and by boosting exports.

2 The EMS today, in the light of the Single European Act

Recognition of the value of the results achieved so far must nonetheless not lead to shortsighted complacency. The EMS has entered a new phase – one which holds out promise of progress towards the final objective of monetary unification in view of the convergence achieved in economic fundamentals, but which is not without dangers and tensions that may require the system to be adapted and strengthened. A first significant step toward this goal came with the changes in the EMS mechanisms decided in September this year by the Committee of the EEC Central Bank Governors, and presented to the EEC Ministers of Finance at the informal meeting in Nyborg on 12 September 1987.[1]

The Single European Act of 17 February 1986 aims at the establishment of an area without internal frontiers permitting the free movement of goods, persons, services and capital by 1992 so as to improve the allocation of resources and put a seal, thirty-five years after the signing of the Treaty of Rome, on the integration of Europe. The liberalisation of capital movements and the creation of a European financial market are therefore key objectives that will influence not only the conduct of monetary and credit policies in the coming years but also the structure of financial systems.

It needs to be recognised, however, that *complete* integration of national financial markets entails exchange rates remaining fixed. Otherwise financial assets held in different currencies will not be perfectly substitutable, an indispensable condition for full integration. Financial integration itself calls for monetary convergence. In principle, sovereignty in monetary matters – which takes the form of autonomy in controlling the money supply and the exchange rate – is not compatible with the objective of creating a *single* European financial market.

On the other hand, the benefits associated with currency integration depend in the final analysis on the ability to ensure (after a period of steady convergence) permanently stable exchange rates within the area – and, ultimately, a single currency. The advantages depend, in practice, on the scope for exploiting money more completely in terms of its three basic functions: as a unit of account, as a medium of exchange and as a store of value. In principle, a common currency reduces information and transaction costs, narrows the gap between private and social rates of return, leads to a more efficient allocation of resources both through space and over time, and diminishes the impact of destabilising shocks insofar as it implies the aggregation of diversified risks. It is obvious, however, that these advantages can be gained only to the extent that the currency area is able to ensure conditions of internal monetary stability, in terms of inflation and interest rates, at least equal to those ruling in the countries with more firmly established monetary discipline. It is also necessary to have – as indeed the Single European Act envisages – freedom of movement for products and factors of production. Otherwise there would be only a switch in risks, in the sense that variable barriers to transactions would take the place of variable exchange rates, in all probability at a higher real cost.

Lastly, it is necessary to limit and prevent rigidities – or even perverse movements with respect to productivity – in wage rates in the countries forming the area. The minimisation of the costs associated with overcoming balance of payments problems cannot be achieved exclusively by exploiting the mobility of the factors of production, but must also be able to rely on fiscal measures that are coordinated at the area level – and, when necessary, on recourse to corrective instruments such as incomes policy.

There is thus a close link between monetary and currency unification and the integration of financial markets. The final objective to be achieved must be clearly defined: in the first place, to permit the related costs to be assessed, with special reference to the renunciation of national sovereignty in monetary affairs and the partial loss of sovereignty in the use of deficit financing, as the budget constraint indicates; in the second, once the choice has been deliberately made, to permit the phases leading to the achievement of the objective to be defined.

The major change with which the EMS will have to come to grips in a period of exchange liberalisation, financial integration and the completion of a single European market is the gradual loss of national monetary autonomy. It will therefore be necessary to mark out a course that will allow controlled progress to be made while new methods and instruments are developed for the management of the monetary autonomy of the area as a whole.

This basic problem raises a number of specific ones that are nonetheless extremely important for the evolution of the EMS in the immediate future.

Progress toward European monetary integration obviously implies the need for participation in the exchange-rate mechanism to be extended to all the countries belonging to the EMS. The question arises principally in connection with the pound sterling, and the tensions that could develop as a result of the London financial market being subjected to the discipline of the exchange-rate mechanism, but the objective of a single market means that consideration also has to be given to the countries that have joined the Community only more recently. The role of the ECU itself, which I shall examine shortly, also suggests the same conclusion: all the currencies linked by the exchange-rate mechanism – and no others – should be included in the European monetary basket. This brings to the fore the issue of a two-speed Europe – with specific reference to monetary and financial integration – a question which will not be taken up here but which may well deserve more detailed study and an unprejudiced assessment of its far-reaching implications.

The present phase of dollar weakness and the need for America's trade balance to be re-equilibrated point to an international scenario that will work against EMS cohesion. Finally, the success achieved throughout Europe in bringing down the rate of inflation may mean that monetary stability will be given less priority among the objectives of economic policy.

3   Some proposals for strengthening monetary integration and achieving monetary stability in the EEC

These considerations lead on to the proposals for adapting and strengthening the EMS that are put forward in this section. For the sake of simplicity of exposition, three main paths for the transition to a single market and a single currency can be outlined. From a substantive point of view these three strands are so intertwined that considering them in isolation would not be appropriate.

The three paths that I identify in the advance towards monetary and currency unification are: (1) the inclusion of all the countries participating in the EMS in a stricter, but not yet rigid, exchange-rate mechanism that would promote the gradual stabilisation of exchange relations in Europe; (2) closer monetary policy and interest-rate coordination, with the monetary effects of intervention – which should be extended to the forward exchange market – in principle not being sterilised; and (3) the integration of the private and official markets for the ECU, which would come to play the role of a real European currency both inside the area and in international relations under the supervision and control of a European Monetary Fund.

a.   Exchange-rate mechanism

As for the exchange-rate mechanism, it will be necessary to avoid responding to the risks of instability outlined above by easing the discipline it imposes. Such action would not be consistent with the progress made so far in the pursuit of monetary stability and smaller inflation-rate differentials; it would have a negative effect on the credibility of the whole system. The survival of the EMS itself could be put at risk. At the same time, it will be necessary to allow exchange rates to move in both directions within the prescribed band with the aim of preventing operators from making easy and relatively certain capital gains by taking open positions on the eve of realignments. The anticipation of sizeable movements in market exchange rates when realignments are made is the most serious threat to the survival of the EMS.

One way to reduce this risk would be to play down realignments by making more frequent recourse to small changes in central rates, with such action even being entrusted to a technical body. This evolution towards a crawling-peg system nonetheless appears unsatisfactory in the light of the final objectives of the EMS. Small and relatively frequent changes in pivot rates would also reduce the emphasis on accompanying domestic policy adjustments, which should instead play an even greater role in fostering the process of monetary integration.

The proposal made here for enhancing the rigour of the exchange-rate system and its ability to act as a direct instrument as well as a catalyst of the monetary unification of EC countries – without, however, exposing the system to destabilising speculative attacks – consists of a two-pronged manoeuvre.

In the first place, the strictness of the system should be guaranteed not only by conformity with the permitted margins of fluctuation but primarily by the commitment of *all* the countries participating in the exchange-rate mechanism – with their currencies included in the ECU basket – to *keep the annual changes in their bilateral central rates within a given limit*, say 5 per cent in present circumstances.

The commitment would not involve the expectation – or, indeed, the likelihood – of real exchange rates getting out of line over time, since it would have to be supported by a parallel explicit undertaking to modify and correct domestic factors of cost–price pressure, notably in respect of wages and the budget.

The emphasis should therefore be shifted to addressing the factors which, at national level, impede or slow the pace towards attainment of the objective of monetary stability and exchange-rate cohesion. Participation in the EMS would thus automatically imply that parliaments, governments and economic agents in general would have to accept, in the light of the Single European Act, the implications for their actions of the process of monetary and financial integration.

In particular, this would involve, in my opinion, closer scrutiny of budgetary situations, with a view to preventing imbalances which might over time represent a major threat to monetary and exchange-rate cohesion, as is clearly indicated by dynamic analysis centred on the so-called government budget restraint.

The second part of my proposal on the exchange-rate front – which should *not* be taken out of context because this could even make it appear contradictory – is prompted by the need to forestall speculative attacks on central rates in the crucial phase of freedom of capital movements before the fixing of the exchange rates.

Applying today's narrow bilateral fluctuation band of 2.25 per cent to *all* the countries whose currencies are part of the ECU, and in prospective to all the countries belonging to the Community would, I believe, place a very heavy burden on interest rates in the task of combating speculative pressures. In turn, this would have negative consequences for growth and a destabilising effect on public debt service, notably in the countries with a large public debt at floating rates. Such margins could also prove too narrow to allow the frequency of realignments to be reduced without this entailing sizeable variations in market rates which, as mentioned above, tend to give rise to destabilising speculation. In the light of these considerations, I would therefore suggest that the constraint on central-rate variations – on which the progress towards monetary integration would primarily hinge – could be supplemented by the adoption of a bilateral fluctuation range for *all* countries in the order of 3 per cent, without in any way loosening the overall discipline of the exchange-rate commitments.

Since this bilateral margin would allow over time a maximum swing of 6 per cent to emerge, it appears suitable in today's circumstances – insofar as it would allow both sizeable movements in interest-rate differentials, without taking forward exchange rates outside the fluctuation band for spot rates, and less frequent realignments of central rates (*on average less than one a year*) – without this implying discontinuities in market rates. Both the constraints – presumptive for central rates and operative for the range of fluctuation – should be *gradually tightened* in line with the objective of monetary and financial unification. The discipline imposed by the system could be further reinforced by reactivating the unilateral ECU divergence indicator in response to the growing interest in 'objective' economic indicators as instruments for the pursuit of convergent economic policies and international surveillance.

Should it not prove possible to agree on the commitment to curb annual changes in central rates, as an alternative to this 'first best' solution, designed to foster the process of monetary unification *in the area as a whole*, it would, I believe, be desirable for the time being for the countries entering in the exchange-rate mechanism to adopt a wider fluctuation band than the present 2.25 per cent. This would still have to be coupled with measures to promote lasting convergence of the economic fundamentals in all the EMS countries in a growth-oriented environment.

If the above analysis is valid, the dilemma gripping the EMS is that, while it is necessary to liberalise capital movements, this process might well be accompanied by such large speculative capital flows in anticipation of central-rate realignments that the cohesion of the EMS itself could be threatened. This approach suggests that there is a need to strengthen not only the exchange-rate mechanism but all the defences designed to prevent, or at any rate damp, any shock waves that might develop. The traditional instruments to be strengthened include the availability of adequate lines of credit and, in the initial phase, the possibility of invoking safeguard clauses, albeit for limited periods, in respect of full freedom of 'monetary' movements across frontiers. In addition to these measures, I attribute considerable importance to the development of broad forward markets for foreign exchange in which monetary authorities would intervene.

Fifteen years' experience with floating exchange rates has reaffirmed lessons already learnt in the period between the two world wars, and rebutted the argument of those who claimed that exchange-rate stability would be ensured by stabilising speculation.

The theory was that extrapolative expectations would have rapidly been dominated by regressive ones regarding the return of exchange rates to their equilibrium levels. But in the short term the trade balance reacts perversely to exchange-rate movements, owing to the inertia with which trade volumes adjust. Accordingly, the expected equilibrium exchange rate in the medium term necessarily becomes a highly uncertain variable dependent on a large number of factors, including the economic policies pursued both at home and abroad. A depreciation of the exchange rate may, for example, lead simultaneously to a surge in the trade deficit and a domestic cost–price spiral, which the downward stickiness of prices subsequently makes it difficult to cure, even with restrictive policies.

On the other hand, any system of fixed but discretely adjustable exchange rates is subject to the risk that exchange-rate expectations will generate very large flows of capital, which may well exceed the defences put in place in the form of foreign-currency reserves and lines of credit.

Offering operators the anchor of forward contracts with monetary authorities that are consistent with the latter's commitments to curb the movements in central rates in the medium term can provide effective support (together with larger and more frequent changes in interest rates) in preventing the development of pressures on exchange rates. With this approach the fluctuations in spot rates within the permitted limits rapidly reduce the potential advantages of speculative movements of funds.

b. Monetary policy and interest-rate coordination

A comparable problem to that of greater strictness in exchange-rate relations is that of strengthening monetary cooperation through the adoption of rules of the game consistent with the objective of unification. A first model could be based on *coordinated management* of individual central bank's expansion of both the *domestic component* of monetary base and domestic credit.

A second model based on coordination foresees an asymmetrical solution: the country whose currency is at the centre of the system keeps the growth in its monetary aggregates consistent with domestic price stability. It is up to the other countries to manage their exchange rates *vis-à-vis* the 'dominant' currency by making suitable changes in their interest rates. The growing recourse made to intramarginal interventions in the EMS has led to some of the features of this 'asymmetric' model being present in the operation of the system. This model has the advantage, which should not be underrated, of providing the system with a nominal anchor to which the discipline and credibility of the leader country extend. On the other hand, the reasons why the other EMS countries would have difficulty in accepting this solution are obvious, especially if it is not set within the framework of an overall design for economic policy based on cooperation and intended to promote the growth of the European economy as a whole. Moreover, the leader country itself might be unwilling to accept the constraint inherent in a passive exchange-rate policy within the area.

In any event, it will be necessary to prevent the formulation of a cooperative model from leading in practice to a weakening of the commitment to monetary stability in the area. One possible defence is the creation – based on standard sets by the Bundesbank model – of a European Monetary Fund with binding institutional guarantees of its adopting a non-accommodating monetary stance in its surveillance of the policies pursued by individual countries and their impact on the EMS area as a whole. This does not imply *immediate* devolution of national monetary sovereignty to the Fund, which should however be able to evolve towards a European central bank. It is worth recalling in this connection that the Federal Reserve System was conceived at the time of the gold standard as a system of twelve federal banks, coordinated but endowed with considerable autonomy in the management of their 'domestic' credit markets.

It would, of course, be an illusion to imagine that the mechanical adoption for all the countries in the Community of an acritically formulated model based on the development of just one monetary or credit aggregate could guarantee monetary stability. Financial innovation, the enhanced sophistication of operators and the global integration of markets all diminish the importance of the effects of the availability of funds in the transmission of monetary policy impulses. By contrast, there is an increase in the importance of the channels connected with the 'prices' of credit and money – interest rates and exchange rates. To complete and strengthen the more flexible management of exchange rates within the fluctuation band, there will therefore have to be a willingness for the impulses deriving from the changes in the external component of the monetary base to be promptly and symmetrically reflected in changes in interest-rate differentials. More generally, the processes whereby liquidity and credit are created will have to be carefully monitored and coordinated, in part through the use of 'objective' economic indicators, and correctly analysed as part of the determination of overall portfolio equilibria.

c.   Integration of private and official markets

A portfolio analysis model clearly underlies the last aspect examined here of the problem of strengthening the monetary system in Europe. At present the official ECU and the private ECU are two distinct monetary entities. In addition to strengthening the official ECU, by removing the limits to its acceptability and broadening the scope for its use in financing intramarginal interventions along the lines set by the Governors' recent decisions, it would also be desirable to integrate the two markets, thereby giving the ECU a truly central role both as an international reserve asset and as a European currency in parallel with national ones. I have recently developed a comprehensive proposal for linking the official and the private ECU markets, without the need for any institutional changes. The proposal is based on the joint role of the Bank for International Settlements as the clearing house of private ECUs and as a recognised holder of official ECUs. By way of this institution, central banks could transform their official ECU holdings into private ECU balances, and vice-versa. The creation of private ECUs would be subjected to similar controls to those existing for individual currencies, and would take account of the growth in the latter.

The European Monetary Fund would be entrusted with the task of supervising the ECU and acting as the nucleus of the system of central banks. The Fund would also be responsible for the centralised management of a part of the European foreign-currency reserves – in accordance with the original plan for the EMS – and for the short-term credit mechanisms for the support of currencies, designed to discourage and repel speculative attacks on the currencies of participating countries.

4   Concluding remarks

The methods and models briefly sketched here[2] could, I believe, help to strengthen the EMS and promote its cohesion, notably in view of the problems that liberalisation of capital movements will bring. However, the key to progress in the fields of European integration and monetary stability remains convergence of the economic fundamentals – and, in particular, the state of public finances and the processes underlying the determination of costs. Without progress in these two areas, it will not be possible to strengthen Europe's monetary cohesion. The first eight years of the EMS have nonetheless shown that the discipline it imposes can exert both a direct influence and act as a catalyst to fostering, through a complex play of causes and effects, the broader process of convergence.

Indeed, the proposal made here for acceptance of a maximum variation over a twelve-month horizon of central exchange rates is advocated on the assumption that it will result in greater discipline in nominal wage demands and in budgetary processes.

I conclude, however, by stressing that the move towards greater monetary discipline, gradual abandonment of the exchange rate as a policy instrument, and full capital liberalisation will proceed only to the extent that this will actually prove the cornerstone for growth and the gradual reabsorption of unemployment.

Price stability, *per se*, will help towards attainment of this objective, but policy adaptations – of a micro and macro nature – may well be necessary also in countries which have already ensured domestic monetary stability, but have failed so far to meet their medium-term growth objectives.

NOTES
* Central Director for Economic Research, Banca d'Italia, Rome. The views expressed are those of the author and should not be attributed to the Bank of Italy.

1 To recall, agreed measures are as follows:

(i) The duration of the very short-term financing (VSTF) on which central banks can draw through the European Monetary Cooperation Fund (EMCF) to finance interventions in EMS currencies will be extended by one month, taking the maximum duration from two and a half to three and a half months. The ceiling applied to the automatic renewal for three months of these financing operations will be doubled – i.e., it will amount to 200 per cent of the central bank's debtor quota in the short-term monetary support mechanism instead of 100 per cent as at present.

(ii) A presumption that intramarginal interventions in EMS currencies agreed to by the central bank issuing the interventions currency will qualify for VSTF via the EMCF will be established under certain conditions; the cumulative amount of such financing made available to the debtor central bank shall not exceed 200 per cent of its debtor quota in the short-term monetary support mechanism; the debtor central bank is also prepared to use its holdings of the currency to be sold in amounts to be agreed and the creditor central bank may request repayment in its own currency taking into account the reserve position of the debtor central bank.

(iii) The usability of the official ECU will be further enhanced. The central banks will accept settlements in ECUs of outstanding claims in the VSTF in excess of their obligation (50 per cent) and up to 100 per cent as long as this does not result in an unbalanced composition of reserves and no excessive debtor and creditor positions in ECUs arise. After two years of experience, the formal rules relating to the official ECU will be subject to review.

These measures form part of a broader strategy to foster exchange-rate cohesion within the EMS: the Governors have agreed in particular to exploit the scope for a more active, flexible and concerted use of the instruments available, namely exchange-rate movements within the fluctuation band, interest rates and interventions. To promote this more effective use of the instruments, the procedure for joint monitoring of economic and monetary developments and policies will be strengthened with the aim of arriving at common assessments of both the prevailing conjuncture and appropriate policy responses.

2 I have developed in more detail these ideas and proposals in some recent works of mine. I refer in particular to Masera (1984), (1986), (1987a), (1987b).

REFERENCES

Masera, R. (1984). 'Introduction', in Rainer S. Masera and Robert Triffin (eds), *Europe's Money: Problems of European Monetary Co-ordination and Integration*, Oxford, Clarendon Press.

(1986). 'Europe's Economic Problems in an International Perspective', Banca Nazionale del Lavoro Quarterly Review (December).

(1987a). 'An Increasing Role for the ECU: a Character in Search of a Script', *Essays in International Finance*, No. 167, Princeton University (June).

(1987b). *Lo SME e l'unificazione monetaria in Europa*, 2nd edn, Bologna: Il Mulino.

Short-term implications of EMS exchange-rate mechanism changes

Wolfgang Rieke

I would like first of all to focus on the short-term implications of the recent changes in certain EMS rules adopted in Basle and Nyborg. Participants in the EMS exchange-rate mechanism agreed that exchange rates should be allowed to respond more flexibly within the band, and should not be pegged at certain positions as had increasingly been the case. Short-term interest rates should also be made to respond more flexibly to deal with any emerging tensions. An important new element is the closer 'monitoring' of exchange- and interest-rate developments to be undertaken by the Committee of Governors and the Monetary Committee. The essential purpose is to detect sources of tension as early as possible. Developments outside the EMS – especially those affecting the US dollar, yen and other currencies – will be closely followed as part of the new procedures, especially insofar as they affect the EMS.

There was also consideration of the arguments for and against smaller realignments that would avoid adjustments of market rates exceeding the width of the fluctuation band. Such 'technical' realignments could then possibly be entrusted to the Committee of Governors or the Monetary Committee. It was felt, however, that realignment of central rates remained a political issue, requiring decisions at the political level. As a matter of principle, central-rate adjustment should be accompanied by other measures dealing with the internal causes that regularly led to tensions and made rate adjustments necessary. Such measures in most cases involve fiscal policy and thus lie outside the realm of central bank Governors. In any case, realignments should not be made too easy, and the system should not be allowed to degenerate into a quasi-automatic 'crawling-peg' mechanism.

I would also point out that it may be rather difficult to diagnose correctly the need for small realignments. One can refer to the IMF concept of 'fundamental disequilibrium' as a precondition of parity adjustment under the Bretton Woods rules, a concept that had never been clearly defined but that limited parity adjustment to cases where the correction of a balance of payments disequilibrium without parity adjustment would have imposed disproportionate burdens on the country concerned, and on the whole system.

As part of the 1987 package of EMS improvements it was agreed also that there should be a presumption in favour of very short-term financing (VSTF) of intramarginal interventions by mutual central bank credits via the EMCF, though within certain limits and provided the partner central bank agrees to the use of its currency for intervention. As Lamberto Dini said in his introductory remarks, the availability of VSTF for intramarginal intervention should not lead to systematically greater resort to EMS credit or to a large build-up of net claims and liabilities within the EMCF.

In the same vein, it had been agreed that the 50 per cent acceptance limit for official ECUs should be suspended, assuming that no large, long-lasting and one-sided net creditor positions of official ECUs were allowed to build up. The new unlimited acceptance obligation for official ECUs in settlement of intervention balances will be reviewed after two years.

The discussion concerning intervention obligations, credit mechanisms and ECU acceptance limits has reflected the concern of some partners that there should be an appropriate balance between adjustment and financing in the system. In addition to the unlimited VSTF mechanism, the credit mechanisms could after all put considerable financing burdens on surplus countries over extended periods, and they could at the same time reduce the urgency of adjustment measures in deficit countries. As President Emminger indicated at one point, this might force the Deutsche Bundesbank to suspend the intervention obligation if domestic monetary control and price stability were at risk.

In my view, the extension of the existing financing and settlement mechanisms to intramarginal intervention would put additional responsibility for the smooth functioning of the EMS on deficit countries to take prompt action when confronted with pressure on their currencies.

Turning to the longer-term prospects of the EMS, two questions are of particular relevance.

(a) How will the system be managed once inflation rates have been reduced to levels, and inflation differentials narrowed to a point, where following the German stability example no longer seems the natural thing to do?

(b) How will capital liberalisation affect the workings of the system, and what are the responses likely to be?

In their Report to Ministers, the central bank Governors stated that as a consequence of the commitment to fixed but adjustable exchange rates and free capital movements, monetary policy will come under increased tensions so long as individual countries' economic policies leave room for substantial internal and external imbalances. This underlines the need for policies that reduce or avoid such imbalances and keep inflation firmly under control. Indeed, fiscal policy should be such as to avoid undue pressures on financial resources and potential crowding out of private credit needs for investment purposes. Monetary policy in all partner countries should be committed to price stability as its primary objective. Their central banks should be put in a position to live up to this objective.

If countries are prepared to do this, it would amount to a strengthening of central bank autonomy in the pursuit of monetary policy objectives at the national level. It could open up the road for further progress leading to the eventual creation of a European Central Bank endowed with an adequate degree of autonomy from political interference at the national or community level. If central bank autonomy were allowed to grow at the national level the transformation into an autonomous Community Central Bank system might be eased considerably.

During the conference it has been argued that the EMS will have to live with differential inflation rates, as far as one can look ahead. In my view, this implies that inflation is still considered as an acceptable price that countries are willing to pay for lower unemployment and higher growth, with the perceived trade-off likely to differ from country to country. If this is the reality, it is highly disturbing, as it would conflict with the joint ambition of all partners to reduce the need for regular currency realignments and the desire to move forward to an ever more closely integrated system. At some point prior to the achievement of economic and monetary union a situation would have to be reached where prices and costs (as major factors determining exchange rates in the medium term) can be said to converge enough to warrant consideration of the final step to permanently fixed exchange rates and monetary union.

Old rules and a new reality?

Luigi Spaventa

The title of this panel discussion refers somewhat ambiguously to a 'new phase in the European Monetary System': is it implied that we have already entered a new phase, or that such phase belongs to a desirable but as yet uncertain future? I believe that both things are true. We have indeed entered a new phase, marked by greater financial integration and by increasing liberalisation of capital movements which have affected the rule of the game. It also appears, however, from a number of statements made during this conference, that this new phase must be conceived as one of transition in which the system cannot rest: unless there is further advancement towards improving its structure, there may arise an inconsistency between the old rules and a new reality.

It is not for me to lay down a new constitution for the day after D-day in 1992. I shall confine myself to considering some issues which run the risk of being neglected in the general enthusiasm for the great leap forward.

If all the talk about convergence leaves us some spare time, we should occasionally ask ourselves whether we are satisfied with the rather narrow specification of the targets of convergence which has prevailed so far.

No doubt, the acceptance of a nominal anchor to the system and limited recourse to exchange-rate realignments in recent years have constrained monetary policies and allowed convergence to lower inflation; and we should be pleased with it. We should, however, ask with more insistence why this process has not entailed also convergence to higher growth. The 1970s taught us that we cannot buy steadily higher growth by pushing up the inflation rate. This correct proposition, however, received an unwarranted extension when it was taken to imply that lower inflation would, by itself, buy us more growth. In the sober OECD prose:

> the medium-term financial strategy adopted by the majority of European countries at the beginning of this decade . . . aimed at an eventual return to growth rates sufficient to bring unemployment down substantially as well as restoring an acceptable degree of price stability. These objectives were to be achieved through a combination of monetary restraint, greater control of public finances, and market-oriented structural reforms . . . It was to be expected that the initial impact of the medium-term policy strategy would be to slow employment growth and raise unemployment. This duly happened, but to a greater and more prolonged extent than foreseen. Between 1980 and 1987 no net new job will have been created overall in Europe [while the average unemployment rate] quickly rose to levels unprecedented in the post-war period.[1]

Note that growth performance of some countries outside the EMS has been (for the US) or is now (for the UK) better than that of the EMS area. As in the case of inflation, also in the case of growth, convergence appears to have occurred towards the lowest rate. The country supplying the nominal anchor is also the one with a low growth record: this is another anchor, which reduces the speed of the whole convoy.

EMS convergence has had one target – inflation – and has affected only one policy instrument – monetary policy. The system has been unable to enforce convergence of fiscal policies, whether in view of a more balanced distribution of domestic demand between the countries concerned, or – more modestly – to restrain the fiscal profligacy of some members. France in 1983 does not provide a counter-example, as that was the case of a sudden imbalance caused by expansionary policies, which found its sanction in the exchange rate and was quickly redressed. There has instead been little or no convergence in the case of structural fiscal imbalances, which affect especially Italy but also some smaller economies (the three highest public-debt ratios in the OECD area are to be found in three EEC and EMS countries). First, unlike in the case of monetary policies, there are no sanctions in the system against persistent fiscal imbalances, while the progress made on the inflation front may have generated too much complacency on the disciplinary virtues of the system. Second, low growth and high interest rates are not the best cure for countries beset by high deficits and debt, both for their consequences on the rise of the debt ratio and because it is more difficult to enforce drastic cuts in expenditure or tax rises in a situation of insufficient growth. In the medium run, as has also been pointed out by Rudiger Dornbusch (Chapter 2 in this volume) growing monetary convergence may turn out to be incompatible with persistent fiscal divergence.

These problems affect the issue of capital liberalisation. There are different views on this issue and its implications. One echoes a counsel of perfection: liberalisation would provide the constraint which has been lacking so far, as, together with continuing monetary convergence, it would compel the authorities in the divergent countries to approach gradually the straight and narrow path of fiscal discipline. The other is a practical and pragmatic view: occasional lapses from the virtue of free capital movements may not lead to heaven, but are a safer way to avoid the temporary hell of runs on the currency and of financial crises which may endanger the stability of the system. There is also an intermediate view, well represented in some studies discussed in this conference and with which I am inclined to agree: liberalisation of capital movements requires a more flexible working of the exchange-rate agreement; it requires, in John Driffill's words (Chapter 8), that 'central rates in the EMS are changed frequently enough and by sufficiently small amounts'.

Recent developments in Italy provide an example of the problems involved. The liberalisation measures taken in May 1987 not only restored the freedom to invest in foreign securities, but also removed a number of restrictions on commercial credits and hence on the possibility of using leads and lags as a vehicle of speculative movements (as has traditionally been the case in Italy). It may be argued that a more gradual approach would have been perhaps more advisable. Still, once the decision was taken, one option was to pre-empt speculative movements by a quick change of parity early in the summer. This was not done and a massive speculative movement against the lira did occur: eventually, the chosen alternative was the temporary suspension of some of the liberalisation measures and the introduction of administrative credit controls.

It is thus likely that a decision to go ahead with full capital liberalisation (affecting also monetary assets) and the adoption of a stricter view on the possibility of invoking safeguard clauses are likely to be accompanied by a greater flexibility of exchange rates within the band and by more frequent changes of parities. If this is the case, the resistance to domestic pressures to restore competitiveness by means of exchange-rate changes will be weakened and the spells of real appreciation of weaker currencies will be shortened. Pressures for parity changes will be stronger now, when the appreciation of the dollar no longer offsets the movements of real exchange rates within the EMS and when, at the same time, greater freedom of capital movements provides additional weapons.[2]

These outline observations on convergence and on the possible consequences of liberalisation of capital movements lead me to some tentative conclusions on the 'new phase'. An interpretation of the new phase according to which its major and only ingredients are full freedom of capital movements *and* less exchange-rate flexibility – possibly with narrower margins (with particular reference to the need to abolish the wider band for the lira) – seems to me neither acceptable nor desirable. It would be acceptable and it may be desirable, only if other ingredients were added to those two, in order to avoid the contradictions arising from the coexistence of fixed exchange rates with full liberalisation of capital movements 'while economic policies continue in point of fact to be unconstrained'. A list of the additional requirements necessary to mark a truly 'new phase' of the EMS is provided in a recent memorandum of the Italian Government;[3] they range from a reform and a strengthening of the EMS financing mechanisms, to the extension of the exchange-rate agreements to other countries, to the provisions necessary to avoid 'the asymmetry which derives from the role of the "dominating" currency and the deflationary bias which results therefrom', to a common policy *vis-à-vis* third currencies. Unless (and until) at least some of these changes in the institutional structure of the EMS are introduced, the attempt to pursue full liberalisation of capital movements and stricter exchange-rate discipline at the same time is likely to be doomed to failure.

Greater ambitions for a new, a stronger EMS, then, require less ambition in this phase of transition. If the emphasis is, as seems to be the case, on full capital liberalisation, the target of greater exchange-rate discipline will have to be postponed, to allow the time necessary to introduce the required reforms.

Purists would argue that this is bad for discipline: governments and parliaments are, in their view, imperfections in the smooth working of the system, whose freedom of action needs to be limited, and the stronger the external constraint the better. This is a dangerous argument in a world where national economic interests still differ so widely and symmetry of obligations is not accepted. Governments and parliaments may react to an excess of external constraint; probably they would

consider the exchange rate a more prestigious target and back-track on
capital liberalisation in the attempt to protect some degree of autonomy.
Is this a desirable outcome?

NOTES

1 OECD (1987). *Economic Outlook*, No. 42 (December), pp. 10–11.
2 See the conclusions of the studies by Vona and Bini Smaghi (Chapter 6) and by
  Mastropasqua, Micossi and Rinaldi (Chapter 10) in this volume. The basic
  problem arising from the growing German surplus towards other European
  countries is examined in OECD (1987), and is forcefully put forward in the
  Italian government memorandum (1988) quoted below: 'Not only is the pivot
  currency of the system fundamentally undervalued, but the growth of domestic
  demand in Germany is lower than average; the result is that that country has
  structural surpluses also *vis-à-vis* the rest of the EEC'.
3 Italian Treasury (1988). 'On "European" Monetary Construction: the Italian
  Position', a memorandum sent by the Italian Treasury Minister in reply to a
  note of the French Finance Minister (February).

The EMS's ambitions fulfilled?

Jacques Waitzenegger

I would like to make a few comments based on my personal experience of
the functioning of the EMS since its creation in 1979. As is known, the
EMS had a twofold ambition: the creation of an area of exchange-rate
stability and the achievement of a European monetary identity.

Has the EMS fulfilled these ambitions? Some of the positive developments have been reviewed in depth during this conference. However, I
would like to underline the relative stability of member countries'
currencies, their reduced fluctuations compared to those of third currencies and the absorption without major trauma of the central rate changes
that have occurred during this period. Furthermore, the efforts to
achieve discipline and adjustment induced by the EMS through
economic rigour and the reduction of inflation – which have been
particularly noticeable in France – have also represented an important
factor. On the other hand, it is often pointed out that the burden of
interventions and the efforts of adjustment are not always symmetric
within the exchange-rate mechanism. Further, realignments are not
always far-reaching enough and therefore tend to perpetuate certain
competitive advantages. Finally, we should recall that we are still in a
transitory phase that was expected to last only two years. Therefore, in a
period of intense liberalisation of capital movements, it must be realised

that the system is still fragile, and that a number of countries have still not adhered to the exchange-rate mechanism.

The immediate conclusion is that we should continue to reinforce the EMS.

We are now entering a phase in which, as Rainer Masera recalls, the Single European Act aims at the establishment of a single market for goods, services and capital by the end of 1992. Although this objective will affect numerous sectors of economic activity, I shall confine my comments to the monetary aspect, with which we are more directly concerned. It should not be forgotten, however, that the harmonisation of financial rules and of fiscal norms will play an important role in the process of an integrated market. Further, the differences in structure of member countries are such that progress towards the liberalisation of capital movements is bound to be unequal. This indicates that safeguard clauses will have to be allowed for.

Nonetheless, I believe that in spite of the difficulties and the differences in speed, progress towards the liberalisation of capital movements should be irreversible. Further, it is important to realise that the consequence of these reforms will not be limited to the Community, since member countries will become open also to financial flows to and from non-EEC countries.

Will this liberalisation of capital movements open a new phase in the history of the EMS?

In my opinion, it would be an exaggeration to talk about a change in nature. It is, rather, a difference of degree. It is not a transformation, but rather a transition towards a more open and integrated market. Some have pointed out the dangers for exchange-rate stability and the autonomy of monetary policy. I know that from a theoretical point of view there may be incompatibility between unrestricted transactions, fixed exchange rates and autonomous monetary policies. However, these theoretical considerations should be seen in the light of practical experience. As regards freedom of transactions, a system of exchange controls does not totally impede capital mobility. Restrictions, when imposed, are applicable only to residents, and financial innovation leads to partial integration of markets. Further, foreign-exchange controls can be effective only in the short run, and serve most of the time only to delay measures that sooner or later have to be taken.

Exchange-rate stability in the EMS does not mean strictly fixed rates. The system is based on fluctuation margins and allows for realignments. The possibility of adjusting to external disturbances is embodied in the system, and should be used. The autonomy of monetary policy is a concept that tends to lose its substance, since it is increasingly difficult to pursue a monetary policy while ignoring the international situation and the reinforcement of European cooperation.

However, I do not deny that the liberalisation of capital movements does involve adaptation of the system to the new environment. Full liberalisation certainly tightens the external constraints that now face us. In giving their approval to the Single European Act, governments have implicitly accepted the idea of reinforcing the coordination of economic policies in order to achieve greater convergence of the underlying economic fundamentals.

At this stage I would like to take up an issue raised by Professor Kenen, and say how much I appreciate his mentioning the need for greater coordination and harmonisation of fiscal policies. This is an important point that I shall not develop here, but which is fundamental if greater progress in economic cooperation is to be achieved.

There is already a fair degree of cooperation in the field of monetary policy. We are not starting from scratch, and important progress has been made. Lamberto Dini has recalled the Governors' most recent decisions; there is certainly the will to press forward in the areas of surveillance and coordination. I hope that this will lead to practical results. Further, I believe that Europe should not remain indifferent to the efforts being made outside the Community. The initiatives of the Group of Seven to ensure better coordination of economic policies represent, in my opinion, significant achievements. The Plaza and Louvre Agreements have given rise to scepticism; the time has come to recognise the importance of these agreements and their impact on the cooperation framework.

Coordination, however, implies dialogue, and the possibility of influencing other partners. This does not mean that we should rely only on the policy of one country, but rather that we should evolve towards a system in which asymmetries are eliminated, without calling into question the need for price stability which is an objective we all accept. In terms of action, this does not imply shifting from national to supra-national monetary objectives. Indeed, I believe that as long as nations exist, monetary policies will still be conducted at a national level. On the other hand, these policies will have to take greater account of the international environment and European solidarity; cooperation must bring countries closer together rather than separate them.

Some remarks on convergence are perhaps now in order. However necessary and beneficial convergence may be, it is not an absolute guarantee. Operators may estimate, even wrongly, that the risks are not equal in member countries' currencies. Liberalisation therefore requires a reinforcement of the EMS and of its solidarity mechanisms. I will not recall here the measures adopted recently in Nyborg; they are in the right direction, and reveal a constructive state of mind in favour of policy coordination among EMS participants.

I believe that the phase we are currently experiencing, which is not the final one, should lead to an improved use of the instruments available to central banks. My experience of eight years of participation in the EMS has taught me the difficulty of foreseeing how foreign-exchange markets will react. The action of central banks should be based on a pragmatic approach.

In my opinion, three courses need to be followed. Firstly, depending on circumstances, recourse to intervention, to the use of the fluctuation margins and to changes in interest-rate levels. Secondly, a mechanism of effective and regular concertation, at different levels, among monetary authorities. Thirdly, I believe it is necessary for our European system to have a concerted and active policy with respect to third currencies.

In conclusion, even though the EMS has been surrounded by scepticism on the part of some economists and operators, it has nonetheless gained the right to exist. It is, however, necessary to appreciate its achievements and to pursue its step-by-step evolution towards monetary integration. At a world level, the goal is certainly to increase the coordination of economic policies. At a European level, the goal is somewhat different, as indicated by the decision to establish a unified market of 320 million consumers and producers by 1992.

A few comments on this unified market, its institutions and currency. Tommaso Padoa-Schioppa (Chapter 12 in this volume) has indicated the possible different stages of this evolution. The idea of a monetary institution that would cement the economic union is frequently put forward under the form of a European central bank. I think we should not give importance only to the notion of a central bank, and its independence. I believe we should also consider the role to be played by a common currency as the nucleus of European integration – i.e., in this specific case the ECU.

A common currency should mean the possibility of performing the three functions of yardstick, unit of account and store of value throughout the Community. We are not yet at this stage with the present instrument. Market mechanisms require – if this currency is to be superimposed on national currencies – that economic agents should have an incentive to use it. If it is to become the common currency, the ECU will need to have, on all these points, identical features to those of the currently circulating currencies. In this respect, it is doubtful that it could continue to be defined as a basket of currencies; the possibility of a fixed link to national currencies would have to be studied.

I believe it would be useful for specialists at this conference and elsewhere to reflect not only on the more fundamental problems but also on the technical aspects and practical conditions of the functioning of such a monetary union. The time is coming for a careful examination of how today's dream can become tomorrow's reality.

General discussion

The discussion focused on two main issues, namely the mechanisms governing exchange-rate adjustments within the system and the effects of capital liberalisation.

Jacques Melitz agreed on the principle that exchange-rate adjustments should be determined in such a way as to discourage speculative attacks against the system. However, he questioned the thesis that realignments should be small and not involve jumps in market exchange rates. If realignments are small, they may have to occur more frequently, thereby generating destabilising expectations. Further, if realignments do not involve jumps in the exchange rate, there may be little scope for capital reflow towards the country whose currency has been devalued, thereby generating the impression that the new central rates cannot be defended. In his opinion, therefore, there are reasons to wonder whether having exchange-rate jumps at realignments would not represent a necessary sacrifice for obtaining longer periods of exchange-rate stability.

Wolfgang Rieke added that having only small realignments might imply that insufficient attention could be paid to the accompanying policy actions that are generally required in these circumstances. This may weaken the stability of the system, and thereby increase the frequency of realignments.

William Branson pointed out that several issues are still not entirely resolved. One relates to the problem of favouring a more flexible use of the exchange rate within the band and at the same time ensuring exchange-rate stability. Specifically, what accompanying policy measures are required in the case of wider fluctuation margins? A second issue is the extent to which fiscal coordination among member countries represents a prerequisite for monetary union. In the United States there is no coordination at all among the fiscal policies of the various states – some states run deficits that are financed through borrowing from the surplus states. The last issue concerns the new entrants to the EMS – i.e., the UK, Greece, Portugal and Spain. It is likely that the differences in structure among these countries may pose serious problems to the system, and threaten its overall stability.

Massimo Russo   questioned the appropriateness of widening the fluctuation band for all currencies; in his view, it could be preferable to have
a wider margin just for the Deutsche mark for temporary periods and on
the basis of a collective decision, in the face of disturbances external to
the system (such as the current sharp decline of the US dollar).

Rainer Masera   shared the doubts expressed by William Branson on the
possibility of other EEC currencies joining the EMS within the present
structure. He specified that the objective of widening member-country
participation, together with the creation of a unified and integrated
goods and financial market by the end of 1992, was at the origin of his
proposal for modifying certain mechanisms of exchange-rate adjustment
of EMS central rates. The goal is to prevent the structural differences
among the various countries – together with increased capital laterali-
sation – from giving rise to disruptive pressures during the system's
transition towards full monetary unification. In his view, agreement on
the maximum size of exchange-rate realignments within a certain period
of time and increased policy cooperation would enhance the discipline of
the system. This, together with wider fluctuation margins, would enable
a more flexible use of exchange- and interest-rate adjustments when
facing periods of tension.

Jean-Jacques Rey   disagreed both with Peter Kenen's proposal for
possible increased use of capital controls and with that of Rainer Masera
for wider margins of exchange-rate fluctuations. In his view, there is a
third path to improving the functioning of the system – i.e., increasing
policy coordination among member countries. Two conditions are
required. One is the full implementation of the unified market by 1992,
which will help resolve the problem of growth of the whole area. The
second is the reduction of inflation rates and the narrowing of inflation
differentials. Exchange-rate adjustments should, however, take into
account divergences in real performance, which could occur within the
present system of 2.25 per cent fluctuation margins. He stated that there
is scope for reinforcing monetary cooperation – in particular, by adopting
a wider concept of community money supply and by attributing less
importance to short-term quantitative targets. Finally, the present financing mechanisms should be utilised more extensively, and not only in the
face of market pressure.

Theo Peeters   expressed his surprise that during the conference no
mention at all had been made of the divergence indicator, and asked
whether this implied that it had lost all significance.

Stefano Micossi   noted that the use of the divergence indicator had been extensively examined by the EEC Monetary Committee's Alternates (that he chairs). The conclusion had been reached that the divergence indicator – which is based solely on exchange-rate deviations from the system's average – could not claim any special significance in assessing the performance of member countries' economies but could at best be regarded as one among several indicators of performance and developments within the system.

Ralph Bryant pointed out that an important dimension in the evolution of the system is represented by developments outside Europe – especially progress in the adjustment of the present huge payments imbalances among the United States, Japan, and Europe. He also noticed that no mention had been made during the conference of the possible evolution of the institutional procedures of the European Community with respect to the problems raised by external developments and the possible emergence of internal real imbalances in the presence of increasing financial integration.

Rudiger Dornbusch asserted that the liberalisation of capital movements may hamper the cohesion of the system if it is not accompanied by a wider coordination of economic policies. He agreed with Peter Kenen that the process of financial integration cannot be considered irreversible, since the various EEC countries may attach to it different scales of priorities.

Index

419